THE EXPATRIATES

OTHER BOOKS BY ISHBEL ROSS

Nonfiction

SONS OF ADAM, DAUGHTERS OF EVE
The Role of Women in American History

TASTE IN AMERICA
An Illustrated History

CHARMERS AND CRANKS
Biographical Sketches of Twelve American Women

AN AMERICAN FAMILY: The Tafts 1678–1964

CRUSADES AND CRINOLINES
A biography of Ellen Curtis Demorest and William Jennings Demorest

GRACE COOLIDGE AND HER ERA

SILHOUETTE IN DIAMONDS
A biography of Mrs. Potter Palmer

THE GENERAL'S WIFE
A biography of Mrs. Ulysses S. Grant

FIRST LADY OF THE SOUTH
A biography of Mrs. Jefferson Davis

ANGEL OF THE BATTLEFIELD
A biography of Clara Barton

REBEL ROSE
A biography of Rose O'Neal Greenhow

PROUD KATE
A biography of Kate Chase

JOURNEY INTO LIGHT
A history of the blind

CHILD OF DESTINY
A biography of Dr. Elizabeth Blackwell

LADIES OF THE PRESS
A history of American newspaperwomen

Fiction

ISLE OF ESCAPE
FIFTY YEARS A WOMAN
HIGHLAND TWILIGHT
MARRIAGE IN GOTHAM
PROMENADE DECK

THE EXPATRIATES

Ishbel Ross

THOMAS Y. CROWELL COMPANY

Established 1834   New York

Grateful acknowledgment is made for permission to reprint quotations from *A Moveable Feast* by Ernest Hemingway, published by Charles Scribner's Sons; *Ernest Hemingway: A Life Story* by Carlos Baker, published by Charles Scribner's Sons; and *That Summer in Paris* by Morley Callaghan, published by Coward-McCann, Inc., copryright©1963 by Morley Callaghan.

Designed by Judith Woracek Barry

Manufactured in the United States of America

L.C. Card 72-101939

1   2   3   4   5   6   7   8   9   10

Contents

CONTENTS

Illustrations

Americans Abroad

The American expatriate tradition flowered in the 1920s and had touched all quarters of the earth by the 1960s, but it had its roots in the era of the Founding Fathers, some of whom passed long periods abroad helping to shape their own dawning civilization in the West.

The age-old impulse to know the peoples of other lands, to see the world and study the arts and sciences abroad, to seek freedom, or to escape from trouble and responsibility at home, springs to life with each successive generation. In the last three hundred years this deeply rooted tradition has brought a rich inflow of expatriates to the United States, fleeing from tyranny in their own countries or seeking wider opportunities in the Western world.

Today the tide flows in both directions, and American expatriates may be found in most of the countries and islands around the globe. Swift travel and easy communication have lessened the isolation of these wanderers, and innumerable lines of contact now keep them closely linked with the heritage they have temporarily abandoned or have sought to foreswear. The solitude that the nineteenth-century exile knew belongs to the past. Yet the more frenzied the pace of contemporary life, the more men long for peace, only to find that it eludes them now, no matter where they go.

1

Nathaniel Hawthorne noted in the 1850s, when he was acting as a consul at Liverpool, that "no people on earth have such vagabond habits as ours. . . ." But the isles of escape have now lost their traditional magic. A radar station is based on the lonely Seychelles in the Indian Ocean. The news of the day streams into the jungle along with American rock and roll. Expatriate escape is a lost illusion in the 1960s, although it has taken on strange new aspects with the wandering tribes of Hippies who turn up in the Himalayas, in Africa, in Peru, in Greece, in the Matala caves of Crete, or wherever the sun shines and the atmosphere is receptive.

But in contrast to the shiftless Hippies and the bemused flower children are the scientists and scholars, the doctors, nurses, and teachers, the businessmen, engineers, and agricultural experts, the Peace Corps and antipoverty workers, who live nominally in exile, while spreading practical aid around the world. Once missionaries were pervasive, and they are still deeply engaged, but only as a part of the complex network of American activity abroad. The expatriates of today are a new breed, closely linked to government operations. Or they are the men and women in business or the arts who have chosen for personal, business, or professional reasons to settle in spots where they feel more harmoniously adjusted than in the turbulent United States. The most glittering of the expatriates are the hedonists who flash from point to point like restless butterflies, calling no place their home and coming to rest in their native land for the briefest possible periods.

The expatriate spirit, grown stronger now than it was in the 1920s, burns powerfully in young men seeking to escape the military draft. But wars have always nourished the feeling of exile, drawing men from their familiar surroundings into new areas and strange lands. This in turn has led to intermarriage, to employment abroad, to the mystical pull of the Orient, and ultimately to a sense of alienation from their homeland. Two world wars, followed by the conflicts in Korea and Vietnam, have been dynamic in their effect, and many of today's young exiles are avowed draft escapees. This, too, is an old tradition, for John Singleton Copley and other artists left America at the time of the Revolutionary War and settled in Europe, partly because of Tory connections at home. The Civil War, with divided loyalties at stake, flooded Europe, Canada, and Mexico with a wave of expatriates. The same rebellious spirit rages fiercely today, when the outcry for peace is overwhelming. The impulse of the young to put an end to wars grows stronger as nuclear weapons become more destructive.

The more casual of today's expatriates are allied to the Hippie legions and are stirred by the same resistance to the political mores of the times. They spurn authority in any form, from that of parents to college presidents. They are worlds away from the nineteenth-century types, who were largely men of arts and letters, seeking to profit from the culture and academic resources of Europe. These earlier expatriates were as eager to expand their horizons as to shake off the conventions and limitations of their life in the United States. Ralph Waldo Emerson pointed out that travel retained its fascination for all educated Americans because of a lack of native culture. But this is no longer a compelling force for exile, since people of all kinds travel extensively now, and there is a strong interplay of the arts, with the United States a focal point for all manner of literary and artistic experimentation. The same desperate need to pursue the classical image in Italy and Greece does not exist.

In earlier days the well-to-do were welcomed by the universities and conservatories of Europe. Even in the years before the Revolution they turned up at Göttingen and Heidelberg, at Oxford, Cambridge, and the Sorbonne. Young medical students studied in Berlin, Vienna, and Edinburgh. Music students gathered in Leipzig, Munich, Dresden, and Vienna. Rome, Florence, and Venice were the eternal haunts of the artists and writers. Gothic architecture was studied at Rouen, Antwerp, and Cologne. London and Paris were the great focal points as these young expatriates explored the British Museum and the Louvre, starved in cheerless garrets, and lived with native families. They found freezing lodgings in faded Venetian palaces, and barren studios in Chelsea.

Many of the students studied philosophy and political economy, and their outlook on life was greatly changed as they learned foreign languages and consorted with the scholars of the university towns. This tradition has persisted, and the American student turns up again today at the old centers of learning—at Oxford, Cambridge, and the Sorbonne, and in Rome, Florence, Perugia, and Athens, at the British provincial colleges, now with strong drawing power, and the ever-popular universities of Edinburgh, Saint Andrews, and Aberdeen. Blacks from the United States study in London and Paris, in the Orient and in Africa, in the Caribbean and on South Sea islands. Many of today's young scholars are backed by scholarships, foundation grants, and government benefits of one kind or another. They need no longer be the sons of the rich. But the academic swing is headed westward now. The United States has its own artistic and musical resources to offer the émigrés who come to its shores, as well as its architectural wonders, its medical and scientific resources, its great universities and laboratories.

For some time after the Revolution interest in the monarchical picture showed itself periodically among the expatriates, diplomatic and otherwise. Americans were zealously cultivated at the courts of Louis XVI and Napoleon III, whose fashionable consorts, Marie Antoinette and the Empress Eugénie, were of compelling interest to the wives and daughters of the diplomats. It became the custom to seek presentation at both the French and British courts, and a number of American girls who married foreigners adopted European fashions and manners and ended up as permanent exiles.

The Grand Tour, which became customary after the Civil War for those who could afford it, fed the expatriate spirit. It often lengthened into long-term or permanent residence. New links were formed. There was a swing away from the insular outlook, but except for the American girls who married abroad, few foreswore their country until the time of Henry James and T. S. Eliot. Yet in the course of time the Grand Tour came under fire as being unpatriotic and an encouragement to the young to live in the Continental fashion instead of in the sterner American way. As early as 1787 Royall Tyler, the young playwright thought by John and Abigail Adams to be an unworthy suitor for their daughter, Abby, made the point, in his play *The Contrast,* that foreign travel was a betrayal of the American spirit. Although he helped many of the young in the foreign field, Thomas Jefferson deplored the American custom of sending sons abroad for their education. The young expatriate, he commented, "loses in his knowledge, in his morals, in his health, in his habits, and in his happiness." Soon after the Revolution, Noah Webster urged that travel abroad should be discontinued if not prohibited. And in 1968 Lyndon B. Johnson, perhaps more for economic than academic reasons, was advising his countrymen to travel in the United States instead of abroad. This critical spirit has emerged from time to time, notably at the turn of the century when international marriages were creating an expatriate community of the most sensational kind, and arousing censure at home.

Many motives for self-exile have repeated themselves through the ages, from the time that Aristotle left for Macedonia to teach Alexander the Great and stayed away for years. The diseased have roamed the world in quest of health, seeking the climate that suited them best, the spas that gave them the most relief. Many have fled simply to get away from themselves, but these, for the most part, have been the drifters, the beachcombers, the café hangers-on, the alcoholics, the drug addicts and wastrels, who at times have loomed large in expatriate communities. In 1860 Emerson observed, "Men run away to other countries because they are not good in their own, and run back to their own because they pass for nothing in the new places. . . ." Yet great works of art have occasionally been produced by men living in a state of personal degradation and despair.

Americans, born to be restless and experimental, have sought refuge abroad for a variety of reasons, and usually with definite motivation. Tories fled to England at the time of the Revolution. Bankers settle today in Switzerland, and film producers and stars live and work in Europe. Escapes from financial difficulties, social disgrace, insoluble domestic complications have been recurrent motives. James Gordon Bennett, Jr., whose papers in New York and Paris would mirror the expatriate world for years, was a prime example himself, having fled to Europe after a duel with his fiancée's brother over a shocking breach of manners.

But the artists and writers have most consistently fed the expatriate flame, a tradition dating from the Revolutionary era. The first to settle in Europe and find great fame were the artists, notably Benjamin West, John Singleton Copley, John Singer Sargent, and James Abbott McNeill Whistler. Early in the 1870s Mary Cassatt, a rich Philadelphian, settled in Paris and did not revisit the United States more than once or twice in her lifetime, although holding firmly to her citizenship. Meanwhile she became famous for her support of the French Impressionists and for her own paintings of mothers and children. Cecilia Beaux, a fellow Philadelphian who won honors in the art world for her portraits, spent years in Europe, first studying, then painting. Bernard Berenson, once he had finished with Harvard in the late 1880s, became a permanent expatriate, with world celebrities visiting I Tatti, his villa outside Florence, to worship at his feet and study his possessions.

Gertrude Stein fostered modern art and pushed the abstractionists for more than forty years at her Paris salon. Creative individualists in any of the arts were fed, encouraged, or condemned in her strange ménage, which was a focal point for the expatriates of the 1920s. Ernest Hemingway was destined to become the most famous. American writers at times have shown their richest talents while in exile, from the earliest days of the Republic down to the 1960s and its savage realism. The work of Washington Irving, James Fenimore Cooper, Herman Melville, William Dean Howells, Nathaniel Hawthorne, and James Russell Lowell enriched the literary world in the advancing years of the nineteenth century, much of it inspired by their travels. Walt Whitman, Henry David Thoreau, and Emily Dickinson resisted the impulse to seek inspiration abroad, but Mark Twain, Edgar Allan Poe, Ralph Waldo Emerson, Henry Adams, Henry Wadsworth Longfellow, and many others traveled to refresh themselves with the art treasures and scenic beauties of Europe and to meet the reigning stars of the literary world.

At the close of the nineteenth century, Henry James and Edith Wharton were the most discussed literary expatriates, while Stephen Crane was running a brief and meteoric course. Soon Willa Cather found her way across the Atlantic as an observant traveler, but with no intention of losing an iota of her strongly native touch. But all the expatriate strings were firmly pulled together in the 1920s with the creation of a new school of American letters, led by Ernest Hemingway and F. Scott Fitzgerald. The twentieth-century renaissance on the Left Bank was nurtured by an assortment of stars, eccentrics, rebels, hangers-on, and inspired workers. They shook the literary world and their ambience spread as they traveled in France, Spain, Switzerland, Germany, and Italy, occasionally shedding stardust along the way, as well as a legendary record of their revels.

At Shakespeare and Company, her bookshop on the Left Bank, Sylvia Beach, a clergyman's daughter, gave aid and comfort to the restless authors and nurtured the publication of James Joyce's *Ulysses* in full view of the American expatriate colony. Isadora Duncan, the most bewildering and dramatic of expatriates, danced and caroused, picketed and sorrowed, as part of the Parisian picture of the 1920s. At Fontainebleau, Elsie de Wolfe (later Lady Mendl) presided in her bijou palace, which was impeccably decorated with an authentic historical touch.

Earlier in the twentieth century, Mabel Dodge Luhan, long before she settled in Taos and became interested in D. H. Lawrence, lived the life of a benevolent exile at her villa in Florence, encouraging and financing young artists, writers, and musicians in a setting of Venetian mirrors and exotic draperies. And on the Riviera, Maxine Elliott, a noted beauty and actress who was born the daughter of a Maine whaling captain, lived the expatriate life deluxe at one of the most dazzling villas on the Mediterranean. The friend of King Edward VII and then of J. P. Morgan, she divided her years abroad between a manor in England and her villa at Cannes.

These were the most widely discussed expatriates of the early twentieth century, but there were others, including transients like Isabella Stewart Gardner of Boston, who passed many months each year at the Villa Barbaro in Venice, surrounding herself with men of wit and talent, while she bought most of the treasures now in the Isabella Stewart Gardner Museum in Boston. These early twentieth-century expatriates were casting off the final shreds of their Puritan heritage and the stifling Victorian influences that discouraged experimentation.

The spirit of revolt that grew out of World War I had some of the characteristics of today's rebellion against the status quo. The young reacted scornfully to political smugness, to the growing materialism of the American scene, to prohibition, to the fundamentalist elements in the church, and to all attempts to stem the consequences of Freudian revelation. The young no longer accepted parental authority as the keystone of their lives, and the first steps were taken toward the wide open schism of the 1960s. Arts and letters strongly reflected this spirit of inquiry and rebellion. Many of the restless and gifted left the United States to turn their backs on inhibiting influences and to breathe what they took to be the freer air of Europe. World War II inspired another energetic outburst in letters, and the long drawn out struggle in Vietnam whipped up a stream of protest on stage and screen, in books, newspapers, magazines, and in the graphic arts. Wars breed their own brand of exile, and this has been true since the days of the Founding Fathers.

Diplomacy in Europe

America's first official expatriates went abroad because of war. Except for a scattering of writers, students, and merchants there was no expatriate life until Benjamin Franklin picturesquely gave it definition. He was followed by John and Abigail Adams, by Thomas Jefferson and other bright wits and statesmen of the day. They all spent long periods in Europe and were the focus of diplomatic maneuverings both before and after the Declaration of Independence was signed. When the war had been won and freedom declared, they forged new alliances, set up a network of merchant trade, and opened diplomatic relations for the new nation in the making.

They were prominent in social as well as in political affairs and were under close scrutiny for their manners, conversation, and customs. The French and British observed them with attention, and they were forced to walk warily along intrigue-strewn paths. Some, who were clever diarists, have left their own picture of their significant days abroad as exiles who often longed for New England or Virginia. Traveling Americans gathered around them, but Mrs. Adams thought it a mistake for such shoals of her countrymen to rush to Europe so soon after the war.

Franklin started with an advantage, because he was warmly welcomed by the philosophers and scientists whom he had met on earlier trips in 1767 and 1769. All Europe knew of the American inventor and philosopher, and he was on intimate terms with the encyclopedists and economists who were fomenting the raging discontent in France that culminated in the Revolution. He was a student of Voltaire, and although conservative in his own official utterances, he was sympathetic to the radical views frequently expressed in his hearing. But he drew away from Mirabeau, the revolutionary leader, because of his scorching tirades. He could not afford to be indiscreet, since his aim after arriving in France in 1776 was to persuade Louis XVI to sign an alliance between France and America. The British, remembering his earlier visits to London as an agent of the Colonies and his part in having the Stamp Act repealed, were suspicious of every move he made. The French king and Marie Antoinette, in particular, were wary of sage Ben Franklin, but he was on excellent terms with the Comte de Vergennes, the foreign minister. The French manufacturers and merchants wooed his favor with prospects of future trade. The military men welcomed him as the foe of their mutual enemy, the British. The scholars respected him. The wits enjoyed him. And the brainy eighteenth-century Frenchwomen, some beautiful and seductive, others witty and waspish, cultivated Franklin with an appreciation that he enjoyed.

He was in France continuously from 1776 to 1785, first as one of a committee of three appointed by Congress to negotiate a peace treaty with France, then as plenipotentiary, and finally as commissioner, with John Adams and John Jay, to effect a similar arrangement with Great Britain. On an earlier visit to France in 1767 he had been seen at Versailles in the chestnut suit of a prosperous peasant. But as plenipotentiary he added the fur cap that became the distinctive Franklin touch. For court appearances he wore black Manchester velvet, or the dark blue silk suit in which he was painted, with his own hair, long and frizzed, dangling to his shoulders. His tiny spectacles, precariously lodged far down on his nose, were considered amusing; they added to his air of benignity.

With the seeds of their own Revolution already gestating, the French people regarded the American "insurgents" with sympathetic interest. But the Comte de Vergennes assured Franklin at the end of 1776 that France would remain strictly neutral, although he wished unofficially to aid them as much as he could. Frenchmen clamoring to join the fighting forces in America plagued him for commissions for themselves or their friends. Franklin saw them all, but promised them nothing.

He had set up the first American diplomatic headquarters at the Hôtel de Valentinois in Passy. Visitors had to journey far to the little village outside Paris to find him, with his printing press in the garden, where he ran off a daily paper in French and English for the benefit of Americans in Paris. These exiles sought him out with their various problems, political, social, or professional. He entertained them for dinner on Sundays and by degrees abandoned his own vegetarian fare for epicurean meals in the French tradition. His guests sat from early afternoon until sunset over boards set on trestles, enjoying game and wine and discussing the course of events in America. Franklin's hospitality was designed to cheer them as things went from bad to worse at home.

There was deep depression when word arrived that Lord Howe had taken Philadelphia. This was home to Franklin, the Pennsylvania Quaker, and he was speechless at the news. But almost immediately the message followed that General Burgoyne's entire army had surrendered. This development was roundly toasted by the homesick exiles. Paris was illuminated for three successive nights, and all the resident Americans turned out to participate.

By February 1778 the treaty with France had been signed, and to celebrate the Fourth of July appropriately, Franklin had fifty guests to dinner, mostly American. Among them were John Adams and Arthur Lee, the irascible Virginian who kept stirring up trouble around Franklin, until he was finally recalled by Congress, along with Silas Deane. Both men were fellow commissioners empowered with Franklin to encourage good diplomatic relations and trade development. But Franklin preferred to play a solo hand on the diplomatic front. Always the individualist, he liked to work directly through the friends he had made in Paris.

Franklin was a keen observer of his surroundings as he lived the expatriate life, and he shared the daily activities of French citizens. He watched the Church of the Madeleine, still a Paris landmark, being built. He attended the opera, which was then housed in the Palais Royal. His fellow exiles took note of him strolling along the ramparts of the Quartier Bonne Nouvelle, surveying the fields bright with wild flowers on one side, and the silvery-gray buildings of Paris on the other. It amused him to watch the jugglers, rope walkers, and mountebanks who gathered around the cabarets and dance halls of this quarter. As he wandered along the narrow streets, with their cobblestone pavements and ancient mansions known as *hôtels*, the people easily recognized "le grand Franquélin," the man who flew a kite, who tinkered with a lightning rod, whose inventions had a touch of the science fiction of the future.

He felt most at home with the scientific community, and John Adams thought that he dissipated his energies with the academicians instead of attending more swiftly to affairs of state. He had been a member of the Academy of Sciences since 1772, and he went regularly to L'Institut de France, to meetings at the Collège Mazarin, or the Collège des Quatres-Nations. He had formed these links during his visit in 1769. His vast correspondence with soldiers, statesmen, merchants, and adventurers resulted in heaps of letters lying about in his untidy quarters.

Some of his most important diplomatic work was done through the good offices of the clever women who sought his company. Madame de Maurepas introduced him to Anne Robert Jacques Turgot, Baron de L'Aulne, the French minister of finance, and through this connection he arranged a large loan to buy arms for the Continental Army. It was Turgot who wrote the inscription widely used on Franklin's portraits: "He tore lightning from heaven and the scepter from the tyrant." The same Frenchman had predicted twenty years earlier that America would break free from Great Britain, saying, "The fruit does not cling to the tree after it is ripe."

Turgot was greatly interested in Franklin, and the gifted Quaker from Philadelphia met prominent intellectuals at his home—among them D'Alembert, Condorcet, and Morellet, philosophers and mathematicians who worked with Diderot on his *Encyclopédie,* a historic work that diffused the advanced ideas of the period and figured significantly in the consummation of the Revolution. Franklin had many conferences with the Marquis de Lafayette at Turgot's home, for America's warmest French ally was in Paris during most of 1779. Madame Turgot persuaded Greuze to do a portrait of the American emissary.

Although Franklin enjoyed the company of clever women, he also liked them to be bright and cheerful, so Madame de Staël depressed him. He first met this formidable writer and political sibyl at the home of the Duchesse de La Rochefoucauld-Liancourt. She was with her mother, Madame Necker, and was already engaged in intrigues that would lead to her exile after the French Revolution.

His own particular favorite for much of the time that he was in France was Madame Helvétius, whose husband, Claude Adrien Helvétius, had written *De l'Esprit,* a book that was publicly burned for its sensualism and anti-monarchical sentiments. Franklin was a weekly guest at her salon, and she dined regularly at his home. She was worldly and witty, playing hostess to a fascinating assortment of guests who enjoyed her excellent cuisine.

Madame Helvétius' loud and hearty approach, however, was somewhat shocking to Abigail Adams, who thought she needed some scrubbing up; Mrs. Adams observed with disapproval her tiffany chemise, her frizzled hair, and the dirty gauze handkerchief anchoring her tiny hat in place. When she flung herself on a sofa after dinner, throwing an arm around Franklin's neck and showing more than her feet, Abigail was censorious. "I hope to find amongst the French ladies manners more consistent with my ideas of decency," she later wrote.

But Madame Helvétius was not intimidated by the disapproving looks of Mrs. Adams, and continued to jest with Franklin, to kiss him in public, to write him racy but quite illiterate letters, and to surround herself with the intellectual élite. Although he charmed so many women during his years in France, Franklin made little impression on Marie Antoinette, and she greeted him coolly when, as De Vergennes had proposed, he was received at court with other members of the diplomatic corps in March 1779. Two years earlier she had spoken of the Continental soldiers as "bad troops," to the dismay of the American colony in Paris. But the tide had turned by 1778, when the queen wrote that Louis XVI had decided that the King of England should be informed of the treaty he had made with America, and in 1780 Rochambeau was sent to America with ten thousand troops.

The other American expatriates in France were continually involved in negotiations of one kind or another. Agents backing American trade interests swarmed around the commissioners, and the officers of merchant vessels and privateers were in and out of the seaports. Franklin stayed aloof from this sort of thing and concentrated on his diplomatic and scholarly interests. Earlier he had had a dramatic public meeting with Voltaire, after the philosopher had been summoned back to Paris from his exile in Switzerland to be honored and to pose for a sculptured bust. They met at the Academy of Science in 1772, and the audience cried out that they be introduced. Voltaire, in a fur-lined, crimson velvet robe with lace ruffles, the gift of Catherine the Great, and a monster periwig, rose and bowed. Franklin peered through his spectacles as he returned the salute. "How beautiful to see Solon and Sophocles embrace," a spectator commented.

Writers of the period linked Voltaire and Benjamin Franklin, and Condorcet wrote that in another hemisphere Franklin, like his French prototype, had been the apostle of philosophy and toleration. He had honored philosophy in the realm of physics, as Voltaire had in poetry. They had great interest in each other, but found it difficult to converse, since the Frenchman did not speak English and Franklin read and wrote French more easily than he spoke it. John Adams observed Voltaire in a theater, attending his own *Alzire*, and noted that the French philosopher had "yet much fire in his eyes and vigor to his countenance, though now very old."

The tone of the American colony in Paris changed to some degree after John Adams arrived in 1778. It was soon apparent to their fellow countrymen that he and Franklin were not in total harmony. Franklin spent much time at the Duc de La Rochefoucauld's city mansion or his country estate. The duke was a revolutionary, who had translated the Declaration of Independence and the Constitution of the United States into French. He went to work on the provisions adopted by the various states as soon as the texts reached Paris. All this was of great interest to Franklin, and they continued to correspond after the emissary returned to America. Eventually the Revolution swept the De La Rochefoucauld family into chaos, and the duke became an émigré.

Tired and discouraged over the realization that he was being supplanted by Adams, Franklin, plagued by boils, scurvy, and gout, retired into the shadows and went back to writing his fables and allegories. Even Madame Helvétius tired him at this point, and he found Madame Brillon, a neighbor at Passy, more restful company. John Adams observed Franklin's official operations with disapproval, convinced that his head had been turned by Gallic flattery. He considered him indolent, indecisive, and more committed to the French than the American viewpoint—in short, an expatriate who had become too involved in the foreign environment.

But in negotiating the treaty Franklin's sense of compromise had worked wonders with the Comte de Vergennes, who had been bypassed by Adams. Franklin succeeded in raising another loan, and when Adams accused him of provoking the commissioners who had come over to effect the treaty with France, Franklin commented blandly, "Mr. Adams is in Paris. We live upon good terms with each other, but he has never communicated any of his business to me, and I have no inquiries of him." It was his conviction that Adams was making secret approaches to George III, although Congress had ordered the commissioners to do nothing about an English treaty without the knowledge of the French government.

As Franklin prepared to return home, Mrs. Patience Lovell Wright, a Quaker from New Jersey who had long been his friend and informer, was in Paris, and she modeled his head in wax. Her son, who was a painter, made a plaster model from this and took it to America in 1784. Mrs. Wright, one of the most extraordinary women of the Revolutionary era, had acted as a secret agent or spy throughout the war. Franklin had known her during his bitter years in England, when he was denounced as a traitor and a spy, and she repeatedly gave him information gleaned from the notables who visited her modeling museum on Cockspur Street in the Haymarket. Before the time of Madame Tussaud she did wax models of men and women of the day, her most famous being one of William Pitt, which was later installed in Westminster Abbey. King George III and Queen Charlotte visited her studio, and she addressed them by their given names, Quaker fashion. The king turned against her when she voiced criticism of his policies on the colonies, and Horace Walpole, who had frequently commented on her operations, was acid about the degree of latitude she was permitted during the war. Her demeanor was so wild and undisciplined that no one took her for a dangerous spy, but as soon as a new general was appointed for service in America, she found access to some member of his family. She was received in the homes of the peers, was a close friend of Catharine Macaulay, the historian, and her museum was as popular as Benjamin West's gallery.

Mrs. Wright was a dedicated Whig and republican, and she was saddened to see Franklin return to America. The French mourned when they learned that he was going home. Innumerable portraits were done of the benign old man, and they hung in many public places. Household utensils, even Sèvres chamber pots, bore the Franklin insignia. Stories were told of the simple ways of the great philosopher. Elkanah Watson, an American merchant traveling through France in the early 1780s, recalled seeing him at Mrs. Wright's, when he sat reading in the familiar pose, his left arm resting on a table, and his chin supported by his right thumb. An experimenter to the end, Franklin showed Watson a harmonica that he had devised so that the music came from a combination of hemispherical glasses. To his visitor's amazement Franklin played some simple Scottish pastorals for him.

On Franklin's return to America, Adams churlishly acknowledged that Ben might be a wit, a humorist, a satirist, a great politician, but he questioned the legend that he was a "great philosopher, a great moralist or a great statesman." He added grimly, "As a legislator of America he has done very little."

But as the first American expatriate of note Franklin had made his presence felt and had won the respect and affection of countless Frenchmen. Like other exiles who followed him, he returned with fresh vision and rare gifts to enrich the culture and customs of his own land.

The American diplomatic picture in Europe came into sharp focus when John Adams became minister to Great Britain in 1785, the first full ambassadorial appointment after the war. He had been in France and Holland from 1778, working as a commissioner on the alliance treaties. In 1785, a year after Franklin's return home, Thomas Jefferson became the American minister to France. Both before and after these appointments a number of clever American wives came into view, with Abigail Adams leading the parade. She arrived in Europe in the summer of 1784 with her daughter, Abby, and two servants. After years of separation she was joining John, who had been busy negotiating treaties, activating commercial arrangements, and steering the diplomatic bark. Her first act when she got to London was to visit John Singleton Copley's studio and pass judgment on his full-length portrait of her husband. She next called on Patience Wright and was greeted effusively by the tall, angular Quaker who was one of the most discussed women in London at the time. Next she paid a visit to the Magdalen Hospital. But she was so anxious to see John that she did not dally over sightseeing on this first visit.

However, the pageant of the streets excited her, and she quickly noted that Englishwomen were less fashionable than Americans. She thought them rather plain and Amazonian, except for some of the court ladies, who seemed exquisite to her, with their delicate features, tiny tilted hats, and Dresden shepherdess air. Her sister, Mary, who was Mrs. Richard Cranch, quickly heard all about it, as Abigail wrote: "True, you must put a hoop on, and have your hair dressed, but a common straw hat with only a ribbon is thought sufficient to go into company. Muslins are the style. Or if not fashionable, blue and white calico."

John, who had crossed from Paris to welcome her to the house that he had taken at Auteuil, escorted her from London. The house was near Passy and not far from the Bois. There were five acres of gardens, formally laid out, a small fountain, and grape arbors. Thomas Jefferson called on them frequently. He drew them into his own particular circle of the scholarly abbés, the Lafayettes, and the French families most friendly to the American cause. They dined together every week, and went to the opera, the theater, and at times the *concerts spirituels* held in the Hall of the French Comedians at the Tuileries.

Abigail was shocked by the first dance she saw on the stage. She reported that it embarrassed her to be seen watching girls clad in gauze with short petticoats springing into the air, their feet flying. They showed garters and drawers as "though no petticoats had been worn." But after a few more experiences Abigail was able to accept these worldly manifestations with less concern.

She got on best with the Marquise de Lafayette, who was quiet, unfashionable, and viewed life much as she did. The Duchesse d'Anville, mother of the Duc de La Rochefoucauld, made a profound impression on her when Abigail was received at the great family house, with its libraries, gardens, and a group of academicians gathered around the learned eighty-year-old duchesse. She rose to greet Mrs. Adams, who noticed that her tall, spare form showed the inroads of age but that she did not fool with paint or other cosmetics, to Abigail's relief. The layers of paint on the other women present offended the New Englander as they kissed her on both cheeks. The duchesse wore a tiny black gauze bonnet, bowed under her chin, and a cape covered a silk chemise with wide sleeves. She did not bother with stays, but a velvet girdle ceintured her waist, and she had lace ruffles at her throat and wrists. Her manner was as vivacious as if she were twenty. She belonged to one of the most ancient and richest families in the kingdom. In company of this kind, Abigail, like other visiting Americans, felt the need to improve her French, and she read Racine, Molière, and Voltaire with zest. She lighted the way for other expatriates who clung to their American habits. "We must all sacrifice to custom and fashion," she noted, as she introduced French table customs and manners at her dinner table.

Before her weekly dinners the *frotteur* went roller skating over her parquet floors, polishing them with brushes attached to his feet. This was not altogether the housekeeping of New England, but it was effective. None of her guests suspected that a social history of no mean order was taking shape at Abigail's desk, as she documented in her letters home her view of the social and political life of France.

Although never wholly at ease with the Gallic nature, Mrs. Adams decided that the "arts of elegance" were carried to a state of perfection in Paris and that the sense of taste was infallible. She thought that Frenchwomen understood the interplay of society better than any other members of her sex. But she could not get used to their habit of playing cards for high stakes all night and then sleeping late, and receiving company in bed, all tuckered up in lace ruffles and with high, powdered coiffures. However, they were accomplished. They were polite and they were witty, if not particularly lovable.

Abigail's own daughter Abby was suffering from a shattered romance at the time, and the young people of the American colony did what they could to console Miss Adams, whose parents had vetoed her romance with Royall Tyler. She was still madly in love with him, and her brother John Quincy Adams walked with her in the Bois, took her to the theater and opera, and tried to divert her.

Abby was a stately girl, taller than her mother, and quiet and reserved in her ways. Her brother John, a future President, was already something of an expatriate, although he was about to head
back to Harvard.

The most fascinating American woman in Paris at this time was
Mrs. Anne Bingham of Philadelphia. She and Abigail Adams were
quite dissimilar, but each was on the periphery of the diplomatic
set. Where Mrs. Adams lent wit, intelligence, and understanding to
her role, Mrs. Bingham had beauty, charm, and a coquettish spirit
that stirred interest in London and Paris. She also had ambition,
and she took what Abigail considered breathtaking liberties with
the conventions. In many ways she pioneered in the spirit of the
restless Beautiful People of the 1960's.

Anne married in 1784 at the age of sixteen, and four years later
she arrived in Paris with her husband, William, and settled at the
Hôtel Muscovy. Both were intensely eager to make a splash socially,
although ostensibly he was on the scene to make business connections. Soon they were at home in both London and Paris and were
functioning much like the members of the international jet set of
today. Mrs. Bingham was presented at the court of Louis XVI and
Marie Antoinette, and with some qualms Mrs. Adams introduced her
at the British court. But Anne's beauty and style on that occasion
disarmed Abigail. "I own I felt not a little proud of her," she wrote,
observing her Paris gown with approval and her winning ways with
satisfaction. The lords and ladies of the court showed more interest
in Mrs. Bingham than in any of the other Americans presented on
this occasion, and one of the men remarked, "You have one of the
finest ladies to present that I ever saw."

Mrs. Bingham undoubtedly was the first great belle of the American expatriate world, and by degrees Abigail viewed her as an asset
to the American cause. "She gains my love and admiration more and
more every time I see her," she wrote. "She is possessed of more ease
and politeness in her behavior than any person I have seen . . . her
excellencies overbalance every want of judgment, or that love for
gay life, which is very conspicuous in her, but which I do not wonder at, at all." Abigail thought her rather young to circulate so
freely among the more dissipated and frivolous of the French set,
and her frugal New England soul could not wholly approve of the
Binghams' extravagance. Their luxurious coach with four horses
and three liveried servants went clanking through the narrow streets
of Paris, carrying Anne, a dream of fashion and good looks—*la
belle Américaine,* she was called. She worked hard and unsuccessfully to get a ministerial appointment for her husband, who later be-

came a noted banker and senator in the United States. But in Paris they lived on a much more costly scale than an American minister of the period could afford. Mrs. Bingham's jeweled lockets, watch chains, girdles, and diamonds flashed ostentatiously against the plain attire of such simple Frenchwomen as the Marquise de Lafayette.

There was no such display for the Adamses, either in Paris or London. Abigail found it impossible to entertain on a grand scale with the means at her command, and she soon decided that only the wealthy could maintain the high style of the era. Even before her husband was appointed the first minister to Britain, however, she had observed carefully the social mores and knew how to proceed. And never for a moment did she forget the democratic heritage of the new nation her husband represented. She was half regretful when they moved from Paris to the Court of Saint James's in the spring of 1785, and she had to leave her white lilacs, her polished floors and glittering chandeliers, her fishpond, and her fountain.

A turbulent world opened up for Mr. and Mrs. Adams when they landed in the hotbed of divided loyalties among the Americans in London. The arrival of John Adams, a prime mover in the Revolution, and his brilliant wife, who had done considerable political work on her own, was the signal for the Tory forces to close ranks against them as the adherents of the new order took over. The court presentation of the new minister was a matter of interest not only in Britain and America but around the world. A good many eyes, many of them glinting with hostility, were focused on the actual event.

Adams met it forthrightly with a prepared statement, which he read to the rubicund George, whose fierce white eyebrows and fumbling speech on this occasion were commented on by observers. The king symbolized the tyranny that Adams had helped to overthrow, and their meeting was dramatic, although quietly effected. When Adams had finished, George III told him that not only was he glad to have this assurance of the friendly disposition of the United States, but that he welcomed Adams personally as the nation's choice of a minister.

In a talk with Queen Charlotte, Adams said, "Another Europe, Madam, is rising in America. It will in future ages be the glory of these kingdoms to have people in that country." Two days later the queen received Mrs. Adams, not in private audience but as part of a general presentation. In a hooped white gown with lilac bows and a lutestring underdress Abigail made her obeisance before two hundred people ranged along the walls of a reception room in Saint James's Palace. The king and his courtiers went round the room to the right, and the queen and her ladies-in-waiting made the half-circle to the left. Mrs. Adams must have been of more than ordinary interest to George III, as he saluted her lightly on the cheek and asked her if she had had her walk that day. The queen, in a purple and silver costume, looked at her coldly and remarked, "Mrs. Adams, have you got into your house? Pray, how do you like the situation?"

This was the first and last time the queen ever addressed Abigail Adams, and there was instinctive antagonism between them. "Never again would I set my foot there if the etiquette of my country did not require it," said the spirited Abigail. It was not her habit to be vindictive, but when Napoleon's armies threatened the future of the British Empire, she said, "Humiliation for Charlotte is no sorrow for me. She richly deserves her full portion for the contempt and scorn which she took pains to discover." The queen was singularly devoid of charm. She was clumsily fashioned, with a stout, awkward figure, and a blunt, roughly chiseled face. She had borne fourteen children when Mrs. Adams met her, and another five followed later.

Abigail, like many of the women in the American colony, was too independent to warm to court life. The war had not been fought to perpetuate the monarchical tradition, and she was not disposed to fawn over the French and British rulers. She expressed herself explicitly on the subject: "I own I never felt myself in a more contemptible situation than when I stood four hours together for a gracious smile from majesty, a witness to the anxious solicitude of those around me for the same. I, however, had a more dignified honor, for His Majesty deigned to salute me."

The queen, apparently, had taken pains to belittle Abigail Adams, but the king continued to treat both Mr. and Mrs. Adams with courtesy, and Abigail soon was enjoying life in London. She preferred it to Paris and felt more at home in the English-speaking world. Their house was in Grosvenor Square, and she liked to think that nearby Hyde Park resembled Boston Common. The flowers and gardens overwhelmed her. Social life was brisk. They took in the opening night of the *School for Scandal* at Covent Garden. Americans instinctively gathered at the theater and opera, and after the dim years of the war they appeared in the most fashionable clothes and jewels. But both Mr. and Mrs. Adams thought that large parties and balls were not in the democratic tradition. They knew that they were setting up precedents for the years to come. Abigail was dismayed to find that Englishwomen were as keen about card playing as the French, and at times she could not avoid being drawn into a round of whist, cribbage, or the popular card game commerce. She thought that London, Bath, and Southampton harbored as much dissipation as Paris, and she regretted seeing so many of her countrymen gambling, dancing the nights away in rowdy resorts, and casting their money fruitlessly on the waters. She preferred to run across them attending services in St. Paul's, or visiting an art gallery.

But there was consolation for her in her visits to the university towns, the beauty spots surrounding London, and the ancient landmarks that summed up the history of Britain. She had her frivolous moments, too. It was dashing news back in Braintree that she had done herself up in an oilcloth cap, a flannel bathing dress, and heavy socks and had dabbled about in the ocean at Southampton. Her son John Quincy Adams was to become one of America's earliest and most assiduous swimming experts.

She was relieved to find that her rather simple clothes passed muster in London, and that she did not need large hoops except for court wear. Abby, recovered from her love for Tyler, married Colonel William Stephens Smith, a Revolutionary officer who had been aide-de-camp to General Washington. The Bishop of Asaph presided at an Anglican service alien to the Adamses and then the young pair settled on Wimpole Street and soon became involved in the British way of life.

By degrees Mrs. Adams adapted herself to the world of the émigré. Her own first official dinner was enlivened by talk about the huge turtle that an American sea captain had brought to her. It was the *pièce de résistance* of the evening. Nevertheless both Mr. and Mrs. Adams were well aware that they moved through thick mists of hostility. Abigail had never before been exposed to such social affronts, many of which came from American Tories who had moved to England before or during the war days. Those who had hoped to return to America in triumph were particularly bitter, and even Jonathan Sewall, an old friend, thought that an American legation in London was absurd. It was easier for the Adamses to understand the enmity they encountered in the drawing rooms and at royal parties of all kinds. John Adams' cold manner did not help this situation, although Abigail worked hard to preserve harmony, without surrendering her pride and independence. Attacks on her husband had wounded her for years, but they had reached her chiefly through the written word. In London they both walked defenseless into gatherings where they were openly insulted or ignored. Robert Pitt and the Marquis of Carmarthen, then British minister of foreign affairs, seemed to be their stoutest allies. Franklin and Jefferson were not able to stand up to the chill in London, but the Adamses survived.

Soon after they settled at the Court of Saint James's, Jefferson crossed from Paris to help push through the treaty negotiations with Britain, but he was snubbed and bitterly offended. The Marquis of Carmarthen received Jefferson and Adams together, and Jefferson decided that the "King, ministers, and nation are more bitterly hostile to us at present than at any period of the late war." The treatment he received rankled for the rest of his life, and he summed it up for posterity: "Of all nations on earth they [the British] require to be treated with the utmost hauteur . . . They require to be kicked into good common manners." He felt that their only feeling for America was one of "deep-rooted and cordial hatred."

While in England, Jefferson toured the great manor houses, from Blenheim Castle to Woburn Abbey, and visited the Duke of Devonshire's Palladian mansion. But much as he admired the architecture, statuary, and treasures in the great houses, he noted that America was richer in natural beauty, with its majestic rivers, valleys, and mountains. He developed profound respect, however, for the "mechanical arts" of England and for its gardens. Like all the other American residents abroad at that time, he visited Windsor Castle, the London Pantheon, which was given over to balls and masquerades, and Astley's, a summer place of amusement more than ten centuries old, on Westminster Bridge Road. The theaters and shops were a revelation, but he preferred the orderly look of Philadelphia to sprawling, dirty London.

Jefferson was entertained by some of his fellow countrymen while in London, and he met Dr. Edward Bancroft at the home of Mr. and Mrs. John Paradise. Mrs. Paradise was the former Lucy Ludwell of Virginia, who had married John Paradise, part English and part Greek. Dr. Bancroft, a scientist from Westfield, Massachusetts, had played a mysterious role during the war, serving as secret agent for the American commissioners in Paris and hiding some of his messages in tree trunks in the Tuileries. He was also credited with selling information on American affairs to the British government.

As in the case of John and Abigail Adams, Jefferson's experiences abroad strengthened his belief in the future of America. All three were conscious of the decadence and extravagance surrounding court life, and they took note of the misery of the poor. In a lighter vein Abigail decided that in spite of the English nightingale the birds of Europe were less melodic than those of New England. The flowers were less fragrant, the fruit less sweet, and manners were "not half so pure, nor their people half so virtuous."

When the time came to return to America in 1789, Abigail wrote to Thomas Jefferson—whom she then regarded as "one of the choice ones of the earth"—that "retiring to our little farm, feeding my poultry and improving my garden has more charms for my fancy, than residing at the Court of St. James's where I seldom meet with characters as inoffensive as my hens and chickens, or mind so well improved as my garden."

But there was more to come. The White House lay ahead of John and Abigail Adams after their expatriate years.

Jefferson in Paris

The expatriate pattern was well established in London and Paris when Jefferson was appointed minister to France in 1785, taking over many of the functions of Franklin. He had already been on the scene for a year, and he fitted smoothly into the official setting, although he never became the beloved figure in France that his predecessor was. The embassy was first in the mansion of the Comte de Languedoc at the corner of the Champs Élysées and the Rue Neuve de Berry, and later high up on Mont Valérien, with an encompassing view of Paris. Jefferson considered it part of his diplomatic role to give aid and comfort to the young exiles trying their wings abroad, and he held open house for his fellow countrymen, seating them pell mell at his dinner table but always serving the best of food and wine. Gouverneur Morris, the New York sophisticate who limped through the best social circles with a wooden leg, approved of his cuisine, although he was not particularly friendly to Jefferson. "Mr. Jefferson lives well," he observed. "Keeps a good table and excellent wine, which he distributes freely, and by his hospitality to his countrymen possesses very much their good will."

A widower who never forgot the memory of his wife, Martha Wayles Skelton, whom he had married in 1772 and deeply loved, Jefferson set up his own *ménage* and assembled treasures that in the future would be the pride of Monticello. With a methodical touch and the advice of some of the smartest women in Paris he bought statuary, furniture, china, lamps, tapestries, silver, and paintings. His walls were hung with blue and crimson damask, and he made free use of the printed fabric *Toile de Jouy,* made fashionable by Marie Antoinette. He had six sofas with gold leaf, and commodes and consoles in Directoire style. Jefferson possessed a silver tea urn that he designed himself, and Mrs. Adams was so pleased with his oval mirror *plateau de dessert,* a centerpiece with a gilt gallery an inch high, that she ordered one for her dinner table in London. It had vermeil candelabra with decorative little baskets for flowers and fruit, and it was from Jefferson that President and Mrs. Monroe picked up their ideas for embellishing the White House with its famous mirror plateau centerpiece and vermeil accessories.

With the social pace quickening around him, Jefferson switched from a simple Virginia phaeton to a painted chariot, upholstered in green morocco. A cabriolet and a more elaborate chariot followed. He had a coachman, a gardener, a cook, a *maître d'hôtel,* a *valet de chambre,* and a *frotteur,* which was par for the more affluent Americans settled in Paris at that time. He entered his daughter Patsy (Martha), who later became Mrs. Thomas Mann Randolph, in the Abbaye de Panthémont, a convent close to Paris. His second daughter, Polly, married her cousin, John Wayles Eppes. Both girls were the wives of young men he had helped through practical advice on their education and introductions to men and women of influence. Randolph, who lived for years at Monticello with Jefferson, became governor of Virginia in 1819.

In Paris the minister did not always dress up to his surroundings and frequently appeared to greet his guests—even fellow diplomats—in muddy boots or bedroom slippers. He kept a copy of the American Bill of Rights on one of his walls, and he had Houdon busts of Voltaire, Turgot, Lafayette, Franklin, Washington, and John Paul Jones. He took three copies of his own bust in plaster back to America. Condorcet, Lafayette, and the writers Grimm and Marmontel all were close friends of Jefferson, who, although on the best of terms with the revolutionaries, seemed to have no inkling of the coming storm. He consorted with other members of the intellectual élite and went often to the Château de la Roche-Guyon, the great estate of the Duc de La Rochefoucauld, who had sympathized enthusiastically with the American revolutionaries. The duchesse and William Short, Jefferson's own protégé and secretary, were in love with each other.

Lafayette and his wife, Marie Adrienne de Noailles, lived in great splendor, for the house, garden, promenades, and garniture of the De Noailles estate were legendary. The marquise, who liked and understood Americans, took Patsy Jefferson under her wing and showed her how to entertain such men as Talleyrand-Périgord and the Comte de Buffon. French clerics interested Jefferson and in particular the Abbé Morellet, an associate of Turgot, Diderot, and D'Alembert, editors of the French *Encyclopédie*.

The abbé held matinees for his free-thinking friends in a huge library overlooking the Tuileries. Literary and political topics were thoroughly aired, and here Jefferson consulted Morellet on the translation of his *Notes on Virginia*. The Abbés Arnauld and Charut were also his intimates, and their conversation ranged from the new scientific theories and animal magnetism to the American theory of government.

Although never as responsive as Franklin to the blandishments of the opposite sex, and remembering always his beloved wife, Jefferson was vastly popular in the salons of the great eighteenth-century hostesses, particularly at Madame Necker's. Most members of the American colony disliked the Swiss wife of Jacques Necker, financier and statesmen, but none could question the importance of her salon as she juggled political, financial, and literary figures with a sarcastic and penetrating touch. Jefferson found her restless, fidgety, prudish, and intolerant. Her Monday morning receptions were sparked by the intellectuals of the period, and the encyclopedists always showed up; Madame de Staël, her brilliant daughter, would drop in, and they would all read poetry, voice critical opinions on the prevailing arts, and relax. Grimm had the last word in matters of taste involving sculpture, letters, painting, and all the fine arts. Jefferson thought him acute, egotistical, and cunning.

Intrigue made the American minister uneasy, but he found it even in the salons of his favorites among the Frenchwomen— Madame Helvétius, the Comtesse d'Houdetot, the Comtesse de Tessé, and Madame de Corny. Like Franklin, he often visited Madame Helvétius, whose home was at Sannois, ten miles from Paris. The Comtesse d'Houdetot, the Julie of Rousseau's *Confessions,* held court with both her husband and lover in attendance. She competed at times with Madame Helvétius and Madame de Staël in luring Americans into the fold, and her charm was outmatched only by her hideous looks. Jefferson leaned rather to the Comtesse de Tessé, who shared his interest in architecture and gardening. She was an aunt to the Marquis de Lafayette and belonged to the De Noailles family.

In 1786 Jefferson met Mrs. Richard Cosway in Paris and was impressed by her charm and her knowledge of the arts. She was a gold-en-haired Anglo-Italian, graceful and accomplished. Born in Florence, she was convent-bred and had studied art in Florence and Rome. Her husband was a painter of miniatures, doing greatly admired ivory miniatures of such women as Madame du Barry and Mrs. Fitzherbert. The Cosways lived in high style in London on Pall Mall, and Maria Cosway was friendly with Sir Joshua Reynolds and Angelica Kauffmann, the Swiss-born artist whom he had painted twice. Giovanni Cipriani and Francesco Bartolozzi, the engravers who worked with Reynolds, were friends of the Cosways. During one of her many stays in Paris Mrs. Cosway drew Jefferson into a little group of artists who explored the treasures of the French capital. Together they visited sculptors' studios, the royal palaces, and the gardens. Jefferson listened with quiet attention to Mrs. Cosway and her friends.

Consorting with so many talented women, and observing the contemporary scene, he came to the conclusion that the French lagged two centuries behind Americans in science but were far ahead of them in the arts. "Were I to proceed to tell you how much I enjoy their architecture, sculpture, painting, music, I should want words," he said. "It is in these arts that they shine."

Jefferson respected French cuisine, learned from it, and applauded the temperance that accompanied the Gallic interest in food. He was keenly observant of the young wives from America who came and went with their husbands as American business affairs flourished, but his particular favorite was Angelica Schuyler Church, whose daughter, Kitty, was in the same convent as his own daughters. Mrs. John Barker Church was less conspicuous on the social scene than Mrs. Bingham, but she was a beauty, whom Jefferson found to be reserved and understanding. She was a sister of Mrs. Alexander Hamilton, and her husband, an Englishman, was an aide to Lafayette during the revolution. Angelica played an active part in having Lafayette liberated from his imprisonment at Olmütz. She appealed to Washington, Jefferson, and Chief Justice John Marshall on his behalf. The Churches had an elaborate establishment in London, during the years that he was a member of Parliament. Angelica corresponded with Jefferson as long as she lived, and after her death Kitty continued this custom.

By the time Jefferson had helped innumerable young Americans who passed his way in Paris with advice, introductions, and suitable posts, he had become disillusioned with the growing practice of sending the young abroad for their education. "The consequences of a foreign education are alarming to me, as an American," he wrote from Paris on October 15, 1785, to John Bannister, a member of the Virginia House of Burgesses and of Congress. "But why send an American youth to Europe for education? . . . He acquires a fondness for European luxury and dissipation, and a contempt for the simplicity of his own country. He is fascinated with the privileges of the European aristocrats, and sees, with abhorrence, the lovely equality which the poor enjoy with the rich in his own country. . . . It appears to me, then, that an American coming to Europe for education, loses in his knowledge, in his morals, in his health, in his habits and in his happiness."

But since the young continued to seek his advice and help, he gave them guidance and started a number on good careers. He told them how to study and how to remember. He reminded them to buy the plan of a town and note the major sights, to walk around ramparts and climb to the top of steeples. He urged them to take note of boats, bridges, and other mechanical marvels; to study the animals and local plants; to give plenty of time to the noble gardens of France and its great architecture. He gave them enlightening information on all the arts, on the courts of Europe and on wines and cuisine, but he assured them that political understanding was a prime necessity for the expatriate. The dilettantish note was missing from Jefferson's counsels.

His advice and admonitions became an essential feature of the education of the young American abroad, and the friendships he formed continued for years. Some of the youths were the sons of men he had known in the Continental Congress, and he saw them as future nation builders. He wrote to Thomas Mann Randolph, Jr., later his son-in-law, while the youth was studying in Edinburgh: "I am glad to find you have fixed on . . . politics as your principal pursuit. Your country will derive from this a more immediate and sensible benefit." Thomas Lee Shippen of Philadelphia and John Rutledge, Jr., of Charleston had worldly tastes, but Jefferson steered them firmly into productive channels. Ralph Izard, John Bannister, and John Wayles Eppes, who later married Polly, all moved in his circle. Aside from Virginians and Philadelphians, two men from Boston were shepherded in Paris by Jefferson—Charles Bulfinch, who would become one of the nation's most famous architects, and John Trumbull, the painter, who did a charming miniature of Maria Cosway at this time.

John Ledyard of Connecticut, a brisk arrival on the scene, had accompanied Captain Cook on his exploratory voyage to the Pacific Ocean, and his bravery, ingenuity, and fund of information were a delight to Jefferson. John Paul Jones, looking dandified and well groomed in spite of his sturdy feats in the Navy, caused a stir among the women of the colony, and surprised the French by discussing women's cosmetics and costume with understanding. He was greatly feted, and Louis XVI gave him a gold-hilted sword, although it would be his ultimate fate to die in obscurity in the French capital.

William Short, a young planter whom Jefferson had known in Williamsburg, was his favorite protégé and his business assistant and secretary. Short was popular with the French and Americans alike, and made such a definite place for himself that he became chargé when Jefferson returned to America in 1789 to serve as the first secretary of state. Short, a soft-spoken scholar, had been one of the founders of the Phi Beta Kappa Society at William and Mary College. Mr. Jefferson's young men helped to create an image in Europe of the American men of the future.

But the bright whirl of young life at the American legation was interrupted by the horrors of the French Revolution. On July 4, 1789, when George Washington became President, all members of the American colony gathered at the legation for a four o'clock dinner in its beautiful garden. The guests of honor were the Marquis and Marquise de Lafayette, who were viewed by the Americans as having the status of compatriots. Army and Navy officers wearing French uniforms circled around Patsy as she poured coffee from the silver urn her father had designed. It was a bright day in Paris for the American spirit.

Within ten days, however, the Bastille had fallen. The holocaust, which had been in the making for a long time, had ignited at last. Jefferson had been close to many of the leading revolutionaries, and he was thought to be sympathetic to their views until the reign of terror began. He had written to Abigail Adams from Paris in 1787, referring to unrest at home, that he liked a little rebellion now and then. It was like a storm in the atmosphere. Some months later he wrote with greater emphasis to Colonel W. S. Smith: "What signify a few lives lost in a century or two? The tree of liberty must be refreshed from time to time with the blood of patriots and tyrants. It is its natural manure."

The Americans were locked in their homes as the terror progressed. Jefferson was shaken by the mounting violence of the revolutionaries. He watched the citizens of Paris flow through the streets, armed with swords, scythes, pistols, and pikes, shouting *Vive la Nation,* no longer *Vive le Roi.* When Jefferson went to Versailles, he saw some of the carnage in the streets, as stones were hurled at the cavalry and heads were mounted on pikes. Gouverneur Morris had trouble getting through the streets when he sought counsel with Jefferson at the legation. The châteaus of their friends were being burned. The aristocratic intimates who had talked of revolution with Jefferson for many months were in flight or already dead.

Jefferson blamed Marie Antoinette for much that had happened, and wrote in retrospect, "Her inordinate gambling and dissipations . . . her inflexible perverseness and dauntless spirit, led herself to the guillotine, drew the King on with her, and plunged the world into crimes and calamities which will forever stain the pages of modern history. I have ever believed that had there been no Queen, there would have been no revolution."

Jefferson was back in America when the king and queen died on the guillotine. He brought riches home with him which flowed into the life of the American people, through his freshly acquired knowledge of the arts and sophistication of the most cultured of nations. His eighty-six packing cases were filled with the books, paintings, and objects of art that would adorn Monticello and his vistas had been broadened by all that he had learned during his expatriate years in Paris. He brought rare plants, flowers, seeds, and roots to enrich the horticulture of his native land, and the rose bushes of Monticello were greatly admired. In Italy he had found a choice type of rice, which was of help to the South Carolina planters. He introduced French cuisine at the White House, as Dolley Madison presided cheerfully over a lavish assortment of foods new to the American palate. The recipes Jefferson had copied, along with the wines and delicacies that he provided as President, created lively talk in Washington. His *pannequaiques,* now known as crêpes or pancakes, his dessert of ice cream baked in hot pastry, resembling today's baked Alaska, his cheeses and wines, encouraged the development of epicurean tastes in the early days of the Republic.

But Madame de Staël, an irrepressible diplomat who had survived temporary exile, continued to entertain the expatriates from the new nation across the sea. The talk now was not of Robespierre but of Napoleon, with his escape from Elba a nine-day wonder. Americans were more interested in the fact that the Treaty of Ghent, signed in 1814, had brought an end to the British-American War of 1812. Ghent was *en fête,* with dances nearly every night. Albert Gallatin, America's former secretary of the treasury, who had played a major role in the peace negotiations, lingered on with his son, James, for the final act of signature. All were glad that the long drawn out bickering over this treaty had come to an end. Gallatin was constantly at loggerheads with his fellow negotiator, John Quincy Adams, and was as censorious of his manners as of what he called his "Yankee tricks." During their dealings James Gallatin feared at times that his father, studying Adams with tightly compressed lips, "would wither him instead of making a clever joke to restore peace." For the most part Gallatin thought "little of his talents and less of his manners."

The Gallatins had already crossed swords with Adams in Russia, when he was serving there as ambassador. There were moments when Americans abroad were as divided as the nations they were trying to serve, and John Quincy Adams, in his various diplomatic posts, was to polish up the native Yankee image with a sincere and forthright touch, which did not earn him any laurels. A scholar, a man of truth rather than of manners, he entered the diplomatic service at the age of twenty-seven and served as minister to the Hague, Berlin, and Saint Petersburg. Added to the seven years he had spent abroad while his father held office, these experiences made him a seasoned expatriate before he became President of the United States in 1825.

Gallatin made no secret of the animosity he felt for Adams. He had been frozen out in Saint Petersburg, then moved on to London as an unofficial negotiator in 1814 before being appointed minister to France in 1816. While in London, Gallatin refused presentation at court since he was not a resident minister. But young James mingled freely with members of the colony, wearing a suit of Chinese nankeen, white silk stockings, and a high white stock, with a seed-pearl breast pin. He visited Lady Elizabeth Stafford at Trentham and thought her home more magnificent than any he had seen in France or Russia except the royal residences. She was one of the great hostesses of her time, a friend of Marie Antoinette and of Madame de Staël. He shot snipe on the Chelsea marshes and went regularly to White's Club and Brook's. Friends took him to Crockford's, the gambling hall in Saint James's, where the young American bloods, as well as such notable members as the Duke of Wellington, Talleyrand, and Prince Esterhazy, gathered at night. Both Gallatins stayed at Chatsworth with the Duke of Devonshire and dined on gold and silver plate with the Duke of Wellington. They attended a reception given in the royal pavilion at Brighton by the prince regent. Red-faced and half intoxicated after a cock-fight, he lay on a divan while he received the Gallatins. Albert Gallatin stiffly answered his questions about the royal family in France, and in particular about the Duc de Berry. Young Gallatin thought the Pavilion appallingly vulgar, with its gilded chandeliers splashed with huge colored dragons.

While the Gallatins were in London, Queen Charlotte was suffering from dropsy and was subject to savage tempers. Every day she visited her husband, then experiencing one of his periodic fits of insanity, but he did not recognize her. He thought he was holding court, and he talked ceaselessly to imaginary companions.

James Gallatin, acting as his father's secretary, was eager to stay in Europe, feeling that the years he had spent with his father in Russia, France, and England had unfitted him for life in America. Paris seemed a seductive billet when his father was appointed minister to France in 1816. The Gallatins were of Swiss-German ancestry, and had migrated to the United States in 1780. One of their forebears had been an intimate friend of Henry IV. Their worldly sense was strong, except for that of Mrs. Gallatin, who had prudish views and read sermons by Jeremy Bentham before driving off to a ball in their glass-fronted carriage, known as a Berline. Red-haired young James, handsome and pleasure-loving, swung around Paris in his own cabriolet. Like most of the more prominent Americans he frequently visited Lafayette, and his parents dined often with King Louis XVIII of the restored Bourbon line.

Mrs. Gallatin gave big New Year's Day receptions at which the members of the American colony might rub shoulders with the aging Madame de Staël, with her daughter and son-in-law, the De Broglies, with Baron Friedrich Heinrich Alexander von Humboldt, the Duc de Richelieu, the Duc de La Rochefoucauld, and other aristocrats who had survived the Reign of Terror. The Gallatins were more pretentious in their ways than Franklin, Adams, or Jefferson, and their servants wore blue and yellow livery with wide silver braid and silver buttons.

The members of the American community all went skating on the Petit Lac in the Bois, and were surprised to find how lacking in skill the French were in this sport. The most knowing of their critics was young Gallatin, who skated superbly. So did most of the Russians and Poles. No French girls were permitted to skate, and James Gallatin broke precedent when he guided his sister Frances over the ice. The Gallatins, having recently been in Russia, supplied two large sledges with tiger skins to propel the French matrons over the ice. One of the sledges was swan-shaped and lined with blue velvet.

It was always a major event in their lives when the Gallatins went to visit Madame de Staël at Coppet, with its magnificent view of lake and mountains. Three relays of horses took them to the château, and young Gallatin observed that she had more influence on public opinion than any other person except the ministers. The Americans went into mourning when she died at Coppet in 1817, hating Napoleon to the end. But she was friendly with Madame Elizabeth Patterson Bonaparte, the American wife of Jérôme, Napoleon's brother.

The Gallatins attended many splendid balls in Paris, and young James danced the night away at the most magnificent of them all. It was held at the Tuileries on February 17, 1818, with the Duchesse d'Angoulême in white velvet embroidered with gold fleurs-de-lis and edged with ermine. A diadem of emeralds and diamonds glittered on her powdered head. The Duchesse d'Orléans was in rose velvet and the Duchesse de Berry in white with a sable-bordered train. Both were members of the French royal family. James enjoyed himself more at Madame Récamier's, where many of the younger Americans gathered out of curiosity about her legendary fame. He found her utterly beautiful and supremely stupid.

Gallatin was still in France when Napoleon died at Saint Helena in 1821, and was astounded, like all his fellow Americans, to observe how apathetic the French were in their reaction to this event. He heard the news cried in the street: *La Mort de Napoléon à Saint Helena . . . deux sous.* "It might have been an ordinary actor who had died," he wrote, "instead of the hero which the whole French nation had worshipped, whom all Europe had trembled before . . . a mighty man indeed he was with all his faults."

Albert Gallatin did not open his doors freely to visiting Americans, but Madame Bonaparte was always welcome. He considered her a woman of brilliant intellect, who had been badly treated. He always enjoyed the visits of both the Von Humboldt brothers—Alexander and Wilhelm. They were worldly and traveled, and he found that they discussed American politics in the most knowing way. But John Jacob Astor upset the Gallatin household with his atrocious table manners. "Father has to be civil to him, as in 1812–1813 he rendered great services to the Treasury," wrote young James. "He came to déjeuner today; we were simply en famille, he sitting next to Frances. He actually wiped his fingers on the sleeves of her fresh white spencer. Mamma in discreet tones said: 'Oh, Mr. Astor, I must apologize; they have forgotten to give you a serviette.' "

Two other arrivals from America who were conspicuous in Paris during the Napoleonic era were Stephen and Eliza Jumel. After leaving his native country at the time of the French Revolution, Jumel had established a flourishing wine business in New York. Madame Jumel, an obscure girl from Providence, Rhode Island, had a somewhat tarnished image when she became the wife of the popular merchant, with whom she had been seen often in public. In the course of her lifetime she was variously known as Betsy Bowen, Eliza Brown, Madame de la Croix, Madame Jumel, and Madame Burr. She was the daughter of a sailor and his wife, who was a vagrant familiar in the courts of Rhode Island. As Betsy Bowen, the future Madame Jumel bore a son whom she named George Washington Bowen after the fashion of naming babies for contemporary men. She abandoned the child at birth, but he harassed her in later years by insisting that he was George Washington's son. This absurdity led him into a legal battle over his mother's fortune. He argued the point unsuccessfully in court, but his claim aroused considerable public discussion.

Jumel was unaware of the existence of this child when he married Eliza Brown, as she called herself when she came to New York. She soon emerged on the social scene as ambitious, intelligent, and ruthless, learning French, educating herself, studying the arts and graces. But although she presided with almost regal style in their mansion on the Hudson, the Livingstons, the Beekmans, the Murrays, the Clintons, and the Astors would not receive her. Jumel was popular with the leading men of the day, but his wife was roundly snubbed when together they planned a dinner party to celebrate the election of Thomas Jefferson as President.

On her first trip to France in the late 1790s Madame Jumel saw that Paris bore the scars of the Revolution, and people still talked of little else. Anthelme Brillat-Savarin, whom she and her husband had known in New York, introduced them to his cousin Madame Récamier. Soon Eliza was basking in the company of wits and savants, and was trying to charm Talleyrand, Joseph Bonaparte (who was Napoleon's brother), and Henri Benjamin Constant de Rebecque, novelist and political agitator.

The Jumels drove to the Bastille. They strolled through what later became the Place de la Concorde, which had recently run with blood. They saw where Marie Antoinette had died. Madame Jumel, who had been frozen out socially on the American scene, was received in the inner sanctums of the Faubourg Saint-Germain because of her husband's connections and his promotion of the wine industry in America.

In 1815, the year of Waterloo, the Jumels returned to France and encountered adventure from the day of their arrival. Madame Jumel liked to tell in her later years of the plan she and her husband had arranged with Joseph for Napoleon to board their brig, the *Eliza,* after his escape from Elba. They were to take him to the United States. Instead, he chose the *Bellerophon* and threw himself on the mercy of the British. Within three months he was on Saint Helena, but in the meantime he had sent his carriage to the Jumels out of gratitude. Thereafter Eliza rode around in this state equipage lined with morocco leather. She had the gold key to the emperor's army chest and his traveling clock with the royal N in gold. The embellishments Madame Jumel gave this story increased with the years, but she kept up her association with various members of the Bonaparte family. She insisted that Joseph Bonaparte had come to the United States because of her, and for a time Prince Louis Napoleon, a nephew of the emperor, was her protégé. But the story of Madame Jumel's loves remains misty and legendary.

The impoverished aristocrats of France welcomed the worldly Jumels when they settled at the Hôtel de la Breteuil on the Rue de Rivoli, facing the palace gardens. Eliza often lent her magnificent coach and eight to the Duchesse de Berry, the Duchesse de Charot, and the Comtesse Henri Tascher de la Pagerie, who was related to the Empress Josephine. Through these relationships she acquired some of the jewels and Napoleonic furnishings that later adorned the Jumel Mansion on the Hudson. The Bonapartists and the Royalists both had her support, but she landed in serious trouble when she hung a victory wreath on one of Napoleon's eagles and flaunted it on her carriage. She was mobbed and thrown into jail, the assumption being that she was a dangerous alien plotting a Bonapartist uprising.

Stephen Jumel used all his diplomatic connections to have her freed, and she fled back to New York, leaving her niece Mary enrolled in a boarding school outside Paris. Jumel stayed on in France for many years, and in 1821 Eliza returned. She had been exonerated, and for the next five years they lived in high style on the Place Vendôme. Louis XVIII always took note of her when he drove past her yellow coach, and she appealed to him to recognize her husband with a title or a decoration, since Stephen had created a demand in the United States for French merchandise and had helped to supply it.

The Bourbon king did not heed her request, but she continued to attend all the court functions, and she was at the coronation ball for his successor, the Comte d'Artois, who became Charles X. With a jeweled comb, which had belonged to the Empress Josephine, in her auburn hair, Eliza outshone all her peers in a gown of gold and white silk. But her extravagance cut heavily into her husband's fortune, and she finally returned to the United States. He followed her some years later, and when he died in 1832 after a fall from a haycart, Eliza was thought to have hurried him out of the world by dislodging a bandage and letting him bleed to death. She then married

Aaron Burr, former vice president, who had known and admired her for years. This marriage, however, did not last. Nevertheless, on one of her many subsequent trips to Europe she stood up in her carriage when halted on a country road by a company of soldiers and proclaimed in high, clear tones, "Make way for the widow of the Vice-President of the United States." The name Aaron Burr had left its echo in European circles, whereas that of Stephen Jumel had been forgotten. In her last years in the Jumel Mansion, now a historical landmark open to the public, Eliza—old, tawdry, and demented—dredged up fabulous tales of her life at the French court. Mrs. Alexander Hamilton sometimes called to see her, although, ironically enough, Madame Jumel had married Aaron Burr, who had killed Hamilton in a duel. Eliza's name had figured in the background of this historic duel, but the story remains vague. She was one of America's most interesting political expatriates of the early nineteenth century, but her own countrywomen abroad shied clear of her and left her to the companionship of the dying aristocracy of France.

The Artist's Quest

Many of the early expatriates frequented the studios of London, Paris, and Rome, beginning with Benjamin West's atelier, which drew a long parade of young Americans in the late eighteenth and early nineteenth centuries. Life, color, and a tide of political feeling swept the artist's world as the American Revolution fomented. It paralleled the great renaissance of British art in the mid-eighteenth century, which had followed the Reformation. Portraiture had become the preoccupation of London's fashionable artists. Sir Joshua Reynolds was in command when West appeared on the scene. Thomas Gainsborough and George Romney were on their way up; William Hogarth, the master satirist, was reaching the end of the road.

The American invasion was a new and powerful force, and the studios where these artists worked were filled with brisk activity, like the London coffee shops. Some of the painters were gossip mongers of the first order, and they could boast of having painted George Washington, John Adams, Benjamin Franklin, and Thomas Jefferson. Visiting celebrities made a point of calling at "Mr. West's gallery," and there they learned what was going on in the *beau monde*. Later in the nineteenth century, when the tide shifted gradually to Paris and Rome, artists were the pet expatriates, discussed, criticized, lauded, and feted. In England they continued to be court favorites, like Benjamin West, or pampered by duchesses, like John Singer Sargent; James Abbott McNeill Whistler was as much a public character as Truman Capote is today. But they were often in trouble, and they rarely paid their bills.

Benjamin West, instinctively an artist, showing promise long before he had had any formal lessons, was born near Springfield, Pennsylvania, in 1738. His father was an innkeeper who had come from England, and the boy listened attentively to the Germans heading along the Delaware in their Conestoga wagons. His simple sketches of children, animals, and flowers were much discussed before he was twelve, and his fame as a child prodigy spread through the region. He demanded paints and canvas when he first saw the harbor masts at Philadelphia, and in 1759 John Allen, a Philadelphia merchant, offered him free passage to Leghorn.

He traveled to Rome, where he aroused interest as a visitor from the land of red Indians—the European conception of America. It happened that West was greatly attached to the Indians, and when he was shown the Apollo in the Vatican, he exclaimed, "My God, how like a Mohawk warrior!" In the salons of Rome he extolled the strong, proud Mohawks. Slow to warm to the classical images, he was as repelled by the emotionalism of the religious paintings as he later was by the voluptuous work of François Boucher, Madame Pompadour's favorite. However, Raphael Mengs, a Bohemian who was fighting the rococo influence, took West into his studio in Rome, and the young American studied there for three years, meanwhile receiving considerable acclaim for his work. When he was ready to return to America, his father urged him to visit England. On his way there he stopped at Parma to copy Correggio's *Madonna of Saint Jerome,* a custom adopted by the visiting American artists who followed him. This became one of their favorite subjects as they studied the masters.

When West reached London in 1763, he had considerable self-confidence. He was affable, assured, and his name was known in Italy as well as in America. For a time he studied drawing at Saint Martin's Lane Academy, haunted the English galleries, and was in and out of Dr. Johnson's club. William Howe, who later commanded the British army, liked his work and urged fashionable Londoners to drop in and see what Mr. West was doing. Benjamin decided to set up his own school when sales were slow, and he soon became preeminent as a teacher. Matthew Pratt was the first of his fellow countrymen to study with him, and he was followed by John Singleton Copley, Gilbert Stuart, Charles Willson Peale, Rembrandt

Peale, John Trumbull, Washington Allston, Samuel Finley Breese Morse, Edward Greene Malbone, Charles Robert Leslie, Thomas Sully, and William Dunlap. These and many other artists paused to study with Mr. West before heading for Paris and Rome.

Prelates of the Anglican Church backed West in his wish to paint pictures infused with piety but not with agonized distortion. In the thirteen years prior to 1776 he turned out thirty-four classical canvases, and King George III, who had become his friend and patron, commissioned him to paint thirty-five large murals for the chapel at Windsor Castle. However, West's close association with the court aroused the jealousy of leading British artists and created complications for him as America shook off the British yoke. The king thought Reynolds and Gainsborough too worldly; plain Mr. West was more his man. The American painter refused a knighthood as not in keeping with the democratic tradition of his native country, but he was elected president of the Royal Academy when Reynolds died in 1792.

Most of the British artists who followed Reynolds took instruction at one time or another from Benjamin West. He was one of the first to acclaim the work of Joseph Turner, and he encouraged William Blake and other artists and writers involved in the pre-Romantic movement. To Byron, West was a dotard, but thirty thousand people visited his studio to admire his painting *The Death of Lord Nelson.* Later *The Death of Wolfe,* exhibited in 1772, was one of the most discussed paintings in the history of British art. Such was his influence with King George that the British Fleet was paraded for his benefit while he was doing *The Death of Lord Nelson.*

West was at times in an uncomfortable position with his compatriots, both at the time of the Revolution and again during the War of 1812. He was suspected of toadying to the king, in spite of his protestations that his sympathies were all with his native land. Nevertheless, Jefferson visited him in 1786, and when Abigail Adams first landed in England, she went to study the picture he had done of her husband. Robert Fulton, who had served with the Revolutionary forces, left before the war was over to study painting with Benjamin West. But Fulton soon moved on to Paris, where he painted panoramas, before devoting himself to the inventions that led in 1807 to the successful run of the *Clermont* up the Hudson River.

The Napoleonic Wars kept many Americans tied to London, and the expatriate life was brisk around Mr. West's gallery. His surroundings were impressive, and the peers of the realm came and went with great familiarity. The artist had added a gallery with two lofty rooms to his substantial house on Newman Street. His own, work lined the walls, and casts of Venus and Apollo were in evidence. A garden with an arcade and statuary suggesting an Italian effect could be seen through small-paned windows.

The young artists who worked and often rollicked in his studio liked to go picnicking at Richmond and Greenwich. They attended the theater regularly, and worshipped at the shrine of Sarah Siddons, the incomparable Lady Macbeth of the nineteenth century, and the subject of Reynolds' *Tragic Muse*. Some of the youths went skating with Mr. West, who was so expert on ice that the nobles and statesmen, as well as plain citizens of London, gathered to watch him dance the minuet on skates in Hyde Park. He never became a sophisticated man of the world, in spite of the company he kept, and his simplicity at times made him a target for hostile comment and the butt of many jokes.

West, above all, was a hard worker. He arose early and planned his day before breakfast. After giving lessons, he painted until four in the afternoon. Then his visitors arrived, many of them American, some English. After dinner he went back to work and study. His studio was a haven for the penniless expatriate because he never turned anyone away, and he gave financial help to many of the young Americans who were his guests and students. Much was made of the story that he had harbored the irrepressible Tom Paine, but West insisted he had merely seen the revolutionary on three or four occasions during Paine's stay in England.

As he became insane, the king turned against West, and the painter's pension and royal commissions were canceled. But his painting *Christ Healing the Sick,* done to help the Pennsylvania Hospital in Philadelphia, renewed his wealth and added to his fame. When he died in 1820, he was buried in London at Saint Paul's, next to his historic rival Reynolds. His influence was felt for years to come among the artists of his native land.

Gilbert Stuart, who was a fugitive from war and sailed from Boston in 1775 on the day before the Battle of Bunker Hill, was taken on by West as his assistant. As well as being one of the Revolutionary War expatriates, Stuart was to become one of America's most noted artists. He was born in North Kingstown, Rhode Island, in 1755 and spent many of his boyhood hours on the seafront of nearby Newport. Like West, he drew and painted almost from childhood, and after being tutored in Newport by a Scottish painter named Cosmo Alexander, he studied at the University of Glasgow. The death of his mother's brother, Joseph Anthony, who was his patron, forced him to return to America. Penniless, he enlisted before the mast on a collier. His parents, who were Tories, had fled to Nova Scotia as Loyalists. Years later Stuart said that he had wanted to fight the British, but his father had advised him to sail again to England. His departure was precipitated by the fact that he was shut up in Boston during the Battle of Lexington.

He vowed he would never seek the help of the king's painter, but lack of funds drove him to the hospitable Mr. West's gallery, where he worked for the next four or five years, earning half a guinea a week at first and painting draperies only. West understood him from the start and made no attempt to curb his bold, arrogant spirit, although Gilbert sometimes created bedlam with his practical jokes and carousing. The young artist deplored West's technique; he frequently made fun of him behind his back, and even in his hearing. He made no secret of the fact that he preferred Gainsborough's work. But West continued to treat him like a father, and when Stuart broke a valuable optical instrument the aging artist mildly remarked, "Well, Stuart, you may pick up the pieces." His pranks added little to the tone of the gallery, but he was welcomed back after each spree.

The peers, bishops, and scholars who called on Mr. West soon observed the wild young man who had so much to say for himself, and Dr. Johnson asked how it happened that a colonial should speak so well. Stuart shot back, "Sir, I can better tell you where I did not learn it. It was not from your dictionary."

Like West, he skated well. His *Gentleman Skating* was exhibited anonymously at the Royal Academy in 1878 and was thought to be by Gainsborough. There was something so dynamic in his work that he was soon loaded with commissions, painting George III, George IV (as Prince of Wales), Sir Joshua Reynolds, Mrs. Siddons, and Benjamin West. "I hear West says that he nails the face to the canvas," young William Temple Franklin reported to his grandfather Benjamin Franklin. He subordinated costume and background to emphasis on character, and he disliked doing children and animals.

Stuart was temperamental and erratic in his work, but he was soon making more money than any other artist in England except Reynolds and Gainsborough. He was also spending it at a livelier pace, living with some magnificence and employing a French chef and a group of Italian musicians. Although he remained on good terms with West, as soon as he had had some success, he set up his own studio and showed great independence from the other academicians. But he could never free himself wholly from his debts, and he landed in a Dublin prison for not paying his bills, after consorting with some of the wildest gentry in Ireland. He returned with his family to New York in 1793, and Sir Thomas Lawrence, the English artist, who knew him well, commented, "I believe that the real cause of his leaving England was his having become tired of the inside of some of our prisons."

He returned to his native land a famous artist, although he had left it in obscurity. From this point on, he painted one political celebrity after another, and notably the generals of the Revolutionary War. However erratic, his expatriate years had been fruitful, and his future was assured. He had studios in New York, Philadelphia, Washington, and Boston. He became best known for his portraits of George Washington, doing five full-length portrayals of the first President. He also painted Martha Washington, John Adams, John Quincy Adams, James Madison, and Thomas Jefferson. Stuart died in 1828, and his name was chosen for the Hall of Fame in 1910.

John Singleton Copley, whose portraits of noted New England men and women became what Oliver Wendell Holmes called the sure clue to ancestry in that region, left his native country after being involved through his wife's family in political moves that preceded the Boston Tea Party. His wife, Susannah Clarke, was the daughter of Richard Clarke, a Tory merchant who was an agent for the East India Company and a prominent merchant in Boston. Although Copley worked for peace, he left for Europe after his home and family were threatened by a mob.

Copley's wife and three of their four children followed him to London. The youngest, left behind, soon died in besieged Boston. By the time five British regiments were quartered there, Copley had decided to stay in England, and he wrote to his friend Henry Pelham, "Could anything be more fortunate than the time of my leaving Boston? Poor America. I hope for the best but I fear for the worst. Yet certain I am she will finally emerge from her present calamity and become a mighty empire."

West welcomed Copley at his studio and introduced him to Reynolds, who took him to the Royal Academy. His reputation had preceded him. He moved restlessly across Europe, garbed in a friar's cloak over a snuff-colored greatcoat, with a French bonnet looped around a brightly patterned silk handkerchief. He was a nervous traveler and carried a sword or hickory stick to protect himself from highwaymen. Copley never habituated himself to the ways of the world, although he mirrored the most worldly of types on canvas. His speech was sharp and abrasive; his manner was suspicious.

The colonials with British sympathies were in the habit of meeting at the New England Coffee House, where they dined on salt fish, or else at the weekly meetings of the Loyalist Club, where they discussed the loss of their possessions and the progress of affairs at home. They called themselves the New Poor. Elkanah Watson, an American merchant from Plymouth, Massachusetts, who traveled across Europe in the late 1770s and early 1780s, was an observer of the two factions in London—those wholly committed to the cause of the Revolution and those who remained vigorously Tory. The artists, with the freedom of all bohemians, touched both areas, and Watson observed Copley and West present with a group of American ladies on the winter day in 1782 when George III announced before Parliament his decision to recognize the independence of the United States.

Artillery roared as the king arrived with all due pomp at the Houses of Parliament. He faltered and choked as he read from a scroll. In admitting the separation of the Colonies from the Crown he observed, "I have sacrificed every consideration of my own to the wishes and opinions of my people." Watson noted the "anguish and despair depicted on the long visages of our American Tories." He walked out with West and Copley and dined that night with Copley, who put the finishing touch to a painting he had done of Watson. It showed the merchant with a ship in the background, but the cautious artist had refrained from adding the flag until King George had conceded independence. It would not have been helpful to Copley had the nobles and members of the royal family who visited his studio seen this symbol in advance.

But now it was a *fait accompli,* and Watson wrote in his memoirs that Copley had "attached to the ship the Stars and Stripes with a bold hand, a master's touch, and I believe an American heart." He decided that it was the first American flag hoisted in England.

Next day Edmund Burke attacked the king's speech as a "farrago of nonsense and hypocrisy." Watson was introduced by Burke to Pitt, Fox, Sheridan, Conway, and other parliamentarians. Many of the exiled Americans consorted with the members of Parliament and the great orators then making history in England. After independence was conceded, Copley swung completely around to regarding the Revolution as a glorious event. He was bored and impatient with the endless criticism he heard of the Americans who had taken this historic step. His quarrelsome and intolerant nature led him to break with the amiable Mr. West, who had given him so much help. In the course of time he helped to drive his old friend from the presidency of the Royal Academy, and the artists and other expatriates resented this.

The vogue for Copley declined in the late 1790s, and his clear, cool work lost favor in an age of opulent backgrounds and aristocratic paraphernalia. He adapted himself to the new fashion to some extent, but remained essentially the realist, catching the sensitive, intellectual face with rare understanding. He was scornful of the colonials who saw nothing beyond the exterior likeness in portraiture. However, all were agreed that his painting *The Death of Lord Chatham* was a historical masterpiece, and Londoners flocked to see it. They also gathered around when he worked on *The Repulse of the Floating Batteries at Gibraltar*. This was such a huge work that a tent housed it in Green Park by consent of the king. Copley stood on a platform with his canvas fixed on rollers, and spectators considered this another of the whims of the strange men from the Colonies.

Copley had a house on George Street, and his son, John Singleton Copley, who had grown up in England and became a jurist, was knighted. As Baron Lyndhurst he became lord chancellor of England. In many ways the older Copley regretted having left New England, and he looked back with nostalgia on the days when he painted his compatriots in their native settings. He died of a stroke in 1815, the year of Waterloo.

Charles Willson Peale, who had learned from Copley how to paint by candlelight, was one of the first American artists to show up in West's gallery, but he was unhappy and homesick. He had financial backing from Horatio Sharpe, governor of colonial Maryland, and ten members of the Colony's council, who expected him to show that America was not solely a land of commerce and materialism. He visited London as a young man and wandered restlessly around the city, going to the theater, touring Windsor, Hampton Court, and Richmond, talking endlessly to West as he posed for the figure of Regulus in West's *Regulus Leaving Rome,* a picture commissioned by the king. While in London, Peale had some success with his miniatures. He modeled in plaster and worked on mezzotints. His style was enriched by his study abroad of costume effects, and he showed skill in painting the rich silks and laces of the day. Peale miniatures were worn in brooches by the great ladies of America for years to come.

Like Gilbert Stuart, Peale painted George Washington, and no less than fourteen times. Rembrandt, one of his three artist sons, all of whom were named after painters—Raphael, Rembrandt, and Titian—did what became the most popular portrait of Martha Washington. Peale named another of his seventeen children after Benjamin Franklin, whom he had visited in Paris. The fact that he

43

tinkered with taxidermy, watchmaking, and wax figures appealed to the multifaceted Franklin. But on the whole, Peale was a lonely exile and was glad to return to his native land.

When John Trumbull, an artist friend of John Adams, reached England in 1784, he hurried at once to Mr. West's gallery, the natural habitat of the painter abroad. He was a veteran of the war and when Jefferson met him in London, he urged Trumbull to move to Paris for further instruction. He was soon appearing in the company of Houdon, the artist Madame Vigée-Lebrun, and Jacques Louis David, court painter to Louis XVI. Trumbull was well fortified by John Adams' advice to all the young American émigrés who passed his way. Adams warned them against indulging too freely in dancing, card playing, and the theater. The behavior of many, he had observed, was not to his liking, and he particularly deplored any surrender of the independent American spirit. "Cultivate the manners of your own country, not those of Europe," Adams told them. "The more decisively you adhere to a manly simplicity in your dress, equipage and behavior, the more you will devote yourself to business and study, and the less to dissipation and pleasure—the more you will recommend yourself to every man and woman in this country, whose friendship and acquaintance is worth your gaining or wishing." He urged urbanity, without ostentation or extravagance.

Not all of the expatriates heeded this advice, and the artists in particular were a law unto themselves. They continued to stir up controversy, excite talk, and get themselves involved in political affairs. After the Napoleonic Wars the American painters ranged over the Continent, forming colonies in Paris, Rome, and Florence, and creating a strong image of the American artist abroad.

Literary Pilgrims

Letters, no less than diplomacy, loomed large in the lives of the early American expatriates. Franklin, Adams, and Jefferson all were seasoned writers and diarists, but it was Washington Irving who set a firm and enduring pattern for the American writer abroad. He was followed by a succession of authors whose talents were enriched by their travels, and who left behind them records of their experiences in foreign lands. The impression at times was that of a banal and repetitious travelogue, but their accounts gave the people of the young Republic a strong sense of life in Europe, from the topography of each country to the personalities of the day. It was period writing of lasting effect, and it encouraged many to go abroad and see the world for themselves.

A deliberate attempt was made by the early Presidents to fill diplomatic posts with men of culture and scholarship. Writers were a likely choice. Their dispatches were informative. They moved with grace among the worldly men of letters. Washington Irving was so successful in this role that the tradition of combining diplomacy with scholarship persists to this day. Irving was an early propagandist of the first order and a man of great charm and distinction. Moreover, he was wholeheartedly committed to the well-being of his fellow Americans abroad, and all who passed his way commented on the hospitality and help they received from him. There was much need of this kind of assistance when Americans first began going abroad.

At different times Irving lived in Madrid, London, Paris, Dresden, Vienna, Salzburg, and Prague, and wherever he went, he reached the inner nerve of the city and moved among the knowledgeable. Spain is the country with which his name is most closely associated, and he started a wave of travel in that direction. Irving was on the embassy staff in Madrid from 1826 to 1829 and was United States minister to Spain from 1842 to 1846. He was splendidly at home as secretary of the United States legation in London from 1829 to 1832, the year in which *The Legends of the Alhambra* came out and added to his fame. He was already well known for his *History of New York . . . by Diedrich Knickerbocker; Bracebridge Hall;* and *The Sketch Book.*

These books brought him popularity, and his personal charm gave him swift entrée to the social life of London. He attended the major parties of the period, invariably well turned out in what he called his "peas blossom" waistcoat, a claret coat, and flesh-colored silk stockings. At all times he was the worldly man about town, sauntering in and out of the best clubs, and consorting with the statesmen, wits, and writers of the early nineteenth century.

Delicate as a youth, Irving was sent abroad by his family for his health in 1804, when he was twenty-one. They commissioned him to bring home a cargo of wine. He toughened up as he took the Grand Tour of Europe—in fact it was he who set the fashion for this finishing course for affluent young men in America. He participated in boar fights in Germany, and roughed it along the highways and byways, taking walking trips in Britain with William C. Preston, later a senator from North Carolina, and in Italy with Washington Allston, the artist, and Samuel Taylor Coleridge, the poet.

In Rome they spent long hours at the Caffè Greco, where the sculptors and artists gathered to discuss their work. They rambled in the Alban Hills, explored the Roman ruins, and discussed art and letters under the pines of the Villa Borghese. Allston, four years older than Irving, was a South Carolinian sent abroad by his family to save him from the ignominy of becoming an artist, the prevailing view at that time of such divergence from the established planter tradition. Edward Malbone, the miniaturist, encouraged the young painter in his work and went abroad with him. Allston had success in his venture and became a productive expatriate. He stayed on in Rome for three years after Irving left, and did several portraits of Coleridge.

While in Europe, Allston helped some of the young American artists he met, as Irving did the writers. The two friends shared a common interest in wild mountain scenery, waterfalls, and medieval castles. Both were acutely conscious of the banditti who were supposed to lurk in the fastnesses, and they conjured up eerie encounters along the highways. Byron shared this taste, but James Fenimore Cooper deplored it. He belittled the dangers of the road, although Nathaniel Hawthorne as late as the 1850s narrowly escaped highway robbery.

Irving was enthralled with Rome and noted that "men discover taste and fancy in Italy." He was keenly observant of the native life, from the Bernini churches "overcharged with ornament" to the bright flowers worn on the hats of the peasants. He found Canova at work in his studio on statues of Napoleon, Napoleon's mother— Maria Letizia Ramolino, "Madame Mère"—and his sister, Princess Maria Paulina Borghese. Prince Torlonia, the banker, invited him to a Roman *conversazione,* a popular form of social gathering in the nineteenth century for the discussion of literature and the arts. He had his first meeting with Madame de Staël, who was then in Italy assembling material for *Corinne ou l'Italie.*

For a time Irving considered staying in Rome to study painting, but instead he pushed on to France, traveling through the romantic passes of the Apennines to Bologna and Milan. He took courses at the Sorbonne and soon showed up in the salons of Madame Récamier and Madame de Staël, establishing another custom for visiting students. He quickly found compatriots in Paris, and John Vanderlyn, a protégé of Aaron Burr's who was taking life classes with students from other countries, painted a portrait of him. He met John Izard Middleton, a South Carolinian descended from a signer of the Declaration of Independence. Middleton's wife was the daughter of a Swiss banker living in Naples, and he had settled in Italy after attending Cambridge University. Charles Eliot Norton described Middleton's *The Grecian Remains in Italy,* published in 1812, as "the first contribution made by an American to the knowledge of classical antiquity." He was the first of the long parade of archaeologists who would cross the Atlantic for "digs."

All these encounters in the days of his youth were profoundly felt by Irving, but no one moved him more than Sir Walter Scott. Irving and Preston toured the Trossachs together, covering the trail of *Lady of the Lake,* and in the end encouraging the passion for Scott in America, and particularly in the South, where the medieval tradition took firm hold. Irving tried to model himself on Scott, but although a hard worker, he could not push himself to write at any hour of the night or day, as the author of the Waverley Novels did. His health sometimes failed him, and during one period he could not write at all until the poet Tom Moore visited him and spurred him on. But when he went to work on the life of Columbus, he wrote continuously for fourteen and fifteen hours a day.

Because of Irving, Spain became a stop on the Grand Tour and was on every American's itinerary in spite of the hardships of travel and the adventures of the road. Irving's path crossed that of John Howard Payne in the 1840s, when the author of "Home Sweet Home" was serving as United States consul to Tunis. The two men had worked together on plays in Paris some years earlier. Payne at that time was fleeing from his creditors, and had not yet written his enduring song.

Irving passed his last years at Sunnyside, his country house near Tarrytown, New York, the region he had immortalized in *The Legend of Sleepy Hollow*. There he turned out his five-volume *Life of Washington* between 1855 and 1859, the year in which he died. He was the first of the literary expatriates, but the fashion he set was well established during his lifetime.

When Henry Wadsworth Longfellow arrived in Europe in 1834, he was well schooled in the Irving tradition and followed the same paths. He was only nineteen when he landed in France, thinking of himself as a pilgrim visiting a holy land. At first he was amused, then disgusted by the customs of the French. The "noise and stench" dismayed him, but conversations with Talleyrand restored his equilibrium. He found Paris dark, gloomy, and muddy, and the struggle to master French at the Sorbonne tired him, although his family had sent him abroad to study languages so that he could teach on his return.

Spain was another story. Following the trail of Washington Irving, Longfellow spent eight months journeying through a land that at first looked cold and uncultivated to him, but soon seemed invested with charm. He wrote romantically of the Alhambra and of trips that lingered "like sunbeams" in his memory. He traveled, sometimes on horseback and sometimes by diligence, over highways that he felt must be overrun with robbers. He was welcomed by Irving, whose *Sketch Book* had inspired his travels. Life seemed a constant adventure to the young student, whose literary career still lay ahead of him. Along the way he collected Spanish devotional poems and Moorish legends.

When he reached Italy, Longfellow decided that Venice was the most beautiful city he had ever seen, but the muddy Arno, almost dry in summer, was disillusioning when he got to Florence. However, he did the customary tourist rounds of the city's art galleries. He walked most of the way from Florence to Rome, with *Childe Harold* in his knapsack. The influence of Byron was strongly felt at this time. Longfellow stayed with a Roman family, and a fellow lodger was George Washington Greene, an early expatriate who had married an Italian girl and become American consul in Rome. Greene, the historian grandson of Nathanael Greene, George Washington's favorite general, spent twenty years in Italy and, like Irving, was always a friend to an American passing through.

Longfellow was entertained in the salon of Joseph Bonaparte's daughter, who played "Yankee Doodle," thinking this would please him, but he was intent on brushing up on classical history. Wherever he went among the ruins of Rome, from the Catacombs to Tivoli outside the city, he pictured Marcus Aurelius, Vergil, and Horace in their natural settings, and recalled the classical allusions from their writings that fitted the scene. It was a scholar's journey, but he found living drama in the Colosseum when he visited it at night, pronouncing it a majestic sight, with torches pouring showers of light on the arches and dimming the pale moon. Lumbering carriages waited at the entrance for the visitors wandering in the great amphitheater.

The poet became seriously ill in Rome and went to Ariccia in the Alban Hills to recuperate. There he read Italian poetry and sauntered through the Chigi woods, a favorite resort for artists at the time. On all sides he saw them at work, sitting on campstools, waving their palettes, or dozing under the shade of their wide umbrellas. The artistic fever caught him briefly, and he did a little sketching before returning to Rome, to sit again in the Piazza Navona or to watch the dancers weaving to the music of tambourines in the park of the Villa Borghese. The chimes of convent bells, the songs of the Italian boatmen, all worked their way into his consciousness, and he talked earnestly to Greene of the literary future he planned for himself.

After exploring Dresden, Prague, and Trieste, Longfellow followed some of his American friends to the University of Göttingen. After three years he was back in the United States and his first book, *Outre Mer,* detailed his adventures. He made many return trips, spending long periods abroad and coming to know Italy intimately. He was ardent for the unification of Italy when he revisited the country in 1868, soon after his translation of Dante had been published. During his years of association with Harvard he spread the Italian mystique among scholars and lighted the path for many expatriates to come, particularly the poets. Lecturing at Harvard in

1851 he said: "Say what ill of it you may, it still remains to the poet the land of his predilection, to the artist the land of his necessity, and to all the land of dreams and visions of delight."

Longfellow, James Russell Lowell, and Charles Eliot Norton widened the horizons of the poet in the United States, and in translating Dante, Longfellow opened a new field of letters for the American student. At the Dante Club, which later became the Dante Society, interest in the Italian poet and his work flowered into a minor renaissance. George Ticknor, the scholar and traveler who had preceded Longfellow and Lowell at Harvard, worked chiefly in the linguistics field, but they deepened the general study of the Italian master. Christopher Cranch, who had lived in Rome, George Washington Greene, and William Dean Howells joined this group, and among the later students were Bernard Berenson, who went forth to live the complete expatriate life and become one of the world's greatest art authorities; Isabella Stewart Gardner, who collected Italian masterpieces on Berenson's advice; and other literary figures who were drawn toward Dante's world and sometimes into permanent exile from the American scene. The Dante Society met first in Longfellow's study, which had Thomas Crawford's bust of Nathanael Greene on display, and then at Norton's house.

Another prominent American author who loved Italy and was instantly recognized there was James Fenimore Cooper. Basking in the success of *The Last of the Mohicans,* he arrived in Europe with his wife and daughters in 1826. He stayed for seven years and turned out books with unfailing regularity—in Rome and Paris, in Dresden and Bern. His prestige for many years was formidable, and each of his books was published simultaneously in thirty-four European cities. Post offices and country inns were named after him. He was besieged with invitations to stay at castles, attend great parties, and represent his country at innumerable functions.

Cooper was vigorously American and republican wherever he went, and in his books he reverted always to his native background, no matter where they were written. Because Cooper's books mirrored Indian life so accurately, Europeans savored them as something novel and informing. In time they also contributed to the prevailing feeling that the United States was more or less overrun with Indians. But during the 1820s and 1830s he helped to illumine the American scene for Europeans who did not wholly understand the Revolution and its consequences.

Traveling extensively and in high style through Italy, Switzerland, and Germany, Cooper met the celebrities in each country he visited, and always left a strong impression of himself. He was apt to be quarrelsome, cranky, and critical, and at times he ran into law-suits. Like most of the other expatriates, he made Italy his mecca. Long before F. Marion Crawford settled at Sorrento, Cooper wrote *The Water Witch* on the terrace of the Casa Tasso. He cared more for scenery than he did for art, although he spent much of his time in Europe with men like the sculptor Horatio Greenough, and he was always ready to give a salty opinion on any work of art. He found the Giotto campanile in Florence "finical" and the cathedral at Pisa a "droll medley." The poet Adam Mickiewicz, a close friend of the Italian patriot Giuseppe Mazzini, and a conspirator for most of his life, rode over the Campagna di Roma with Cooper, and he spent much time with the author's family. The Polish poet viewed him as "that star of the other hemisphere who sweeps across (ours) like a comet." Cooper's books were popular in Poland, as elsewhere in Europe, and along with Lafayette, who backed the Polish rebel-lion against Russia in 1830, he did what he could for this cause when he moved from Rome to Paris. He was close to Lafayette and often visited him at his country estate.

Usually Cooper went from one country to another with expecta-tion rather than regret, but it pained him to leave Italy, and his wife noticed that it was the only country he ever left looking over his shoulder as he went. "Italy is the land I love," he said, after he had savored its beauties and its art for two years. He left many friends behind him in Rome, but he was cordial to his fellow coun-trymen, whether he met them journeying between Moscow and Warsaw or at his own dining table. In Paris he made a point of serv-ing meals suited to the American taste, and gave breakfasts with buckwheat cakes and strong coffee for those who hungered for the native touch. This paralleled the efforts of Mrs. Alphonso Taft, mother of William Howard Taft, to train her servants in Vienna to make French toast and corned beef hash for her husband's breakfast while he was minister to Austria. The expatriate's wife of an earlier day had many problems of this kind to solve.

Samuel F. B. Morse, subsequent inventor of the telegraph, had left America in deep depression when he failed to make headway with his art. He was the constant companion of Cooper in Paris. They took long walks together, and Morse helped Cooper choose paintings for his home. They spent hours in the Louvre, with Morse painting laboriously and Cooper directing operations in a dogmatic way from an adjoining stool. Morse was a member of the American Committee in Paris to aid the Polish insurgents, and the two men were politically sympathetic.

Cooper's popularity faded when he returned to the United States.

His earlier republicanism seemed to have faltered, and he viewed his native land with a critical eye. Just as he had been scathing at first about European customs and manners, he now belabored the land of his birth and focused on the materialism of his compatriots. He had scorned the tyranny and show of Europe, but on his return the impression prevailed that he had succumbed to pomp and ceremony and had lost his egalitarian view of mankind. The man who had extolled the lack of guards, processions, wands, and robes at the inaugurations of James Monroe and John Quincy Adams projected a new image that Americans did not like. He expressed his critical views in his books and won several libel suits against newspapers before his death in 1851. His defenders insisted that his democratic spirit had remained intact.

In spite of the years they spent abroad, Longfellow and Cooper were not true expatriates like Washington Irving or James Russell Lowell, who also combined belles lettres with diplomacy. Much in the lives of these two men was comparable. Lowell, poet, essayist, diplomat, and editor, was United States minister to Spain from 1877 to 1880, and to Britain from 1880 to 1885. Both men wrote of their travels, and Lowell made sensitive notes on his impressions of the Italian scene. His first sight of Rome affected him as it did Henry James many years later. The dome of Saint Peter's, constructed from designs by Michelangelo, was his first impression, and later he wrote of it, "The dome is to Rome what Vesuvius is to Naples; only a greater wonder, for Michelangelo hung it there."

Lowell commented on the drifts of wild hawthorn and honeysuckle scenting the air, on the nightingales singing as he drove from Palestrina to Monte Cavo, on the chestnut trees on the hillsides and the flowing stretches of the Campagna. He admired the girls in the mountain villages, balancing copper water jugs on their heads. He commented on the white evanescence of the fountains at Tivoli, and the "silent hovering iris." Lowell thought Florence the noisiest town he had ever been in, but he preferred his Florentine to his Roman walks. Close attention to nature was typical of the expatriates, and most of the nineteenth-century exiles tramped the countryside with the zeal later devoted to fast motoring. But aside from his delight in the natural beauty of the countries through which he traveled, Lowell had some knotty diplomatic problems to untie as Minister to Spain from 1877 to 1880. During this period he had the complicated job of overseeing the judicial rights of American citizens in Spain and its possessions, a thorny question from the time of the Cuban Revolution of 1868.

It was noted that Lowell's dispatches from Spain, beginning in the summer of 1877, were singularly like those that Washington Irving had sent thirty years earlier. Conditions had changed little between 1845 and 1878, when General Ulysses S. Grant made his world tour and was enthusiastically entertained at the autumn military maneuvers near Vitoria. The general dined with the king and rode by his side during one of the reviews, and Ulysses and Mrs. Grant visited the Escorial and Toledo. In the following year Lowell attended the marriage of King Alfonso XII and the Archduchess Maria Christina of Austria, who later became dowager queen when the king died, leaving a posthumous heir who reigned as Alfonso XIII.

The ministers and consuls who moved from post to post, and lived so long abroad that in some instances they acquired full expatriate status, were inevitably involved in the political developments and court ceremonies of Europe. Nathaniel Hawthorne was never happy in his official role, yet much of his literary inspiration developed in Italy. He wrote his first draft of *The Marble Faun* in Florence. Trips through churches and museums were infinitely wearying to him. He had little interest in art, but his clever wife, Sophia Peabody, saw that he did not neglect any sightseeing. She was tireless herself in her pursuit of culture, while Nathaniel observed the ways of the people. Sophia had taught drawing and considered it a moral duty to absorb what she could at the Louvre while her husband watched the passing crowd and ignored the pictures. He did not suffer in the least when Mrs. Anna Jameson, a productive Irish writer who constantly crossed the path of the American exiles, with helpful wisdom or boring persistence, said that she could give him "no credit for knowing one single simplest thing about art." She took him driving along the Appian Way and showered him with the riches of her accumulated knowledge. He considered her a sensible old lady, but with characteristic skepticism he questioned her own perceptions and was not impressed, even after she had dragged him through churches and museums.

Mrs. Jameson was one of the candid ladies in the elite circle of the Brownings, with a special place in their lives, for it was she whom Browning had begged to help Ba on their journey to Italy when they eloped from Wimpole Street in 1846. They settled in the Casa Guidi near the Pitti Palace, where they lived for thirteen years when they were not in the hills of Fiesole, until Elizabeth Browning died in 1861. Mrs. Jameson stayed on in Pisa and Florence, writing on religious art, and she became as noted an authority on the old churches as she was on the contemporary studios and art collections. She seemed to be the perfect person to shepherd Hawthorne through the churches and galleries of Rome, and to pinpoint for him the vegetation of the Alban Hills. No landmark escaped her sharp eye. Sophia, a member of the intellectual Peabody family of Salem, was disposed to involve Nathaniel in the growing tide of feminism, and at different times they were hosts to Fredrika Bremer, the Swedish novelist, and to tall, gaunt Maria Mitchell, the Nantucket astronomer who had discovered a planet and entertained the Hawthorne children on a long carriage drive out from Rome by telling them all about it.

By degrees the majesty of Rome touched Hawthorne's sensibilities, and he viewed Saint Peter's as "the world's cathedral." He was less resistant to Bernini than Longfellow had been, and he passed much time with the sculptors in Rome. The rush of fountains and the fall of sparkling waters became music in his ears. The dirt and refuse in the streets appalled him as much as the quiet courtesy of the Romans impressed him, and he wrote of the Eternal City, "The intellect finds a home there more than in any other spot in the world, and wins the heart to stay with it."

But Hawthorne did not find true peace until he rented a forty-room villa in Bellosguardo, close to Florence, and went to work on his first draft of *The Marble Faun.* "I hardly think there can be a place in the world where life is more delicious for its own simple sake," he wrote. The idea for this book had come to him after visiting the Villa Borghese. "The faun is a natural and delightful link between human and brute life, with something of a divine character intermingled," he wrote. Although he finished this work in England, it took shape and form in his villa at Bellosguardo, from which he could see Galileo's tower in the distance, and listen to the "liquid melody" of the bells of Florence.

Hawthorne did not concern himself with the turbulence of the Risorgimento that was shaking up many of his compatriots, although he took note of the social evils and of the more somber elements in Italy, shadowing the idyllic and the innocently gay. His long conversations with Browning and Hiram Powers, the sculptor, stimulated Hawthorne as the days slipped past in dreamlike beauty. Like all the visiting Americans he was profoundly interested in the woman whose love story had become a legend. He was surprised to find Mrs. Browning such a "pale small person," with speech that would have seemed shrill but for the "sweet tenuity" of her voice. The Brownings attracted every visitor of note, and Browning refrained from going anywhere that Elizabeth could not go.

In *The Marble Faun* Hawthorne summed up the ambivalent state of the true expatriate:

The years, after all, have a kind of emptiness, when we spend too many of them on a foreign shore. We defer the reality of life . . . until a future moment, when we shall again breathe our native air; but, by and by, there are no future moments; or, if we do return, we find that the native air has lost its invigorating quality. Thus, between two countries, we have none at all, or only that little space of either in which we finally lay down our discontented bones. It is wise, therefore, to come back betimes, or never.

Most of the nineteenth-century expatriates, particularly those who settled in Italy, lived in this dream world, and were never wholly at ease when they returned to America. Time and again they came back, in quest of the old enchantment, but Europe was changing too, and by 1900 a new crop of expatriates sought out the antiquities, enjoyed the unchanging landscape, but found a deep shift in the arts, the ideals, the politics, and the ways of the people.

The Italian Mystique

In the nineteenth century the Italian mystique enveloped the young sculptors, artists, writers, and musicians who had left the United States to study abroad and to drink at the fountains of antiquity. They formed their own colonies in Rome, Florence, and Venice, usually around one central figure, but they interlocked at various points with the artists of other nations. Both the American and British writers were inevitably drawn to the romantic Brownings.

The sculptors were the first to assemble in numbers, clustering around Bertel Thorvaldsen, the Dane who had a studio in Rome from 1768 to 1844. Since he succeeded Canova in the classical revival of sculpture, his training was sought by such Americans as Thomas Crawford, Hiram Powers, and Horatio Greenough. All three were men of personality, who soon became conspicuous in Rome and Florence. Many of the sculptors who flocked in from Vermont, Massachusetts, New York, and Ohio had been stonecutters or plaster molders. They had carved tombstones and mantelpieces. Some had specialized in figureheads for sailing ships, and nearly all had attempted portrait busts or wax models of famous men. Their work may be found today in many of the parks, squares, and cemeteries across the United States.

Greenough, a Harvard graduate of 1825, went straight to Italy from college and had his own studio in Florence from 1828 to 1851 after studying with Thorvaldsen in Rome. Bearded and of striking appearance, swinging along with a greyhound at his side, he always made an impression as a man, aside from his skill as a sculptor. He was in and out of Thorvaldsen's studio in Piranesi's old house below the Pincio Gardens. Marble gods and goddesses were lined up in orderly rows indoors, but those outdoors stood in romantic disorder in the tangle of wild roses and mallows in the sculptor's studio garden —a common state of affairs in Rome at the time, when broken bits of statuary and archaeological finds seemed to fit naturally into the ruins. The archaeologists were having one of their abundant periods, and the sculptors were alert to their discoveries. The mythological image was in full flower, and the Englishman John Flaxman and the Welshman John Gibson, who had studied with Canova, were fostering it when Greenough appeared on the scene.

As a boy in Boston he had learned to use a chisel and had modeled in clay. Washington Allston urged him to go to Italy. Fenimore Cooper took an interest in him and gave him his first important commission—two nude little boys who seemed faintly shocking when they reached Boston. It was through Cooper that Greenough's statue of Washington was commissioned by Congress. He did a bust of his benefactor, and also one of John Quincy Adams. It was a growing fashion for the men of the day to have this form of recognition before photography became an accomplished art. But Americans were slow to recognize the talent of their own sculptors, until statesmen like Charles Sumner and writers like Cooper, traveling in Europe, saw what they were accomplishing at the very fountainhead of statuary.

Greenough was avant-garde for his day. He believed in the functional effect and was scornful of the Greek influence in temples, banks, and stations. Such buildings, he argued, should accord with the climate and the uses to which they were put. The battlements and towers of the Smithsonian Institution, where his colossal Washington was installed, were deplored by this picturesque expatriate in Florence. He was friendly with Walter Savage Landor, the explosive English writer who lived intermittently in Paris, in Como, and in Florence, after he had outworn his welcome in his own country and fled from lawsuits and abuse. From 1826 Landor lived in Fiesole, and Greenough took Emerson to visit him at his villa in the hills. Emerson found him more kind than violent, although all the members of the British and American colonies were aware of Landor's undisciplined rages. But Landor thought Greenough a "great man and glorious sculptor," and shared with him a common republican interest in the cause of Italian freedom. Mazzini and Garibaldi were Landor's heroes, and Greenough was friendly with Giovanni Niccolini, the patriot playwright, and with Giuseppe Giusti, the satirical poet. Landor found the members of the American colony irresistible, and was always at war with them or enjoying their company. Elizabeth Barrett Browning could usually soothe him. Greenough's brother, Richard Saltonstall, who did the colossal bronze statue of Benjamin Franklin that stands in front of Boston City Hall, studied in Florence for a time and then had a studio in Rome.

All the sculptors paid tribute to Thomas Crawford, a New Yorker who studied with Thorvaldsen in Rome in 1835 and remained a resident of the Eternal City for most of his life. Charles Sumner gave him his start when he strolled into his studio one day and ordered one of his sculptured figures for the Boston Athenaeum. Crawford was lonely and discouraged when the handsome senator from home paid this visit. Important government commissions followed, for Sumner was dedicated to the promotion of the arts in the United States, as well as to the abolition of slavery. Some of the sculptural decorations of the Capitol are Crawford's work. The pediment and the armed figure of Liberty on the dome were done from his designs. Another government commission was for the statue of Washington in Richmond. His work drew the attention of people in the United States to the talents of American artists in Italy, and a wave of official statuary followed. It had begun with busts and wax models in the time of Benjamin Franklin.

Crawford became such an important figure, with the Capitol involved, that a warship was sent to Italy to bring his work across the Atlantic. The skeptical Hawthorne, somewhat immune to art, thought his work commonplace, and Emerson was as cool to it as he was to all sculpture and painting. But Crawford, his brilliant wife, who was the sister of Julia Ward Howe, and their son, F. Marion Crawford, were citizens of the world in Rome.

Hiram Powers from Woodstock, Vermont, became the best known of all the sculptors who found their destiny abroad. Before establishing his studio in Florence in 1837, he had already done portrait busts of Jackson, Calhoun, Webster, Marshall, and other noted political figures. His statues of Franklin and Jefferson are in the Capitol, but his most discussed work was the *Greek Slave,* which was a *succès de scandale,* as well as a work of art. Mrs. Browning wrote a poem about it, and it was carefully scrutinized by censorious eyes in America before being exhibited to the general public. The clergymen of Cincinnati were asked to give their approval of the nude figure after one section of the community had suggested discreet veiling. But replicas of the *Greek Slave* were soon on display in British, Russian, and American mansions, and the sculpture was a sensation at New York's Dusseldorf Gallery in 1858. Powers' *Eve Before the Fall* passed muster, too, in the Victorian climate, and Landor wrote to Emerson that "sculpture at the present day flourishes more than it ever did since the days of Pericles, and America is not cast into the shadow by Europe."

Hawthorne downgraded Powers, as he did Greenough, describing him as a "mechanic" in his work. Hiram was noted for his dexterity and skill, perhaps due to his early training in Cincinnati, where he worked in a clock factory and repaired wax figures for shows. In Florence he functioned rather like Benjamin Franklin in Paris, tinkering away with curious inventions of one kind or another, and he talked glibly about flying machines. He was a particular favorite with the English colony, and Mrs. Browning wrote of him, "Mr. Powers, the sculptor, is our chief friend and favourite. A most charming, simple, straightforward and genuine American." He was rugged in build and blunt in his conversation, but he could show tenderness of spirit. As he worked, he wore a sculptor's cap tilted on one side of his bald head.

Powers preferred Florence to Rome, which he found ponderous and oppressive. But he kept up his friendship with Thorvaldsen, who said that his work "constituted an era in art." Emerson was struck by the fact that so many of the artists preferred Florence and considered it their home. It seemed to him to be much more comfortable to live in than Rome or Naples, with its "good streets, industrious population, spacious, well-furnished lodgings, elegant and cheap cafés." As he saw it, the cathedral, Giotto's campanile, the splendid galleries, and the absence of the all-pervasive beggars, made it the favorite of strangers.

But the mecca of the sculptors, artists, and writers in Rome was the Palazzo Barberini, designed by Bernini, and lived in for forty-five years by William Wetmore Story, a Salem man whose father, Joseph Story, had founded the Harvard Law School and been a Supreme Court Justice. William first visited Rome in 1847, intent on studying sculpture, and he was drawn back to live in Italy in 1856. After practicing law in Boston, he had studied painting, sculpture, and music, so he was dedicated to all the arts, and he welcomed the young Americans who were carving their way to fame in Rome. All the celebrities passing through visited the Palazzo Barberini, and Story was a particular friend of the Brownings, Landor, Hawthorne, and Charles Eliot Norton.

He was a brilliant host and invested his home with charm and talent. He was small, witty, restless, and informed in all the arts. Hawthorne, who knew him well, wrote, in his *French and Italian Notebooks,* of Story: "Rich, in the prime of life, children budding and blossoming around him . . . with sparkling talents . . . who should be happy, if not he?" Nathaniel considered him the "most variously accomplished and brilliant person, the fullest of social life and fire, whom I ever met."

Mrs. Henry Adams was skeptical. "Call him a genius!" she wrote to her father from Paris on April 20, 1873, "I don't see it."

Story had a statue of Thorvaldsen in his garden. The children of his noted guests were as enthusiastic about the palazzo as the adults. With his own children growing up happily in this environment, he devoted much thought to their entertainment, and turned one of the vast rooms of the palazzo into a theater. Sometimes he wrote the plays that were staged. In one he acted with Tommaso Salvini, the Italian tragedian, who was a friend. Hans Christian Andersen read *The Ugly Duckling* to the Story children, and Robert Browning recited the *Pied Piper of Hamelin* as he led a grand march through the palace. In 1853 Thackeray wrote *The Rose and the Ring* for the Story children.

In his own person and career Story summed up some of the Italian mystique. The early Roman characters he had come to know through his textbooks in Boston were alive for him in Rome, from Tasso under the cypresses to Horace in his villa in the Sabine Hills. The echoes of Keats and Shelley were still strong in Rome when Story arrived, and he did a bust of Shelley for Eton. The Spanish Steps, which would be romanticized in the films of the twentieth century, were already alive with artists' models in costume. Brigands and martyrs, marchesas and contadini, chattered as they waited for the artists to select them for work.

Story patterned himself after Browning, who in turn took lessons in modeling from Story. He chose to write about the free open life of the road, and his verse often dealt with the street musicians, the ballad singers, the beggars, the street scenes of Rome, and the infinite variety of the Campagna di Roma. His essays and poetry were in the mood of the era, but his special genius lay in his relations with others. He was the host par excellence for the gifted young expatriates in Rome.

A favorite gathering ground for the sculptors, artists, and writers was the Caffè Greco, the Dôme of its day, on the Via Condotti, not far from Saint Peter's. There was more lounging in cafés in Rome than in Florence, and here the artists of many countries gathered in smoke-darkened rooms and sat at little round marble tables, discussing professional problems and their own inner joys or melancholy. Sometimes they wound up reading their new papers over sunrise coffee by the light from wax tapers. Even today it remains the most picturesque coffeehouse in Europe, and in 1953 it was proclaimed a national monument. The decor has changed little in two hundred years, and the walls are covered with memorabilia of its history. The early habitués called themselves the Grecisti, and at one time they had their own Free University there. The café was so dark and smoky that conspirators felt free to discuss their plans without fear of police surveillance. And penniless artists were always staked to pastry and coffee. It was first made famous by the Germans living in voluntary exile in Rome. After 1779 Goethe had his own corner table in the café. King Ludwig of Bavaria visited the Caffè Greco frequently, and Felix Mendelssohn complained that the habitués talked ceaselessly of art rather than music. Rossini composed some of his music in the surrounding bedlam, and Hans Christian Andersen wrote two novels in an apartment over the coffeehouse, where he lived for two years. Thorvaldsen and his American friends were in and out at all hours of the day and night, and Nikolai Gogol wrote part of his *Dead Souls* on one of the marble tables. Both Wagner and Liszt spent hours drinking coffee in the narrow, smoky rooms. Shelley, Keats, and Byron kept to themselves, but at different times Sir Walter Scott, Thackeray, Hawthorne, Henry James, Browning, and Tennyson lounged in the Caffè Greco, and Mark Twain called it his favorite haunt in Rome, "because it had nothing by Michelangelo." Caruso, Toscanini, D'Annunzio, Sarah Bernhardt, and Paderewski all patronized it at different times.

Today the Caffè Greco is surrounded by such high-fashion houses as Gucci, Bulgari, and Buccellati. It is run through family inheritance by Signora Gubinelli-Grimaldi, and the international set mixes in its smoky interior with the artists and writers of today. The American expatriates of the nineteenth century settled happily in the Caffè Greco, and so did the Russians. All were avid for English and French newspapers and magazines. James Russell Lowell, passing through, observed that it was easy to pick out the Americans by their shabby dress coats with rumpled tails. The Europeans were more apt to go in for befrogged effects, and all manner of odd hats, like the French stovepipe variety or the conical black felt with velvet ribbons. The Americans were disposed to be clean, and Herman Melville, visiting Rome in 1857, noticed with disgust that John Gibson had filthy hands. Gibson was the Welsh sculptor who often went straight from his studio to the café, and sometimes he had with him Harriet Goodhue Hosmer, the American sculptor from Watertown,

Massachusetts, who had made herself a valued part of the artistic community, both in Rome and Florence. She had studied with Gibson and had inherited from him Canova's old studio adjoining his own. This proximity gave her an advantage, for wealthy patrons visiting the Welsh sculptor were usually steered next door for a look at Miss Hosmer's work.

Rome had never seen anything quite like Harriet. The police finally dissuaded her from riding all over the city alone at night, thinking her a Yankee show-off who attracted too much attention to herself. She was a self-avowed feminist and scorned the protective concern of men, although she had a good many celebrities looking out for her. With her brown curls bunched under a black velvet cap, a prim blouse, tie, and neat skirt, Harriet lacked the air of a bohemian. She summered with the Storys at Siena, and that brought her into close touch with the Brownings when they had a villa there. The cast she did of their clasped hands was a period piece of interest to her fellow Americans.

Harriet was always close to the seat of the mighty. When in Florence, she dined habitually with the Brownings, and in Rome they picnicked together in the Alban Hills, riding on donkeys. She was always clever enough to bring along Browning's latest poem, and on one expedition she persuaded him to read all of *Saul*. He, in turn, tutored her in Greek and called her his "dearest Hattie." Mrs. Browning studied Harriet with interest and appraised her feminism neatly: "She lived the life of a perfectly emancipated female free from all shadow of blame, by the purity of hers." They had many happy evenings together, playing and singing until midnight, and they encouraged her in her work—not that Harriet needed this support, for, though little known in the United States, she had become quite famous in Italy.

She was decorated by the Empress of Russia and the King of Bavaria. The Prince of Wales bought her *Puck* for his rooms at Oxford—it was a current fad for students to decorate their rooms with contemporary art. Tennyson proclaimed her *African Sibyl* the "most poetic rendering in art of a great historical truth" that he had ever seen. Harriet's work was exhibited all over Europe, but it was considered even more remarkable that she should ride on horseback from Rome to Florence at night and alone. She became one of the wonders of Rome and was carefully observed by George Bancroft, William Cullen Bryant, Henry Ward Beecher, and other prominent Americans passing through. Her *Zenobia* was reassuring to Bostonians, a trifle dazed by some of the art and sculpture that was reaching America from its gifted sons in exile. It became fashionable in the

1840s and 1850s for well-to-do Americans to winter in Rome, and with the growing tide of culture at home, many of them haunted the studios and galleries to pick up treasures for their Victorian parlors or for the great halls and staircases of their Greek Revival mansions. Life-size figures of Apollo and Venus, romping cupids in marble, busts of Washington and Jefferson, and large paintings displayed on easels became increasingly fashionable as the century advanced.

Since Rome in the middle of the nineteenth century was as much the refuge of the American expatriates as Paris in the 1920s, they had ample scope for buying. The New England influence was all-pervasive, and Florence came to be known as the Boston of Italy, a truism that Margaret Fuller acknowledged but deplored when she said, "Florence is a kind of Boston with the same good and the same ill —and I have had enough of both. I do not like it . . . because it seems like home."

But Miss Hosmer was not the only American woman who lived in the soft golden light of the Italian mystique. Fanny Alexander spent a lifetime following the New England way of life in an ancient palazzo in Florence.

Her father was Francis Alexander, a portrait painter who settled in Florence in 1853 when she was still in her teens. When he died, she and her mother remained in their spacious quarters in the old palazzo, speaking Italian with a Boston accent, keeping their accounts in Boston stores, dining off the East India china that had come to New England on a sailing vessel, and tending a little roof garden bright with sweet alyssum, larkspur, mignonette, and lemon verbena.

"Cast down your eyes," Mrs. Alexander whispered to Fanny when they approached a nude figure in an art gallery. Ruskin called her a saint, but she was no fool, and she made a lively, useful life for herself in the midst of the Italian mystique. She ran a soup kitchen for the poor in Florence and employed seamstresses to make clothes for them. Her own basques and cloaks still came from Boston, and her mother continued to crochet her hairnets. They attended a Lutheran church run by a cousin of Rossetti's.

Fanny was an artist and writer, and she collected the songs of the mountain singers along with legends of the peasants when she and her mother summered in the Apennines. Prim and proper, she walked briskly through the olive groves, and talked in her Bostonian Italian to the sun-kissed Tuscan girls and the youths at work in the fields. She nursed the ailing children in the hills and sent many to the seaside. When her *Roadside Songs of Tuscany* came out, illustrated with her own flower drawings, Ruskin was charmed, and even more so when he learned her story and met Francesca (as he called her) and her mother. He lectured on her work, and so did George F. Watts, the English painter and sculptor who worked in Rome from 1843 to 1847. Through them Fanny became well known in England, and her drawings were picked up by Oxford youths for their quarters. Cardinal Manning thought her book "as beautiful as the Fioretti of St. Francis," and the clergy made much of it. Both Lowell and Whittier added to her fame with sonnets addressed to Fanny, and Charles C. Perkins, the Boston art historian, spread the tale of her extraordinary progress as the protégée of Ruskin.

Constance Fenimore Woolson, another American woman well known in the expatriate world, was less assertive than Fanny, but she was a novelist who knew Florence as few Americans ever did, and she wrote with sharp perception of her compatriots in the Italian setting. Constance was the grandniece of James Fenimore Cooper. She was forty years old and fresh from New Hampshire when she settled in Florence in 1880 and wrote *East Angels,* a novel set in Saint Augustine in the days following the Civil War. Most of her novels about the South were written in Venice, but she swung gradually to observing the contemporary Americans in Florence and Venice, in Sorrento, Rome, and Florence, in Switzerland, and in England. Henry James was intensely interested in her work, because it was so much in his own field and was done with considerable perception. Miss Woolson turned a cynical eye on the exiles who had come to study art or to have their children educated and stayed on year after year, never admitting that they were not going back to America.

She had stayed in the faded pensions on the Lungarno and knew the American picture well—the healthy, beautiful girls studying music and art, their restless, ambitious mothers, and the rootless women quite obviously seeking romance under the blue Italian sky. When she took a pale yellow villa at Bellosguardo, with vineyards and olive groves below her and a distant view of the Apennines, she succumbed slightly to the Italian mystique in spite of her efficient and thorough exploration of all the churches, galleries, and ruins within range. Henry James was her guide at Uffizi, the Pitti, and the Boboli Gardens, and he soon found that, like Edith Wharton, she had an excellent grasp of her surroundings and a sense of historical perspective that pleased his fastidious nature. Miss Woolson found him "quiet, almost cold in manner," but she learned a great deal from him, and his praise of her work gave her standing in the American and English communities. As time went on she nursed a hopeless passion for him, and James was deeply shocked when she committed suicide in Venice after fourteen years abroad.

Harriet Hosmer, Fanny Alexander, and Constance Woolson all were remarkable expatriates in their several ways and had potent backing. Harriet had the gifted John Gibson to promote her work. Fanny had bewitched John Ruskin, who gave her the status of a saint. Constance had Henry James, who ranked her among the most knowing of his many women friends. All three American women moved with considerable success in the Italian glow. They were individualists, widely dissimilar in their aims and conduct, but all were enveloped in the Italian mystique.

Like other American residents Constance was often at the home of Marie and William Stillman in Florence. Stillman was an artist and journalist who was art critic for the *New York Evening Post* and then became special correspondent for the *London Times* in Herzegovina, Montenegro, Albania, and Italy. He was consul in Rome from 1862 to 1865 and in Crete from 1865 to 1868. But interest centered chiefly in his wife, and Constance Woolson applied her satiric touch to the romantic Mrs. Stillman, who floated about in pre-Raphaelite draperies and could afford to live in high style, since she was the daughter of a rich London banker. She was part-Greek, part-English, and she was much discussed as one of the identifiable figures in Disraeli's novel *Lothair*. Stillman was a pet of Isabella Stewart Gardner's, and she sometimes used him to promote her finds in the world of art and music. When one of her protégés, a violinist named Pier A. Tirindelli, was appearing in the opera *Atenaide* in Rome, she asked Stillman to cover the performance, for she was wise in the ways of publicity. At the moment the critic could not leave his bureau, so the spirited Isabella telegraphed her own critique, and was always proud of the fee she received—the only money she ever earned in her life.

Florence, being small, was much more gossipy than Rome. Americans could walk all over the place and greet each other several times in the course of a day. Villas in the hills were passed from one to another, and Fanny Alexander had spent seventeen summers in Miss Woolson's villa, where she enjoyed the magnificent view described by Elizabeth Browning in *Aurora Leigh*. Henry James, another tenant, had celebrated the completion of the facade of Giotto's Duomo by donning a black velvet cap and a crimson *lucco*. These were the touches that made Florence so fascinating to traveling Americans. The Renaissance seemed near at hand along the Arno, and George Eliot's *Romola* was studied attentively by the artists, poets, and sculptors. They could follow the paths known to Botticelli, study the Florentine faces in Ghirlandajo's frescoes, and visit Romola's house, which became a place of pilgrimage. The Ponte Vecchio was a charmed bridge with rich echoes of the past, and the artists watched with horror the growing rush of American tourists buying miniature alabaster statues of Hebe, lockets and caskets, silver and enamel baubles.

The lives of the writers inevitably crossed those of the artists and sculptors. Many whose work would never attract attention reveled in their happy days among the titans of the arts—both past and present. The artists were always recognizable, with their velvet jackets and artists' caps, their beards and paraphernalia. With folding stools, easels, and palettes they wandered about in quest of likely subjects. Everything in the Italian setting was conducive to artistic inspiration, except the languorous golden aura of sunshine and the awesome inheritance of the past. Some of the most vigorous American artists came and went, and returned for short stays, but continued their careers at home or in more bracing climates. A few reacted to the Italian mystique by going back to the United States to do regional interpretation, but nearly all enjoyed the time they spent in Rome and Florence. Thomas Cole, who fostered the American school of landscape painting, spent four years in Italy in the early 1830s, painting the dreamlike tinge of the Campagna di Roma, the Arno in its many moods, the temples of Sicily. On his return to America he settled in the village of Catskill and became closely identified with the Hudson River school.

When Rembrandt Peale arrived in Rome at the end of the 1820s, he found about three hundred students assembled from every European country, but Americans were coming in small batches of two or three at a time. He listened to the chatter of the bearded men at the Caffè Greco, did a painting of the mighty Thorvaldsen, and his second portrait of Georges Cuvier, the French naturalist. Peale was disappointed in the paintings in the Sistine Chapel, and his American colleagues were equally disrespectful.

One of the most picturesque of the expatriates seen around Rome for many years was Elihu Vedder, the illustrator whose murals are on the walls of the Library of Congress, but who is best remembered as the artist who brought the *Rubáiyát of Omar Khayyám* into prominence, giving it great popularity in America. He was staying in a villa at Perugia when Edward FitzGerald's translation of the *Rubáiyát* in rhymed verse was brought to him by Edwin J. Ellis, an English painter who had worked on William Blake's hand-illustrated lyrical poems. Vedder was interested at once, and began to plan his famous illustrations for this classic, which were made later in his studio in Rome, outside the Porta del Popolo, and close to the medieval walls of the city.

Vedder's garden had gnarled trees and ducks swimming in a pool screened with bamboo. After he started work on the *Rubáiyát* visitors were conscious of spidery illustrations hung on his studio walls. Earlier, when he was busy working on his mosaic panels for the Library of Congress, Julia Ward Howe would call to have tea with him and to watch him at work, his black skullcap perched precariously on the back of his head, and his mustache ferociously military beneath a long mane of white hair. In his conversation with her Vedder would frequently revert to the Civil War. Plagued with a feeling of guilt while it raged, he had returned home for a period and had tried to enlist. Turned down because of an arm injury, he shared the uneasiness common to other artists and writers who had questioned their own expatriate status during the Revolutionary War and the War of 1812.

Popular illustrators flourished in the late nineteenth and early twentieth centuries. Vedder was not alone in this field. The wandering writers liked to have their books illustrated by their artist friends. Joseph Pennell, who illustrated William Dean Howells' *Tuscan Cities* and Henry James's *Italian Hours,* accompanied these writers on their travels. He went with Howells to Lucca, Siena, and Pisa, sketching along the country roads and doing etchings in the street. It was Pennell's custom to ride on a tandem bicycle with his wife, Elizabeth.

The painters and sculptors took expeditions periodically to Palestrina, or night rambles among the Roman ruins. Like all other American residents of the Eternal City they picnicked on the Campagna di Roma, and they were always interested in the patient work of the archaeologists. They had everything in the world to delight their senses as they roamed the city and spotted the unaccustomed detail, as well as the historic and magnificent effects.

Eager American students soon learned to slow down to the pace of Rome. They had to wait their turn before they could copy pictures, and Thomas Gold Appleton, a Bostonian and an amateur artist, wrote from Florence in 1833, "I patiently (impatiently) wait my day. Titian's mistress will soon be mine. As for the Pitti, only seven are admitted at a time, and an artist who is to copy some Salvatores for Mr. Perkins has been waiting for eight months."

By the time American girls were arriving in groups, Louisa M.

Alcott's sister May had compiled a handbook for their benefit called *Studying Art Abroad*. They needed it as they coped with the problems of renting studios, making the proper art connections, marketing, tipping, and cooling the ardent Italian spirit. There were always the strong ones among them, like Vinnie Ream, who had been commissioned by Congress to do a statue of Lincoln for the Capitol Rotunda. Mrs. Nathaniel Hawthorne and other New England matrons looked after Vinnie while she worked on her statue. There was usually a helpful hand for the American girl in Rome, and many were aided by Julia Ward Howe, who came so often and lived so long in Italy that she had almost full expatriate status after her husband's death.

Her daughter Maud had married John Elliott, a young mural and portrait painter who had trained at the Académie Julien in Paris when Carolus Duran was one of the masters there, and John Singer Sargent a student. Elliott had known Longfellow in Paris, and his links with the American artists and writers continued after he moved to Rome in 1882. He studied at the San Lucca Academy and took a studio on the Via Flaminia outside the Porta del Popolo. Returning from Egypt, Mrs. Howe and Maud called on Elliott one night in 1879 as spring was breaking over Rome, the almond trees were in flower, and the bells of Saint Peter's were ringing the "Ave Maria."

Maud and Jack fell in love. They gathered violets together in the Villa Pamfili Doria, anemones in the Borghese, and wandered through the gardens of the Medicis, listening to the nightingales sing. Elliott was introduced to the lavish life of the Palazzo Odescalchi where Mrs. Luther Terry presided on the grand scale. No one knew more about Rome than she. Her sons, F. Marion Crawford and Arthur Terry, were in and out of Rome when Elliott became a regular visitor at the palazzo. Their sister Daisy Terry was still in her teens and was studying music and Latin. Anyone taken up by Mrs. Terry in Rome was a fixture socially, and Elliott flourished. Jose Villegas of Seville, one of the outstanding painters in Rome at the time, gave him lessons in art in return for instruction in English. Because of Villegas, Spaniards were predominant in the International Artists Club, which was dear to the students in Rome. Its frolics at carnival time were unique, with a five-mile procession of costumed students through the streets, many dressed as Roman senators wearing wreaths and togas. They played pipes, drums, guitars, and mandolins as they marched. The frolic ended with a riotous costume ball. But all was tinged with the Italian mystique, and it only faintly resembled the Beaux-Arts balls of Paris.

Years later, when Elliott went to Madrid to see Villegas again, he found him director of the Royal Museum of the Prado and court painter, a different man from the gifted bohemian he had known in Rome. He went to the gala bullfight with Irene Langhorne Gibson, the original Gibson girl, who was in Madrid that winter with her husband. Charles Dana Gibson was concentrating at the time on Velasquez, but he became an ardent aficionado before the time of Hemingway. He was ashamed of himself, he said, but could not resist the spectacle, especially when the bull was being led into the arena.

The 1890s was a decade of splendor in Rome, but the American influence was in its dying hours, and Elliott watched the changing course of events from the Palazzo Rusticucci where he had taken quarters after his marriage to Maud Howe in Boston in 1887. It was a spot where Raphael had once lodged, and its lofty carved ceilings and thick walls bespoke its history. The Elliotts' fountain cast its spray through orange trees, and they dined under a pergola on the terrace. Henry James considered the view from this vantage point unsurpassed. They looked down into the Square of Saint Peter's, or as Elliott put it, "our windows looked into the Pope's." Beyond that they could see the Pincio and the Villa Borghese, and in the far distance the Alban and Sabine hills.

But Elliott took care to install a fireplace and a bathtub in their frigid palace. It was often the fate of the expatriates to live in marble halls when they did not starve in garrets, but in Italy they more often settled in spacious palazzos with a few medieval chairs, refectory tables, and credenzas to fill up space. Elliott also had a huge studio in the Palazzo Giraud Torlonia in the Vatican quarter, close to his home. It dated back to 1503 and seemed as large as a church. He kept pets like a tortoise and a falcon in the courtyard, but his friends sought him out at the Palazzo Rusticucci, often to admire his terrace garden as one of the sights of Rome. Each season of the year had its own display, and the range was from red honeysuckle to passion flowers. The scent of jasmine and oleanders was ever present in the Elliott ménage, although Maud returned so often to America that Jack continued to be a somewhat lonely exile. He did not thrive or feel well adjusted on his few visits home. This was true of many of the expatriates when they tried to find their bearings in America after years passed abroad.

Sam Ward, the fascinating cosmopolitan who was Maud's uncle and Julia Ward Howe's brother, was one of Elliott's first patrons, posing for him in the last year of his life. Mrs. Potter Palmer gave him his first important commission—to decorate the dining room of her fabulous mansion on Lake Shore Drive in Chicago with a frieze of cupids gathering grapes and treading the wine press in Dionysian rites. In 1894 he returned to Boston to paint the ceiling of the Boston Public Library. His theme was "The Triumph of Time." But he was glad to return to Italy, where the air was "full of roseate prophecy" with the coming of the new century.

Julia Ward Howe enjoyed her last Roman season with the Elliotts in 1898, exactly half a century after her first visit to Rome. In the interval she had become known around the world. She was a cosmopolitan as much as an expatriate. Wayne MacVeagh was American ambassador at the time, and the first secretary was the genial Larz Anderson, whose anecdotes and expansive spirit delighted the Americans who gathered around Mrs. Howe. In 1910 he presented to the nation Elliott's *Diana of the Tides,* which was installed in the National Museum.

But by that time the Americans who had lived so long under the spell of Rome and Florence had scattered or died. "How homesick I was for the golden Rome during long months after my flight," Henry James wrote to Maud from Lamb House on April 17, 1901. "That little marriage feast in your hanging garden on that wondrous June afternoon gathered the whole thing up in a bunch and stuck it in me, as with a golden nail. . . ."

The mystique cloaked the greatest of the scholars as well as the simplest of the students who had sought inspiration in Italy for the better part of a century.

Students and the Grand Tour

Aside from the artists and literary pilgrims the most significant expatriates have been the students who have swarmed over Europe with the eagerness of youth and the plasticity of their immature years. Many formed close ties with the countries in which they studied. Some became permanent exiles; others returned with their ideals, their political philosophy, their knowledge of the arts and sciences, shaped and expanded. A few became drifters who could no longer adjust themselves to life on either side of the Atlantic.

Germany had the greatest drawing power for scholars in the early nineteenth century, and many American youths studied at Göttingen and Heidelberg, Berlin and Leipzig, Jena and Halle. Some moved from one to the other, and the Sorbonne drew many to Paris. The flexibility of the curricula at most of the universities enabled them to sample a variety of courses, but philosophy and political economy were the strong drawing cards in Germany. The entire system of American education was affected by these young exiles who returned to urge the establishment of graduate schools modeled after the German; or, as in the case of those who studied in Italy and France, to foster the arts and linguistics. The British universities continued to be a fountainhead of the rounded education, although it was some time after the Revolution before American parents showed any enthusiasm for sending their sons to Cambridge or Oxford, which later became receptive to the Rhodes scholar.

American youths had little zest for the dueling of Heidelberg, but the hearty social life of Germany had strong appeal for them. Lincoln Steffens, who tasted the Teutonic university life before starting on his adventurous career as a journalist in the late nineteenth century, pictured the American students at Heidelberg "beer drinking, dancing, swimming and boating, walking, talking and exploring the world and one another." It was a happy, carefree life, although the academic demands made on them at German universities were stiffer than those made elsewhere. Their futures were often influenced by the social life they experienced in the ancient capitals of Europe. While George Bancroft, the historian, was American minister to Germany, he helped the American students as Jefferson had done in an earlier era. In all the capitals they had every opportunity to share in the best of music and the theater, to meet celebrities, attend court functions, and observe the political developments and diversions of the period. They were courted by hostesses with marriageable daughters, and since a number of them had great charm and suavity, they were pampered to some degree. Many, however, lived an utterly Spartan life in freezing quarters, with indifferent food and few comforts. They were prodigious walkers, striding through mountain passes as well as the marble corridors of the great museums. Above all, they were exposed to the wit, learning, and experience of the great nineteenth-century scholars.

Quite often students were sent abroad to combine the Grand Tour with their university life. Perhaps the most noted example, because of the use he made of his opportunities and his detailed record of his adventures, was George Ticknor, who would eventually become professor of linguistics at Harvard. None of the students of the day covered more ground than Ticknor, or described his expatriate years with more precision.

Ticknor landed in Europe in 1815 with Edward Everett, to study at Göttingen and to tour the Continent between semesters. Joseph Green Cogswell, who later became Harvard librarian and bibliographer of the Astor collection, joined them at various points. All three were men of substantial background. Everett was the first American student to get a Ph.D. degree at Göttingen. Later he became a famous Unitarian clergyman, orator, and statesman. His speech at Gettysburg would attract more attention than Abraham Lincoln's short and memorable address. For the time being, however, Everett was a blithe young man, taking fencing lessons with Ticknor, reading German diligently, and in the evenings meeting other students at Blumenbach's, Heeren's, and Eichhorn's, the popular cafés in Göttingen.

These youths, like many others of the period, went abroad with strong family backing, letters of introduction, and money to spend. Their families expected them to get all they could out of the Grand Tour, then becoming a fashion, but some were caught up in the expatriate tradition and lost all desire to return to America—like James Gallatin of New York, who had moved in the diplomatic milieu of his father, Albert Gallatin. Ticknor differed from his fellow students by being an ardent note-taker and diarist, in the fashion of Irving, Longfellow, and Hawthorne. Wherever he went, he met the notables of the day, and he moved about in London with assurance, dash, and considerable charm. He had his first glimpse of expatriate life, like so many other visiting Americans, at Mr. West's gallery, where he was warmly welcomed as a young American of substance. He soon joined the loungers at Murray's Literary Exchange and picked up the bookish chitchat of the period. There was genuine interest in these young men arriving from America so soon after the Revolution. They were sounding boards for the political impressions of the day, and Europeans, particularly men of letters, were inclined to cultivate and study them. Ticknor, in turn, observed the manners, customs, attitudes, and social graces of the people, as well as the topography of their countries.

The statesmen who had watched the long drawn out struggle in America studied Ticknor with particular interest. He was well aware that there was still a faint chill in the air toward Americans, although the writers and artists of both countries seemed to move in a nimbus of their own. Ticknor soon learned that statesmen and men of letters circulated around Lord Henry Holland, and he was often at Holland House, although he disliked Lady Holland intensely. The former Elizabeth Vassall Fox was a much discussed hostess, and as Lady Holland she drew fire from many quarters. But Lord George John Spencer, who became the second Earl of Spencer, and his famous sister, Georgiana, Duchess of Devonshire, were apt to be at Holland House, and Ticknor felt he was in the thick of things when he met the Duke of Wellington, fresh from his victory at Waterloo. Ticknor stayed with the Marquis of Salisbury at Hatfield, a historic mansion built in Hertfordshire for James I. He consorted with Lord Russell and with Thomas Robert Malthus, who was already engrossed in studying population. Washington Irving, then at the British legation in London, took him to see *The*

The first American expatriate of note, Benjamin Franklin won the affection of the French and the respect of the European intellectual community in general. Arriving in France in 1776 for his third trip abroad, Franklin established the first American diplomatic headquarters at the Hôtel de Valentinois in Passy, where he turned out a daily newspaper for the benefit of the Americans in Paris.

In order to cheer his fellow Americans when the war was going badly at home, Benjamin Franklin entertained frequently at his house in Passy. Visitors sat for hours discussing the course of events in the States and enjoying good French food and wines. (Victor Hugo's sepia drawing of Franklin's house, Passy; Manuscript Division, New York Public Library)

When Mrs. John Adams arrived in London in the summer of 1784, she met open hostility from American Tories and the British and was forced to endure numerous social affronts. Abigail Adams's sojourn abroad increased her belief in the strength of America and in the future of the burgeoning nation. (Gilbert Stuart, National Gallery of Art, Washington, D.C.)

Benjamin West's studio attracted a long parade of Americans in the late eighteenth and early nineteenth centuries. West established a school in London and many prominent artists, among them Gilbert Stuart, paused to study with him before continuing their journeys to the Continent. (Gilbert Stuart, National Portrait Gallery, London)

Washington Irving first went abroad when he was twenty-one and set the fashion for the Grand Tour as the finishing touch to an affluent young man's education. Irving developed a special affinity for Spain and served as United States Minister to that country from 1842 to 1846. His efforts to popularize Spain started a wave of travel in that direction. (Sleepy Hollow Restorations, Tarrytown, N.Y.)

After his release from Fortress Monroe in the summer of 1867, Jefferson Davis fled to the village of Lennoxville in Quebec. The bitter winters in Canada soon forced Davis to take his family to Europe, where they led a lonely and impoverished life. (Walter Fleming papers, Manuscript Division, New York Public Library)

As the first American female foreign correspondent, Margaret Fuller covered the Italian Revolution for the *Tribune*. Margaret's dispatches were avidly read in the United States, but she was dropped from the paper when her personal behavior abroad caused a great scandal. (Chapel portrait of Margaret Fuller)

Travel became more comfortable as steamships replaced sailing packets. Shipboard conveniences and food were improved, and Americans enjoyed seawater baths in marble tubs and Victorian plush in the saloons.

James Abbott McNeill Whistler's personality was discussed as much as his art, and he was considered to be more of a showoff than a serious artist. Whistler's manner of dress was so eccentric that Aubrey Beardsley drew him as a fop, an image that stuck. (A. E. Gallatin Collection, Print Division, New York Public Library)

John Singer Sargent's daring portrait of Madame Gautreau caused a great deal of controversy. It became known as "Madame X" because the original Madame Gautreau was so incensed by the painting that she refused to be associated with it. (The Metropolitan Museum of Art, Arthur H. Hearn Fund, 1916)

Bernard Berenson's success as an art expert was strongly linked to Isabella Stewart Gardner's collection of Italian art, and both did much to familiarize the American public with the Renaissance masters. Berenson purchased forty-six important paintings for Mrs. Gardner between 1894 and 1914. (Simon and Schuster)

One of Isabella Stewart Gardner's protégés, Anders L. Zorn, depicted her with her arms outstretched as he had once viewed her in the doorway of her palazzo balcony. Zorn painted Mrs. Gardner all in yellow with her famous rope of pearls swung to her knees. (Isabella Stewart Gardner Museum, Boston)

Degas painted Mary Cassatt in a brown dress and a tan hat, trimmed in green. Miss Cassatt disliked the picture intensely, and it was lost for many years. The portrait turned up in 1951 at the Wildenstein Gallery in New York. (Andre Meyer Collection)

Henry James's renunciation of his American citizenship aroused a storm of criticism, and as a result the term *expatriate* took on a bad connotation. However, James found that his talents flourished abroad, and he drew the inspiration for much of his work from his travels in England, France, and Italy. (Max Beerbohm, Bettmann Archive, New York)

After a duel with his fiancée's brother, James Gordon Bennett, Jr., journeyed to Europe to avoid social disgrace. Bennett, whose papers mirrored the expatriate world, was notorious on the Left Bank for his wild escapades and pranks. (Nemo, Culver Pictures, Inc.)

Italians. He noted the shouting and hooting from the pit and the showers of orange peel aimed at the actors. The play was withdrawn, for Italians were unpopular at the time.

Ticknor attended the music festival and the Doncaster races, and he visited the famous castles, gardens, and landmarks of Britain. Much as he enjoyed the hours he spent in the House of Commons, watching Sir Robert Peel (a dandy in white pantaloons, blue surtout, and black cravat) orate, or hearing Benjamin Disraeli make witty ripostes when plagued by his critics, Ticknor found his greatest satisfaction in consorting with writers. From Joanna Baillie's windows in the unpretentious house belonging to this Scottish poet and dramatist at Hampstead, he caught a magnificent view of London, with Saint Paul's towering "like a vast spectre to the clouds." He dined at the home of William E. Godwin, author and philosopher, and attended a convocation of the Saturday Night Club at Leigh Hunt's. He found William Hazlitt living in Milton's house, where *Paradise Lost* had been written. The whitewashed walls were covered with phrases, broken lines of poetry, references, and notations of one kind and another which had flowed from the mind of the blind poet.

Like countless others who followed him, Ticknor made a literary tour of the Lake Country. When he visited Robert Southey, he was introduced to Mrs. Samuel Taylor Coleridge, and they talked at length of America, Spain, and Portugal, special interests of her husband's. Southey showed him the prospect described in one of Thomas Gray's letters and drove him sixteen miles to call on William Wordsworth. Young Ticknor thought that Wordsworth displayed Roman dignity and simplicity in his bearing and manner. His grave and tranquil exterior was quickly broken up, however, when they discussed poetry. Then he became the "Khan of Tartary again, and talked as metaphysically and extravagantly as ever Coleridge wrote." Wordsworth discussed the reviewers and praised the poetry of Robert Burns. They climbed hills and admired the lakes, and Ticknor noticed that children took off their hats to Wordsworth and the peasantry bobbed as they passed.

But the high point of his literary tour for Ticknor—as for many of his compatriots who followed him—was the time he spent with Sir Walter Scott, both in Edinburgh and at Abbotsford. Scott always took time to entertain a visiting American, and Ticknor watched his heavy features brighten as he recited poetry and discussed the history of Scotland. The poet, six feet tall and robust, but with a slight stoop, took him to the theater to see the play *Rob Roy*, fashioned from his novel. He showed him around Edinburgh, pointing out the houses of Hugh Blair, David Hume, Adam Black, and other men of scholarship and letters. Scott treated Ticknor to a rich flow of anecdotes about the people who lived in the lanes and closes they passed. His daughter Sophie, an unaffected girl in her late teens, played ballads for them on the harp, while the talented and pretty Anne looked on. They were piped in to dinner, and reels were danced afterward. The young student from America was getting a thorough indoctrination in Scottish ways.

Mrs. Anne Grant of Laggan, an American by birth, a confirmed Tory, and the great lady of letters in Scotland at the time, made a point of entertaining all the visiting students from the United States. She was particularly impressed with young Ticknor. On June 24, 1819, she wrote to an American friend: "The American character has been much praised among our literary people here, by a constellation of persons of brilliant talents and polished manners, by whom we were dazzled and delighted last winter. . . . They were all very agreeable persons, Mr. Ticknor preeminently so, and I can assure you ample justice was done to their merits here."

Joseph Green Cogswell, who often traveled with Ticknor, was another of her favorites, and she also singled out Hugh S. Legare of South Carolina and a "handsome and high-bred Mr. Ralston from Philadelphia, whose mind seemed equal to his other attractions and who left also a very favorable impression of Transatlantic accomplishments."

Thus the literary rapport between the two nations was strengthened, as Washington Irving charmed his European hosts, and young men like Ticknor spread enthusiasm for the newly created republic. They were early and successful expatriates, nourishing their own personalities and creating a good image of the land from which they came. Ticknor went to Ireland to visit Maria Edgeworth, who wrote so productively of Irish life and later gave practical aid to the peasants during the famine of 1846. He found her established at Edgeworthtown, sixty-five miles from Dublin, in a mansion surrounded by clumps of oaks and beeches, with a great lawn and a conservatory.

Ticknor called on Lord Byron and was struck by how well-informed Lady Byron was on things American. He found her diffident, talented, and on the defensive. Byron, discussing France and Greece with him, talked of his early follies with considerable frankness, and told young Ticknor he had written *The Corsair* in eleven days and had copied it on the twelfth. While they were talking Sarah Siddons, the tragedienne, came to call, commanding in presence, a contrast to the fragile Lady Byron.

Continuing his student travels, Ticknor flourished in Paris and basked in the company of such men as Chateaubriand, Baron von Humboldt, Alexis de Noailles, and Talleyrand, who was still smarting from the suggestion that Washington had told Alexander Hamilton he did not wish to receive Talleyrand at his receptions. Talleyrand spoke admiringly to Ticknor of Alexander Hamilton, but was scathing about Aaron Burr. The young student found the French statesman original and graceful in his conversation. Ticknor went to the Duchesse de Gramont's Saturday night soirées for the liberals before going on to the Tuileries. The Duchesse de Broglie gave a dinner in his honor, which was attended by Baron von Humboldt, the Marquis de Lafayette, and others friendly to the new America. Von Humboldt seemed to be everywhere, a man of boundless vitality, sleeping as little as Thomas A. Edison did many years later. His conversation was always spirited and contemporary, and he was particularly alert to American personalities and interests.

None of the scholars could pass through Paris without attempting to see Madame de Staël. She was dying when Ticknor saw her, but her face lit up as she told the young American, *"Vous êtes l'avenir du monde!"* He was as restrained about the beautiful Madame Récamier as some of the other students who had found her somewhat lacking in her legendary charm. She, too, looked faded and old, but her conversation was vivacious, and he commented on her "mild eyes full of expression, and her beautiful arms and hands."

Chateaubriand, short and dark-complexioned, poured out a "torrent of rich and various eloquence," and Benjamin Constant was consistently witty. Ticknor felt that he was under scrutiny in France for consorting with these radical thinkers. As minister at the time, Gallatin called on him to apologize for the note of supervision. He expressed the hope that Ticknor had not been inconvenienced or embarrassed. When the young student moved on to Venice, he found it beautiful but dull after the stimulating scene in Paris, but when he arrived in Rome in 1817, he thought it "worth all the other cities of the world." He explored the churches, the palaces, and the ruins, by moonlight and in the sun. The visiting Americans were expert walkers, tramping through miles of gallery corridors and over cobblestones, armed with books on art, architecture, and music. The Germans, the British, and the French had separate societies in Rome, but the Americans did not yet make up a solid community of their own. The literary gatherings known as *conversaziones,* and the *accadèmia,* involving both the cardinals and the scholars, brought out the intellectual elite of all races, talking their own languages. It seemed to Ticknor, viewing this, that Rome was still as much the capital of the world as in the time of Hadrian or Pope Leo X. But the contemporary pope told him that the time would come when America would dictate to the Old World.

The English seemed to dominate the social scene, with the Duchess of Devonshire giving *conversaziones* and directing excavations in the Forum. The Bonapartes were carrying on the Napoleonic tradition, and the Princess Borghese, Napoleon's sister, lived in her palace in high state and was coquettish with visiting young Americans. Before leaving Rome Ticknor, who missed nothing along the way, had a private audience with the pope.

From Italy he proceeded to Spain, where he tried to make connections with Washington Irving, whom he had met in the first place through a letter of introduction from Thomas Jefferson. He had a rocky trip through Spain and Portugal, traveling mostly on horseback with a postilion who took care of his luggage and guarded his Greek Testament and his Shakespeare, Milton, and Dante, the reading he felt was suitable for his travels. But Don Quixote soon seemed to fit Ticknor's case better as he encountered the hardships of the road. The highways were sometimes almost impassable. There were no taverns along the way. He dined twice with mules and slept only twice on a bedstead. Usually his resting place was a stone floor with straw and a blanket. But when he reached Madrid, Irving took hold of all arrangements for him, found him lodgings, and showed him how to gain the most from his surroundings.

Ticknor was impressed, and noted that he was glad to find America represented by a man who was so much respected by the diplomats, the government, and the people. He commented that Washington Irving never asked for favors, but insisted on what he thought was a right, and the young student wrote of him: "In his own house I found him very pleasant, for he has talent, a clear head, and considerable knowledge, though very little literature. His establishment was elegant ... quite on a par with most of the ministers there. In short, I am clear there was not one of the diplomats who understood his business better, or, taking the whole capital together, was more respected than Mr. Irving."

The ancient Spanish costumes were an inexhaustible source of interest to young Ticknor, and he thought the Paseo del Prado the finest walk he had seen within the walls of any city, except for those in the Tuileries and the impressive Chiaia promenade in Naples. He considered the Spanish theater next best to the British. Although he deplored the life of the nobles as "monotonous, gross and disgraceful," the Spanish population as a whole seemed a "great and generous people." His first bullfight affected him so greatly that he had to be carried out. He could not share the general enthusiasm for bullfighting and thought the *fiestas de los toros* a natural setup for licentiousness and popular wit of the cruelest kind. The pastoral life of the Spaniards had great appeal for him, however, with the people dancing the fandango and the manchegas to their pipes and castanets, while lovers serenaded their mistresses with guitars.

Ticknor found the people of Madrid orderly and well-behaved, and he was struck by the literacy of the population as a whole. The children of the poor were taught in schools run by women. Princess Prossedi, the oldest child of Lucien Bonaparte, took the youth in tow and showed him the best features of the land, including its great art. From Madrid Ticknor proceeded to Cordova, Granada, Gibraltar, and Seville, following in the footsteps of Washington Irving, and refreshing himself with barley water in coffee shops along the way. He proceeded to Lisbon with a band of smugglers, armed with pistols and dirks. They were protection in themselves from the robbers that he was told plagued the traveler in Spain and Portugal. Nearly everyone spoke English in Lisbon, because of years of trading with Britain. Ticknor thought it a splendid city, with a multitude of ships crowded in the harbor and, all around it, an amphitheater of hills crowned with country houses, gardens, convents, and churches.

After four years of studying, touring, and enjoying the social life of Britain, France, Italy, Spain, Switzerland, Holland, and Germany, Ticknor returned to the United States with William Preston, who also had charmed Mrs. Grant of Laggan. No one at the moment was better versed in Continental affairs and personalities than Ticknor, and he was back in Europe again in 1835. This time he found August Schlegel feeble and aged, and Goethe, whom he had visited years earlier at Weimar, was dead. Much had changed in Germany, and there was now much talk of slavery in America. Ticknor had many questions to answer about William Ellery Channing's book *Negro Slavery*, which had just come out. Joanna Baillie and Mary Somerville, both well-known writers, were singing hosannas over it. The Whigs were restrained, having abolished slavery in the West Indies with less trouble than they had expected. The high Tories, as always, disliked things American.

Ticknor wrote from Dresden to William Hickling Prescott, who was then busy with his book on Spain, that traveling Americans were being bombarded with questions about this situation, and they found it hard to explain all the constitutional provisions and local situations. "In general," he wrote on February 8, 1836, "the naked fact of the existence of a slave population, under a government that rests entirely on the doctrine of equal rights, with the additional fact that it is thought wrong to do anything in the purely free States to promote immediate emancipation, is all that is understood; and on these two grounds we are condemned in a tone that would surprise you, I think, if you were here."

The German papers accused Americans of humbug and hypocrisy on this issue. But in spite of all the criticism, and the mob riots in America, Ticknor wrote cheerfully, "Notwithstanding the reproaches of now and then a philanthropist who has heard about the Cherokees, it is still very comfortable to be an American; and is, on the whole, an extremely good passport to general kindness and good-will. At any rate, I would not change my passport—for any one of the fifteen hundred that are lying with it at the police in Dresden, from Russia, France, and England."

Ticknor was disappointed in the state of the arts in Dresden. The work being done by students in sculpture was poor, but he thought they were excellent lithographers. The court of Saxony was not only moral and respectable but it was intellectual, in his opinion. He saw *Hamlet* in Schlegel's translation, attended a regents' ball, and various court happenings, meeting the princesses of the ruling house. He moved on to Berlin, with stops at Leipzig, Dachau, Wittenberg, and Potsdam, where he saw a great military review of twenty thousand men, with the Duc d'Orléans and the Duc de Nemours present. In Berlin he dined with Lord Russell, the British minister, and was entertained by his old friend, Baron von Humboldt. Ticknor preferred the magnificence and architectural style of Prague to that of Berlin.

Soon after returning from this second trip to Europe, Ticknor helped to found the Boston Public Library. He had used his earlier travels to good advantage, teaching French, Spanish, and literature at Harvard. As a result of his expatriate years Ticknor spread linguistic skill and general European culture among a generation of the young as did Longfellow, Lowell, and Norton among those who studied belles lettres. From these sources flowed a fresh expatriate generation, intent on living abroad through the golden years of the late nineteenth century, when arts and letters in the classical tradition flourished.

Charles Phelps Taft and Peter Rawson Taft, the half-brothers of William Howard Taft, were two of the students who followed Ticknor's course in the mid-nineteenth century. The youths of Ohio in growing numbers joined the New Englanders and Southerners in pursuit of a broader education and the Grand Tour. Charles Taft, who later owned the Cincinnati *Times-Star* and became an important political figure, took a degree in Roman law at Heidelberg in 1868. He traveled from country to country, taking in the traditional sights, hearing the finest music, attending the theater, viewing the great art of Europe, and perfecting himself in French and German. His experiences all took root and affected his taste in the future. He returned many times to Europe with his rich wife, Annie Sinton Taft, a noted patron of the arts, who fostered the Cincinnati Symphony Orchestra and established the Taft Museum, with a collection of noted paintings.

Peter Taft, who had graduated from Yale with the highest score on record there and was class valedictorian, was in frail health during his years abroad. He tried to toughen himself with exercise, walking in the woods and climbing mountains. Peter joined Charles in Paris, where the brothers had quarters overlooking the garden of the Hôtel de Cluny. Peter lived through the exciting days of 1870, writing to his father of the breathless moments when the plebiscite was adopted. Paris was illuminated that May night as he drove around, viewing the public buildings. The emperor gave a big reception, but smallpox raged in the city. The Taft brothers entertained visiting Cincinnati girls from well-known families, like Elisabeth Perry and Mary Shillito.

No American ever felt more at home in the foreign milieu than Alphonso Taft, the President's father, during his expatriate years as minister to Austria. His method was to ignore completely the protocol of his mission and to function with total simplicity. His wife, Louise Torrey Taft, mother of the President, wrote to young Will about this unusual procedure: "He believes in the good old Vermont way of doing things by 'main strength and awkwardness.' Your father borrows no trouble and says there is no mystery about etiquette, that it is just as it was in Washington. He does not realize the embarrassment of not understanding the languages which makes it impossible to obey signals and save ourselves from blunders."

With uniformed figures, ablaze with decorations, whirling around him, bowing, clicking heels, going through the social gestures of the regime, Alphonso Taft quickly decided that a baron in Austria was the equivalent of a justice of the peace in Vermont. He disliked the toadyism and hand-kissing of the court, and so did another son, Horace, who had followed his half-brothers to Europe in 1883, and was destined to found the Taft School in Connecticut. Will, already a graduate of Yale and a lawyer, took a walking trip in Switzerland in the same year. The whole world—and the presidency and chief justiceship—lay ahead of him. Henry Cabot Lodge, a young Bostonian whom he would know well as a noted senator in later years, preceded them by touring with his family and a private tutor in 1867. Lodge's grandson, bearing the same name, would become one of America's notable public figures a century later.

Even before American youths went abroad to study, merchants and businessmen made up an important group of expatriates. One of the first to leave a record of his activities was Elkanah Watson, who traveled in the 1770s to study the agriculture and husbandry of Europe. He was a New Englander from Plymouth, and Adams, Franklin, and John Jay all welcomed him as a herald of reviving commerce. He came to be well known in expatriate circles as a man of affairs and imagination. Commissioned by the Continental Congress to procure army supplies, and knowing virtually no French when he landed in Nantes, he soon had a fleet of six ships and brigs lying at the mouth of the Loire, and employed seven clerks to handle his mercantile business. He visited Ghent, Brussels, and Ostend, and moved about so freely that the postilions on the road to Paris shouted when they saw him, *"Voilà encore Mon Bostone!"* He strolled with John Adams under the lofty oaks at The Hague, where a peace treaty was being negotiated, and he listened to much advice on the dangers of gambling, dancing, playing cards, and wasting time on frivolity. The departure of a Dutch vessel from Rotterdam with more than a thousand German emigrants aboard was of great interest to him. They were heading for the United States—the expatriate picture in reverse.

In Nantes Watson lodged in the same house as Tom Paine, and he found Paine a tiresome egotist—"coarse and revolting." Yet he conceded that Paine had been an instrument of providence in hastening the Declaration of Independence. Watson found more affinity with another traveling American, Louis Littlepace, who stopped in Nantes in 1779 on his way to Madrid under the wing of the diplomat John Jay. Littlepace was popular at the court of Versailles, and also with the Empress Catherine when he went to Saint Petersburg.

With the aid of Benjamin Franklin, Watson, too, was warmly welcomed at the court, and the Comte de Vergennes, the foreign minister, recognized him as an instrument of trade for the expanding civilization across the ocean. He had a passing glimpse of Louis XVI and Marie Antoinette departing on a hunt, with their courtiers riding in a cloud of dust. As a New Englander, the levity of the Sabbath in Paris was shocking to young Watson, who could not get used to the dancing and music in the crowded cafés. The Palais Royal struck him as being a "mass of moral corruption." He was impressed with the gardens and monuments of Paris, but deplored the narrow, muddy streets without sidewalks. He stayed at the Hôtel d'York on the Rue Jacob, where four years later the British and American peace commissioners signed the treaty affirming the independence of the United States. Watson found his approach to the city thrilling, as he drove through the Place Louis XV, which had yet to become the Place de la Concorde, saw the blaze of color in the Tuileries, and crossed the Pont Neuf.

Benjamin Franklin, whom he often visited, helped Watson get to England in 1782, bearing letters to Edmund Burke, Lord Shelburne, and to the peer's librarian, Joseph Priestley, a clergyman and scientist who had to flee to the United States after the French Revolution. The London houses struck him as being "neat and elegant," but the streets seemed dimly lit after the brighter lights of Paris, which were suspended overhead and benefited from reflectors. London streets were wide and clean, however, and had the pavements lacking in Paris. But the general effect of the city, to Elkanah, was one of gloom and smoky brick.

Watson hastened north to conduct his business affairs and found Liverpool, Manchester, and Birmingham in a frenzy of industrial activity, with many American expatriates on the scene, working for the Tory or Revolutionary cause, as the case might be. Wherever he went, he found the Tory refugees vindictive and bitter. Among others he looked up Andrew Oliver, who had been lieutenant governor of Massachusetts, and Thomas Hutchinson, the royal governor who had upheld the legality of the Stamp Act. As a businessman Watson tried to avoid discussions of politics, but he observed that the Tories treated him with more respect as the tide of battle turned in favor of the revolutionists. He encountered Edward Bancroft, the American scientist from Westfield, Massachusetts, who had settled in London and discovered important dyes for use in the manufacture of textiles. Watson described him merely as an "ardent Whig," but it later developed that Bancroft during the Revolution was a secret agent for the American commissioners in Paris, and was also credited with selling information on American affairs to the British government —an early example of the counterspy working for both sides.

While in Britain, Watson often encountered James Watt, then busy with his steam-engine projects. Watt had tin mines in Cornwall and worked at the Soho Engineering Works in Birmingham. His great invention still lay ahead of him. As Watson traveled, he took note of the social conditions, like many of the visitors from abroad. He was surprised to find highway robbery so common in the country, and footpads and pickpockets busy in the cities. In Liverpool he had a dirty little attic bedroom at the Golden Lion, and decided that the famous inns of England were not necessarily the best. On his way to Manchester, the great cotton center, he lingered to watch a country frolic at a farmhouse. Four-handed reels, not unlike the New England variety, were being danced to merry fiddling. In London Watson did the conventional sightseeing of the American traveler. He dined with John Singleton Copley, visited Mr. West's gallery, followed all the expatriate paths, and noted the British love for pugilism. The Irish Giant, named Burns, eight feet two, sitting near Saint James Park on a high chair and breathing fire, gave him one of his more amusing moments.

On his return to America in 1784 with Rufus King and Elbridge Gerry, on their way to the Continental Congress, Watson was surprised to find so many masts massed at the docks in New York, which then had about fourteen hundred houses and a population of twenty thousand. His own return had been hastened when the National Bank of France, squeezed by collapsing finances, suspended all payments in 1783. Watson's commercial interests were heavily involved. But before long he was running up another fortune at home, making superfine broadcloth and merino from the down of his own sheep. The President and other public men wore this fine cloth, which marked a new development in American manufacture. Like many of the early expatriates he had brought back something of lasting value from his travels, aside from his personal development. He gave America its first county fair, with a cattle show which preceded the incorporation of the Berkshire Agricultural Society.

Watson's business operations merged happily with tourism, and during his five years abroad he covered more than two thousand miles in England, France, the Netherlands, and Austria. His was the Grand Tour of the businessman, as Ticknor's later one was that of the scholar, and both were early examples of the waves of Americans who in the next two hundred years would swarm across the face of Europe and, eventually, around the world.

The Grand Tour became a status symbol for the well-to-do. It had flourished in the Elizabethan age before it took root in America, and Dr. Samuel Johnson, who had not gone far beyond the hated Hebrides, remarked, "A man who has not been in Italy is always conscious of an inferiority." Then, as later, taking the Grand Tour involved the acquisition of possessions, and one early traveler returned with 878 crates and bags. Life moved at a leisurely pace, and the tour could last six months or six years, depending on the mood of the traveler and the state of his purse. It was considered a choice thing to use boats as well as coaches, and the barges of Holland, traveling at four miles an hour, delighted the early American nomads. The thirty-mile sail from Ghent to Bruges cost roughly fifty cents.

It was also possible to travel through much of France by waterways—from Paris to Rouen, or from Lyons to Avignon on the Rhône in a *diligence par eau,* which had to be towed upstream by oxen. Passengers slept in a huddle on bales and chests. There were many alarms along the way, and in Italy the passion for carrying firearms for defense was curbed by a ruling that swords and pistols must be checked in the cloakroom. Tipping was formidable on the Grand Tour, since the servants lined up in solid rows with open palms—a not unfamiliar custom at a later date. Passports were huge, and detailed in their information. Customs examinations were exhaustive, with a constant quest for watches, tobacco, or silk hose. Currency presented problems. There were Italian, Milanese, and Austrian lire to befuddle the innocent abroad, not to mention the British half-crown and florin.

One of the American traveler's problems was adjusting himself to consuming wine and cake for breakfast in Italy, even though the wine was served in cut-glass Venetian goblets. In Holland he could be sure of excellent coffee and familiar food. In Amsterdam English was spoken in the coffeehouses, and American tastes were understood. There was no such thing as a hectic schedule, but it was commonplace to arrive late at some destination and find doors locked, no food available, and even city gates unyielding to pressure. A sense of time did not shake the calm or diminish the discomfort of the Grand Tour.

Britain, France, and Italy were the points of concentration at first, although there was a swing to Spain as the Washington Irving vogue developed. Padua, Siena, and Milan drew visitors as early as the 1830s, and the pinching habits of Italian men were apparent to Catharine Sedgwick even in the 1840s. She noted how relentlessly the girls she chaperoned were pursued, and how they clung to her for protection, making her feel uncomfortably like a duenna. Rome, Florence, and Venice were the major points of interest, and Lucca, to the northwest of Florence, reminded the traveling correspondent Nathaniel Parker Willis of Saratoga. It was popular before Fiesole became the writer's retreat. By the middle of the nineteenth century the Grand Tour had an established pattern, and business and professional men joined the army of artists, writers, and musicians who concentrated their energies on culture and learning.

Wives and daughters by this time shared in the pleasures of the Grand Tour, haunting the Vatican, Saint Peter's, the Colosseum, and the Villa Borghese. The pope received visiting Americans,

Roman Catholic or not, regularly. Switzerland became a land of special scenic delight, of mountain drives and dramatic vistas, of the thrilling carriage drive over the Saint Gothard pass, of Byron's Castle of Chillon. When Harriet Beecher Stowe reached the Hospice of Saint Bernard, she found a crowd of men smoking cigars and watching her approach, "just as any set of loafers do from the porch of a fashionable hotel." The stern New England touch was often applied by visiting commentators to the places of recreation as well as the dens of sin in Europe, but all were prepared to rave over the beauties of the south of France, to listen to music in the beer gardens and *Kursaals,* to sail up the Rhine, and to tone up their bodies at the spas, a European custom rapidly adopted by the more prosperous Americans. The most popular spas were Wiesbaden in the 1830s, Vincenz Priessnitz's health establishment in Silesia in the 1840s, and Carlsbad and Baden-Baden in the 1890s.

Many Americans went abroad to look; a surprising number stayed, settling in chalets in Switzerland, in villas outside Florence, in hotels in Paris, in dream castles with turquoise urns and green jalousies on the Riviera, in comfortable English homes. Many came to enjoy the gourmet food of France and to drink the wines. American women learned to buy their clothes in Paris, London, and Berlin, to seek their silks in Lyons and their leather in Rome and Madrid. While the acknowledged art collectors bought knowingly and in increasing numbers from the 1870s on, the average American and his wife followed their instincts in their choice of carved woodwork and Persian carpets, icons and bronze vases, majolicas and Della Robbias, triptychs and illuminated manuscripts. Many dubious paintings, credited to the great masters, were hung in the mansions of unsuspecting owners. When Stanford White went into action, he kept a sailing ship at Leghorn to convey the treasures he bought for the Renaissance buildings he was putting up in America. Architects, builders, and decorators worked hand in glove in the days of Palladian magnificence.

Collectors or mere spectators, Americans abroad learned to weather the ridicule they sometimes encountered over their own alien customs, even when it came from their fellow countrymen. Charles Sumner, scholar, antislavery crusader, and later a senator, was one of the worst offenders in this respect on his first trip to Europe in the 1830s. He deplored his compatriots' strident speech, their rumpled linen, and their "want of manner either of the scholar or the man of the world." Later, when he became a settled expatriate, after being physically attacked in the Senate over his antislavery stand, he was more temperate in his judgments as he haunted the best homes and clubs of Britain, enjoyed country weekends, was welcomed at Windsor Castle, and consorted with Lord Palmerston and Disraeli, with Dickens, Thackeray, and Carlyle. The social barriers of the Victorian era were let down for him as for Emerson and Harriet Beecher Stowe, for Samuel Gridley Howe and his wife Julia, for General and Mrs. Grant. Queen Victoria received Daniel Webster at court, and Edward Everett, American minister at the Court of Saint James's in the 1840s, saw to it that visitors from New England received their due.

Longfellow also was critical of his countrymen abroad and deplored the tourist to whom a Roman aqueduct, a Gothic cathedral, two or three churches, and an ancient ruin or so were only breakfast fare. It was true that many compared the sacred Rhine unfavorably with the great and rolling Hudson, the Alps with their own western mountains, the exotic foods of Europe with simple American fare, continental shops with A. T. Stewart's in New York, and the belles of Europe with their own chic and beautiful women.

William Tudor, the author who helped to establish the Boston Athenaeum and founded the *North American Review* in 1815, took note of the fact that even before 1820 the people in the eastern states had become great travelers. Both sexes were showing up in London, Paris, Rome, and Naples, and most of the bright young men had been to Greece, too. Tudor felt that the Puritan spirit was relaxing slightly under European influences and that the humor, ardor of thought, and energy of the American character were becoming apparent in the foreign field. Civilization had reached a pitch by this time where "every man wore a watch, every lady carried a parasol, and every house had a piano," or this was how things seemed to Tudor. America was growing up, but the true expatriates still felt that it had a long way to go. They had no means of knowing that Noah Webster, buried in books in London and Paris, was working on obscure points for the classic dictionary he would soon bring out, or that Jared Sparks was in France rounding up material for his books on the American Revolution.

Another wanderer who would be heard from in a convincing way was John James Audubon, the naturalist, known best at the time as the "American Woodsman." He crossed to Europe in 1826 with John Swift of Saint Francisville, Louisiana, who was bound for Dublin to visit his parents. Passengers lay about on the deck of the sailing ship and on cotton bales, "basking like crocodiles," Audubon noted, "while thousands of large Petrels displayed their elegant aerial movements to me."

Audubon was sailing to Europe to get subscriptions for his book

The Birds of America, and he was soon in Edinburgh discussing the habits of the turkey buzzard with Professor Robert Jameson. His drawings were displayed in Manchester and Liverpool, and he could not resist making witty sketches from the inn where he stayed at Matlock, and at other spots along the way. His wolfskin coat and hunting attire were a trademark, but his delicate aquiline profile suggested the scholar or poet.

By degrees the boundaries of the Grand Tour expanded, and expatriates grew in number as transportation quickened and improved in the nineteenth century. The two big advances were the development of railways in the 1840s and 1850s and the arrival in New York in 1838 of the *Sirius* and the *Great Western,* the first steamships to cross the Atlantic. The discomforts of sailing ships and the horrors of seasickness had previously limited travel to the hardier souls. It was rough going in the early days, although some of the bright young students managed to travel in style. William Preston and a party of friends went rollicking from Paris to Rome in a private coach and four. When they arrived, they took over an empty palace, rented furniture, and hired a large staff of servants. On the other hand Bayard Taylor, poet and diplomat, supplied his own bedding and food on a sailing packet in 1844 and tramped across Europe with knapsack and staff. He wandered through Germany, Italy, Switzerland, France, and England on next to nothing, but later garnered his reward with his writings and lectures.

Preston preferred the French diligence to the English coach, for wine flowed and there was much fun and laughter in the diligences as they thundered over macadamized roads with six horses, or rattled on cobbled streets. But a later generation of Americans, growing up with the *Pickwick Papers,* saw more romance in the stagecoach, with its postboys and liveried coachmen, its guard with bugle, and its prize assortment of passengers. The *vettura* was favored in Italy, and guidebooks, good and bad, abounded. Baedekers came out in English in 1861, as the Civil War began, but Murray's handbook, first published in England in 1836, remained a standby. Thomas Cook & Sons eased the picture from the 1850s on, and American Express moved into this field in 1897. A popular handbook was *The Tourist in Europe,* published by George P. Putnam in 1838. The red tape of travel was considerable even then, and the customs officials inspected an extraordinary collection of portmanteaux, trunks, carpetbags, hatboxes, dressing cases, jewel cases, Gladstone bags, hold-alls, steamer rugs, and *portefeuilles.*

There was less travel during the Civil War years, and the Grand Tour was in eclipse until the 1870s, when it was more popular than ever. It had become more comfortable to travel. Steamships had taken the place of the sailing packets. Shipboard conveniences and food were much improved. By the close of the nineteenth century more than 100,000 Americans went abroad each year. They had become used to seawater baths in marble tubs on the liners, and Victorian plush in the saloons. The cuisine was heavy, but it pleased the trenchermen who abounded during this era. Gymnasiums, deck games, betting on the day's run, and daily newspapers added to the excitement of the voyage.

European hotels had learned to cater to this opulent trade, and the appearance of cigar-smoking, whiskered men in fur-collared overcoats, and beautiful girls steered around by chic but assertive mothers, was a welcome sight anywhere between London and Vienna. They exuded an air of luxury as they closed in on the Parisian fashion houses and bought baubles on the Rue de Rivoli and silver on the Rue du Bac. Galignani's Reading Room was a good place in Paris to receive mail until Thomas Cook & Sons and American Express took over this function for later generations. The German spas were in high esteem, and railroad agencies moved in to make life simple for the traveling American, or the permanent expatriate.

Henry James was skeptical of arranged tours, like many Americans who followed him, but he conceded that his countrymen, with their bad French, their multilabeled luggage, their search for sitz baths and pale ale, needed professional help of some kind, and so he did not frown on Thomas Cook and its successors. It was a happy state of affairs that the wandering American in 1882 could bed down in one of Cook's hotels for $2.10 a day, with table d'hôte, lights, attendance, and a substantial breakfast thrown in. Sometimes resident Americans latched on to this happy way of having a few days of comfort away from their chilly lodgings. But the bohemians and the professional expatriates remained cold to the packaged tours, a point of view that did not wholly change even in the 1960s. Bicycles were a carefree way of getting away from it all in the 1890s, and Americans old and young whizzed through country lanes in England, and followed the highways in Italy, France, and Germany.

European inns, hotels, and restaurants in time became accustomed to the invasion from America. The writers and artists, always discursive on what they saw and enjoyed, whipped up interest in certain hostelries and bars. In Paris the Hôtel de France et Choiseul, the Louvre, the Grand, and the Hôtel Meurice attracted many Americans in the late nineteenth century, just as the Crillon, the Georges Cinq, and the Continental were popular after World War I, the Hôtel Scribe during World War II, and the Lancaster and

Plaza-Athénée in the 1960s. James Russell Lowell's liking for the food at Véfour drew many Americans to this restaurant, and in London such diverse characters as Mark Twain, Andrew Carnegie, and Mrs. Hetty Green set their seal on the Langham Hotel in the Victorian era. Switzerland established a solid reputation for its orderly and well-run hotels. The Riviera, bathed in sunshine, bright with bougainvillea and mimosa, and washed by the blue Mediterranean, became the playground of the rich toward the close of the nineteenth century.

Political Refugees

The Civil War led to a great expatriate wave of political refugees. It resembled the exodus during the Revolutionary period, but was more intense and highly concentrated as the war ended and the Confederacy fell. Long before the war began, while the clouds were gathering, American consuls, commercial agents, and minor diplomats worked tirelessly in Britain and France on behalf of Southern interests. The cotton and tobacco trade, which was their lifeline, was involved. The agents of the North were equally persistent in their efforts to win support for their side, and the British statesmen were divided in their responses. Many swung to the South in the early stages of the Civil War, until it became clear that the North was winning. As the war progressed, the counterspying intensified, and the Confederate network of commercial agents was particularly strong in the northern industrial areas of Liverpool, Manchester, and Birmingham, where the cotton interests were centered.

After Gettysburg the diplomatic game had been won by the North, and James Mason and John Slidell, American commissioners in London and Paris, were checkmated at every turn. Charles Francis Adams in London and John Bigelow, consul-general in Paris, were the two strong men from the North who nullified their efforts. Both Mason and Slidell had worked closely with two of the most noted agents of the Civil War period—Matthew Fontaine Maury, world-famous scientist and geographer, and Rose O'Neal Greenhow, a Maryland aristocrat, long resident in Virginia, who charmed many of the British peers and boasted of the period she had spent in the Old Capitol Gaol in Washington after Allan Pinkerton, emerging as America's number one detective, had nabbed her as a Confederate spy.

The exiles in England and France were stirred up when Mrs. Greenhow appeared in their midst in 1863. She had long been known for her operations in Washington as a fascinating woman, who, with her persuasive arguments and manner, could conjure up sympathy for the Southern cause. Now, with the halo of her imprisonment around her, she showed up in London and Paris, and proceeded to operate openly and freely, conducting herself with her old dash and pride. The other Confederate agents had been campaigning with more discretion and secrecy for supplies and money to help the failing Confederacy.

When she crossed from London in 1864 to push the Southern interests in France, the emperor received her in a small salon in the Tuileries on a somber winter day. It was an official audience, and she pleaded her case with ease and eloquence. She was treated courteously, but she had come too late. The open door between France and the Confederate States was closing decisively at the very moment she was asking for aid.

Slidell reported to Judah Benjamin, who was secretary of state for the Confederacy at the time, that the emperor had indeed received Mrs. Greenhow, and he enclosed confidential details of the meeting. Rose, who spoke French fluently and had long been one of the most accomplished hostesses in Washington, was the final card played by the Confederacy with the emperor. She was working closely with Commander Maury in his efforts to get ships from France. They were desperately needed since the British government had held up the ironclads known as rams that were ready to sail from Liverpool for the Confederate States.

But the defeat of the South at Gettysburg had affected the French viewpoint deeply. It was becoming apparent that the Confederates were losing. Mrs. Greenhow did all she could on Maury's behalf, knowing the importance of the ships he sought. Aside from her private audience with the emperor, she was formally presented at court. Empress Eugénie, of mixed Spanish, Scottish, and American blood, was thought to lean strongly to the South. She knew that Mrs. Greenhow had long been a favorite of the Comte de Sartiges, French ambassador to the United States. Rose had done France some favors, and she sought some in return. In Paris she was singled out for press attention when she attended a magnificent ball given by the emperor and Eugénie. She entered her daughter Florence in the Convent of the Sacred Heart, which the daughters of many other transplanted Americans were attending. Mrs. Slidell, with Creole grace, paved the way for many of them, for her husband still functioned importantly in Paris.

But the American rush of presentations at court tapered off, with the planters and financiers who had once abounded in Paris returning to serve their country, and a new crop of exiles moving in, more quietly, and not seeking attention. Many of the American girls remained in the schools where their parents had placed them, and they watched the fortunes of war from afar. They attended literary and scientific lectures, and some married Frenchmen, including Slidell's daughter Rosine, who became the Baroness d'Erlanger. An observer of the American colony in Paris at this time remarked, "Utterly self-reliant, they walk as daughters of a conquering race, who have made themselves a place under the sun."

American war news could be picked up through the papers in the reading room of the Grand Hotel. Rose followed it eagerly, as she made appointments with bankers and diplomats to discuss the trading in cotton and tobacco that she and other Confederates were promoting. She had little time to waste on the shops, although it was her first visit to Paris, but she found time to drive in the Bois with Florence in the late afternoon. Old friends whom she had known at the French legation in Washington received her, but the chill was settling deeper on the Confederate cause. Mrs. Greenhow had always been one of the most elegantly turned out women in Washington, but her months in jail and her saddening days in the South after her release had dimmed her interest in dress. Now Florence helped her to buy smart clothes again for herself and for her younger daughter, Rose, who had shared her imprisonment. Rose was entered in the convent, too, but before she had turned eighteen, this beauty, famous always as "Little Rose," married a West Pointer whom she later divorced. She returned to an expatriate existence in France, became deeply religious, and retired from public view.

Mrs. Greenhow was received with some acclaim in England. Her book, *My Imprisonment and The First Year of Abolition Rule at Washington,* published just before her arrival in 1863, was read with a combination of interest and skepticism. On a lesser scale it stirred up talk as *Uncle Tom's Cabin* had done, but from the opposite viewpoint. Describing Lincoln and three of his chief aides— Seward, Wilson, and Stanton—in stark and abusive terms, it differed from Harriet Beecher Stowe's book by discarding the veil of fiction. Mrs. Greenhow's prejudices came into view on every page, and she became an overnight celebrity in London. She made no secret of her own guile as a Confederate agent, and her romantic drive was apparent to all, but her genuine devotion to the South endeared her to those who were on her side.

The moderate-minded felt that Mrs. Greenhow's denunciation of everything Northern was wildly overdrawn, and that her sense of wrong rose almost to the pitch of frenzy. She talked, wrote, and lectured with flaming passion, approaching every statesman who would listen to her. Through Rose the English had a strange view of the statesmen of the North. In the 1960s she would have been known as an effective political hostess and propagandist, like Mercy Warren Otis at the time of the Revolution. But in the 1860s she was regarded as a fascinating woman serving her country, a beguiling link in the ring of agents and commissioners working busily for the South.

The press, cotton men, and many of the peers leaned her way until the final days of the war. The British working class was sympathetic to the North, and Adams had John Bright, Richard Cobden, the Duke of Argyll, Richard Monckton Milnes, and other able and eloquent statesmen behind him. Lord Russell and Lord Palmerston wavered for a time and then came out for a neutral stand. Although Lord Russell came under fire for receiving Mason and Slidell in the beginning, he was eventually accused of being influenced by Charles Francis Adams. There was no doubt that Adams had some fast work to do for the North after the Proclamation of Neutrality was issued, for the Southern agents had been working long and assiduously and could call on plenty of support.

Rose's writings were pushed hard in the cotton and shipping centers of northern England, where much of the Confederate backing lay. Three Southern clubs in Liverpool, Manchester, and Birmingham were collecting money and clothing for the Confederates. Rose was much in demand to speak at the public meetings they held in towns and villages. She was equally popular as the star attraction at bazaars and other functions promoted by the peerage for the Southern cause. In fact, for a time, with all this wealth and prestige behind her in England, she floated on a golden cloud.

Modishly gowned in the clothes supplied by her daughter Florence, Mrs. Greenhow whirled around in the London ballrooms as she once had in Richmond and Washington. Wherever she went, she found sympathy for the Confederacy, and she fed the blaze with skill and energy, in spite of the frightful news arriving from America of the slaughter at the battles of the Wilderness, Spotsylvania, and Cold Harbor. She planned a quick return trip to take money and clothes to the Confederates, and to make a personal report to their president, Jefferson Davis. Dispatches were continually being lost at sea, and she wished to give him her own account of her interview with the French emperor. It was her intention to return later to England, for she had promised to marry the widowed Earl of Granville.

In high spirits, and looking rejuvenated, she sailed on the *Condor* from Greenock on an August day in 1864. Blockade-running was at its peak, and no woman crossed the Atlantic at this time without a compelling cause. But Rose had one. A heavy leather reticule, which she never let go, hung from a long chain around her neck. Underneath her clothes she was heavily weighted with English gold for the Confederacy, some of it sewn into her underwear. The *Condor* was skippered by Augustus Charles Hobart-Hampden, a younger son of the Earl of Buckingham. He had won the Victoria Cross in the Crimean War and was a favorite of Queen Victoria's. As a blockade runner the admiral used the aliases Hewett, Roberts, Gulick, and Ridge, the name he bore when Mrs. Greenhow came aboard. Just before sailing he received dispatch bags from James Mason with instructions to give them to Rose, who intended to go straight to Richmond. She was joined at Halifax by James B. Holcombe, a Confederate commissioner who had been working in Canada for the Southern cause.

The *Condor* was within two hundred yards of Fort Fisher and the protection of its guns when it grounded on the New Inlet Bar close to Baltimore, while trying to elude what Hobart-Hampden mistakenly took to be a blockade runner. Rose dressed with frantic haste. There was much confusion on board and no one knew what was happening as the ship lurched, guns were fired, and rockets went up. Thinking of another term in prison lying ahead of her if captured, and of the golden loot and dispatches she was bearing, Rose insisted on being sent ashore along with Holcombe. The towering admiral tried to dissuade her, but she would not listen to his assurances that she would be safe if she stayed aboard the *Condor*. When persuasion failed, she stormed at him, and they had a shouting match on the bridge in the wavering light of lanterns.

Soaked to the skin, wrapped in a heavy black shawl, clutching her reticule tightly, Rose finally was lowered into the lurching boat as dawn broke. She demanded the dispatch bags, which were lowered beside her and were never seen again. The boat capsized. Holcombe swam ashore, but the waves quickly broke over Rose's head, and she was lost to view in sea and spray. She sank at once, weighted down by her golden sovereigns. Her body was found by a Confederate soldier from North Carolina. Her reticule lay on the sand beside her, still linked to her neck. He saw the glitter of gold as her sovereigns spilled in a golden shower around her. Holcombe was saved, but Mrs. Greenhow, who had always said that she would gladly die for the Confederacy, had achieved that end through her impulsive nature. Among the political exiles she was perhaps the most handsome, guileful, and persuasive of her sex.

She had worked closely with Maury, a scientist of great distinction whose expatriate life in England, France, and Mexico was laced with grief and misunderstanding. Mrs. Greenhow had much in common with this Virginia oceanographer who had contributed so much to the early success of the Confederate navy. In some respects he reminded her of her late husband, Robert Greenhow, who had worked for the State Department, and done brilliant exploration in the West. She and Commander Maury made a powerful combination when they proselytized for the South in the drawing rooms of Victorian England. His prestige in Europe was great, but he was a practical man of scientific bent who found his work as an agent frustrating and disappointing. He had arrived from America with money to buy gunboats, but all the other agents at the time were offering cotton in exchange for ships and other war supplies. This created a certain disharmony and cross-purpose, but in the end neither cotton nor Confederate money counted.

Maury organized a commission of Confederate naval officers in London who tried to get ships on any terms. He hoped to persuade shipbuilders to sell him vessels already under construction. Every kind of craft was needed to run the Northern blockade. The Confederate agents claimed that 792 vessels entered or cleared the Southern ports in the first year of the war. Fort Fisher, where Mrs. Greenhow died, was the last to remain open. Soon most of the cotton shipped was lost at sea. So was every other kind of commodity, and much human life. Maury worked ceaselessly abroad on his electric mines, torpedoes, and other new devices, some of which he had used effectively at the beginning of the war.

He had his headquarters close to Manchester, where he used both cotton experts and propagandists. James Spence, a writer and businessman who had long been an expatriate, ran an agency in Liverpool for the sale of Confederate bonds, and aided Maury on ships, mines, blockade operations, and the shipment of cotton. He was the author of *American Union,* a treatise on the South. Both he and Henry Hotze, another agent, published a weekly review known as the *Index,* which gave space to the work of Mrs. Greenhow, Maury, and other prominent Confederates. They supplied the English newspapers and magazines of the day with material favorable to the South.

George McHenry, another of these "commercial agents" who doubled in brass as writers and traders, took Mrs. Greenhow's book north with him to Manchester "to buttonhole a few of the leading manufacturers and talk cotton with them." McHenry and his fellow traders were active in the Society for Obtaining the Cessation of Hostilities in America, which met regularly on Regent Street and had more than five thousand members in 1864, many of them American expatriates. It had a roster of prominent Parliamentarians, from Lord Robert Cecil to A. J. B. Beresford-Hope. But Maury, who had been influential in organizing this group, carried the olive branch in one hand and the sword in the other. He worked with intense concentration on his torpedoes, which had aroused some skepticism in the citizens of Richmond, even after Maury had mined the James River successfully in the early days of the war.

But he lost hope for all his plans in Europe after the defection of the French emperor. Maury had worked hard on the elaborate coup, which would have involved the United States with France in the affairs of Mexico. Archduke Ferdinand Maximilian of Austria, like most European rulers, was familiar with his work as a geographer, and Maury counted on him to help swing French support to the Confederacy when he was established by France in 1864 as emperor of Mexico. Maury envisioned a plan to separate California from the Union and restore it to Mexico, should the South win. Emperor Maximilian was deeply interested, but Louis Napoleon swung away from these intrigues when England declined to join him in recognition of the Confederacy. In her interview with the French emperor Mrs. Greenhow had backed Maury's plan. Few Americans were more familiar with Mexico than she, for she had spent a great deal of time there, spoke Spanish, and knew all the political complications.

When Britain banned the departure of the ironclads that were to help the Confederacy, Maury knew that Adams had used powerful measures to stop them. He decided on a secret trip back to Richmond to report to Davis on the shipping situation and on the various moves involving Maximilian. The time had passed when such communications could be contained in dispatches because they were now likely to be lost at sea, or read by the enemy. On May 2, 1865, he sailed from Southampton under orders from the Confederate secretary of the navy. When Maury reached Saint Thomas, he heard of the collapse of the South and the assassination of Abraham Lincoln.

He went on to Cuba, sending a son who was with him back to Virginia. At this point he surrendered his sword and resigned as a commander of the Confederate navy.

Meanwhile Maximilian, who was the brother of Francis Joseph, Emperor of Austria, and his wife, Princess Carlotta, daughter of Leopold I of Belgium, functioned uncertainly on the throne given them by France after Mexico had been partially conquered. They extended a helping hand to the stranded Maury when he wrote from Havana, offering his services to Mexico. In keeping with his scientific reputation he was appointed director of the Imperial Observatory.

But Maury was soon in trouble when he launched a colonization project, hoping thereby to give refuge to many of his Southern friends who were scattering in all directions. At first Maximilian was sympathetic to his plan and appointed him imperial commissioner for colonization, and two shiploads of immigrants arrived from the Southern states. Maury's idea was to admit immigrants of all nations, and those who so desired could bring laborers with them, or induce them to come in considerable numbers. The laborers would be subject to protective regulations but would be allowed to take care of themselves after seven years of training.

Maury planned to get land surveyed and create a "New Virginia" in Mexico. But his project carried the implication of revived slavery, and soon he was under heavy fire. Maximilian abandoned the Department of Immigration and the colonization scheme after General Philip H. Sheridan vowed he would break up the "Maury nest of Confederates." Maximilian's brief reign on the throne of the Montezumas was cut short when the United States government demanded that Napoleon III withdraw his troops from Mexico. Left to his fate, Maximilian persuaded Carlotta to return to Europe. He was taken prisoner and shot in 1868, and after his death she lost her reason.

The scientists of Europe found that Maury had aged incredibly when he returned there in 1866 after the fiasco in Mexico. He was feted by them, and Von Humboldt pointed out that he had created a new science. His work on currents influenced the commerce of nations, shortened sea voyages, and strengthened the security of navigation. He was elected an honorary member of many of the learned societies in Europe. Medals were struck in his honor.

Toward the close of Maury's expatriate days the French emperor invited him to become a Frenchman, but Maury decided that he would rather pursue his scientific interests in England. He opened a school of instruction on electric torpedoes and wrote a series of geographical textbooks for the use of schools. Along with Tennyson he received an honorary degree from Cambridge in 1868, and was specifically cited for his "attentive observations of the course of the winds, the climate, its currents of the seas and oceans." When political barriers to his return to the United States had been removed, he accepted the chair of physics at the Virginia Military Institute. Robert E. Lee meanwhile had become rector of Washington and Lee, and they were friendly neighbors. January 14, Maury Day, became a school holiday in Virginia, and eventually Maury was elected to the American Hall of Fame.

But many of the expatriates of the Civil War period never returned to the United States. They felt they would not be happy in the North, and the misery and poverty in the South dismayed them. They found new lives, new homes, new interests, in Europe. Their children grew up with the knowledge that their parents had once been exiles. They, in turn, married abroad and brought up a generation that still heard tales of the bitterest of American wars. The image of North and South was never blurred in their identity, however, and the soft accents and characteristic ways emerged even in the great-grandchildren of this expatriate generation.

The experiences of the Civil War exiles immediately after Lee's surrender were dramatic, embittering, and sometimes painful in the extreme. Their wives and families suffered with the men who were cut off from the normal flow of their lives. Mrs. Maury stayed in the United States when her husband fled to Mexico.

The worst off was Jefferson Davis, the man who had been president of the short-lived Confederacy. He was the most notable, as well as the most unhappy, of fugitives, and his brilliant wife, Varina, who had known both social and political power, suffered in full measure. She stayed close to his side through all his tribulations. When he was released from Fortress Monroe in the summer of 1867, after undergoing harsh treatment there, he decided to go first to Canada. A number of other Confederate leaders had already fled there, or to England, in addition to the few who had gone to Mexico.

Davis was reunited with his family when Varina and his children —Winnie, always known as "The Daughter of the Confederacy," Margaret, Jefferson, Jr., and Billy—joined him in the village of Lennoxville in Quebec. He had stopped on his way there to visit Mason in the summer cottage the former commissioner had at Niagara Falls. The days passed slowly in that first year of exile, and Varina was distracted, trying to comfort the shattered man still suffering from the humiliations of his imprisonment. The voices of people sounded like trumpets in his ears. He could not endure the slightest noise or excitement. "The trees and flowers bloomed for others," Varina wrote. "I knew they were fair, but they were not for me or mine." The Davis horizons, once so wide and diversified, now were bounded by a village street.

The boys attended a good school outside Lennoxville along with the sons of other Southerners who had had to leave their native states because they would not take the oath of allegiance. In the evenings the children gathered to sing and play games, and Varina felt that she was experiencing a semblance of home again, but this did not comfort her anguished husband as he worked feverishly on his own history of the Civil War. Davis called his existence vegetation, not life. He was experiencing political exile at its most painful, with the crushing knowledge of the disastrous defeat of the South weighing on him day and night. His case was unique. He was the unsuccessful leader of a hard-fought cause. Probably no other American expatriate in history bore the burden of responsibility that Davis did. He was consumed with anger as he brooded over mistakes made, errors of judgment, and the shattering charges leveled against him. Both he and Varina realized that ahead of them lay a period of melancholy wandering, of rootlessness, of the bitter dregs of defeat, of impoverishment, of the acute loneliness of a ruler in exile.

The Canadian winter so affected his health that he was advised to seek a warm climate after he had appeared in court in Richmond for the *nolle prosequi* proceedings on a charge of treason. The Davises went to Havana at this point, then to New Orleans, where he was greeted by old friends. The state of the South depressed Davis further. After returning to Lennoxville in 1868, he and Varina made plans to go to England.

The arrival of the former head of the Confederate States at Liverpool that same summer aroused great interest in Britain, and wherever he went, the tall, gaunt man, whose disastrous history was still so fresh in people's minds, was recognized. The Davises were entertained by many of the statesmen who had been friendly to the South during the war, but they were constantly running head-on into Americans from the North who were traveling in great numbers now that the war was over. Varina, like Abigail Adams after the Revolutionary War, found herself surrounded by antagonistic spirits. She fared best with the Englishmen she had entertained in Richmond. The Marquis of Westminster, a great favorite of hers when he was their guest in the high days of the Confederacy, welcomed them with warmth. Lord Shrewsbury, another of their Richmond visitors, invited them to Alton Towers for the "flower show for laborers," a significant note for the future. Lord and Lady Leigh had them at Stoneleigh Abbey, and they were entertained by Lord Percy, Lord Lovell, Lord Lytton, Lord Lothian, Lady Brownlow, and the Duke of Sutherland.

Lady Eardley offered them her house on Lancaster Street, in which Davis's portrait already hung. Her father had strong feeling about the war, for he had been dismissed from his post as consul at Mobile for showing sympathy to the Southern cause. Varina enjoyed her stays with Mrs. C. E. Barrett-Leonard, who had a Tudor house in Essex with secret chambers, a Cavalier hiding place, and a legendary ghost in the tapestry room. Davis became godfather to her niece, who was baptized Anne Varina Jefferson Davis and was known as Winnie, like his own daughter.

The Confederate cause was still being discussed from all angles in the stateliest homes of England, but the Davises were profoundly unhappy and isolated, suffering the despair of the vanquished and the ever-present knowledge of the misery in the South following the war. Varina, worldly at heart, found it hard to forego the social pleasures and brilliant conversation that she instinctively enjoyed, but her husband felt that they must live without ostentation. He was well aware of his position as a man without a country, without an occupation, without the sense of destiny that had been his from his earliest days in Washington. For years he had figured prominently on the national scene, and he was now a leper, worn out in body and soul. The Davis children were not adjusting well to the change of scene. The boys had been sent to a school at Waterloo, close to Liverpool, and Jeff was taunted by young Theodore Roosevelt when he came to visit a cousin who was also enrolled there. Teddy noted in his diary that he "had a nice time but met Jeff Davis' son and some sharp words ensued."

Davis's doctor ordered him north for the bracing air as his health declined. In Glasgow he visited James Smith, a philanthropist who had lived in Mississippi and had given a battery to the Confederacy. Smith's brother had died fighting for the Southern cause. When Davis visited Robert Burns's birthplace near Ayr, he found his own portrait hanging beside that of the poet. At Saint Andrews he stayed with John Blackwood, the magazine editor, in September 1869, when the heather was in bloom and the shooting season in full swing.

The Davises crossed to France and entered Winnie at the Convent of the Assumption outside Paris. They were not presented at court because of their ambiguous position. Northerners were in the ascendancy abroad, and Varina observed with some bitterness Americans "bowing the knee" quite regularly to the emperor and empress. In her *Memoir* she acknowledged that the emperor was attentive to her husband—"in a manner." He sent a staff officer to offer Davis an audience, and Empress Eugénie let Varina know that she would be glad to receive her. But proud Jefferson Davis, according to his wife, "felt that the Emperor had not been sincere with our Government. He did not wish to say anything uncivil, and could not meet him with the cordiality his Majesty's kindness warranted."

Reviews were held in Davis's honor, however, and he received official attention. He and Mrs. Davis had cards to attend chapel in the Tuileries. In Paris they were surrounded by Confederate friends, including John Slidell, who had long represented the Davis government in France; Senator William McKendree Gwin from California; A. Dudley Mann, who had been a trade commissioner in Europe for the South; and other expatriate Southerners. They dined with the Slidells on New Year's Day, and recalled the receptions they used to have in Richmond. Rosine Slidell, who had often been intermediary for her father in the transmission of dispatches, had married Baron d'Erlanger.

Mrs. Davis was struck by the luxury in which many of their old friends were living, in spite of the disaster that had overtaken them all. She felt somewhat out of the swim as she watched skating on a pond in the Bois, and the coroneted carriages bowling past, with wigged and powdered footmen in elaborate liveries. Now and again the empress appeared on the ice, with the aid of a baton held by two court attendants. Varina watched Cora Pearl, the famous demimondaine and actress whose true name was Emma Crouch, drive along the Champs Elysées with a lapdog dyed to match her hair, and she listened again to Adelina Patti, whom she had heard singing when she first settled in Washington as the wife of Jefferson Davis.

In Paris, too, a great loneliness descended on the Davises. The silver-gray buildings of the French capital, the manor houses of England, the men's clubs to which Davis was invited, the gardens in which he was perpetually interested, the literary landmarks that commanded his attention, the Welsh mines, the Scottish moors, the House of Commons—all would have interested him in other days, but now he moved like a ghost among them. It seemed to Varina that wherever they went—even among their own expatriate group in Paris—their welcome had a forced ring. They were no longer at home anywhere on the face of the earth, for they were true political refugees.

The faint chill in the air seemed even to affect their relations with Judah P. Benjamin, formerly the most brilliant member of the New Orleans bar, one of the architects of the Confederate government, and a close political associate at Richmond of Jefferson Davis. Mrs. Davis, in particular, influenced Benjamin on many issues, and she was a potent figure in the Confederacy. After General Lee surrendered to General Grant, Benjamin escaped capture under the most extraordinary conditions. Disguised as a Frenchman, he traveled south by horse and buggy, enveloped in a cloak, his face half hidden behind huge goggles. A drooping hat completed the effect. When he reached Florida, he donned the homespun of a farmer, and in this attire he sailed for the Bimini Islands on a sloop which foundered. Transferring to another vessel he reached Nassau, then proceeded to Havana, and finally arrived in Southampton three months after the war ended.

When the Davises reached Europe, Benjamin was already beginning to make his way at the British bar. Specializing in mercantile cases, he had much important business in the Liverpool region, where Confederate cotton interests had been strong. By 1870 he was queen's counsel for Lancashire County, showing that he had proved himself as a senior member of the bar and had been recommended to the queen by the lord chancellor. The Davises saw much of him during their first winter in London, and he joined them in Paris when they stayed with Mann for the celebration of the New Year. But he was reluctant to discuss the war with Jefferson Davis after one long and exhaustive talk. He had turned his back on it all, and did not wish to do anything that would imperil his growing prestige in British legal circles.

Varina observed that her old friend and ally was enjoying the worldly pleasures of Victorian England. Although his success at the bar was sensational, she was in no way surprised, since she had boundless respect for his talents. When Edward A. Pollard's savage book on the Davises came out, pillorying Varina as a "coarse Western woman" and attacking her husband unmercifully, the Davises discussed legal action with Benjamin, but he advised them to ignore it. He felt sure that the book "would drop into oblivion" unless they advertised it by taking notice of it.

There is no proof that Benjamin did anything to help Jefferson Davis in England other than to maintain pleasant social relations with him and Varina. Davis was a proud man in any event, who would not accept favors, and he stood by while a number of his old associates flourished in Europe as his own fortunes declined.

Louis T. Wigfall was among the dispossessed who sought refuge abroad. Although born on a South Carolina plantation and married to a Charleston girl named Charlotte Maria Cross, he had long been identified with Texas. He was a spectacular figure at Fort Sumter and was one of the more conspicuous rebels, noisy and self-assertive. After being close friends, Mrs. Davis had wrangled with the Wigfalls, and Wigfall had become one of Jefferson Davis's severest critics. Although all were in the same plight when they fled from the storm, the Wigfalls ignored the Davises in London. When they settled on Portman Square, they entertained all the Confederate leaders except Davis and Benjamin. Most of the exiles, however, were curious to see their fallen leader, and a few who had been habitually critical of Mrs. Davis in Richmond watched her social course in London with some malice.

But Mrs. Davis was no longer a woman who loved pomp and circumstance. She had suffered too much, and had learned that anonymity was a better state for her stricken husband. She was well aware that tales of any extravagance on their part would be magnified in the United States, and they could not match the luxurious life of the peers in any event, for they were now without funds. After visiting various country homes, they took modest rooms in Dorset Square in the spring of 1869, and Varina wrote to her relatives in Mississippi, "We refuse all invitations to go out to fine parties, or to fine people. Lord Campbell and Sir Henry Holland, and Lord Abingdon have been very civil in their pressing invitations to us to go to them for dinner, luncheon, etc., but we cannot afford to associate on those intimate terms with such rich people."

When Varina's sister Margaret married Chevalier Charles de Wechmar-Stoess, an Alsatian who was consul at Liverpool, the Davises gave her as fine a wedding as they could afford. It was held in Saint Peter's Church, Belsize Park, but Jefferson Davis was already planning to return to the United States in the hope of making a living for his family. His funds were at a low ebb. A commission-house venture in the North, on which he had depended, had failed. He returned to Memphis in 1870, when a post as president of an insurance company was offered to him. Varina and the children stayed on in England and lived the life of a number of other Southern exiles during this period. Little Maggie walked with her governess in Regent's Park; Winnie studied her primer industriously, and liked to listen to poetry and music; Billy and young Jeff, who knew all too much about the roar of cannon from their Civil War days, were startled by the fireworks and cannon fire in Liverpool on Guy Fawkes Day. Wherever they went, they were recognized as Jeff Davis's children, and their mother felt that the expatriate life was demoralizing for the young. They were all handsome and bright, and she was a martinet about their manners.

Mrs. Davis moved with a touch of her old hauteur among the shifting scenes around her, passionately upholding the Confederate cause to all who would listen. She was still consumed with her old resentment over the treatment her husband had received at Fortress Monroe and his indictment for treason. Her face had a look of suffering and melancholy, but her dignity was unimpaired, and her pride was as strong as ever. Glad as she was to see Benjamin climbing the social ladder and becoming rich and successful, she suffered for her disheartened husband.

At first Benjamin had thought of settling in Paris, where his adored but indifferent wife, Natalie, and his daughter, Ninette, lived. He was introduced by Slidell to bankers who might help him, and Madame de Pontalba, an old friend from his New Orleans days, urged him to stay in Paris. But he was at heart a lawyer, and he quickly decided on the course he should follow. He was introduced to Gladstone and Tennyson, who were sympathetic, and to Lord Campbell (Stratheden) and Sir James Ferguson, both friends of the Confederacy, who helped him. He worked briefly for the *Daily Telegraph,* writing editorials on international affairs. Benjamin lived in simple fashion at first, eating in cheap restaurants and on Sundays dining with old friends from Louisiana who were also exiles during this painful period in American history. The gourmet and sophisticate of New Orleans, who spoke Spanish, English, French, and Latin, seemed to have fallen on lean times. But at the beginning of 1866, less than a year after the collapse of the Confederacy, Benjamin enrolled at Lincoln's Inn and rose thereafter like a rocket.

Suave, polished, and genial in manner, he cut corners and moved fast, with strong influence behind him. Dispensing with the usual three-year legal apprenticeship, he became an English barrister at the age of fifty-five, thirty-four years after his admission to the Louisiana bar. The way was made easier for him when it was established that he was a British subject, born in Saint Thomas of Sephardic ancestry, like Disraeli and Spinoza (his parents had moved from the Virgin Islands to Charleston in 1822). Benjamin later went to Yale, and just before the Civil War broke out, he rented the famous Decatur House in Washington, designed by Latrobe, and lived in at different times by Henry Clay, Martin Van Buren, Edward Livingston, and Howell Cobb. Benjamin furnished it with a perfect period sense for his wife, Natalie, but she preferred to live in Europe and soon left him.

When Benjamin rose so quickly to fresh legal eminence in Britain, his old enemy Wigfall wrote bitterly of him to Clement Clay, another Confederate leader who had not joined the exiles:

> As to Benjamin he turned out to be an Englishman & he has plenty of money and can attend the clubs, entertain friends & extend his acquaintance. He found no difficulty in being admitted after six months at the Inns. . . . On his arrival here he reported himself authorized by the President to take charge of financial matters & my own belief is that he and the agents have divided among themselves all that was left of Confederate funds. . . .

This was an unproved charge, born out of old animosities, but the world of the political expatriate has always been one of rumor and uncertainty, and the deep and bitter feelings engendered by the War Between the States was unparalleled in this respect. Benjamin was soon making $150,000 a year at the British bar by his own unaided talents. He had many tough cases to fight for compatriots, and he was known as an able defender of lost hopes. His bizarre dictatorial manner mellowed to easy geniality as he argued with the princes of the British bar. Moncure Conway, the Cincinnati clergyman and antislavery spokesman who was a pastor in London from 1864 to 1884, and a well-known expatriate himself, observed in the Cincinnati *Commercial* that Judah Benjamin had become the "most famous advocate at the English bar." Conway felt that his manner and his power had improved during his years of exile, and he was much sought after for cases involving international law. One of his clients in 1878 was Cyrus McCormick, of Chicago, who consulted him in Paris about the European sales of his reapers. His Confederate role in America was forgotten by the new millionaires who invaded Europe after the war.

Benjamin disliked anything that roused memories of his past. He never returned to the United States, and when Davis wrote to him about an old wartime controversy as he was compiling his autobiography, Benjamin told him rather sharply that he had no wish to mix in any way in the controversies of the past, which for him were buried forever. "If at any time your character or motives should be assailed and my testimony needed," he assured Davis, "I should be indeed an arrant coward to permit this feeling to interfere with my prompt advance to your side to repel the calumny. But in any other case, I long only for repose."

Davis did not appeal to him again. Benjamin was a conservative politically in Britain and was disappointed when the Disraeli ministry was overthrown in 1880 and the Liberals were returned to power. He won his last case before the House of Lords in 1882 and died two years later at his house in Paris. His life, said the *Times* of London, had been as various as an Eastern tale, "and he had carved out for himself by his own unaided exertions not one, but three histories of great and well-earned distinction."

The Ladies Travel

In the eighteenth and nineteenth centuries few American women abroad were considered true expatriates, yet hundreds of wives in diplomatic, business, and artistic circles lived in country houses close to London, in trim dwellings in Passy, in picturesque palaces on the Grand Canal in Venice, in vast Roman mansions; or in the frigid discomfort of Chelsea, the Left Bank, or chilly lodgings along the Arno.

The scholars' wives settled in unfamiliar university towns and considered the advantages for their children compensation for their own deprivation. Their transplanted lives involved a tremendous change of pace and they were usually less at ease and adjusted than their men. Nostalgia for the United States burned like a high fever in many of them, and the daughters of pioneer stock were apt to resent the endless protocol and servility of court life, and to long for their homes in Indiana, Ohio, Massachusetts, or Tennessee.

The more worldly might entertain famous writers, artists, and statesmen and win brief mention in their memoirs of a good dinner served, a becoming Worth gown, a sparkling wit, or handsome children. Beyond that they did not count, except for the strong individualists who wrote their own histories or took a hand in political and artistic movements. As wives they sank into the general picture; yet it is a historical fact that many of the most noted expatriates among the men have been bachelors.

The women settled abroad might look enviously at their compatriots on the Grand Tour, shopping in Paris, driving along the Riviera, attending the opera in Vienna, and the theater in London. After a brief term these transients would go home, and come again, and then go home. Their children would grow up in the American pattern. Their days would be spent among their own. The American heiresses who curtseyed to Queen Victoria and the Empress Eugénie and ended up marrying titled Europeans garnered endless publicity, but little sympathy was felt for them when their marriages failed. They were less representative of their country than the anonymous American wives scattered all over Europe, with growing families and ambitious husbands.

Wherever they were, American women were known for their style, vivacity, and healthy good looks. European women marveled at their independence, their wealth, and the casual way in which they treated their men. They thought American children were ill-disciplined brats and that their mothers' manners lacked polish. The American accent, regardless of its regional timbre and distinctions, was always an irritant to the critical European. But the American woman abroad continued stubbornly to be herself—a true native of her own land till the day she died. The few who slid into pretension and affectation were discounted by their compatriots. In general a bright spirit burned among them, which occasionally exploded in revolutionary activity embarrassing to their men and to their country. The women writers in particular left a record that testified to their individualism, and the social reformers took back to the United States some new causes and a strong strain of feminism.

Many of the diplomatic wives were chic, clever, and witty in their own right. They were sometimes studied with care when their husbands were being chosen for ambassadorial duties. A perfect example of the American woman in action on the diplomatic front at a crucial time in history is Mary King Waddington, who was part of the official life of the American set in Paris during the vivid 1870s. It was swinging at high pitch, as travelers poured in after the Civil War. They had money to spend, and the city was overrun with American women busy with social activities, entering their children in French schools, and having them drilled in languages, dancing, music, and all the available arts. Mrs. Waddington was the American-born wife of William Henry Waddington, French archaeologist and statesman who served in turn in the French Assembly, the Senate, as minister of foreign affairs, as premier, and as French ambassador to Great Britain. His mother was a Scot named Chisholm. He had attended Cambridge University and was a favorite of Queen Victoria's.

Mrs. Waddington was able to observe the social scene at close range, both in Paris and London, since the resident expatriates, the visitors, and the official set turned up with unfailing regularity at the Quai d'Orsay and the embassies. Lord Richard Lyons, the British ambassador in Paris, who gave splendid dinners himself and never invited a cardinal and an ambassador to the same function, thought that American women were more adaptable than French or English women; in fact, he told Mrs. Waddington (possibly with tongue in cheek) that he had never met a stupid American woman. He knew them well, since he had been the British minister in Washington during the Civil War. But Mrs. Waddington needed to be smart, because she had to cope in turn with the Conservatives, the Royalists, the Bonapartists, and the Republicans.

At the time of her marriage in the 1870s the Assembly was sitting at Versailles, and Louis Thiers was first president of the Third Republic. When he was overthrown in 1873, he was followed by Marshal MacMahon. The French were embittered by their defeat in the recently fought Franco-Prussian War, and Mrs. Waddington watched with interest the struggle between the Republicans and the Monarchists. Political feeling was intense, with the younger generation asserting itself and gaining influence. Waddington's personal friends were mostly scholars who valued his archaeological achievements, or Orléanists, the monarchists who supported the Bourbon line.

Mrs. Waddington soon decided that the American women in Paris were not profoundly interested in foreign politics, but many of her friends joined her with true native curiosity to see a phase of French life that was novel to them—the interplay of social and political forces. Like other diplomatic hostesses, she faced many social crises, since her countrywomen were apt to ignore the rules of court etiquette. Invading charmed circles, they approached the sacrosanct without waiting for notice and proceeded to talk in an uninhibited way about whatever occurred to them. "The Americans do just as they like," she commented, "and no one is surprised. The explanation is quite simple—they're Americans." After watching the outcome of some of the international matches, she was convinced that her compatriots remained thoroughly American, no matter whom they married or where they lived. On her drives to the Chamber of Deputies to bring her husband home, she ran into them everywhere—in the streets, at the fashion houses, the *pâtisseries,* and in the small curio shops. They were intent on buying old furniture, prints, and china. It was an era of acquisition for their houses at home and abroad. The Civil War had created a number of new millionaires.

Mrs. Waddington reflected that the concentrated intelligence of France passed through her quarters at the dinners and receptions held at the ministry. There were parties without end, and her petit salon was close to the long suite of rooms in the Palais d'Orsay. The red carpets and blue brocaded walls, the tapestries and pink roses in tall crystal vases, made an effective setting for the women of many nations gathered to dance, to talk politics, and to take stock of one another's gowns.

The Russian and American women seemed to their hostess to be the most spirited. Mrs. Waddington observed that the number of tiaras had increased and that American women were beginning to wear them, in spite of the new republican spirit that prevailed. Their gowns and jewels were magnificent, and they were always distinguishable at the opera or the Comédie Française. American girls wore lace and jewels, in contrast with the austerity of their French friends, and as soon as they married, they blossomed out in long velvet gowns, with feathers in their hair. Tickets for the Sunday afternoon concerts at the Conservatoire, where classical music was presented at its best, were much prized by the American girls, who were as eager to improve themselves in languages, art, and music as they were to enjoy the parties and the good-looking men around the embassies.

Marshal MacMahon received visiting Americans in a salon overlooking the gardens, and his wife, a practical and energetic woman, was particularly kind to the artists who flocked to these gatherings. The Americans who called at the Quai d'Orsay were deeply interested in everything relating to the unforgettable Lafayette, and Mrs. Waddington made many pilgrimages on their behalf to the Château de la Grange, where the general had spent his last years. It pained her to see the neglected state of the lawns, but geraniums, pinks, and sunflowers made a blaze of color in the disordered grounds. She often went to the Thierses' gloomy house in the Place Saint Georges, a gathering place for the Republicans and some of the Orléanists, both diplomats and politicians. With the end of the National Assembly in 1876 and the beginning of a new regime, members of the Orléans family turned up at all the big parties given by the Waddingtons.

A round of magnificent entertainments began in 1889 when the

Universal Exposition opened at the Trocadéro on the centenary of the Revolution. The Eiffel Tower was a new landmark, and all Paris glittered with pomp and uniforms. Foreign princes attended the dinners and receptions, and the Chinese, Japanese, Persians, Greeks, and Romanians wore their native costumes. Epaulets and aiguillettes abounded, and spurs jingled with the cavalcade along the Champs Elysées. Germany alone was not represented. The scene suggested to many the last days of the empire, and Americans enjoyed it to the full.

The theater and opera were at their best. The Prince of Wales (later Edward VII) made himself popular by going to the small theaters and speaking the argot like a native. The Empress of Austria, perfectly tailored, rode in the Bois on magnificent horses, and Queen Isabella of Spain, who lived in the Palais d'Espagne that later became the Hotel Majestic, held court, with all her gold plate in evidence and an orchestra of guitars and mandolins. Louis Tiffany was a popular figure at the exposition, and visiting Americans bought many pieces of his silver as souvenirs of the occasion. It was a departure from the heavy, classical silver of France, and it created a vogue for Tiffany designs.

By the time the exposition closed, Mrs. Waddington longed for the simpler way of life she had had in Rome. The protocol and stiff ways of the French tired her. As a girl she had spent much time in Italy, and she preferred the informal ways of Rome. In that city there were few notes to write or formal invitations to send out, for she met her friends each day, hunting, riding on the Campagna di Roma, driving to the villas in the afternoons, and finishing at the Pincio for music. They made their plans on the spot for their next meeting, and the American women, like everyone else, seemed to be more relaxed under the Italian sun.

The diplomatic picture, aside from court formalities, varied in the different capitals, and it was at the embassies that one saw the flow of expatriate life, although many of the permanent residents never went near the courts or the embassies. A constant change of emissaries followed the fall of monarchies and the overthrow of governments, but the United States had a long succession of able ministers in its foreign service. Moving from capital to capital, some achieved full expatriate status in spite of their official role. A few had remarkable wives, among them Abigail Adams, Mrs. Whitelaw Reid, and, in the 1940's, Mrs. Rose Kennedy, mother of President John F. Kennedy. All three represented a style quite different from that of the bright young embassy wives of the 1960s.

During the 1870s and 1880s one of America's most glamorous political hostesses, Kate Chase Sprague, was in and out of Paris and London, still a powerful figure in social circles, but late in the 1880s she returned to France, this time to live the expatriate life. Her fortune was gone; her father, Salmon Portland Chase, was dead; and her reputation was clouded because of her divorce and a notorious affair with Senator Roscoe Conkling. She lived in a villa at Fontainebleau and took an interest in the artists of the Barbizon School, who had retired to the forest to live close to nature. She bought a Corot, a Rousseau, a Courbet, and other Impressionist works. She was still dressed by Worth, for she had long been one of his most prized customers. She took her daughter Ethel to see Sarah Bernhardt at the height of her fame, and Bernhardt's performance as Camille encouraged Ethel to train for the stage. In the Bois they watched the actress Réjane driving in a phaeton drawn by white mules.

Mrs. Sprague's old enemy, Mary Todd Lincoln, ended a period of exile in 1879 when she returned to America after lonely years spent in Pau and Nice, following her release from an American asylum. A crowd waited at the dock when she stepped ashore in New York, and Mrs. Lincoln came to life again, but for a moment only. She quickly saw that no one recognized her. They were waiting for Sarah Bernhardt to step down the gangplank. But if Mrs. Lincoln and Mrs. Sprague, so prominent during the Civil War, had lost status, all the doors that mattered in Europe were open to their contemporaries Julia Ward Howe and her husband, Samuel Gridley Howe.

Beautiful and eloquent in her youth, Julia had a gift for being in the right place at the right time, and she interested the aristocracy, while her husband fostered humanitarian causes and, like Byron, served in the Greek war for independence from Turkey. They spent long periods abroad, and Europeans were as familiar with Dr. Howe's work for the blind and the miraculous story of his ward, Laura Bridgman, as Americans were. Julia, with her many gifts, was best known for having written *The Battle Hymn of the Republic* at the Willard Hotel in Washington after watching Civil War soldiers parading past. She became an ardent worker for peace and for woman suffrage.

Julia was a New York girl of Huguenot ancestry who lived at Bowling Green and drove around the city in a coach with a pale yellow lining. She met Washington Irving several times at the home of John Jacob Astor. When she married Dr. Howe, she fitted smoothly into the intellectual life of Boston, and was equally at ease attending the Dante Club or presiding over the New England Women's Club. She "discovered" Italy as early as 1843, and for the rest of her life she spent a great deal of time in Europe. She studied Dante with Felice Foresti, the Italian scholar and revolutionary, and in Turin she met his sister and Silvio Pellico, a fellow member of the Carbonari (charcoal burners), a secret society whose members blacked their faces to conceal their identity when they plotted army mutinies. Mazzini was one of them. With all these influences at work, Mrs. Howe was soon committed to the cause of freedom and, like Margaret Fuller and Catharine M. Sedgwick, was inevitably drawn into the Italian political movement known as the Risorgimento.

Always beautifully gowned, fascinating as an orator, and ever ready to speak up for the downtrodden or to uphold the rights of women, Mrs. Howe created an impressive image in Europe of the American woman. She had many links abroad. Her brother, Sam Ward, a friend of Lord Rosebery, was a bon vivant with a multitude of interests and a rich crop of legends surrounding him. Her sister, Mrs. Luther Terry, lived in the Palazzo Odescalchi in Rome and was a woman of great charm and beauty. She was popular in cosmopolitan society, and her son was the well-known author F. Marion Crawford. Mrs. Howe's daughter Maud was married to John Elliott, the artist who also lived in Rome. All this made her as much at home in Rome as in Boston or London.

Mrs. Howe, an advocate of prison reform, spoke at congresses on this subject in England, Geneva, Paris, and Faneuil Hall in Boston, where she later pled the cause of Greece. When she visited Europe in 1877, she breakfasted with the Gladstones and found her host disputatious. But she enjoyed her fellow guests—William Black, the novelist and war correspondent, and John Richard Green, the historian. In Paris Frédéric Passy, who founded the International League of Peace, took her to a meeting of the French Academy, where she saw the Immortals in their armchairs, wearing long coats faced with palms embroidered on green satin. She visited Paul Gustave Doré and attended a women's rights convention in Paris. While in the French capital, she attended the reception that Marshal MacMahon gave for General Ulysses S. Grant on his world tour. Léon Gambetta, the French lawyer and statesman, escorted Mrs. Grant in to dinner.

In Italy, during this visit, Mrs. Howe showed many facets of her striking personality. She watched King Umberto take the oath of office before the Italian Parliament in 1878, and she spoke on suffrage in Florence. She wrote poems in Italian and made speeches in French. She studied Hebrew, and she sang and played charades at musical parties that brought the Anglo-American visitors together.

Mrs. Howe was the chosen poet at a number of festivals, and once she gave a reading with the tragedienne Adelaide Ristori. She was a prominent figure at the expositions on both sides of the Atlantic. When she and Dr. Howe were in London in 1843, Edward Everett, American minister at the Court of Saint James's, noted that no visiting Americans had ever excited more interest or received more attention. This was a period when the statesmen, writers, and artists of Britain were studying the visiting Americans with appraising interest. Mrs. Howe's worldly charm had great appeal for the eloquent parliamentarians. During the Franco-Prussian War she started a women's peace crusade, issuing an appeal to women throughout the world. Although a convinced suffrage worker she took care not to become militantly aggressive on the question. She was always a well-bred observer with smoother means of furthering a cause.

In 1867 the Howes were in Greece, and the Turks had set a price on the doctor's head because of his long involvement with the Greek struggle for independence from Turkey. On their return, Julia gave parlor readings at the home of Henry James to raise money for the Cretans. When Dr. Howe died in 1875, the Greeks sent a helmet and a sword of violets to honor their champion. Julia continued to travel and live abroad. She was only slightly less well known than Mrs. Harriet Beecher Stowe, whose *Uncle Tom's Cabin* had made her a world-famous figure. When Mrs. Stowe entered a shop or a church in Europe, she was recognized at once, for her book had been translated into many languages. Moreover, she had just spread Lady Byron's story of her unhappy life with the poet in an article written for the *Atlantic Monthly* in 1869. Many of her British friends were shocked by this breach of confidence, but they welcomed her to their homes and lionized her during her stay. While in Italy, Mrs. Stowe was drawn to the ritual of the Roman Catholic Church, and she began to write *Agnes of Sorrento* when a storm detained her at Salerno. Like Elizabeth Barrett Browning she was a believer in spiritualism, and the two famous women discussed this subject by the hour. Both were interested in the rappings and strange effects evoked by Daniel Dunglas Home, a Scottish medium who had found a haven in Connecticut. He was the subject of Browning's *Sludge the Medium,* written in 1864, and many notables believed in him, including William Cullen Bryant, who succumbed easily to a belief in the supernatural. Sir William Crookes, the scientist who had been led astray by Kate and Florence Cook, two English mediums, and Kate and Margaret Fox, spiritualists from the United States, gave Home clearance after testing him in the daylight. Alexander Dumas was Home's best man when he married a Russian countess, and Balzac's widow was one of his disciples. His exhibition at the Tuileries delighted Paris when he made chairs dance around the salon for Napoleon III and an accordion play melodious airs by itself. The Empress Eugénie was persuaded that one of the hands he "materialized" was that of her Spanish father.

Mrs. Stowe was an indefatigable sightseer who observed on her travels that virtually every country in Europe was undergoing a revolution to establish the rights of humanity against the old order. She had cut considerable ice herself, and when she visited the *bottega* of the Castellani brothers, who were goldsmiths, they gave her the head of an Egyptian slave, chiseled in black onyx. One of them said, "Madam, we know what you have been to the poor slave. We are ourselves but poor slaves still in Italy; you feel for us; will you keep this gem as a slight recognition of what you have done?"

Americans living in Rome and Florence clustered around Mrs. Stowe, although it was not until 1910 that she was elected to the American Hall of Fame. Her collected works, *The Writings of Harriet Beecher Stowe,* came out in 1896, the year of her death at the age of eighty-five. She was a star among the travelers—not for the length of time she stayed abroad, or for her literary excellence, but because she was a vivid and compelling personality and had shaken up the social body.

An exile who drew attention everywhere and by all odds was the most distinguished of Horace Greeley's correspondents was Margaret Fuller, who managed to get involved in the Risorgimento and to gallop through the streets of Rome after Garibaldi's lancers, wearing the Garibaldi tunic of bright red cloth and the plumed Greek cap.

Margaret's literary reputation was well established before she became one of the most interesting of all feminine expatriates. The British writers, who viewed some of the female correspondents from the United States with disdain, recognized her qualifications as an editor of the *Dial,* an acknowledged transcendentalist, a friend of Emerson's, and a first-rate critic and book reviewer for Greeley. It was inevitable that she should be taken into the inner circle, for she had strong social connections in New England as well as literary standing. Hawthorne and Theodore Parker disliked her. She had helped Thoreau and knifed Longfellow, but the poet bore her no ill will. Her sharp criticism of Lowell's work struck flint, however, and he lampooned her in his "Fable for Critics." Harriet Martineau found Margaret a graceless guest when the American visited her at Ambleside. But Miss Fuller introduced Robert Browning to the American public, helped to popularize Goethe's work, and was the best conversationalist of her day, even if her mannerisms and abrasive voice did not help her on the platform.

Margaret favored full social and political equality for women, but she was not an avowed feminist, and she stayed aloof from the growing tide of agitation as the antislavery advocates worked strenuously and at the same time for woman suffrage. She was heavily committed to the mesmerists, fortune-tellers, spiritualists, phrenologists, food faddists, and other cultists who abounded in this era. Margaret was convinced that she had second sight. Her wretched health was ascribed by Greeley to her habit of drinking too much strong tea, but her own theory was that she worked best when in pain, which she said acted "like a girdle and gave tension to her powers." It also resulted in her work always being late, an affront to the energetic editor of the *Tribune*. However, he valued her political dispatches from abroad when she became involved in the Roman revolution, just as he cherished her literary acumen and style.

From childhood she had been a classical scholar, pushed by an exacting father who demanded that his small daughter be up at five in the morning to study French, Greek, Latin, and philosophy, as well as practice her scales. Later, at her Dante classes given for young ladies and her *conversaziones* on Greek mythology, Margaret emerged as an American George Sand and became known as the "Yankee Corinne." She had the outward bearing of an intellectual snob as she brandished her lorgnette and made pronouncements. In black mousseline, with a blue chenille chord knotted around her hair, and a carbuncle ring flashing from her hand, Margaret seemed the essence of the New Woman then coming into view in America.

Love chastened her to some extent after she became an expatriate, and with a political cause to cherish involving her lover, Giovanni Angelo Ossoli, she found a new outlet for her energies. But first she made the grand tour in Britain, visiting Stratford, the Inner Temple, Kew Gardens, Parliament, Saint Paul's, and the Lake Country. Her social conscience, always alert, had full play as she visited the coal mines of Newcastle and talked to the mill girls of Manchester. The industrial picture, as she saw it, was graphically presented to the American public through Horace Greeley's newspaper. Writer expatriates like Margaret Fuller did much to shape opinion at home during this period, when fewer people traveled than a century later, after tourism had become more widespread.

Margaret met Thomas De Quincy in Edinburgh and found him old and confused. Wordsworth made her welcome amid his daffodils, and in London the Carlyles gave a dinner for her, at which she met George Henry Lewes, who later became the constant companion of George Eliot. More importantly, here she established her first contact with Giuseppe Mazzini, the republican lawyer who aimed to free Rome and who later helped to organize Garibaldi's expeditions. Mazzini was then teaching at a London school for impoverished Italian boys. He lived near the Carlyles and at their dinner table indulged in what Carlyle called "rose-water imbecilities" but Mrs. Carlyle considered to be living truth.

Carlyle seemed to Margaret arrogant and overbearing but without "littleness or self-love." He was boisterous, while Jane Carlyle sat like a dim and silent shadow. Reporting back to his friend Emerson on his impressions of Miss Fuller, Carlyle wrote, "She is very narrow, sometimes, but she is truly high." He conceded that she was unique, "an excellent soul," and rare among the women of her day.

George Sand, receiving Miss Fuller in Paris, was well aware that she had been caricatured in the *Dial* as Minerva, driving a team of the new *illuminati,* as the transcendentalists were known. A ball at the Tuileries meant less to Margaret than the hours she spent talking to this famed French author in a thickly carpeted room, shaded in café au lait with flowers in Chinese vases and a rosewood piano hallowed by Chopin's touch. While the American Corinne displayed her powers as a conversationalist, she noticed that George Sand challenged any remark she made that specially interested her. Later Margaret went to Chopin's quarters on the floor above and he played for her. She thought him "frail as a snowdrop" in his pearl-gray suit, with pastel effects all around him in his salon.

But Margaret found the true breath of life when she reached Rome in the spring of 1847. She was soon picnicking on roast chestnuts, bread, and wine, and watching the sun go down over the dome of Saint Peter's with the Marchese Ossoli, a slender youth, gentle in manner, belonging to the papal nobility, but a stout-hearted liberal in his political convictions. He was younger than Margaret, who was then thirty-seven, but he brought romance into her life after a long correspondence with a New York man who in the end abandoned her for other interests.

Ossoli was heavily involved in the revolutionary movement simmering in Rome at the time, and when Mazzini, long an exile, stole in quietly and on foot to avoid a demonstration, he visited Margaret in secret and conferred with Ossoli, who was at odds with his family but who knew what was going on in conservative Vatican circles. Margaret, always the alert journalist, caught the timbre and mood of both the liberal and conservative factions, to the satisfaction of Horace Greeley and the *Tribune* readers. She was also in touch with Adam Mickiewicz, the Polish poet and political conspirator who had been friendly with James Fenimore Cooper. Mickiewicz was familiar with the American scene. He had lectured on Emerson in

Paris and had circulated copies of the *Dial* among his students. He was well aware of Miss Fuller's importance, and he urged her to strengthen her association with Ossoli to further their political interests. Mazzini thought Mickiewicz the greatest poet in Europe, and Ossoli was so dedicated to Mazzini's cause that Margaret's love affair was half political and half romantic.

Margaret shared the fate of lesser women by becoming pregnant at a time when Ossoli could not marry her openly because his family objected to the match. She retired to Rieti in the Umbrian mountains to live with the peasants and wait for the birth of her child. The coming of little Angelo was a great event in her life, and she wrote, "I find satisfaction for the first time to the deep wants of my heart." She rode on donkeys over the bridle paths fringing the vineyards and took long walks through the olive and mulberry groves, but soon she was back in Rome in time to become part of the great drama staged when the troops of Napoleon III bombarded the city and the pope fled. Ossoli commanded a battery on the Pincian Hill as Margaret watched the city turn into an inferno. She sent the *Tribune* a stirring dispatch on the demonstration at the Quirinal palace preceding the departure of the pope. She watched the door of the palace swing open and the leaders of the revolutionary party enter, demanding the withdrawal of the Swiss Guard.

During the siege of 1849 she directed the work in one of the hospitals and read to the wounded in the gardens of the Quirinal. But she wrote despairingly to Emerson that their cause was already lost. She watched Mazzini sink into melancholy, but he lingered on after the French troops entered Rome on July 4, 1849, until Margaret and Giulia Modena finally persuaded him to leave the city. She and Ossoli, who were assumed to have married to legitimatize their child, escaped to Florence, where their close association with the Brownings developed. They visited the two poets frequently in their apartment overlooking the Piazza Santa Maria Novella, while Margaret worked on her history of the Roman Revolution, which was subsequently lost at sea. She had many talks with Hiram Powers, Horatio Greenough, Harriet Hosmer, and other sculptors and writers who moved in the Browning set. However, with the fall of Italy to the French she seemed to have lost much of her will to live, and she sailed for America on a May day in 1850 with "dark presentiments" typical of her extrasensory leanings. She was with the Brownings on the night before she sailed, and she gave small Pen Browning a Bible as a parting gift from her own Angelo. It was prophetically inscribed, "In memory of Angelo Eugene Ossoli." All three of the Ossolis drowned when their ship, heavily loaded with Carrara marble, was wrecked off Fire Island near New York. Their bodies were never recovered, but the work of Margaret Fuller was her monument.

A New England friend, Catharine Sedgwick, was as ardent a supporter of the Italian movement as Margaret Fuller, and she resented the restraints imposed by the government, from the need for special permission to cross the frontiers of the small Italian states to the lack of concern for the welfare of the people. Miss Sedgwick, spending many years in Italy, knew the country as well as any American of the period. She studied the villas around Milan and Como with the eye of the novelist and the knowledge of the historian, long before Mrs. Wharton started exploring villas and gardens. She was deeply versed in the history of the gardens to which "nature, climate, art, and wealth had given the last touch of perfection."

Miss Sedgwick thought that to Americans Italy was all a stage, with the Italians like actors playing parts in some poetic drama. It always surprised her that they could never distinguish between an American and an Englishman, true though it was that they heard the Boston accent more often than any other from across the Atlantic. She took careful note herself of the gay costumes of the peasants, with their scarlet bodices, embroidered petticoats, coral necklaces, and baskets of grapes, often borne on their burnished hair. She was less sympathetic to the King of Piedmont's soldiers galloping through clouds of dust in scarlet uniforms. But all wayfarers were observed by Miss Sedgwick, from the pilgrims with shaggy beards, sandals, and colored robes to the Americans on the Grand Tour, traveling in large coaches.

A more glamorous expatriate for a number of years than either Margaret Fuller or Catharine Sedgwick was Kate Field, a St. Louis girl who was considered a great beauty when Elihu Vedder painted her in Italy. She became well known all over Europe as an actress, writer, and general gadabout, but she was only seventeen and already ardently committed to the cause of Garibaldi when she first called on the Brownings at the Bocca di Leone. She was to see them often after that and to find in Florence a number of her compatriots, including Robert C. Winthrop, the Stowes, James T. Fields, the publisher, and an English couple of great interest to her—George Eliot and George Henry Lewes, a man she considered ugly but possessed of charm as a conversationalist. When Kate landed in Europe in 1859, she was well fortified with letters of introduction—to the Brownings, the Trollopes, the Hawthornes, and Franklin Pierce, who was then in Rome, his days as President behind him.

On Christmas Day 1860 Kate Field was in Florence, dining with the Trollopes, and she brought in the New Year by attending a great ball at the Palazzo Vecchio. Anthony Trollope later described her as his "most chosen friend," and while in Florence she always attended the Trollope Monday evenings. She came to know Walter Savage Landor well. He taught her Italian, and Adelaide Ristori, then the Marchesa del Grillo, made such an impression on her that she decided to devote her life to the theater. Along with the actress Charlotte Cushman and Harriet Hosmer she took singing lessons. Meanwhile, she sent letters home to the Boston *Courier* and later to the New York *Herald* and the New York *Tribune*. She was another of Horace Greeley's traveling correspondents. Kate had known Charlotte Cushman, Julia Ward Howe, and Edwin Booth at Newport, where her aunt, Mrs. Milton T. Sanford, had a villa.

Kate thought Rome more beautiful than Paris, where she attended a ball given by James Mason, the Confederate diplomat who was treading delicate ground as the nation headed toward civil war. Kate wore white tulle with a blue sash, and her curls were tied back with blue ribbon. "Not Rome," she said, "but the seventh heaven." Paris had been transformed by Napoleon, and it looked splendid to her American eyes. Kate, slender and blue-eyed, with a Boston accent and intellectual as well as worldly interests, was noticed on her way through Paris. She had keen understanding of the nature of Elizabeth Barrett Browning, and on March 29, 1860, Browning wrote to her, "You are not only the delightful Kate Field, which I always knew you to be, but the perspicacious creature to whom I am suddenly found bowing down before you as the sole understander of Ba in all Florence."

When Elizabeth died in 1861, Kate Field attended her funeral and noticed that Browning could scarcely stand up. His face expressed "the most terrible grief." She felt desolate herself and wrote to her aunt, "My hold upon Italy has gone. The Brownings were dear to me; she was a guiding light, and will ever remain so, wherever I may be."

Everything at the Casa Guidi was as Ba had left it—a half-opened fan, the desk where she had written her poems, the last *Nazione* that she had read. Browning told Kate that he would never have a home again but would rove about the world. For the time being she went back to the United States and found a great flowering of letters there. She lectured gracefully on "Women in the Lyceum," costumed in blue and white silk, with flowers at her belt and a cascade of curls resting on her neck. Her purpose was to raise money to maintain John Brown's farm as historic ground. But she was soon back in Europe again. After her mother's death in 1871 she traveled in Germany and Switzerland and then settled in London on Half Moon Street. She lectured on Dickens and attended the séances held by Margaret and Kate Fox, the two American mediums who were drawing in all those interested in spiritualism.

In the 1870s Kate alternated lectures and newspaper correspondence with the stage, appearing in New York in *Peg Woffington* in 1874 and flopping badly, but having a two-year run in London in *Extremes Meet*. Her stage name was Mary Keemle. She became internationally famous overnight when Queen Victoria first picked up a telephone receiver. Disraeli had asked Kate to sing for the queen over the telephone. Alexander Graham Bell wrote thanking her, and Kate wryly remarked, "I'm considered a great creature because I've sung to the Queen." It was a transatlantic gesture that made a fortune for Kate, since she received early stock in the Bell Telephone Company. The life she loved, however, was the literary one, and in London she strolled along the Embankment with Carlyle and consorted with Herbert Spencer, George Eliot, George Henry Lewes, John Tyndall, Anne Thackeray, and others with scientific and literary interests. She wrote a memoir for the *Tribune* when George Eliot died. Back in Paris in 1882 she saw Sarah Bernhardt in *Camille* but preferred Modjeska's performance. From 1883 to 1890 she went in for a ceaseless round of lecturing and traveling. Since she was known to all the diplomats on both sides of the Atlantic, she decided to publish a paper of her own. *Kate Field's Washington* first appeared in 1890, a political weekly that covered literature and drama, and ran a good deal on the occult, to the dismay of her general readers. She campaigned for dress reform, for the abolition of polygamy by the Mormons, for the abolition of a tax on paintings and statuary; she tried unsuccessfully to found a national art association, an ambition born out of the years she had spent in Italy.

Kate was wandering away from home again when she died. She had gone to Hawaii to study Oriental immigration, visit the leper colony, and foster free kindergartens. She was blown off her horse while crossing a lava bed in a hurricane. Kate was injured and developed pneumonia, from which she died in 1896. In his autobiography Anthony Trollope wrote of her, "She is a ray of light to me from which I can always strike a spark by thinking of her." Kate's own estimate of herself was precise: "If I am anything," she said, "I am a Woman of Tomorrow."

She was only one of many Americans abroad who went to the séances run in London by Margaret and Kate Fox. A séance they had held at the Carlyle house was the talk of England in the 1870s. They were both a fad and a fashion at a time when Sir William

Crookes, the physicist, was investigating all such phenomena. He backed them and stuck to his convictions even after Margaret pronounced herself a fraud on their return to America. But their expatriate years were filled with excitement, and celebrities poured into their parlors. They were most noted for the strange rappings that came from ceilings and walls, from tables and chairs, when they were in a room.

The Cook sisters, English girls who also were sponsored by Sir William, put on a more glamorous performance for the celebrities who visited them. The sitters saw semiluminous figures in veils, flickering through darkened rooms, holding bunches of roses. Invisible hands touched them; angelic-looking children floated through the air; tambourines were shaken; and stringed instruments made unearthly music. Dickens, Browning, John Bright, and other celebrities watched the magic projected by Florence and Kate Cook.

The Fox sisters had simpler methods. They could make a room seem to rock with their mysterious rappings. When Sir William Crookes did his tests of Kate, he announced that for "power and certainty" he had never found a medium to touch her. She did mirror writing, too. "It seems only necessary for her to place her hand on any substance for loud thuds to be heard in it. . . . I have heard them on a glass harmonica. I have felt them on my own shoulder and under my own hands," said Sir William. "I have heard them on a piece of paper held between the fingers by a piece of thread passed through one corner. . . ."

Margaret, who had been dragged all over America from her childhood days to exploit the famous rappings, enjoyed being a pampered pet in Victorian drawing rooms. She had a firm hold on the public imagination and some personal fame as the common-law wife of Dr. Elisha Kane, the distinguished explorer and scientist, whom she had met in Philadelphia when she was sixteen. He was then thirty-two and about to set out on his Arctic expedition in quest of Sir John Franklin and his party. Margaret's claims on Kane led to much litigation, but he died in 1857, and the story was forgotten when she appeared on the London scene, dining happily with men and women of note. One night it would be Hensleigh Wedgwood, grandson of Josiah Wedgwood, who had founded the famous pottery firm; another night it might be someone from the House of Lords. Statesmen, churchmen, scientists, writers, and men and women of many interests were groping for communication with the spirit world at this time, but there had been so much charlatanism that many of the mediums were on the run. Not the Fox sisters, however. They were solid in the public estimation. Kate had married H. D.

Jencken, a barrister of Dutch ancestry, and they lived on Brompton Terrace in the house where Sir William Crookes tested her so exhaustively.

Margaret renounced spiritualism on her return to the United States after her years abroad, and publicly proclaimed herself a fraud at a meeting held in the Academy of Music in New York in 1888. She disclosed that the famous rappings were done by snapping the joints of her toes, and she demonstrated her technique on the spot to an awed and incredulous crowd of believers. Kate was less convinced of the wisdom or necessity of Margaret's confession, but no amount of recantation blotted out the memory of this drastic revelation. In forty years the rappings had never been satisfactorily explained, although all manner of sages and scientists had tested the sisters from Buffalo.

Their halo still surrounded the Fox sisters among believers in spiritualism, however. Sir William did not give an inch of ground, but insisted that Kate was one of the truly inspired mediums. Eventually the sisters completed their own ruin by becoming hopeless alcoholics. Kate died penniless in New York in 1892, and Margaret followed her in another year. But in their expatriate years they had notoriety of the most lurid sort and were known around the world wherever psychic phenomena came under discussion. Their older sister, Mrs. A. Leah Fox Underhill, had exploited them in their early years, but had broken with them when they became flagrantly notorious.

The sisters had something in common with two of the most controversial expatriates of the nineteenth century—Victoria Claflin Woodhull and Tennessee Claflin. Vicky had several claims to fame, not the least being the fact that she had run for nomination to the presidency of the United States against Ulysses S. Grant. After a squalid childhood the two wild witches from Ohio became the lady brokers of Wall Street, backed by Cornelius Vanderbilt and other financiers of the day. Vicky was beautiful and eloquent; Tennie was a frivolous coquette. They were both committed to spiritualism, and Vanderbilt believed he made money on Tennie's tips from the stars. When Vicky announced that she would run for the presidency, she established *Woodhull & Claflin's Weekly* to back her cause. It soon became a muckraking sheet and brought Henry Ward Beecher into court to defend himself in a suit charging alienation of affection, brought by Theodore Tilton, one of his most prominent parishioners, who accused Beecher of having an affair with Mrs. Tilton. The jury found the charge untrue, but the bloom had been scraped from the reputation of the great Brooklyn divine. With Anthony Comstock, the guardian of public morals who had confiscated copies of the slanderous *Claflin's Weekly,* in pursuit, and their standing with the leading suffrage workers much impaired, the Claflin sisters sought exile in England. A new life began for them there. After their rickety career in America they both made good marriages, with wealth, family, and respectability to help them on their way, once they had dusted off their native soil.

Tennie married Sir Francis Cook, and Vicky made a third try at marriage with John Biddulph Martin, a banker and scholar who was impressed when he heard her lecture. Although they were not received in the inner social circles, they had a standing of their own and were shunned only by visiting Americans who knew too much about them. Tennie gave large garden parties outside London at Richmond, wearing gossamer gowns and wide-brimmed hats. When her husband died in 1901 she inherited his estate and a quarter of a million dollars. She founded a bank called Lady Cook & Company, with memories of her days on Wall Street, but it did not prosper. England was not yet ready for a lady banker. Next she turned her attention to establishing schools and supplying clothes and food for the needy. Since eugenics was then a fashionable topic, she advocated the legal recognition of illegitimate children and proposed opening a home for them, but the people of Richmond vetoed this. Tennie died in 1923 and Vicky survived until 1927.

Vicky was busy until her death playing Lady Bountiful. After her husband's death in 1897 in the Canary Islands she inherited a fortune of $850,000, gave up her London house, and lived at her country place, Bredon's Norton in Worcestershire. She fostered flower shows, the Froebel kindergarten system, and carol-singing by the village choir at Christmas. Nor did Mrs. Martin forget her American heritage. She contributed generously to the purchase of Sulgrave Manor, the home of George Washington's family in England. By that time she had given up lecturing on "The Scientific Propagation of the Human Race." In this area she was one step ahead of her generation on the population explosion, and twenty thousand people on one occasion waited in the street to hear the beautiful Mrs. Martin lecture. She brought a suit against the British Museum for harboring books and pamphlets relating to the Henry Ward Beecher case. Believing them to be derogatory to her reputation, Vicky and her husband took action against the trustees. There was much hilarity in the British press over the first libel suit ever brought against the British Museum. The verdict was for the defendants, with costs.

Always a little ahead of her time, Vicky was interested in aviation and offered five thousand dollars for the first man or woman to fly the Atlantic. She lived to learn that Charles Lindbergh had made it—just three weeks before her death on June 10, 1927.

Even better known than Victoria Woodhull was Mrs. Frank Leslie, who spent much of her time abroad in the latter part of the nineteenth century. For years after the death of her husband she ran a magazine empire, using his name as her own. She was known for her style, ambition, competence, and romantic interests. She had four husbands and was on the point of marrying a fifth, a Spaniard who had been gentleman-in-waiting to the King of Spain, when he died in Paris in 1907. One of her husbands was William G. Kingsbury Wilde, brother of Oscar Wilde. Most of her friends were men of fame or stature, and her salon was likened to Madame Roland's. Her linguistic skill and business enterprise were discussed on both sides of the Atlantic in the Elegant Eighties.

Her life from first to last was one of high drama, and at different times she lived in Peru and Spain, France and England. As a publisher and correspondent she crossed the Atlantic innumerable times and was usually found where historic events were taking place. She reported Queen Victoria's jubilee and was a conspicuous figure at the Paris Exposition while she was still Mrs. Ephraim Squier, wife of a well-known scientist, and was working for the Leslie publications. The Squiers and Frank Leslie, whom she would marry after divorcing Squier, were invited to all the state functions, and Mrs. Squier danced with Bismarck at the state ball given at the Tuileries in honor of the czar. Her readers in the United States had a detailed view of the Empress Eugénie wearing a twenty-thousand-dollar purple satin gown at the opening of the exposition. Her own gowns were newly ordered from Worth, and Leslie added a gift of emeralds. The full splendor of the era seemed to be concentrated in Paris at the time, with rulers and celebrities from all parts of the world in attendance. Like Kate Field, Mrs. Leslie made the most of it. At a Fourth of July gathering at the Grand Hotel she was toasted as "the most beautiful woman in Paris." She had a sixteen-inch waist, prominent blue eyes, and alabaster skin.

Mrs. Leslie became well known in London, Paris, Rome, Madrid, and the spas as she moved about with the sophisticates of the era, but always with an eye to business. She rounded up artists and writers and picked up news and comment wherever she went. She had more acclaim in London and Paris than she had in the United States. In this respect she somewhat resembled Victoria Woodhull. By the 1890s, having sold her publishing properties, she spent most of her time abroad. She liked San Sebastian and often visited the Queen of Spain. Before her death in 1914, at the age of seventy-eight, she had assumed her ancestral name, the Baroness de Bazus, a throwback to her Creole ancestry.

Meanwhile in Hastings, England, another expatriate of high ideals and serious purpose was lecturing and writing on eugenics, sex education, and subjects never referred to in the Leslie publications. Dr. Elizabeth Blackwell, the first woman doctor to graduate in America or anywhere in the English-speaking world, had come originally from Bristol, but her youth and early maturity had been spent in the United States. The last half of her life was an expatriate existence. Her small, dignified figure was a familiar one in medical circles, and she had many imposing friends in literary and reform circles. She was on good terms with Rossetti, George Eliot, George Henry Lewes, and Frances Power Cobbe, philanthropist and writer. She counted Florence Nightingale among her friends.

Dr. Blackwell, who had been turned down by twenty-nine medical schools in America before being accepted by Hobart College at Geneva, New York, held court for years at Rock House in Hastings, with visitors coming to see her from various parts of the world. Although never a militant worker for woman suffrage she was the sister-in-law of two of the most noted pioneers in this field—Lucy Stone and Antoinette Brown Blackwell, earliest ordained minister in the United States. The 1870s were preeminently the decade of reformers, with women fighting for the vote, for temperance, for sex education, for prison reform, for moral reform. Elizabeth cheered them all on, but with dignity and reserve. She was a quiet and thoughtful worker, with profound experience in the humanities behind her. On her return to Europe the old "doctorial sack" she had worn when she walked the wards of Guy's Hospital had been abandoned for soft velvets and lace fichus.

She tried to reform the muncipal government in Hastings and to have the local brothels closed. She joined the Moral Reform Union and went to France to speak in drawing rooms on vice and ignorance. She badgered members of Parliament, who were inclined to listen to Dr. Blackwell when they would not heed the other moral reformers. All the cumulative wisdom of her life and experience flowed into her lectures.

Her health was frail, and in the 1880s she and her adopted daughter, Kitty, wintered on the Riviera. They belonged to the great wave of sojourners who moved along the Mediterranean coast from Antibes to San Remo year after year. Dr. Blackwell settled in Menton, and then in Bordighera, traveling from point to point with steamer rugs and spirit lamps, with books, cushions, and picnic baskets. She tried the Tyrol and Switzerland. She wandered through Padua and

Verona with Shakespeare's plays in her satchel. When she was eighty-five, she revisited America, where her great creation—The New York Infirmary for Women—was flourishing under the direction of her sister Dr. Emily Blackwell.

Her sister Anna, another expatriate and correspondent for Horace Greeley, spent years in France. In 1856 Anna wrote to Elizabeth from Paris about the balls and receptions, and the illuminated opening of the theaters in honor of the birth of an imperial heir. She watched the emperor review 150,000 troops in the Champs de Mars, with Count Orlov of Russia riding beside him on a magnificent charger. Two years later Anna took Dr. Elizabeth to a reception at Compiègne, where she saw Eugénie in a cherry velvet dress covered with Alençon lace. Fontainebleau was overrun with Americans, Anna noticed, and they were all bowing and scraping and getting invited to the receptions. Most of them stayed at the Hotel Louvre, and they all went to the Théâtre Français to see the famed actress Rachel.

In 1870, during the siege of Paris, Anna nailed the Union Jack across her door when she left the city, and she found it intact on her return. She finally retired to Montivilliers in the Pas-de-Calais, where she sewed under the shelter of a hedge and watched the shepherds riding in their straw huts on wheels after their wandering flocks of sheep. In the end she and another sister, Marian, lived in Hastings, next door to Elizabeth, who had always been the lofty and selfless member of the family. In 1910 Elizabeth died at the age of eighty-nine and was buried at Holy Loch in Scotland. The *Times* of London ran two columns on her history. She was one of the most influential of America's women expatriates.

Perhaps because of her British birth, Dr. Blackwell had found it easy to adjust herself to life on either side of the Atlantic, but Emma Willard, touring Europe in 1830, remarked that "as an American and a woman" she could never be happy in English society. Mrs. Willard, who had founded the Troy Female Seminary in New York State and was particularly interested in the schools and colleges of Europe, was shocked by the low state of female education, even in Holland. Lafayette, who never failed to look after the interests of visiting Americans, made arrangements for her presentation at court and an invitation to a ball at the Palais Royal. Recalling her early life in a Connecticut village, Mrs. Willard wrote, "How could I then have believed that a time would come when I should enter the court of France alone, pass through long rooms, guarded by files of soldiers, officers, and royal attendants."

The reformers had much to learn during their years abroad. Britain was experiencing an industrial revolution in the midst of Victorian opulence. The slums were attracting comment and attention. Growing concern was shown for the housing, education, and health of the poor. Settlements were established, and Jane Addams found inspiration for Hull House in Chicago when she visited Toynbee Hall in London. Frances Willard toured the world promoting the temperance cause. Carry Nation made herself heard in Albert Hall. Dorothea Dix pursued in Europe the campaign she had started in the United States for reforms in prisons and asylums.

Clara Barton worked for the wounded during the Franco-Prussian War, repeating what she had done in the Civil War. In Alsace-Lorraine she saw the International Red Cross at work and made up her mind to start an American chapter, which she did, by founding the American Red Cross in 1882. Out of her years abroad had come a great humanitarian organization for her country. She soon became an international figure, traveling around the world to attend congresses or lead relief expeditions. In 1893 she was in Constantinople, directing four relief expeditions spread out through Turkey and Armenia. It was one of many large relief programs that she managed personally, at home and abroad. Later, during the Spanish-American War, *The State of Texas,* flying the flag of the Red Cross and laden with food for the starving at Santiago, led the naval parade into the vanquished city, with Clara Barton aboard. The American woman had found many ways of making her presence felt in the world at large.

Sargent and Whistler

The most discussed as well as the most enduring of the expatriate artists were John Singer Sargent and James Abbott McNeill Whistler, who created interest and stirred up talk on both sides of the Atlantic after the Civil War. Visiting Americans took a personal pride in these two dissimilar men, and sought them out to an exasperating degree as they went their separate ways. Whistler was thoroughly grounded in Europe, an immovable expatriate, but Sargent returned to the United States from time to time. The two artists— one so reserved and realistic, the other so foppish and affected— were on good terms, and Sargent defended his erratic countryman when the storms roared around Whistler. He would not permit anyone to speak ill of the terror of the art world.

Sargent was the most courteous, orderly, and in many ways the most successful of the expatriate artists, leading the field until his death in 1925. While Whistler's career was linked with Paris and London, Sargent found his most natural background in Italy. Although his parents were American, and most of his ancestors sprang from Gloucester, Massachusetts, he chanced to be born in Florence in 1856. As a small boy he went sketching with his mother in Rome. Before long he was copying the old masters in the galleries of Europe, and he studied briefly in Germany. At the age of eighteen he enrolled at the famous Parisian atelier of Carolus Duran on the Boulevard Montparnasse.

Sargent soon made his presence felt in this rigorous school. There was none of the skylarking that Gilbert Stuart had indulged in at Mr. West's gallery. He was reminiscent of a Van Dyck portrait himself, with his pointed beard and bright blue eyes. Tall and formal in his manner and attire, his subtle and witty spirit made him a good companion. Although intensely reserved, he circulated freely in social circles and got on well with his fellow artists of any nationality. When he settled in 1884 at 31 Tite Street in Chelsea, he was within close range of good friends and expatriate spirits. Whistler, Henry James, and Edwin A. Abbey, who did illustrations for *Harper's,* lived nearby, and the turbulent Carlyle home was always open to the American exile. Sargent often visited Abbey at Broadway in Worcestershire, and always found fellow Americans there. He could count on Henry James being present, as well as Mary Anderson, the American actress who had married Antonio de Navarro and settled in England. She eagerly sought out her countrymen when she could. Neither James nor Sargent suffered fools gladly, and the company usually ran to intellect and talent. The Americans found kindred souls among the British men of arts and letters. Edmund W. Gosse, English author, poet, and critic, often crossed swords with Sir George Henschel, the singer and composer. Frederick Barnard, who did black and white illustrations for Dickens' books, compared notes with Alfred W. Parsons, illustrator and landscape painter. Sargent was apt to play the piano tirelessly, working his way through a stiff recitative, or improvising when he was in the mood. These were the mellow 1880s, when the arts were flowering in the romantic vein, and Sargent liked to relax in the country and to punt from Oxford to Windsor.

As his fame grew, Sargent became part and parcel of the social life of the period, but he kept his American identity strongly alive. Between 1884 and 1916 he crossed the Atlantic at least a dozen times, as well as journeying in Italy, France, Spain, Norway, Switzerland, Morocco, Egypt, Palestine, Turkey, Greece, Corfu, and Austria. He visited the United States almost every year after 1895, finally establishing a studio in Boston and spending much time in Isabella Stewart Gardner's circle. In England he kept his American image brightly polished, appearing at all the official parties, introducing visiting Americans to those who could best help them in their aims, and taking considerable pains with aspiring painters and writers from the United States.

Sargent had entrée everywhere. He belonged to the exclusive Atheneum Club and was active in the New English Art Club. He was a member of the council of the Royal Academy, and he preferred the company of artists to that of peers. His portraits had elegance and style, and were in great demand; the French critics caught the robust quality behind the sheen and approved his work. But his portrait of Ellen Terry, done in 1889, was called the best-hated picture of the year, and Sir Henry Irving disliked it so much that he cut it to pieces. *Madame Gautreau,* now in the Metropolitan Museum, and considered one of his finest portraits, roused a storm of talk. For a time it was known as Madame X, and Madame Gautreau herself disliked it so much that she would have nothing to do with it. "I chronicle, I do not judge," Sargent remarked, when he was accused of bringing out the worst in his subjects.

Isabella Stewart Gardner, who became one of the great patrons of the arts, first showed interest in the expatriate painters when Henry James took her to call on Sargent so that she could see his portrait of Madame Gautreau. From then on they were close friends, and he painted an equally daring portrait of Mrs. Gardner on one of his trips to America. It dramatized her stunning figure but gave cruel emphasis to her homely face. He had tried seven times to catch a likeness of her before he succeeded, and she often tried to get him to say that it was better than the portrait he had done of Madame X. Sargent held his peace but did not agree. Isabella's black velvet dress was looped with her joined pearl necklaces. For background Sargent used an exotic print suggestive of a halo around her worldly head. Her husband was deeply shocked and refused to let it be shown, but today thousands pass by it each year at the Isabella Stewart Gardner Museum in Boston, and her low décolletage and well-defined figure no longer cause a ripple. Sargent was frequently Mrs. Gardner's guest at the Villa Barbaro in Venice, and he advised her on many of her art purchases. She usually arrived in Italy like a whirlwind and was immediately surrounded by waves of expatriate life—mostly young artists, writers, and musicians, eager for her patronage and captivated by her charm.

Sargent and Henry James were good friends, and although Sargent did not approve of the author's giving up his American citizenship, he was a man of tolerance. Since his own speech was that of an Englishman, and he had spent much of his life abroad, the question was sometimes raised whether or not he was truly American. Those who knew him well considered him American to his roots, and he was less critical of his native country and fellow Americans than Henry James. He was at his best painting beautiful women, and his most dismal failures were with Woodrow Wilson and Charles William Eliot, president of Harvard, an old friend to whom he wished to do justice. The artist's famous portrait of four Johns Hopkins doctors painted in London was the great success of the Royal Academy exhibition of 1906. The study he painted of Henry James shortly before the author's death in 1914 was destined to hang in the National Portrait Gallery in London. It seemed to be his fate to have critics attack his work, and a militant suffragette, looking for trouble, literally slashed James's portrait, but it was successfully restored.

Sargent died at his Tite Street house in 1925 at the age of seventy. He had been reading a book by Voltaire, and his spectacles were pushed up on his forehead—a quiet exit for one of America's most admired expatriates. But he had lived long enough to catch the tide of criticism that greeted a retrospective showing of his work in New York in 1924. Although the traditionalists stood by him firmly, his work was disparaged by the avant-garde critics.

Unlike Sargent, Whistler was cold to his fellow expatriates and showed little interest in their well-being. He deplored the raw Americanism of Joaquin Miller, known as the Bard of the Sierras, who swaggered around London with a ten-gallon hat, high-heeled boots, pistols, and long hair. To Londoners this was no more strange than the foppish Mr. Whistler himself, with his tilted hat, long narrow trousers, monocle, tall cane, and lavender gloves. Aubrey Beardsley had drawn him tellingly as a frilly fop, and the image stuck. He was thought to be more of a show-off than a serious artist. He dyed his hair black except for a white forelock, which on special occasions was tied with a ribbon. His signature was a scorpion-tailed butterfly.

There was never any question of Whistler's expatriate status, since his entire life from the age of twenty was spent abroad. His grandfather, John Whistler, arrived from Ireland with a British regiment just in time to share in Burgoyne's surrender at Saratoga. On his return home he eloped with Anna, the daughter of Sir Edward Bishop, an Englishman, and brought her back to America. Their grandson James was born in Lowell, Massachusetts, but he became a traveler early in life, for he spent more than five years of his boyhood with his family in Saint Petersburg. Ever afterward he had visions of the Chinese Room at Tsarskoe Selo, the palace of Catherine the Great. His interest in Oriental art, which was to affect the artistic trend of the late nineteenth century, had its start at that time.

He flunked out of West Point, after attending Pomfret School on his family's return to the United States. Next, he drew somewhat fancy topographical maps for the United States Coast and Geodetic

Survey in 1854 before deciding to head for Paris and a career in art. Whistler enrolled at the studio of Charles Gabriel Gleyre and was soon romping around Paris with American and British students. George du Maurier, destined to become a successful artist and novelist, was one of his fellow workers. His grandparents had fled from Paris during the Reign of Terror, and he was much at home in the French capital. Another of the roisterers was Edward John Poynter, later well known as a historical painter and director of the National Gallery in London. When they all attended artists' parties in the British colony, Whistler's model "Fumette" danced and recited from De Musset while he played the guitar and sang plantation songs.

All this carousing had repercussions when Du Maurier's *Trilby* was serialized in *Harper's Magazine* in 1894. One of his characters, Joe Sibley, was reminiscent of Whistler. The artist threatened the magazine with a libel suit unless Joe was dropped from the serialized version and from the book itself. The editors of *Harper's* apologized, and Joe vanished from the serial and the book. Du Maurier, by this time a highly successful illustrator, was blithe over Whistler's fury and explained that he was merely being nostalgic for the good old days in Paris. A million copies of the book were sold, and Trilby dolls, Trilby shoes, Trilby violets, and Trilby luncheons became the vogue. Without doubt Whistler's eccentricities and affectations had helped to give the Left Bank some of its bohemian fame and flavor.

Long before *Trilby* came out, Whistler had settled in London and was one of Chelsea's notable figures. His narrow house was on Lindsay Row, ten minutes' stroll from Cheyne Walk. His neighbors included Thomas Carlyle, with whom he passed a good deal of time, Dante Gabriel Rossetti, George Eliot, and Algernon Charles Swinburne. Rossetti was dependent on laudanum and chloral hydrate at this time, and auburn-haired Swinburne, with his glittering green eyes and errant ways, was rarely sober. Although warmly welcomed at first, Whistler's own personality discouraged his fellow artists. Sir John Millais took him up, but found him difficult and dropped him. Whistler cultivated Aubrey Beardsley for a time, but his own toughness of spirit did not lend itself to the extreme aestheticism of the Burne-Jones group. For all his irresponsibility Whistler usually found time to work and study. He spent hours copying the masters, painting his misty pictures, and turning out sharp-edged prose, for he was as eager to write as he was to draw. His speech, a blend of American and French, was not as anglicized as Sargent's. Henry James once observed, after dining with Whistler, that his wit was the crystallization of his bitterness and that the pearls he cast had been "cultured and polished by acid and gall."

Whistler was inclined to regard the interest shown in his affairs by James and Sargent as unwelcome patronage, and he was often rude to them. On one of Mrs. Gardner's visits to Paris, Sargent asked William Rothenstein, noted art authority and dealer, to show her around. He took her to Whistler's studio, and she immediately decided she wanted a seascape that hung on the wall. It was not finished, and the artist told her he could not let her have it. But when the irresistible Isabella set her heart on something, there was no denying her. She was looking at his famous *Harmony in Blue and Silver: Trouville.*

"Why don't you put it under your arm and carry it off?" Rothenstein whispered. When Mrs. Gardner told Whistler that she was going to take it off the wall and carry it away with her, he laughed and did not try to stop her. She told him he could finish it at her hotel, and he finally put his butterfly seal on it there, and let her have it, after some collusion with T. Jefferson Coolidge, the Boston art expert and diplomat who was minister to France from 1892 to 1893. In the end Mrs. Gardner, always keen for a bargain, paid three hundred dollars for this little gem.

Whistler's personality was as much discussed as his art, and he deserted his pastel-tinted background on Lindsay Row to dramatize the library of F. R. Leyland's mansion in Princes Gate, after he had pointed out to its owner that he could not bear the sight of the *Princess of the Land of Porcelain* in its heavy Spanish setting. Leyland engaged him to change the decor according to his own ideas. He lived on the premises and covered every inch of the room in blue and gold, using a peacock design. When Leyland, a wealthy shipowner who fancied himself as a patron of the arts, thought Whistler's price too steep, the artist worked a caricature of him into his design, in the guise of a peacock with his claws on a pile of guineas. The Peacock Room eventually became one of the treasures of the Freer Gallery of Art in Washington. At the time it was all in the spirit of the pre-Raphaelites, or of Cecil Beaton today, and Whistler never failed to play the role of poseur in an aesthetic setting. But he was in such serious financial difficulties when he moved from Lindsay Row to Princes Gate that he pawned his most famous picture, *Arrangement in Gray and Black* (better known as "Whistler's Mother"). It was bought ultimately for the Louvre, on the advice of Clemenceau, the French statesman, who had an American wife.

This study, which has become known the world around, was first exhibited in 1872. When it was shown in the United States, it stirred up great interest, and Whistler joined Sargent and Henry James as the third of a trio of brilliant expatriates constantly sought out by visiting Americans. He usually provided them with better gossip to take home than the stuffy James or the reserved Sargent. A puritan by nature, who ate and drank abstemiously, smoked little, and worked hard, Whistler nevertheless had a knack for making news, and he lent himself to caricature, an art that was highly developed among the exiles.

The American colony was deeply stirred when he brought a libel suit against John Ruskin in 1878. Ruskin, who disliked Whistler and his work, wrote of the artist's *Nocturne in Black and Gold* that he was "flinging a pot of paint in the public's face." Henry James, then writing for *The Nation,* attended the trial and watched Whistler fume. Ruskin did not appear, but Burne-Jones testified for him. William Michael Rossetti, brother of Dante Gabriel, was a witness for Whistler, whose painting of Henry Irving was exhibited in court to emphasize the strength of his work. Ruskin tried to prove that Whistler was an amateur and a charlatan. In the end Whistler won the case, with damages of one farthing, a coin that he wore thereafter on his watch chain. The art world was fascinated by the array of celebrities in court, and Whistler's image became fixed in the public mind.

To many the painter's work suggested that of the early Impressionists. Although the French as well as the English artists disliked him, Pissarro conceded his skill as an etcher, and Toulouse-Lautrec believed that he had made a contribution to the art of his day. Beyond that they ignored him. Whistler took up lithography in 1877, fourteen years after his first brush with fame when the Salon des Refusés hung *The White Girl,* which had been rejected by the Royal Academy in 1863. His model, a red-haired Irish beauty named Joanna Heffernan, who also managed his household, posed for Gustave Courbet as well as for Whistler when he took her with him to Paris.

In 1887 he married Beatrice Godwin, the widow of E. W. Godwin, editor and author, and soon afterward they settled in Paris, where Whistler became an outstanding member of the expatriate world. Both in London and Paris Beatrice smoothed the social path for her impulsive and irascible husband, until she died of cancer in 1897. Many honors came his way during the 1880s and 1890s, but he remained too bitter to allow his name to be presented at the Royal Academy, which had cold-shouldered him.

Young artists and writers flocked to 110 Rue du Bac on the Left

Bank, where Whistler's atelier was an eighteenth-century pavilion in a courtyard. A white and green door led into a sparsely furnished studio with Empire pieces, old silver, and a Japanese birdcage on a table. The garden behind the pavilion adjoined a convent, and the chanting of the nuns was a dim obbligato to Whistler as he worked. William Rothenstein, then studying at the Académie Julien, often called on him. He considered Whistler eccentric in his tastes, particularly as he watched him entertaining American friends in his garden on Sundays. With a palette in his hand the painter moved jauntily among them, wearing white duck trousers and white shirt, with a short black velveteen jacket.

This was the outfit he had worn while in Venice in 1879, etching and doing pastels for a government commission. His wide-brimmed brown hat, worn far back on his head, his long black tie loosely knotted under a low collar, Whistler seemed the epitome of the far-out artist to the young men of his generation. Americans, Russians, Poles, and Dutch hailed him at Florian's in Saint Mark's Square, or visited him at his freezing room in the Casa Jankovitz. It amused him to hire a barge and have it sail the length of the Grand Canal, with musicians playing *Yankee Doodle* and floodlights focused on a display of his pictures. Whistler was still smarting from the Ruskin trial, and he took care to avoid the paths traveled by Ruskin in *Stones of Venice*. He felt lonely, homesick, chilly, and alien in the city of canals. Italian food did not agree with him, and he haunted the American consulate and the English Club. But his two series of Venetian etchings added substantially to his fame. He had become expert in the graphic arts as well as in portraiture. His misty effects were characteristic of his paintings and reflected the years he had spent on the banks of the Thames in London.

Whistler was as cold to Rome as he was to Venice, and he sometimes shocked worshipers of the Italian mystique when he repeated his bon mot that on his one visit to the Eternal City he noticed a "bit of an old ruin alongside of a railway station where I saw Mrs. Potter Palmer." Apparently his impression of this art patron and collector from Chicago was stronger than his feeling for Rome. Mrs. Palmer was collecting work by the Impressionists at the time, and she had acquired her first Degas for five hundred dollars in 1889—*On the Stage*.

Degas happened to be one of the French artists who had a poor opinion of Whistler but a grudging respect for his work. Strolling over to him in a Parisian café one day, Degas remarked, "My dear Whistler, you have too much talent to behave the way you do." Whistler was much more understandable to his compatriots Joseph and Elizabeth Pennell, of Philadelphia, who were such admirers that they later became his official biographers. Pennell, a distinguished etcher in his own right, spent a great deal of time with Whistler. Logan Pearsall Smith, a Philadelphia writer who also chose to live abroad, watched Whistler as he worked on his painting of Comte Robert de Montesquiou-Fezensac. A more unlikely visitor from time to time was Richard A. Canfield, the gambling czar from Saratoga, who showed a lively interest in Whistler, and eventually bought Graham Robertson's collection of his work.

Two other Americans whose visits were of the utmost significance were the noted art collectors Henry C. Frick and Charles L. Freer. When Freer first walked into Whistler's studio in Paris in 1894, he was captivated by what he saw, and he visited the artist regularly after that on his trips abroad. Whistler's etchings interested him in the art of the Far East, and he became a collector, bringing the artist many treasures from the Orient. Whistler's paintings on silk and his fan designs encouraged a vogue for Oriental art objects that spread rapidly in the late nineteenth century. Freer became the major collector of his friend's work, and the Freer Gallery of Art in Washington is Whistler's most enduring memorial today in the United States. Frick's important backing helped him at a time when his work was going into eclipse.

In the closing years of his life, Whistler traveled restlessly, seeking warmth and sunshine, but he was alone in his studio in London when he was found dead on a July day in 1903, just as Freer was about to call for him and take him for a drive. He was buried in Chiswick churchyard, with two Americans, George Vanderbilt and Freer, serving as pallbearers, along with the British portrait painters Sir John Lavery and Sir James Guthrie. A simple monument to the painter's memory was installed at West Point, and the Whistler home in Lowell became a public shrine. In 1908 a project to erect in Chelsea a memorial, designed by Rodin, failed. He suggested that ten thousand dollars be raised by subscription, but there was little response. Sargent was opposed to the whole idea. He did not approve of this sort of thing for artists, and he felt that Whistler would have hated it, for he remembered that his gifted friend "never was funnier or more sarcastic than on the subject of the monument to Rossetti on Cheyne Walk."

Collectors and Patrons

All American expatriates, and particularly the artists, knew of Isabella Stewart Gardner, and many had benefited from her interest and support. She visited Europe so often and made such long stays in Venice that she acquired expatriate status herself. There were so many facets to her personality that she never ceased to make headlines on both sides of the Atlantic. In the words of Henry James, with whom she dined, walked, and drove in London and Paris in the early 1880s, her life was a "dense splendid tissue of adventure." There were few celebrities in contemporary art and letters whom she did not meet at one time or another, and she would back a struggling young artist—but only if he had talent. She had no taste for the amateur in any field, being a perfectionist by nature.

Her interest in art took root in the 1880s, when she attended classes given by Charles Eliot Norton, the medievalist who had returned from England to teach the history of art at Harvard. Norton had been one of the questers himself, meeting Darwin and Dickens, Ruskin and Rossetti, Burne-Jones and William Morris. The beautiful Julia Ward Howe and the homely Isabella Stewart Gardner exchanged notes at these meetings with Henry and William James, Henry Adams, Oliver Wendell Holmes, and F. Marion Crawford, Mrs. Howe's nephew. Also in the group was an auburn-haired young Lithuanian-born American with greenish eyes. This was Bernard Berenson, whose career as one of the world's leading art experts would be indissolubly linked with Mrs. Gardner's collection of Italian masterpieces.

Instinctively a patron of the arts, Mrs. Gardner backed Berenson from the day he left the United States in 1887, newly graduated from Harvard, until her death in 1924. Theirs became one of the famous associations of the art world, and Berenson bought forty-six important paintings for Mrs. Gardner between 1894 and 1914. He was one of the true expatriates, and he never returned to the United States except for rare visits of a month or two.

His success was meteoric, and from lunching off chestnuts and coffee in Paris and deploring the "horrible solitude" of the French capital, he soon moved up to a world of luxury and authority. Mrs. Gardner wrote him encouraging letters as he sent her his first impressions of Paris. He detested the *Mona Lisa* and never came to like this painting by Leonardo. He interpreted her inscrutable face as being "watchful, sly . . . with a pervading air of superiority." He thought that all of Leonardo's women were appalling; nor did he think better of his men. *The Last Supper,* to Berenson, had too many faces, all of them uncanny and too big.

Berenson felt more at home in London than he did in Paris, and he flourished at Oxford, taking courses but not a degree. At this time he turned his back coldly on the American scene, and Mrs. Gardner was aghast when he wrote to her that there was something "crude and vulgar and stupid about many if not most Harvard men." He turned against Thoreau, whom he had once enjoyed. Emerson, another of his early gods, seemed to him an amateur philosopher. Longfellow, Berenson wrote, was as much of an amateur in the world of poetry as Nathaniel Hawthorne was in the sphere of romance.

But by the time Berenson had toured all the big galleries of Europe and found his way to Italy, his sense of perspective developed. And when he began to buy for Mrs. Gardner, his reputation was soon made. She was an astute bidder herself, and two decades before Andrew Mellon came into the field, she was picking up bargains that are legendary today. With the lowering of a handkerchief held to her face, her customary sign to her agent that the bidding had gone far enough, she bought for six thousand dollars Jan Vermeer's *The Concert,* one of the gems of her collection. Mrs. Gardner was so intense about getting what she wanted that Berenson warned her she could not expect to own all the great paintings that came on the market. She lost the *Blue Boy* to Henry Huntington but landed Titian's *Rape of Europa,* a triumph, since Dr. Wilhelm von Bode of the Berlin Museum was determined to have it.

For years Mrs. Gardner spent half her time abroad, buying Italian masterpieces and rare furnishings for the Venetian palace she built in Boston on the Fenway after her husband's death. She bought in the fashion of J. P. Morgan, Henry E. Huntington, W. K. Vanderbilt, Henry C. Frick, Harry Payne Whitney, and Andrew Mellon, all of whom were assembling old masters for their American mansions, often on the advice of Sir Joseph Duveen, the world-famous art dealer. Mrs. Gardner had a wide personal range. She roamed through Italy, spotting columns and capitals, reliefs and frescoes, pilasters, arches, fountains, balconies, and mirrors. From a convent grille she bought in Florence to her staircase from Dorigo and the Fior di Persica columns, which visitors to her museum view today, Mrs. Gardner showed an instinct for the perfect note. "Her taste was infallible," said Ellery Sedgwick, a fellow Bostonian. "Of course she had the advantage of the wisest advisers of her time, Whistler, Sargent and Berenson among them, but to take the best advice is as rare as to give it, and in the making of every choice she was the guiding spirit."

Henry James heard all about her purchases, and so did F. Marion Crawford, the novelist, then a lonely expatriate wrestling with his own discontent at Santagnello di Sorrento, his home in Italy. Crawford and Mrs. Gardner had become friendly through Dr. Norton's course and they shared a lifelong interest in Dante. Often he sent her his manuscripts for a reading before giving them to his publishers. His writings were serialized, and he worked prodigiously. "I hope you are enjoying everything, as you always do," he wrote to her. "People envy you for many reasons, but you are most enviable for that marvellous power of getting grapes from thorns—and sugar plums out of paving stones."

The collector's early association with the poets, authors, and artists who took the Norton course led to some of her subsequent links with the expatriates, and her own extended stays abroad. Her reputation as a well-off patron of the arts brought many to her door. She met Brahms and Johann Strauss at Ischl and led the funeral procession for Liszt in Bayreuth, with his daughter, Frau Cosima Wagner. In Paris Massenet played his new opera *La Navarraise* for Mrs. Gardner. Sargent found her a constant source of inspiration and attached himself to her train of admirers. After visiting Daniel Curtis, a fellow Bostonian, at the Villa Barbaro in Venice, she decided that this would be her home abroad, and summer after summer she turned it into an American salon. When Berenson visited the villa in 1923 as the guest of Cole Porter, who had it that year, he wrote to Mrs. Gardner, who was then on the brink of death, "If I ever sigh for anything in the past it is for those days."

The Villa Barbaro became a focus of artistic life, where men of letters, musicians, and world-famous artists clustered around the vivacious Mrs. Gardner. She was a plain woman with infinite charm. Although noted for her superb figure, which Sargent defined so effectively on canvas, she had a blunt, combative face and a chilling, distant look. Her bluish-gray eyes were faintly blurred and rather stony. Her reddish hair matched her quick-tempered nature.

Each Fourth of July Mrs. Gardner rounded up the American residents for a Venetian serenade outside her palazzo. They floated along the canals, with music, lanterns, flowers, and moonlight. Among her guests was Anders L. Zorn, the Swedish artist whom she had met at the Columbian Exposition in 1893. She promoted his work, and he did many sketches of her that she did not like, until finally he saw her one night stepping in through French doors from the balcony of her palazzo. Her beautiful arms were outstretched, and her pose was so dramatic that he cried out, "Stay just as you are. That is the way I want to paint you."

She was all in yellow. Her famous rope of pearls, held by one large ruby, swung to her knees, and the Venetian night showed faintly in the background. The critics found this portrait one of Zorn's best when it was exhibited in Paris. "Your letters make me love life," he wrote to her. Isabella's zest was boundless. Wherever she went in Europe, she was recognized as the most indomitable patron of the arts—the American who defied convention, who drove through the streets of Boston with two pink-bowed lion cubs in her carriage, who attended prize fights and drank beer at baseball games, who imported Italian masterpieces and statuary, pillars, and entire rooms for what today is the Isabella Stewart Gardner Museum in Boston. Her parties always expressed her current taste: Oriental dress and food when a world tour gave her a keen interest in Oriental art; Spanish dress for her El Greco period; and on countless occasions Italian costume with simple Italian food served in the costliest dishes.

Berenson, who was her adviser from 1884 until 1906, when he tied his fortunes to Joseph Duveen, understood her well. He occasionally advised her even after that, but he shut her out of his personal life when he fell irrevocably in love with Mary Costelloe, wife of Frank Costelloe, a devout Catholic who could not divorce her. She was the daughter of Robert Pearsall Smith and Hannah Whittall Smith, Philadelphia Quakers who had inherited a fortune made in glass. Mary's brother, Logan Pearsall Smith, was a Fabian author and her sister Alys was Bertrand Russell's first wife. Mary, born in 1864, joined a little band of pioneers (Gertrude Stein was one of them) who attended lectures at Harvard. They called themselves the Harvard Annex, and from this nucleus Radcliffe College came into being.

In 1885 Mary noticed Berenson at a Harvard concert, and she was told that he was the most brilliant member of his class. She did not meet him again for three years, and by that time she was Mrs. Frank Costelloe and had two daughters. Her life as an expatriate had already begun. She had worked at Toynbee Hall, the famous London settlement house, and had come under the influence of the socialist writers Beatrice and Sidney Webb. Before long she deserted her husband and children and joined Berenson in Fiesole. He never mentioned this new liaison to Mrs. Gardner until he visited her at the Villa Barbaro in 1897. Two years later, soon after Frank Costelloe's death, Berenson and Mary were married by the Mayor of Florence at the Palazzo Vecchio, followed by a ceremony in a little chapel close to I Tatti, the Tuscan manor that was to be their eventual home.

At this time Berenson wrote to Mrs. Gardner: "For ten years Mrs. Costelloe and I have been constantly together, sharing every thought and almost every feeling. Marriage can bring our minds and our ways of feeling no nearer than they already are. . . . She understands me and my needs and my interests as no other person, and I am sure she will try to make me happy—I am too shy to say more."

In all of his voluminous writings Berenson never referred to Mrs. Gardner except as Boston's "first pre-cinema star" and "The Serpent of the Charles." But his correspondence throws ample light on their business transactions and their unique teamwork as collectors of great art. Mrs. Gardner saw to it that her dollars were not wasted. Berenson made sure that her instinctive sense of taste was fortified by his own professional acumen. Their partnership was much discussed in the art world, and there was also speculation on their personal relationship; Mrs. Gardner's love interests were so diversified that she was often a target for gossip.

Berenson's home, I Tatti, in course of time became the mecca of the art world. Experts, students of all the beaux arts, statesmen, and celebrities of various kinds visited him in his Florentine retreat. Mary maintained a brisk social life, but in spite of her origin she veered more to the British than the American expatriates. Berenson had a fondness for New Englanders, and he kept up with the social and topographical changes in Boston. He had a strong taste for the gossip of most of the capitals of the world, particularly for artistic tittle-tattle.

For centuries Italy had attracted enterprising travelers. In the early seventeenth century foreign scholars had studied astronomy and mathematics with Galileo, and medicine at Bologna. Archaeology, architecture, and all the fine arts brought Americans to Rome, Pompeii, Florence, Sicily, and Venice in the nineteenth century, and writers flourished around the Brownings, the Trollopes, Walter Savage Landor, Edward Bulwer-Lytton, and George Eliot. Books, art, music, sculpture, were constant topics of conversation among the resident Americans. But by the turn of the century this era was dead, and expatriate life was largely social until Berenson revived it at I Tatti.

He brought high scholarship to bear on the scene, as he ran something of a formal court, with fixed rules and little leeway for the bohemian spirit. Neither a telephone nor a cocktail party was permitted at I Tatti after 1920. He was cold to Norman Douglas, who had lived for years in Florence before settling in Capri, and whose book *South Wind* had made it an isle of escape from life's conventions. The cultists, the alcoholics, the expatriates who seemed to be going nowhere, found solace at Capri but cold comfort at I Tatti, which became the repository for forty thousand volumes in half a dozen languages bearing on art, literature, history, and travel. Berenson's books filled two halls and ten rooms. The villa's library of photographs, its pictures and bronzes, its gardens and farms, were viewed by thousands while he lived. His personal retinue included Geoffrey Scott, his private secretary for twelve years, and then Nicky Mariano, half-Baltic and half-Italian, who was secretary, assistant, and friend from 1917 until Berenson's death in 1959.

Berenson's collaboration with Joseph Duveen, which had begun in 1906, ended with a disagreement in 1936. In the intervening years, however, the two associates placed many of the great paintings of the Renaissance in American homes and galleries. Duveen paid Berenson twenty thousand pounds sterling a year and a 10 percent commission on every picture sold that he authenticated. The men broke over Giorgione's *Nativity,* now one of the treasures of the National Gallery in Washington. Andrew Mellon, who did not want another Titian at that time, was on the point of buying it from Duveen as a Giorgione when Berenson refused to authenticate it. He was sure then that it was the work of Titian in his youth, but before he died, he acknowledged that it might have been painted by Giorgione with the help of Titian in his early days. This dispute ended a friendship and business association that had made history in the art world. But their mutual dissatisfaction had been building up for some time.

The picture was later sold to Samuel H. Kress, one of the art collectors sent to I Tatti by Duveen. Solomon Guggenheim was another warmly welcomed patron, and when he arrived in the summer of 1926, Mary described him as a "little man with a kind smile and a gentle voice." She noticed the gorgeous pearls worn by his wife, and commented on his son's "terrific American accent." Guggenheim was just beginning to collect, and Berenson was of the opinion that he had fallen into the hands of some dubious dealers. Otto H. Kahn's wife, Addie, was a close friend, whose sparkling presence was always welcome at I Tatti. She was worldly, rich, and as conversant with the arts as her brilliant husband.

When Belle DaCosta Greene showed up in the spring of 1920, Berenson was on his mettle. As presiding genius of the Pierpont Morgan Library, she was known for her blunt speech and uncompromising views. Never one to mollify, she let him know with the utmost candor that she thought Duveen was exploiting him. But she proved to be vivacious and amusing as they traveled to Ravenna and then to Genoa, where she sailed for home. Miss Greene was to reappear on the scene, always with fresh and cutting judgments. The knowledgeable in the art world were fascinated by the interplay of these two strange personalities.

The customary day at I Tatti was broken up by hours of study, a siesta, walks on the grounds or drives into the hills, above Vincigliata, and sometimes into the Arno valley in late afternoon. Guests came in for tea, and they were likely to include Gladys Deacon, who would succeed Consuelo Vanderbilt as the Duchess of Marlborough; Vernon Lee (Violet Paget), empirical in her art judgments; Flora Priestley, whose mother was believed to be the original of Sargent's *Carmencita,* now in the Metropolitan Museum; and the Braggiottis, pictured in *The Constant Nymph* as *enfants terribles* but later well known on the American scene as musicians, writers, and social celebrities.

Elsie de Wolfe, the noted interior decorator and a fellow expatriate, upset the Berenson ménage by being highly critical of the decor at I Tatti. When she drove down from Paris in a big car, she reacted with some disdain to the villa's comfortable chairs, its credenzas and cassoni, its mixture of Oriental sculpture with Renaissance paintings. Miss de Wolfe briskly told them how the rooms should be arranged. She left an eighteenth-century mirror behind her as a gift. Miss Mariano suffered acutely through this visit and later wrote, "She seemed not made of human flesh and blood but of wire and metal and although I met her again and again in Paris and admired her enchanting house I never forgot this first impression of her."

Edith Wharton visited I Tatti at regular intervals, and although Berenson enjoyed her presence, she proved to be an upsetting guest with her many fads and prejudices. But her close friend Daisy Chanler, who was the half-sister of F. Marion Crawford, was an expatriate brought up in Rome with a perfect blend of the American and Italian civilizations. She was a frequent visitor in the 1920s and toured Palestine and Syria with Berenson in 1929.

Favored guests stayed for dinner at I Tatti, and they sat outdoors on summer nights at a long table under the cypresses, with electric lights swinging from the trees. At eleven camomile tea was served, and Berenson, an early riser, retired for the night. His guests, however, could stay at will, or go visiting in the hills, if they so desired. Four languages were spoken over the luncheon table, and scholars fared best at I Tatti. There was no lack of them, both men and women. Miss M. Carey Thomas, president of Bryn Mawr, was Mary Berenson's cousin, and in the summer months she often visited Florence. Miss Thomas was a formidable presence, unlike her gentle brother, a Baltimore physician, who sometimes came with his wife. They were the parents of Mrs. Millicent McIntosh, later headmistress of the Brearley School in New York and president of Barnard College. All three Thomases were Quakers and had known Mary from her earliest years.

Berenson's youngest sister, Rachel, was the wife of Ralph Perry, a philosophy professor who had been a pupil of William James and continually reminded Berenson of his days at Harvard. Both witty and pedantic, Perry gave flavor to many of the gatherings at the villa. Among the other professors, art specialists, and historians particularly welcome at I Tatti were Chester Aldrich, director of the American Academy in Rome, and his assistant John Walker, who later became director of the National Gallery. The great collection of art treasures at I Tatti was of professional interest to Frederick Mortimer Clapp, poet and art connoisseur, who became director of the Frick Collection in 1936; to Walter Cook, specialist in Spanish art, who founded and headed the Fine Arts Institute of New York University; and to Harold Edgell, director of the Boston Fine Arts Museum.

The range of company was wide. Thomas William Lamont, banker and an overseer of Harvard, brought John Masefield to visit. Samuel Barlow, the composer, and his gifted wife, Ernesta, often came to stay. When Ruth Draper, the monologuist, visited the villa, she gave performances in the library. James Thomas Flexner, fresh from the staff of the New York *Herald Tribune,* and busy in Florence assembling material for his books on art, was a frequent visitor in the 1920s—young, blithe, and red-haired. Walter Lippmann, who had met Berenson at the Versailles peace conference and also in New York in the early 1920s, stayed at I Tatti a number of times. Another journalist who stirred the waters at the villa in the early thirties was Dorothy Thompson, the blue-eyed and Junoesque correspondent who was briefly the wife of Sinclair Lewis. She had just come from Germany and was predicting the holocaust ahead. Through the Perrys Berenson met Timothy Spelman and his wife Leolyn from Cleveland, who lived on the Via San Leonardo. Spelman was a composer, and his wife symbolized the wealthy American woman to the conservatives of Florentine society. They lived with some magnificence and had one of the first private swimming pools in Florence carved into their garden. Berenson found their library uncommonly good.

Berenson saw little of George Santayana in their expatriate days in Italy, well though he had known the Spanish-born philosopher at Harvard, but all his visitors from Cambridge liked to gossip about Santayana at lunch in the eighteenth-century dining room of I Tatti, or over coffee and liqueurs in the lemon house that sheltered them from the wind. During more than a score of years at Harvard Santayana had lectured to such men as William James, T. S. Eliot, and Van Wyck Brooks. When he came into money in 1912, he decided to live abroad. Although born in Madrid, he was only nine when he was taken to the United States, so he had true expatriate status when he returned to Europe. But he did not consort with his fellow countrymen, and was thought of as being more Spanish than American. He drifted away from Berenson, who, in turn, observed that there was something of the philistine about Santayana— "above all about his catholicism . . . something without pity and without humanity. He was utterly intellectual."

Santayana grew bored by 1904 with the "soulful tourists and weary dilletanti" he came across in Florence, and he moved to Rome as "larger, nobler, more genuinely alive and most appealing to wide reflection." He returned there after World War I and spent the last thirty years of his life in the Eternal City, while his friend Berenson presided at I Tatti. Most of the time Santayana lived on the Piazza Barberini, within sight of Bernini's Fountain of the Triton. In Italy this philosopher found "nature and art most beautiful and mankind least distorted from their complete character."

Although the Spanish philosopher passed some of his time in France, he was at the Convent of Santo Stefano Rotondo in Rome for the last decade of his life, dying there in 1952. During his expatriate years he had written twenty-three books in English, including *The Life of Reason*. He stood aloof from the fierce political battles of the period.

As Mussolini rose to power, some of the American residents were pro-Fascist in their sympathies before they saw where things were heading, and the Spelmans had this reputation. However, they returned to America during World War II. When it was over they were soon back in Florence and were critical of Berenson for having remained in Italy throughout the occupation. Others shared this feeling, and at one point he was accused of having been an agent for both sides. After the attack on Pearl Harbor William Phillips, the American ambassador, arranged through Count Ciano, Mussolini's son-in-law, for the preservation of I Tatti as a repository of art. But in 1943, when Germany and Italy were losing ground, the count said that he could no longer control the situation in Florence.

At this point Berenson, who had been living quietly without any telephone communication, left I Tatti and went into hiding in the villa of the Marchese Filippe Serlupi, minister of the republic of San Marino to the Holy See. It was above Careggi, two miles from Florence. The yellow and white papal flag proclaimed diplomatic immunity. Mary Berenson was too ill to be moved, and she was sequestered on the third floor while the Germans occupied the first and second floors of I Tatti. Rumors spread that Berenson had fled to Portugal, but actually he was never far from his own villa. Influential Italian friends like Countess Marina Volpi helped to cover his whereabouts. All the more valuable pictures were stored at Fontanelle, the official name of the Serlupi villa. Others were kept at Quarto, the villa belonging to Baroness Kiki Ritter de Zahony, who was the mother of the Marchesa Gilberta Serlupi. The remainder were in Giannino Marchig's studio. The less valuable pictures were distributed artfully through I Tatti to give the impression that things were in order. The books that were not sent to the Fontanelle were walled up in their own quarters.

The Serlupi villa was a no-man's-land between the retreating Germans and the advancing Allied forces. There was machine-gun fire, and Berenson for a time did not know if I Tatti was still standing or if Mary was alive. Although Rome had been declared an open city, Florence was not. When the war ended, Berenson returned to I Tatti. His American passport was regained, and two hundred of his Renaissance pictures were back in place on the walls, having been skillfully restored in Florence after suffering the wear and tear of packing, transit, and—in some cases—less than optimum storage. But Mary, who had long been ill from a nervous breakdown, died in 1945.

Life became brisk again at I Tatti, as it had been in the 1920s. Busloads of American tourists arrived, often bearing letters of introduction. They toured the villa and gardens, were entertained at one meal, and had a chance to discuss their work and interests with Berenson. But the more favored guests moved deeper into the life of I Tatti and were well entertained by their host. Statesmen and the members of ruling houses now began to appear. President Truman paid his respects to Berenson in 1955. The King and Queen of Sweden, Prince Paul of Yugoslavia, and the former Queen Marie of Romania were among his guests. For the hot summer days Berenson would retreat to a little mountain house in Vallombrosa and live quietly amid the tall pines, on fruits and vegetables brought up from I Tatti. Nicky Mariano, vital and understanding, directed his complicated ménage and kept the secretarial strings in order. She reported that he felt equally at home with an American millionaire, a French countess, a German scholar, or a British explorer. He knew plenty of millionaires, and after his break with Duveen he used some of his expertise for J. Paul Getty and Georges Wildenstein, the art dealer, in Paris. He refused to countenance modern art and thought that Picasso hid his true gifts when he found that it paid "to deform and remodel the human face and figure."

Berenson finally decided to give I Tatti with all its art treasures to Harvard, but serious complications arose over its future upkeep, and the final agreement was not signed until 1955, with an endowment of a million dollars by its owner and other arrangements for its maintenance. It was difficult to raise additional funds after Berenson's death. He had foreseen some of the complications when he said, "One cannot project one's own personality beyond the grave as Isabella Gardner and others have tried to do. Everything changes, currents of taste, interests, methods of study. One must trust those who follow us to make the best possible decisions or at any rate the least bad ones."

Isabella, lacking Berenson's flexibility, had decreed that her own paintings should not be rehung or rearranged in any way, and that nothing should be disturbed in her museum. The image of her happy expatriate days in Venice remains strong and evocative in the Isabella Gardner Museum, as the image of Berenson does at I Tatti. Between them the two associates did much to familiarize the American public with the masters of the Renaissance.

Mrs. Gardner had little interest in modern art. In this respect she differed from another great hostess and art collector, Mrs. Potter Palmer of Chicago, who introduced the French Impressionists in the Middle West and was an early Degas patron. With her husband she drove out to Barbizon to watch the masters at work. She climbed to the attics of Montmartre and chatted with Clemenceau, Edmond de Goncourt, and the Comte de Montesquieu at Raffaelli's studio. She was in and out of Raoul Heilbronner's in Paris, running into such fellow purchasers as John Wanamaker, Baron Henri de Rothschild, Clarence H. Mackay, Pierre Lebaudy, and Stanford White, who before long would be murdered by another art collector, Harry K. Thaw.

Early in the twentieth century women of wealth and fashion, like their husbands and fathers, showed an unprecedented interest in the acquisition of art treasures, and Mrs. Palmer helped to arouse interest in the Impressionists and the Barbizon School. Mrs. Charles Phelps Taft of Cincinnati, sister-in-law of William Howard Taft, had invested in a Rousseau, a Corot, a Troyon, and Jean François Millet's *La Maternité,* as well as in a Reynolds, a Gainsborough, and others of the traditional school. Mrs. Taft, a vivacious and immensely wealthy Ohioan, bought emeralds at Cartier's and gowns at Doucet's in Paris, and she and her husband turned up regularly in London at Sotheby's and Christie's, where they exchanged notes with Cincinnatians permanently based abroad. The Californians were much in evidence, too, at a time when William Randolph Hearst was amassing treasures for his castle at San Simeon, California, and Mrs. Leland Stanford was a collector of note. In 1907 it was estimated that $228 million was spent by 300,000 tourists from the United States, and art dealers reported a great surge of buying. "It has become the mode to have taste," commented James Jackson Jarves, a collector in his own right. "Private galleries in New York are becoming almost as common as private stables."

Two collectors who were expertly guided to the best in Impressionist art, as well as to many of the old masters, were Mr. and Mrs. Henry O. Havemeyer, whose fortune was made in sugar. Mary Cassatt, the Philadelphia artist who lived most of her life abroad, was their guide and adviser as they amassed one of the truly notable American collections of modern and classical art. Mrs. Havemeyer was only sixteen and spending a summer abroad when Miss Cassatt took her to look at Degas's pastel *Répétition de Ballet* and urged her to buy it. The technique was new and strange to her, and she thought it had the firm effect of a primitive, with planes and perspective handled in masterly fashion. Degas struck her as a man of the world, compact, dignified, and with fine eyes. There was nothing of the "artistic negligé" about him, Mrs. Havemeyer observed. Like Whistler, he was always reluctant to part with his pastels, but the Havemeyers wound up with more than fifty of his paintings and thirty Courbets, including *La Belle Irlandaise,* the portrait of Joanna Heffernan, a red-haired model who posed for both Courbet and Whistler. A Degas pastel they bought for $100 in 1873 was sold in 1965 for $410,000. They visited Whistler in London and bought the original set of his Venetian etchings, which they later gave to the Freer Gallery in Washington.

In 1901 the Havemeyers started touring Europe systematically with the knowledgeable Miss Cassatt, who seemed to them to have the "flair of an old hunter, and her expert aid made her as patient as Job and as wise as Solomon in art matters." They traveled together through Italy, Sicily, Spain, and France, collecting Goyas and Grecos in Spain, and their Lippi, their Del Sarto, their Raphaels, and others in Italy. They soon had eight Rembrandts hanging in their library in New York. The inspired lectures given them in the Uffizi Gallery and elsewhere bore fruit. Mary Cassatt, never a flatterer, although she was Havemeyer's instructor, remarked, "He learned with leaps and bounds; there will never be another collector like him."

The Rockefellers, the Havemeyers, and Frick all were members then of great trusts that were later broken up. They concentrated heavily on art, but it took experts like Berenson, Duveen, and Mary Cassatt to detect the false. James Jackson Jarves, an American known for years around Florence as an expert in Italian and Japanese art, came under fire at a time when all manner of pictures were being regilded, varnished, and shipped off to America as genuine Correggios and Titians. For years he collected early Tuscan and Umbrian pictures, following the trail to monasteries, churches, palaces, and old family collections. Passersby could see his finds strung up in various stages of disrepair opposite his house as he did retouching. It was not until Berenson's judgment was applied to his finds that their value was recognized. In the end the Jarves collection went to the Yale Art School, and he gave his Venetian glass to the Metropolitan Museum.

Although one of the most brilliant and individualistic of the American artists abroad, Mary Cassatt showed little love for her fellow exiles. Even the suave Sargent annoyed this spirited Philadelphian who settled in France in the early 1870s and returned only briefly to the United States in 1898 and 1908. She had little regard for Henry James and detested Edith Wharton, whose roots were somewhat similar to her own. Miss Cassatt thought that Mrs.

Wharton had no literary distinction and that her husband was a parvenu. Mary was unyielding to her fellow artists, and had snubbed Cecilia Beaux on the steps of the Pennsylvania Academy of Fine Arts. Cecilia, a fellow Philadelphian with a considerable reputation in her own right, painted women and children, a field in which Mary Cassatt excelled.

The salon of Gertrude and Leo Stein in Paris disgusted Miss Cassatt, and she refused to go to their receptions, feeling that she was "too old a bird to be caught by chaff." No sound artist, in her opinion, "ever looked except with concern at those cubists and Matisse." She was, however, the friend and promoter of the Impressionists, and worked with unlimited enthusiasm for Cézanne, Sisley, Pissarro, Monet, Manet, and others. Gauguin thought Mary Cassatt had more talent as well as more charm than Berthe Morisot, the great-granddaughter of Fragonard and the leading Frenchwoman of the Impressionist school. These two women were on friendly terms, and each admired the work of the other.

Miss Cassatt's long association with Degas was a matter of great interest to members of the American colony in Paris, and to the art world in general. They quarreled over the Dreyfus case, for Mary was a fierce defender of Dreyfus. Long before his death, they had gone their separate ways, but this was one of the significant friendships of the art world. Mary first became conscious of his work in 1873, when she saw some of his pastels in an art dealer's window on the Boulevard Haussmann. Years later she wrote to Mrs. Havemeyer, "I used to go and flatten my nose against that window and absorb all I could of his art. It changed my life. I saw art then as I wanted to see it."

Some time later she met Degas, and he urged her to show her work with the Impressionists, who were his friends, rather than at the Academy. He was reluctant to admit that a woman could draw as well as Mary Cassatt did, but he was steadfastly committed to her work, as they quarreled and made up, and enlivened the troubled world of the Impressionists. She considered him the last great artist of the nineteenth century, and she pushed his work for the American market. It worried her as he grew older and wandered half blind along the boulevards that his paintings and little-known sculpture should gather dust in his disordered studio. When Whistler visited Degas in his studio, twirling a tall cane and swinging his monocle, Miss Cassatt remarked bluntly that Whistler was an idiot. But when she was in London in 1883, she visited his studio and admired the painting he had done of Lois Cassatt.

None of the nineteenth-century expatriates, except Whistler, stayed as consistently in Europe as Mary Cassatt, yet in her last years she deplored young Americans going to Europe for their art education. In her youth it was essential, she said, since so little was offered in the United States in the way of sophisticated instruction, but she told Forbes Watson, of the Whitney Museum of American Art, she had come to believe that "expatriatism was not only unnecessary for the American student of a later period but was actually detrimental because of the uprooting involved."

The French critics were often sharp with her work, and Miss Cassatt felt that they resented her because she was an alien, deeply committed to American ideals. But André Mellerio, the art historian, wrote of her, "She is wholly original and belongs to her own race. Her art expresses her nation, young, full of new force; she is without prejudice, vital; although she is familiar with the culture of the old world, there is the freshness of a new nation in her art. She expresses the character of the American people, a people awakening to all that is best in art and eager to possess it in abundance."

Miss Cassatt's milieu was far removed from the life of the Left Bank. She was seven when she first saw Paris, and the Second Empire was in process of formation. Her father, Robert Simpson Cassatt, a stockbroker of solid family, was horrified when his young daughter said she wished to go abroad to study art. "I would almost rather see you dead," he told her. But he compromised by letting her study at the Pennsylvania Academy of Fine Arts. She learned nothing and decided that she must go to France. Without any regret she turned her back on the tennis and boating parties, horseback riding, theater, and opera, and hungrily absorbed artistic inspiration in Paris.

After a brief interlude at home during the Franco-Prussian War she sailed for Italy in 1872 and at Parma studied Correggio's style. She visited the galleries of Spain and Holland and by 1873 was back in Paris. Soon after that her association with Degas began. She haunted the Louvre, a slim, dark-haired girl with a piquant face, ruffled muslins, and delicate parasols. Her parents and her sister, Lydia, joined her in Paris in 1877. Mrs. Cassatt was inclined to be scornful of the American colony and wrote to her son, Alexander J. Cassatt, later president of the Pennsylvania Railroad, that she made "no acquaintances among the Americans who form the colony, for as a rule they are people one wouldn't want to know at home." Among them was Mrs. John W. Mackay, a great individualist and the grandmother of Mrs. Irving Berlin. This dowager had found social success in London and Paris as an expatriate, having failed to win it in America because of her beginnings in the kitchens of the Comstock Lode mines.

The Cassatts lived with considerable style on the Rue de Marignan in the 1870s and 1880s, and after 1893 in the Château de Beaufresne, a seventeenth-century manor in the Oise valley, or at Mary's villa in Grasse. By that time she was seeing less of Degas. Mary was at her best in the country, where she cherished her horses and dogs, and raised Belgian griffons. Her gardens were singularly beautiful, and she stocked a pond with trout. Her guests dined on the fish they caught, and she liked to sit at the water's edge, watching the trout flip about while she painted friends and relatives seated in boats. The Cassatts were an abundant family, and friends and relatives were always showing up. Although Mary was a vegetarian and ate quite simply herself, she served the finest food in the French manner, and with well-chosen wines. She would not smoke, nor allow anyone in her presence to light up a cigarette. When she went to Paris she dined at the best restaurants and bought her own clothes and costumes for her models from Doucet, Redfern, and Paquin, the leading couturiers of the period. She liked the large plumed hats made for her by Reboux and went in for antique jewelry, with her lorgnette always dangling on a long amethyst chain.

Except that she was a constant worker and interested herself in the local French elections, Miss Cassatt lived the life of the typical affluent American expatriate in Paris in the late nineteenth and early twentieth centuries. She kept a vigilant eye on American politics and, as a main-line Republican, thought ill of Woodrow Wilson. Clemenceau, who had married an American, often visited her, and they discussed politics at length. She frequently reminded her French friends, "I am an American—definitely and frankly an American." She firmly believed that her expatriate status and the fact that she was a woman kept her from getting full recognition as an artist.

Although it embittered her that Philadelphia did not give her her due, she was partly responsible for the chill surrounding her work in her native city. She scorned juries, medals, and awards, since she belonged to the original Independents, the Impressionists who had broken away from the French Academy. Proud and stubborn, she refused the Lippincott Prize at the Pennsylvania Academy and the Harris Prize at Chicago. She felt that Corot, Courbet, and Manet all had been victims of the jury system, and she would have none of it. Some deplored her bitter tongue, but the portraitist Paul Helleu, a close friend of Sargent's, the writer George Moore, the poet Mallarmé, and Berthe Morisot were her faithful admirers, as were the artists she had helped.

Other Americans besides Mrs. Havemeyer consulted her about the pictures they bought. When Degas quarreled with the other Independents and refused to exhibit at their seventh show in 1882, Mary Cassatt followed his lead. When Mrs. Havemeyer asked her how she got along with the difficult Degas, Mary replied, "Oh, I am independent. I can live alone and I love to work," summing up their strange association, which was woven into the fabric of the artist life of Paris.

Just as Degas faded out of Miss Cassatt's life in her later years, so did Mrs. Havemeyer. Their long and fruitful friendship came to an end when her patron questioned the authenticity of some prints designed for the Metropolitan. She thought that Mary, then becoming blind from cataracts, might have failed to notice that they were proofs from worn-out plates. Mary could not forgive this lack of trust, and she died in 1928 without relenting. But Mrs. Havemeyer had rambler roses spread over the grave of proud Mary Cassatt. She had figured in so many of the Impressionist purchases that the artists had come to regard Miss Cassatt and Mrs. Havemeyer as heaven-sent. After the crash of 1882 in France Mary bought many of their pictures herself. She lent money to impoverished artists and even to Durand-Ruel, the dealer who fostered their work, thus spreading their fame in the United States. Her brother, Alexander, became a collector of the work of Pissarro and Monet as early as 1881. She advised James Stillman, president of the National City Bank, on his purchases, and Mrs. Potter Palmer listened to her advice as carefully as Mrs. Havemeyer.

Mrs. Palmer's first purchase of modern art was Degas's ballet study *On the Stage,* a possession that she cherished and hung in her bedroom. While Miss Cassatt's name was still little known in America, Mrs. Palmer commissioned her to do a giant mural for the Women's Building at the Columbian Exposition in Chicago in 1893. Some of the lady managers of the fair, who had expected Mary's representation of *Modern Woman* to be shocking, found it merely flat. But visitors at her château had followed with interest her progress in the glass-roofed building she had had erected on her estate to enclose the huge scaffolding she needed for the mural. The canvas was lowered into an excavation in the ground as she painted the upper stretches.

In 1908 Durand-Ruel held an exhibition of Mary Cassatt's own work in Paris, but she was never told that he had given her *Mother and Child* for exhibition at the epoch-making Armory Show in New York in 1911. She would have hated this association, because of her distaste for the cubists and Dadaists. By the time World War I broke out, her work was being shown in London and Manchester, Paris, Rome, Berlin, Munich, and across the United States. In the first week of the Somme offensive George Biddle, a fellow Philadelphian, arrived at her château on a bicycle, along with Abram Poole. They lunched to the booming of artillery, and Miss Cassatt calmly served her guests Philadelphia White Mountain cake and old Burgundy.

Biddle, who was both an artist and critic, said that she had influenced his work more than any other artist he had ever known. Vernon Lee, the pseudonym of Violet Paget, English essayist and art critic and a friend of Sargent's, was rather patronizing when Miss Cassatt asked her to write a preface to a series of her pastels. She described Mary as being very nice, simple, and almost childishly garrulous "in the fashion of the American provincial." Apparently Miss Cassatt wished to make art inexpensive and to bring it within reach of the comparatively poor!

But few others who knew Miss Cassatt thought her either simple or provincial, and in the end she was ranked with Courbet, Pissarro, Manet, Cézanne, Monet, Degas, Renoir, and Daumier. Her aquatint and drypoint prints attracted much attention in the 1890s and were part of the growing interest in Oriental art. During the Civil War John La Farge and John Bancroft had imported Japanese prints, and in 1886 La Farge went to Japan with Henry Adams to pursue his studies in this field. Both Miss Cassatt and Degas had responded enthusiastically to the exhibition of Japanese art held in 1890 at the École Nationale des Beaux-Arts. Mary was also influenced by Indian and Persian art, and many Persian miniatures hung on her walls. She worked in graphics from 1879 until her sight began to fail her in 1911. But she was best known for her mother and child studies, which she started doing in 1890.

When she died in the summer of 1926, all the villagers close to her castle walked in the funeral procession. In spite of her long residence abroad, she was staunchly American to the end, and her will read, "I, Mary Stevenson Cassatt, having my legal domicile in the city of Philadelphia, state of Pennsylvania, United States of America . . . ."

Miss Cassatt was an expatriate of stature, accomplishment, and style, and none but Whistler lived so consistently in Europe. Cecilia Beaux, who was of Puritan stock, spent her childhood in New York and at a country place on the New Jersey Palisades, but her ancestors had come from Avignon, and her mother knew more French than most of the women of Philadelphia, where the Beaux family finally settled. Like Mary Cassatt she attended the Pennsylvania Academy of Fine Arts, and when a friend took one of her pictures to Paris, it was hung in the Salon. Inevitably Cecilia followed this lead and was soon in Paris studying at the Académie Julien. She found a mixed assemblage of students there; many were from the Slade School in London. Julien, an ex-prizefighter, haunted the cafés and boulevards and visited the artists in their studios. An aunt tried to lure Cecilia over to the studio of Carolus Duran but she stayed with Julien, and gradually became accustomed to the life class, prudish though her upbringing had been.

The Salon was always a gathering ground for the expatriates. The *Vernissage* brought out all the celebrities in the various arts, as well as the French aristocrats and resident Americans. Miss Beaux marveled a little when Sarah Bernhardt walked in one day with the entire upper part of her bodice made of fresh violets. She watched Puvis de Chavannes in his black silk cap, and Renoir, Raffaelli, and Jean Paul Laurens sauntering around. As a newcomer to the French capital she was invited to have tea with an enduring expatriate, Mrs. Anna Green, who made a point of feting young American students. She tactfully drew Cecilia's life story from her as she presided in creamy satin and old lace in a Louis Quinze boudoir. By the next winter Miss Beaux had her own studio in the Rue Notre Dame des Champs, and she was soon visiting Italy and England, where she stayed with an old school friend who was married to George Darwin, the oldest of Charles Darwin's sons. They wandered together through Cambridge and studied the Gothic towers, gateways, and bridges over the Cam.

Many other young Americans also traveled across Europe in search of the culture they felt was denied them at home. But of the many hundreds who followed the expatriate pattern only a few emerged as artists of stature, and Mary Cassatt and Cecilia Beaux led the field among the women. Most of the students enjoyed their freezing attics and sparse fare, their view over the rooftops of Paris, their croissant breakfasts, and the camaraderie of the studios and cafés. Hard though they worked in Paris, they were often footloose and wandered at will until Rome and Florence took the place of Paris and London as the firm centers of the art world. Cecilia found delight in Avignon, the home of her ancestors. She was welcomed in London by Mrs. Robert Chapin, a New Yorker living in Queen's House, where Rossetti had lived and died, and the pre-Raphaelites had gathered. The Richard Watson Gilders, who had introduced her to Mark Twain, Saint-Gaudens, Paderewski, and other celebrities at their Friday evening salons on East Eighth Street in New

York, were now in London, and since they knew everyone in the world of art and belles lettres, they saw to it that Cecilia met the people she needed to know. She was soon lunching with Sargent at his club. Expecting to find him a slouchy figure in velveteen, she was amazed at his conventional attire and manner. But he struck her as being shy, and he stammered as he showed her the bas-reliefs he was doing in his studio on Tite Street for the Boston Library. "I saw that his worldly appearance, manner, and speech were a sort of armor for his sensitiveness," Miss Beaux commented.

Sargent's style had an effect on her during the time she was developing into a well-known portrait painter. Even if Mary Cassatt did not appreciate her work, others did, and Cecilia was considered particularly successful with her studies of mother and child. Mrs. Theodore Roosevelt and her daughter Ethel posed for her in the Red Room of the White House, with the President stirring up commotion around them. During World War I she was commissioned to do portraits of outstanding heroes for the United States government and settled again in Europe to fulfill this task. Cardinal Mercier of Belgium, Clemenceau, and Admiral Lord David Beatty were among her subjects, and Henry White and Brand Whitlock, American ambassadors in Europe, paved the way for her. She painted Cardinal Mercier at Malines in the Salle des Éveques, while the cardinal told her what Marshal Foch and he had said to each other in the days of heavy bombing. Cecilia felt at times that she would rather have recorded his words than have painted the cardinal.

Rosamond Gilder accompanied her when she went to paint the fierce old tiger Clemenceau. When the time came to do Lord Beatty Miss Beaux was conscious of the American influence in his surroundings, as she studied the furniture and antiques in his drawing room. His wife was Ethel Field, daughter of Marshall Field of Chicago. After divorcing Arthur M. Tree, Ethel had moved to England and married David Beatty. She was one of a group of fashionable American expatriates from Chicago. The three beautiful daughters of Levi Leiter had British husbands: Mary married Lord Curzon in 1895, Daisy married the Earl of Suffolk, and Nancy became the wife of Major Colin Campbell.

Cecilia Beaux's later years were passed at Green Alley in Gloucester, Massachusetts, but she was one of the expatriate artists who had flourished in Europe. Encounters she had with Sargent at the Chilton Club in Boston and at Fenway Court in later years were reminiscent of her life abroad. The expatriates were always surprised to meet one another on home ground.

The International Set

The fashionable American expatriates who married abroad became numerous before the turn of the twentieth century, but the most dazzling of all appeared on the scene as early as 1874, when Jennie Jerome married Lord Randolph Churchill, son of the Duke of Marlborough. By the end of that year she had borne a child destined for fame—Winston S. Churchill. In her own way she was as remarkable as her gifted son—dynamic, eloquent, ambitious, and witty. She traveled from Brooklyn to the inner councils of the Victorian court with extraordinary speed and grace.

In his mature years Britain's great hero recalled his mother as "exciting, furiously outspoken, and always conscious of her power." Sir Shane Leslie, the Irish poet and critic, who was her nephew, observed that she was a woman of tremendous power who never lost heart. He thought that she had a touch of Cleopatra in her, and he wrote of the fabulous Jennie, "I don't think any wife could have played a greater part than Jennie did." A prime minister's wife said of her, "She could have governed the world."

Jennie married for love. Hers was not one of the Anglo-American matches founded on an exchange of wealth and title. Queen Victoria was less enthusiastic about these alliances than her son the Prince of Wales, who became King Edward VII, but she warmed to Lady

Churchill. The prince thought American women clever, charming, and witty. None was so widely accepted in all sets as Lady Churchill, not only a beauty and a noted *amoureuse* but also a political genius. She was perceptive enough to view the international marriages as an unpopular development on both sides of the Atlantic. Democratic Americans did not feel like applauding some of these loveless exchanges, and the British aristocrats thought them as "experimental as mating with Martians."

The game was played for high stakes and with great magnificence. The daughters of America's newly minted millionaires attended court functions all over Europe, from London to Saint Petersburg. They went in for sports, great fetes, and entertainments of all kinds. They wintered in Egypt and at a given season went to their favorite spas. They shopped in London, Paris, Vienna, and Rome. They were a restless breed, but could not move with the speed of the jet set of the 1960s. Yet in many respects they set the pattern for international society as it is known today. The great ocean liners brought them home occasionally for such special family events as weddings, baptisms, or funerals. But once caught in the Continental social orbit, they were apt to stay permanently abroad. By 1909 a cynic estimated that the international marriages of about five hundred American women had involved the transfer of $200 million from the United States to Europe.

Jennie, independent and always strongly native in her basic instincts, resented the recurrent salutation from other peeresses, "I should never have thought you were an American." She observed that no distinction was ever drawn between one type of American and another. "They were all supposed to be of one uniform type," she wrote. "The wife and daughters of the newly-enriched California mines, swathed in silks and satins, and blazing with diamonds on the smallest provocation; the cultured, refined and retiring Bostonians; the aristocratic Virginians . . . all were grouped in the same category, all tarred with the same brush. . . ."

But Lady Churchill soon emerged in a category of her own, audacious about court procedure, flouting the conventions, but keeping the outer image intact, charming such men as Lord Curzon, Lord Rosebery, Disraeli, Charles Parnell, Bismarck, and the Prince of Wales. Statesmen, writers, scientists, and musicians crowded Jennie's salon, and she stayed on friendly terms with most of the peeresses, too. They realized in time that her décolletages—the most daring in London's smart drawing rooms—and her high kick in the can-can she danced in Dublin were an instinctive part of her spontaneous nature. She was, before all else, a glittering figure among them, and her love affairs were conducted with discretion. The most potent statesmen of the era were deeply conscious of her power.

Jennie's inheritance was a vigorous one, and she was reared in luxury. She was the most scintillant of the three Jerome sisters—the others being Clarita and Leonie—who spent their early years in Brooklyn Heights. Their father, Leonard Jerome, was noted for his love of racing, gambling, and high living. He sponsored young singers and theatrical beauties, and Jennie was named after Jennie Lind, the Swedish nightingale. His wife, Clara, considered by many a snob, was a brooding, handsome woman, with flashing dark eyes and black hair. Her looks suggested the dash of Indian blood that she was supposed to have. Jerome became a millionaire by selling short during the panic of 1857, and he promptly rented a summer home in Newport, invested in a yacht, and swept his handsome family into the social stream. He was variously known as the "Father of the American Turf" and the "King of Wall Street."

When the Jeromes went to Paris and settled in a house on the Champs Élysées, Jennie was presented at the court of Napoleon III and the Empress Eugénie. The ball she attended at the Tuileries set the pattern for many that were to follow in her life. Her personality made itself felt even in her early teens. She had great dark eyes and a dazzling smile. She was never at a loss for a witty observation, and she studied constantly to improve herself. By the age of sixteen she was being wooed by Lord Randolph Churchill, whom she had met on a yachting party attended by the Prince of Wales. "An American connection is not one that we would like," the Duke of Marlborough protested as the romance developed. The Jeromes were equally cold to the match at first, thinking Churchill unworthy of their brilliant Jennie. But the young pair were married at the British Embassy in Paris on April 15, 1874, and Jennie soon forgot all about Mrs. Astor's Four Hundred and the fact that her parents had entered this charmed circle. On November 30 of the same year Winston Churchill was born in a plain brass bedstead in Blenheim Palace.

Through his growing years, he suffered considerably from the austere and sometimes neglectful attitude of his parents. His father would have nothing to do with him, but Winston adored his beautiful mother, and if he did not see her often, she kept a close check on his work, sent him suitable books to read, and worried considerably over her "naughty, sandy-haired little bulldog" of a son. The little bulldog was irresistible, however, when he wrote her beguiling letters, slightly sonorous in tone, and suggestive of the great rhetoric of the future. His masters were always at fault. Why didn't they ask him things that he *knew?* It was humiliating to his brilliant mother to have the headmaster of Harrow tell her that his "irregularity was so regular" that they did not know what to do with him. He was slovenly, careless, unpunctual, forgetful, and an all-round problem. He could stare at an exam paper for two hours, writing his name, smudging the page with blots, and failing to answer a single question. Knowing that he was not lacking either in brains or grace, Lady Churchill wrote to him severely, "Your work is an insult to your intelligence." But she remained a lovely vision to her adoring son, even if seen only from a distance, and Lady Warwick, one of Jennie's friends, shrewdly remarked that while Jennie tried to organize Winston's mind and discipline his behavior, she never tried to stifle his spirit. "True to her American training, she did not check Winston when he asked questions or argued with her," said Lady Warwick.

Winston played up to his mother's American ancestry, too, and when taking his exams for Sandhurst, he wrote to her that she would be pleased to know his paper had been on the American Civil War. Even then his army of toy soldiers was impressive, and she urged his indifferent father to give him a gun he was pining for as a reward for having passed his examinations. In later years Churchill commented bitterly, "I owe everything to my mother; to my father nothing." As he grew older, Jennie saw to it that he listened to the talk of great statesmen at the family dinner table, and that he was nourished on the best of books.

Unaware of the enormous significance her son would have for the British Empire, she devoted most of her energies in the 1870s and 1880s to advancing the political fortunes of the languid and ailing Randolph Churchill. Both Gladstone and Disraeli watched her operations with interest, and Gladstone, approaching her after seeing her in an extended conversation with the Prince of Wales, remarked, "Tell me, my dear, what office did you get for Randolph?"

Her drive at times was ruthless, even though it was ringed with charm. Step by step she strengthened his course until he became one of the most important Conservative leaders of the era. When his father, the Duke of Marlborough, became Viceroy of Ireland in 1876, young Randolph went to Dublin as his secretary. Jennie loved Ireland. She rode magnificently and shared in many great house parties. Randolph became deeply sympathetic to the Irish people and startled his fellow parliamentarians with his charges of misgovernment and neglect of Ireland. A frequent escort of Jennie's during her years in Ireland was John Strange Jocelyn, whom she had met at Blenheim Palace. He was the son of the third Earl of Roden and was in the Scots Fusilier Guards. When a second son was born to her in 1880, she named him John Strange Spencer-Churchill.

The Churchills were back in London on Saint James Place in 1880, and a general election was underway. At this time Jennie's political power became manifest. She talked, lectured, and staged a political campaign on behalf of her husband, both privately and in public. Jennie was the most distinctive member of the Primrose League, a political-social organization open to Conservatives of all classes for discussion of issues and for active electioneering. With two million members the League was a powerful arm of the Tory party, and Lady Randolph, dubbed a Dame by the organization, created the Ladies' Grand Council. She not only accompanied her husband on his campaign trips but went all over Britain establishing Primrose Habitations, groups created to spread the new movement. Sometimes the speeches of husband and wife sounded so much alike that the legend spread that Jennie was the author in both cases.

She reacted with "passionate delight" when her husband became chancellor of the exchequer and Conservative leader in the House of Commons under Prime Minister Salisbury. The way seemed clear for him to become prime minister, but, unaccountably and without consulting his wife, he resigned precipitately in 1886 when he was thirty-seven years old. After John Bright died in 1889, Jennie persuaded Randolph to run for the vacated seat in Birmingham, hoping for a political revival. But Joseph Chamberlain, whose territory this was, dissuaded him, and after that, in the words of Lord Rosebery, Randolph "died visibly by inches in public."

Jennie's reign continued as she fascinated the men of power in England. She was not only one of the PB's (Professional Beauties) of the era, along with Lillie Langtry, but paradoxically she belonged to The Souls, an intellectual group so named by her. The PB's were mostly women in the court circle, whose photographs were sold all over Britain. In some respects they resembled the Beautiful People of today. The Souls, on the other hand, were an elite and lofty group who met for literary discussion and "to talk about each other's souls." They spurned bridge, baccarat, and idle gossip. With Arthur Balfour and Lord Curzon as members, The Souls had prestige while they lasted. Jennie was the most beautiful and forceful member, and Margot Tennant, who later became Mrs. Herbert Asquith, was the most waspish. When they all gathered at Sir Percy Wyndham's for one of their meetings, Lady Warwick remarked that they were "more pagan than soulful," and Sir William Harcourt was struck by the fact that some of "The Souls had very beautiful bodies."

Gertrude Stein's lifelong association with Picasso began around 1905, when he painted her portrait in his studio on the Rue Ravignan. Picasso found Miss Stein to be a difficult subject, and he finished the portrait from memory in her absence. The painting marks Picasso's transition from his Rose Period to cubism. (The Metropolitan Museum of Art, Bequest of Gertrude Stein, 1946)

With his long hair and reddish beard, Ezra Pound was a familiar figure in the expatriate haunts on the Left Bank. He could frequently be found at his favorite restaurant, Émile's, an Alsatian café near the Bal Bullier. (Boris de Rachewiltz; courtesy New Directions Publishing Corp.)

Isadora Duncan's individual style and her innovations had a major influence on the dance tradition of her generation, but her flamboyant personality and scandalous behavior impressed the public as deeply as her art. The Left Bank was a natural setting for Isadora, and she was often at the center of the revels which took place there. (Pastel by Jules Grand 'Jouan. Courtesy, Dance Collection, New York Public Library at Lincoln Center; Astor, Lenox, and Tilden Foundations)

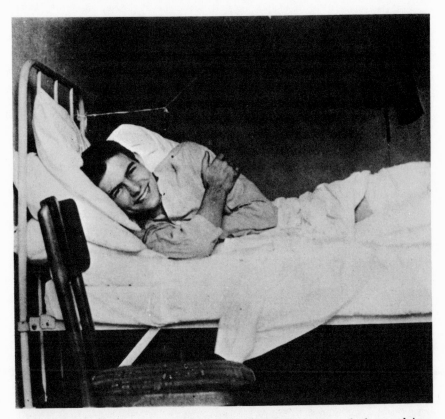

Ernest Hemingway was wounded while serving as an ambulance driver on the Italian front during World War I. Hemingway's war experiences provided the basis for *A Farewell to Arms*. (Henry S. Villard)

F. Scott Fitzgerald was legendary as a gilded youth who typified the gay, devil-may-care attitude of the twenties. Fitzgerald is pictured in 1928 with his daughter, Scotty, who later became a popular writer and hostess in Washington. (Culver Pictures, Inc.)

Jazz spread to Europe in the twenties, bringing a wave of American Negro entertainers to the Continent. Josephine Baker, with her famous pagoda headdress, became a leading lady at the Folies-Bergère. (Bettmann Archive, New York)

The Duke of Windsor gave up an empire and became an expatriate for love. The Windsors move with the seasons, but consider Paris to be their home. (United Press International)

Having left the United States for political reasons, Charlie Chaplin settled with his fourth wife and his children in Switzerland. Chaplin leads a quiet life in exile and tries to maintain his anonymity. (United Press International)

Jennie's romances came in quick succession as the years advanced. Her husband's health declined to a disastrous degree. He traveled much of the time—sometimes, but not always, with his wife. The Prince of Wales, Lord Curzon, Sir Charles Dilke, the Marquis de Breteuil, and Herbert Bismarck all were among Jennie's admirers. But perhaps the great love of her life was the dashing Count Charles Andreas Kinsky, twenty-five years old and four years younger than Lady Churchill when they met in the New Club at Covent Garden at a dance attended by the Prince of Wales and the King of Greece. Count Kinsky was honorary attaché at the Austro-Hungarian Embassy in London, and when they danced to tzigane music that night, he was on his way to becoming a major force in her life. In 1889 she spent much time in Paris visiting her mother and sisters. There she met Paul Bourget and other literary lions, but she was seen most often in the company of Kinsky.

After a world tour Randolph Churchill died in a coma in 1895 at the age of forty-five. Jennie's beloved father had died penniless in 1891, his substance wasted, his wife estranged from him, his sporting friends no longer interested in his fate. His last message to Jennie was characteristic: "I have given you all I have. Pass it on." She had always been his favorite child, and she had inherited his intense drive and ambition.

After her husband's death Lady Churchill expected to marry Count Kinsky, but was shocked to find that two weeks earlier he had married Countess Elisabeth Wolff Metternich zur Gracht, twenty years her junior. With unquenchable honesty she wrote to her sister Léonie, "He has not behaved particularly well and I can't find much to admire in him but I care for him as some people like opium or drink although they would like not to. . . ." The Marquis de Breteuil also failed her by marrying an American heiress.

Romantic though she was, Lady Churchill was a woman of many interests, widely read, musically gifted, as well as politically inclined. She fostered the arts and for a time edited a magazine, *Anglo-Saxon Review*, persuading Henry James to write for it. She organized a pilgrimage to Bayreuth for the Wagner festival, and played duets with Paderewski, who was charmed by her. In his school days Winston had watched his mother dramatically daubing paint over large stretches of canvas. On his return to school he fell into the habit of painting little bridges and roadways, a taste that came to florescence in his later years.

Jennie approved his going into the army and followed his adventures during the Boer War with the closest attention, helping him get his newspaper assignments through her political friends. She organized a hospital ship and went to South Africa to meet the first shipload of wounded. Winston entered Parliament in 1901, at the close of the Boer War and shortly after his mother's marriage to George Cornwallis-West in 1900. Thirteen years later, as another and greater war, which would make her son famous, was about to begin, she and her husband went their separate ways, and in 1918 she married Montague Porch, who was younger than Winston.

Jennie was sixty-seven when she died in 1921, courageous and witty to the end. As she faced amputation of one of her much admired legs, she told her doctor, "Make sure you cut high enough." Jennie had rarely revisited her native land, but her American identity was self-apparent and was frequently referred to by her son as he sought to strengthen the bonds between the home of the Marlboroughs and the home of the Jeromes.

Another American girl who married into the Marlborough family, twenty-one years after Jennie Jerome, lived to regret it and found that the exchange of wealth for a title, forced upon her by an ambitious mother, Mrs. William K. Vanderbilt, had bitter consequences. Consuelo Vanderbilt became the symbol in the eyes of the public of the American heiress sacrificed to social ambition. When she was married to the Duke of Marlborough in Saint Thomas's Church in 1895, she spent the morning of her wedding day in tears. "We were twenty minutes late," she recalled years later in her autobiography, *The Glitter and the Gold*, "for my eyes, swollen with the tears I had wept, required copious sponging before I could face the curious stares that always greet a bride."

Although she was madly in love with Winthrop Rutherfurd, an old Newport friend, her mother had locked her up and treated her like a prisoner until she agreed to marry the English duke. Consuelo observed the social rules meticulously, but found that being a duchess at nineteen—and an American at that—forced her into the company of much older people and kept her constantly on parade. She lacked Jennie Jerome's dash and ambition, but she was a girl of singular beauty—uncommonly tall with a swanlike neck and retroussé nose. The French had called her "La Belle Mademoiselle Vanderbilt au long cou," when as a debutante she attended her first ball in Paris at the Duc de Gramont's in 1893. Both John Singer Sargent and Boldini found her a fascinating subject for portraiture as the Duchess of Marlborough, and Sargent would not let her wear her famous pearls lest they break the classic line of her neck. She was so tall that when she was presented to Queen Victoria at Windsor in 1896 she almost had to kneel to touch Victoria's outstretched hand with her lips.

As Duchess of Marlborough she was immediately welcomed in the inner court circle, but like Lady Churchill she was dismayed to be told repeatedly that she was not like an American. Throughout her long expatriate years she never felt that this was a compliment, and after two marriages she regained her American citizenship.

Consuelo disliked Blenheim Palace from the start. She was used to magnificent houses. Richard Morris Hunt had designed for the Vanderbilts the Renaissance château that was a landmark for many years at Fifth Avenue and Fifty-second Street, and Marble House, their villa at Newport, inspired by the Grand Trianon in the park of Versailles. But Blenheim, with its vast acres and countless rooms, left her cold. She agreed with Alexander Pope, the poet, who had written of it, "I never saw so great a thing with so much littleness in it." She felt that they slept in small rooms with high ceilings, dined in dark rooms with high ceilings, dressed in closets without ventilation, and "sat in long galleries or painted saloons."

The duke instructed her carefully in the protocol involving a "hierarchical society in which differences in rank were outstandingly important." She had to catch the distinctions among at least two hundred members of a social establishment that was truly formidable in the days of Queen Victoria. But in her own family circle she found comfort in young Winston Churchill and his mother Jennie Jerome. "Lady Randolph Churchill was a beautiful woman with a vital gaiety that made her the life and soul of any party," Consuelo wrote. "She was still in middle age, the mistress of many hearts. . . . Her constant friendship and loyalty were to be precious to me in adversity." Since Winston was next heir to the dukedom at that time, she had wondered how she would be received by this mother and son.

The young duchess preferred her gallops across the countryside visiting tenants to her drives in landaus to pay formal calls. When they moved to their house in South Audley Street for the London season, she "watched a pageant of beautiful women and distinguished men performing a stately ritual." The duke and duchess rode in Hyde Park in an elegant hooded phaeton, and for ceremonial occasions used a crimson state coach, with footmen whose livery was stamped with the double-headed eagles of the Holy Roman Empire, of which Marlborough was a prince. She enjoyed the great balls of the period, but this type of party was not new to her either, for a ball her mother had given at Newport, when the Duke of Marlborough had arrived in America to woo Consuelo, had become one of the historic fetes in American social history, with such cotillion favors as old French etchings, fans, mirrors, watch cases, and other bibelots of the Louis XIV period, as well as lanterns that were a facsimile of Marble House, and bagpipes which squeaked amusingly.

The Duke of Marlborough was a thoroughly worldly peer, who liked women of wit and sophistication. Consuelo thought him good looking and intelligent, but she never loved him. He had prominent blue eyes and graceful hands, about which he was most fastidious. He had little appreciation of her quiet wit or understanding of her forthright nature. Her manner was quiet, discreet, and unobtrusive, in spite of her proud bearing. By degrees she became deaf, like Queen Alexandra, and this led to some withdrawal from the social scene. She was canopy-bearer for the queen, and she and the duke went to India for the Durbar as the guests of the viceroy, Lord Curzon, and his beautiful and adored American wife, the former Mary Leiter of Chicago. Consuelo thought Lady Curzon "had shed her American characteristics more completely than I was to find myself able to do." The vicereine was so absorbed in her husband's career that she had subordinated her personality "to a degree I would have considered beyond an American woman's powers of self-abnegation," Consuelo observed.

She felt that Lady Nancy Astor of Virginia, first woman to sit in the House of Commons, was the only member of the British aristocracy who had preserved her Americanism intact, even though her husband, William Waldorf Astor, later Viscount Astor, had given up his citizenship. It seemed to Consuelo that Lady Astor's sense of humor, high spirits, courage, and self-assurance were all of the American variety. As one of the three famous Langhorne sisters, even her looks seemed American to the Duchess of Marlborough.

It was at her dinner table that Nancy and Winston Churchill had a historic clash, often cited in later years. Churchill abhorred sparkling Lady Astor and made no secret of his dislike. "If I were your wife, I would put poison in your coffee," Nancy dared to say to the unflappable Churchill in his own setting at Blenheim.

"And if I were your husband I would drink it," he replied without a moment's hesitation.

Lady Astor continued to be something of a bombshell and aroused great criticism in the late 1930s for fostering what was known as the Cliveden set—gatherings at the Astor country seat of men who sought to appease Hitler as the war clouds gathered.

The Marlboroughs visited the Russian court, and Consuelo attended a great ball of three thousand at the Winter Palace with the Duchess of Sutherland, one of her closest friends. Some members of the peerage were already looking into the future, and these two beautiful and impressive duchesses were staggered, as Consuelo described it in her book *The Glitter and the Gold,* when Czar Nicholas said to them, "I know everything you have done since your stay in Russia, for my secret police send me a dossier on the movements of foreigners, but will you tell us why the Duchess of Sutherland goes to see Maxim Gorky when she knows he is in temporary exile."

The court scene changed radically after Queen Victoria's death. King Edward's liking for American women became marked, but in 1907, the season in which they were most in the ascendant, it was noticed that one of the leading duchesses was missing from Ascot, the Devonshire House dinner, and the Royal Ball given that year in honor of the King and Queen of Denmark. The Marlborough marriage was in trouble, and Consuelo was in retirement on the Continent. Divorce was still regarded as an unfortunate American custom, so at first they merely separated. The duchess stayed on at Sunderland House, a mansion the Marlboroughs had built for themselves in London, and her mother joined her there. The chestnut-haired Alva Vanderbilt from Alabama, who had forced her daughter into this marriage, was now separated from W. K. Vanderbilt, and she seemed to be genuinely sympathetic to the deserted duchess.

Consuelo turned her back on the empty social round and engaged in philanthropic and political tasks. She worked for children's playgrounds, and lodging houses for indigent women and prisoners' wives. She met some of the Fabians and found Bernard Shaw looking "like Jupiter and his words like thunderbolts." Like Jennie Jerome, she attended meetings of The Souls and came to know H. G. Wells, John Galsworthy, and Sir James Barrie, who said to a friend of hers, "I would stand all day in the street to see Consuelo Vanderbilt get into her carriage." Consuelo considered W. B. Yeats, George Wyndham, and Shaw the most brilliant conversationalists of the literary world. Many of her weekends were spent at Crowhurst, a Tudor manor in the north Wolds which she had taken, much preferring it to the grandeur and chill of Blenheim.

Along with the other American-born women living in London, she was active all through World War I, working energetically with Mrs. Whitelaw Reid, wife of the American ambassador, and her daughter, Jean Reid, who became Lady Ward. During the zeppelin raids the basement of Sunderland House became the refuge of friends and neighbors. Consuelo pitched in energetically on behalf of the American Hospital, and the Y.M.C.A. opened for American troops. In the next few years she studied housing conditions, toured the slums, did medical work, and tried to forget her personal worries as she and her husband faced divorce proceedings.

In the spring of 1921 the Duke of Marlborough married Consuelo's old friend the beautiful and clever Gladys Deacon, an American girl in whom he had been interested for some time. A few weeks later, on July 4, Consuelo quietly married Jacques Balsan in the Chapel Royal Savoy in London. This was a true love match, and her life was happy with the young aviator, who had commanded a group of Scout planes during the war and had helped to form the Escadrille Lafayette, the American aviation corps serving in France before the United States entered the war.

The Balsans were devout Catholics and could not receive Consuelo formally until she approached the Rota in 1926, pled that her marriage was performed against her will, and was granted an annulment. Her mother, who had married Oliver H. P. Belmont in the meantime and become an ardent worker for suffrage, sustained the grounds, to everyone's surprise, since she was the culprit. Consuelo then had a Catholic wedding ceremony and was received into the Balsan family circle.

The newlyweds had a house in Paris overlooking the Champs de Mer and a château at Saint Georges-Motel in Normandy. They built a villa, Lou Sueil, across from Eze on the Riviera and led a cosmopolitan life. Winston Churchill often visited them there and painted in their garden, making much fuss about his paraphernalia as he settled himself for the day, complete with easel, parasol, and stool, canvases carefully chosen, brushes cleaned, the right hat on his head, and the cigar box replenished.

Consuelo rarely revisited America, but when her mother died in Paris in 1933, she returned to New York for the funeral ceremonies in Saint Thomas's Church, of bitter memory for her, with recollections of her wedding day. She noted that the suffrage societies flew their banners as they marched down the church aisle. Her mother had done much for the suffrage cause, but Consuelo poured her own energies into her philanthropies. At the time of World War II her Norman castle was turned into a sanitarium for refugee children, and the Paris house became headquarters of American Aid to France. Like other expatriates caught abroad at this time, she shared in the great exodus along the cluttered roads, going first to Spain, then to Portugal, and finally flying from Lisbon on a Clipper. Madame Balsan had never flown; she dreaded it, but as they moved through the waters and rose into the air "I looked at the blue sky above and the slowly fading coast beneath and felt I had embarked on a celestial passage to a promised land," she later recalled. Consuelo had lived under three flags, but it gave her great reassurance to regain her American citizenship.

Another famous American hostess, rich, philanthropic, and gifted, had had to flee back to the United States in much the same way when World War I broke out. Mrs. Potter Palmer of Chicago was at her house on the Rue Fabert as the big guns roared close to Paris. She hastily packed her jewels, art treasures, and furs and drove to Cherbourg in her Rolls Royce to sail home. She knew both Lady Churchill and the Duchess of Marlborough, and her own social reign had been powerful in expatriate circles, as in America, where she was the leading hostess of the Middle West.

Mrs. Palmer was the focus of American social life in Paris in 1900, the year of the great exposition. The American colony was *en fête* while it lasted, and President McKinley had appointed Mrs. Palmer the one woman member of the national commission that represented the United States. Her husband took an impressive mansion on the Rue Brignole near the Trocadéro, where they entertained much as they did in their noted castle in Lake Forest. Mrs. Palmer flourished in this cosmopolitan world, and the French delighted in a commissioner who was also a woman of beauty and elegance, gowned by Worth, speaking their language with total familiarity, spreading charm and hospitality as she coped with practical matters affecting the exposition. She maneuvered Jane Addams, the great humanitarian who founded Hull House in Chicago, into an important post, over the opposition of the French director, who thought that no woman should hold such office. Some of her American colleagues also resented her omnipotence, but she sailed on without real opposition and won a place for women on the award juries, an issue she had battled out in Chicago at the time of the Columbian Exposition in 1893.

Ultimately the Legion of Honor was bestowed on Mrs. Palmer for her work at the exposition of 1900. Only two other women had then received this decoration—the artist Rosa Bonheur and England's Florence Nightingale. Her enemies hit hard when Mrs. Palmer won this distinction, and an American banker's wife gave the New York *Sunday World* an interview showing clearly the rivalry and animosity between the women of the Eastern Seaboard and this dowager from Chicago. She described Mrs. Palmer as the most ambitious woman in America and charged that she was trying "to amalgamate and control the high life of our continent," in the manner of Armour, Carnegie, Gates, and other big industrialists from the West. But Mrs. Palmer was so sure of herself that attacks of this kind did not dismay her. She regretted the bickering among the expatriates, feeling that Americans abroad should show a united front. She might be arrogant, but she also was forgiving.

While the Paris Exposition lasted, there was warm esprit among the expatriates on the whole, and the established American residents, diplomatic and otherwise, gave great balls and dinners. Horace Porter, who had been aide-de-camp to General Grant, was at the United States Embassy at the time, and he gave general receptions once a week for visiting Americans, and smaller dinners and receptions for a limited circle. Mrs. John W. Mackay, who had won her way years earlier in London and Parisian society by sheer personality and warmth of heart, was a permanent expatriate to be reckoned with and was one of the most popular hostesses of her day. Mrs. Pierre Lorillard, whose husband was the first American to be called a millionaire, had a château near Versailles. The William Thaw family had arrived from Pittsburgh with young Harry Thaw, already rich with railroad millions and destined to murder the architect Stanford White on the roof of Madison Square Garden six years later.

American girls married to European men of title abounded in Paris, as they did in London. They had permanent expatriate status, and they entertained lavishly in the year of the exposition. Fifty-seven such matches were recorded up to 1903. The Baronne de Seillière, stepdaughter of John O'Brien, a New York banker, was a close friend of Mrs. Palmer's. The Duchesse de La Rochefoucauld was Mattie Mitchell, daughter of Senator John H. Mitchell. The Duchesse de Dino was Adele Simpson, who had originally married Frederic William Stevens and divorced him to marry the Marquis de Talleyrand-Périgord, who became the Duc de Dino. Madame Clemenceau was American. Baronne de Brin was from New Orleans. The Comtesse de Choiseul was a New York girl. The Comtesse de Pourtalès and the Comtesse de Rohan were both American. The Baronne de la Grange was from Carrollton in Maryland, and the Baronne de Blanc was another compatriot.

The Countess of Craven was Cornelia, daughter of Bradley Martin. He had left New York to live abroad after the savage censure he and his wife experienced for the ball they gave in 1897 at the newly opened Waldorf-Astoria. It was the most discussed party of the era, and brought an end for the time being to the great extravaganzas that had angered a public suffering from hard times. But the most conspicuous American heiress on the scene at this time was Anna Gould, who had married Count Boni de Castellane in 1895, the year of Consuelo Vanderbilt's equally noted nuptials. Four thousand uninvited guests had crowded around the New York church in which Anna Gould was married, and Victor Herbert's twenty-piece orchestra played at the wedding reception. But at the time of the Paris Exposition her sorrowful air was commented on by visiting Americans. Her husband was spending her great fortune at a fast clip, on palaces, travel, and race horses; he was also making her profoundly unhappy.

Meanwhile, the great fetes and cotillions continued in Paris, and Americans, both resident and transient, danced to the pace they set. J. P. Morgan, then busy assembling with the help of Duveen the great art collection that would be valued at his death at $60 million, drove in the Bois, looking aloof and formidable to his celebrating compatriots. He bought with drive and purpose—$200,000 casually paid for a Cellini cup, $484,000 for a Raphael altarpiece.

The more worldly Americans haunted Auteuil and Longchamps and dined at Pailliard's, the Ritz, the Pavillon d'Armenonville, or the reopened Cubat's near the Rond Pont. They drove along the Avenue des Acacias in a stream of carriages, and met for afternoon tea in Empire tearooms near the Rue Royale and the Boulevard Haussmann, or in the Bois. Motorcars had begun to appear on the boulevards, along with the omnibuses, coaches, fiacres, and cabriolets. Soon luxurious models with dust-colored satin linings jammed the entrances to the perfumed salons on the Place Vendôme, where previews were held of the fashions to be worn at the exposition. Paquin, Callot Soeurs, and Doeuillet were the big names of the moment. The women they dressed wore enormous picture hats burdened with artificial fruit and flowers or neat little toques to match their bolero costumes. Their swirling skirts covered layers of ruffled petticoats. Gossamer tulles sparkled with *diamanté* on the ballroom floor and women shone and glittered, even in the daytime, wearing jeweled stockings and wide elastic belts studded with rhinestones. It was noted that no other women handled their lacy parasols with the style of the Americans. Their men exuded an air of well-being and wealth. The younger generation was inclined to be foppish; the mature contented themselves with the well-tailored suits and overcoats of Savile Row, with heavy watch chains hung with seals. They were addicted to expensive cigars, and conventional hats.

This was the Edwardian world of the millionaire and the American peeresses at the turn of the century, and it was on full display at the exposition. Correspondents from the United States did ample justice to the charms of Paris in one of its great years. The treasures of the Louvre, the graces of Versailles, the Tuileries gardens, the fragrance streaming from the bright-hued flower stands, the fishermen of the Seine, the book stalls along the quais, and the boutiques were of endless interest to Americans. Montmartre was its most characteristic self in 1900. Pale yellow light streamed at night from round gas globes over the Moulin Rouge, the cabarets, the clowns and equestrians, and the restless crowds.

After her husband's death in 1902 at the age of seventy-six Mrs. Palmer became more or less a permanent expatriate. She was fifty-three at the time and inherited his fortune without binding strings. For a time she traveled back and forth across the Atlantic, but she finally settled on the Rue Fabert in Paris in a house that differed in all respects from her mansion on Lake Shore Drive in Chicago, so noted for its Turkish, Moorish, and Oriental decor. Her rooms were white and gold, with graceful Louis XVI pieces and her favorite Impressionist paintings hung as part of the decor. Visiting Americans soon became familiar with the Degas circus girls hanging in her bedroom, with the misty effects of Raffaelli, Cazin's Norman landscapes, and Corot's sun-infused haystack. Mrs. Palmer collected faience, Fabergé boxes, jeweled clocks and trinkets, as well as Chelsea statuettes, a taste she shared with the Duchess of Roxburgh, the former May Goelet of New York, and another fashionable expatriate. Mrs. Palmer also took up Mrs. Mackay's fad for collecting silver tankards while she occupied Hampden House in London and became one of the clever American women in King Edward VII's circle shortly before his death in 1910. Her niece, Julia Grant (granddaughter of Ulysses S. Grant), who had married Prince Cantacuzène (a handsome young Romanian, well established at the Russian court), joined her in London and Paris.

The social season of 1907 was one of special magnificence as Britain moved inexorably toward the horror of World War I and the gradual decline of the empire. It seemed to be an all-American season in London, and King Edward, greeting Mrs. Palmer as she strolled about on the lawn at Ascot on a June day, remarked, "I never saw so many Americans in all my life. We outdo New York surely." She and Mrs. John Jacob Astor were invited to the royal ball under the top classification of distinguished foreigners on a par with ambassadors, while *the* Mrs. Astor's name appeared on the secondary list—a shock and surprise to the great Caroline Schermerhorn Astor, supreme hostess of the Eastern Seaboard, who had long regarded Mrs. Palmer as an upstart from the Middle West.

Mark Twain was the American lion of the moment as he swaggered around at the king's garden party at Windsor that wound up Ascot Week. Sir Thomas Lipton, always a figure of interest to American residents abroad because of the International Cup Races and his own good fellowship, drove the humorist back to town.

Bradley Martin gave a dinner for him and so did Whitelaw Reid, the American ambassador. Among her other social duties Mrs. Reid had the task of presenting the American debutantes at court.

"American Cash Floods Europe," the New York *World* reported on June 16, 1907, as the English-speaking world basked in prosperity. It was estimated that $228 million was spent that year by 300,000 tourists from the United States. Mrs. Palmer brought Olive Fremstad over from Paris with her entire cast to sing *Salomé* at Hampden House. The Strauss-Wilde opera was then under a censorship ban, but she daringly introduced it to Londoners at a party given in honor of Mr. and Mrs. Reid. The king asked to have it repeated for him, and he visited Hampden House unostentatiously next morning for a private showing.

Mrs. Palmer persuaded Chaliapin to give a concert at her London home, and his voice was so massive that it seemed to her he shook the walls. She had Pavlova dance at her house on the Rue Fabert in Paris, at the same time entertaining the entire Russian ballet. This party was given in honor of her son Honoré, who had racing stables outside Paris. His bride, Grace Greenway Brown, member of a prominent Baltimore family, was a horse lover, and both of the young Palmers were well adapted to expatriate life.

The social round of these fashionable nomads was as fixed as the stars. Mrs. Palmer took a house at Cowes on the isle of Wight. She was in Scotland for the opening of the shooting season on August 12, and on the Riviera or at Biarritz in spring. She visited Paris whenever the spirit moved her. Although the life at spas did not interest her, she followed the parade to Carlsbad and Marienbad. She was invariably in London for its three-month season, and she moved easily among her fellow Americans at Ascot, Henley, Lord's, and Goodwood. They all attended such fashionable races as the Derby and the Oaks, followed the polo matches, went yachting, and spent long country weekends. In 1907 hansoms, victorias, and barouches were giving way to landaulets and motorcars. The fashionables danced to "The Merry Widow Waltz" and wore Trilby violets in their furs.

In London as in Paris Mrs. Palmer was surrounded by American friends in permanent residence abroad. Among her intimates was Lady Paget, the formidable Minnie, daughter of Paran Stevens, at one time Potter Palmer's chief rival in the hotel business. Lady Paget had lived abroad so long that few traces of her American speech or origin remained. The beautiful Consuelo Yznaga, who had been one of Mrs. W. K. Vanderbilt's bridesmaids, had married Viscount Mandeville, who in time became the Duke of Manchester.

She was witty and gifted, and was popular in the American colony.

May Goelet, another of Mrs. Vanderbilt's bridesmaids, soon married the Duke of Marlborough's cousin, the Duke of Roxburgh; they lived at Floors Castle in the border country. May was committed to salmon fishing, needlepoint, and bridge when she was at home, but she circulated freely and kept up her American friendships. They all gathered at the same sort of parties the Beautiful People attend today, but without the emphasis on philanthropy, and they crossed the Atlantic intermittently. Mrs. Palmer sailed on the *Lusitania* on its maiden voyage at the close of the brilliant season of 1907. The 47,000-ton liner had 550 first-class passengers aboard, including a number of millionaires with their wives and families. Mrs. Palmer tramped the decks energetically with Cyrus H. McCormick, the Robert Goelets, and other friends, all hoping that the new ship would break the speed record. But it ran into fog off the American coast and was slowed down. It was the ship destined to be sunk on May 7, 1915, by the Germans, leading up to the United States entering World War I in 1917. Mrs. Palmer died in 1918 at the age of sixty-nine.

The most beautiful and at times the most discussed of the American expatriates from the 1890s until she died in 1940 was Maxine Elliott, a favorite of King Edward VII and, after the king's death, of J. P. Morgan. Daughter of a Maine whaling captain, Maxine's beauty, ambition, and personality brought her fame in the theatrical world, wealth, and the friendship of gifted men. Asquith, Balfour, and Winston Churchill all enjoyed her conversation. Lord Curzon proposed to her after the death of Mary Leiter. Bernard Shaw called her a "tornado," and Thomas L. Chadbourne, the New York lawyer, said of her, "If Maxine had been a man, Schiff would have been her secretary and Carnegie an office boy."

Her sister Gertrude was married to Sir Johnston Forbes-Robertson, the distinguished actor, and for a time Maxine was the wife of Nat Goodwin, the American comedian. Her name was identified with the theater from 1890 until World War I. A theater named for her and modeled after Le Petit Trianon was opened in New York in 1908, with Nellie Melba and Geraldine Farrar present to celebrate the occasion. But although she appeared repeatedly on the New York stage and toured the country, playing with William Faversham and Nat Goodwin, her life was essentially that of the American expatriate. She attended the suppers, garden parties, and great balls of the period, given by such fashionable hostesses as Mrs. Reginald Keppel, Mrs. Arthur James, Mrs. Ronald Greville, and other favorites of King Edward. Her knowledge of finance endeared her to such tycoons as Sir Ernest Cassel, Sir Reuben Sassoon, and Alfred de Rothschild. Observers noted that her witty conversation amused the king. Her beauty at the time was legendary: She had enormous eyes of ultramarine blue, tea rose skin, and a superb figure, clothed by the most fashionable couturiers of the day. She had a nervous breakdown before World War I, but from her bed she organized a group of sewing women to cut up her gowns to make clothes for the war orphans. Later she was godmother to two hundred Provençal children.

France became her permanent home, and she was often a guest on the yacht of J. P. Morgan, who, like Aristotle Onassis today, liked to entertain attractive women on Mediterranean cruises. Maxine's villa, the Château de l'Horizon, became a rendezvous for the famous and the gifted in the 1930s. Rocks were blasted and leveled near Cannes for the $300,000 villa, which looks like a Moorish fort and eventually became the home of Aly Khan. It was the showplace of the Riviera, and droves of guests arrived for lunch or dinner parties or to stay as guests. Swimmers zoomed down a chute from the pool to the Mediterranean. Elsa Maxwell, Noel Coward, and Clifton Webb visited frequently, and Winston Churchill liked to stay at the villa and paint. Maxine talked politics and finance as few women did. Toward the end of her life she put on excessive weight and spent most of her time playing bridge. She gave the château to the Duke of Windsor for a holiday before his abdication, and Mrs. Simpson was with him.

Her pet lemur, Kiki, was a great annoyance to Elsie de Wolfe, when this fellow expatriate visited her at her villa. Miss de Wolfe, daughter of a Halifax doctor, also had been on the New York stage but had taken up interior decoration and cut across Victorian clutter with the simplicity of her decor. She had won the Croix de Guerre and the Legion of Honor for work she had done during World War I with Anne Morgan and Elisabeth Marbury, a knowledgeable theatrical agent. Miss de Wolfe took special training in the treatment of burns and did valuable work in this field. These three women had taken the Villa Trianon in Versailles, an architectural gem, and Miss de Wolfe had redecorated it in classic fashion. Its music pavilion and avenue of roses were admired by countless guests in the years to come, but during the war it was turned into a hospital, and the atelier at the end of the garden was converted into a chapel.

In 1918 Miss Marbury, whose life was devoted to the exchange of plays and the promotion of playwrights on both sides of the Atlantic, returned to the United States to live but continued to visit London and Versailles. Miss de Wolfe shared a house with her on Sutton Place and kept her decorating quarters in New York through the 1930s, accepting contracts on an international basis. But after her marriage to Sir Charles Mendl in 1927 her life was centered in Europe, and she was one of the best known of the expatriates. Miss Morgan stayed abroad, working zealously for the reconstruction of areas damaged during the war. From this came the American Committee for Devastated France. She added the Morgan wing to the Trianon, and during the peace negotiations René Viviani, the French minister of justice, and the statesmen of all the countries involved, visited the famous villa.

Another American who acquired her own particular nimbus as an expatriate was Mabel Dodge, who later had her own colony at Taos in New Mexico and became the wife of an Indian, Antonio Luhan. Her life was in full flower at the Villa Curonia outside Florence early in the twentieth century, and her Italian decor and fine cuisine were enjoyed by many struggling young artists, writers, and musicians, as well as by the seasoned American expatriates who lived in villas on the hills around Florence. Mrs. Dodge had the generous instincts of a Perle Mesta, and the feeling for talent that Mrs. Gardner had, but her personality was distinctly her own, and many viewed her with bewilderment. She was a Buffalo girl who had sailed for Europe early in the century with two school friends, Mary and Violet Shillito, Cincinnati heiresses who were out to see the world. Mabel was a widow, her first husband, Carl Evans, having just been shot while out hunting ducks. In Paris she met Edwin Dodge, a Boston architect, and they were married before a small group of Americans. They traveled to the Riviera and then to Florence. When Mabel saw the cypress trees soaked in sunshine, the damp old stone, and the boxwood and laurel in the gardens, she cried out, "I will make you mine." She soon came to know the Americans, English, Russians, French, and Germans who lived in the old Italian villas buried among the somber cypresses. Before long, box hedges and stone paths adorned the grounds of the Villa Curonia. Dorothy Perkins roses climbed up the walls, and an iron pergola stood in front of the library, smothered in ilex and rose vines. Terra cotta tubs held gardenia bushes, and the scent of jasmine was everywhere, inseparable from the sybaritic Mabel, who was always drowned in luxury and softly attired in floating draperies. Her *Grande Salone* was done in ruby red, with red damask walls, and Venetian mirrors too faded to reflect the glowing Mrs. Dodge. Her husband had a room of his own, ninety feet long, banked with deluxe books, many on architecture, and opening through French windows on a brick-paved loggia, with stone stairs leading to the terrace below. Together they watched Florence lie in a pale huddle of opal as night fell and the Apennines turned purple.

Their visitors from the United States always wanted to see the galleries, palaces, and gardens, to study paintings, architecture, and landscape. The Dodges felt at times as if they ran an art school. The expatriates in the hills were known as *forestières*. There were separate groups, representing the arts they pursued, but Mrs. Dodge felt at home in all areas, and welcomed them indiscriminately at her villa. She instinctively attracted the more rootless types. But this could not be said of the musical group, represented by the Braggiottis, the Albert Spaldings, Paul and Muriel Draper, and the D'Alexandrowskys. All were hard workers and highly gifted. The Spaldings lived on the Lungarno in a palazzo, and they often had their son, Albert, and Luba d'Alexandrowsky play concertos. Luba was then in her teens—tall, with an oval face and long thick braids wound around her head. Her Russian mother's glittering green eyes darted inquisitorial gleams as she sat behind a samovar, serving cakes and pastries with an inexhaustible supply of Russian tea.

Spalding, who had made a fortune on his sporting-goods store, made his son Albert practice all day long on his Stradivarius, and Luba and Albert would run through duets half asleep from the exhaustion of their day's practicing. Paul Draper would sing and Luba would play at teas given by Mrs. Frances M. Wolcott, who had rented a small villa near the Dodges. Paul and Muriel Draper were everywhere in Florence. Mrs. Wolcott had known them in New York and had taken them under her wing. Muriel came from Haverhill in Massachusetts, but Henry James could never quite accept the fact that she was a fellow New Englander. "An alarming young woman —amazing," he said, after attending one of her parties. Muriel left a wake of bon mots behind her, and Paul liked to drink and bet on the races. He had come to Florence to study music with Isidor Braggiotti, and he was constantly at the piano, playing Bach and Beethoven, when he was not driving Muriel around in his Renault at ninety miles an hour. Motoring had become an intoxication for some of the expatriates, and the Drapers would go tearing through Siena and Perugia, reach Rome in time for dinner, and then drive back to Florence through the night.

On the other hand Russian residents who were part of the music world, like Luba d'Alexandrowsky and her mother, preferred to spend hours in the Piazza, seated at café tables, or at Giacosa's and Doney's, the pastry shops on the Via Tornabuoni. Mrs. Spalding liked to drive around in a huge victoria and to give conventional parties in the American fashion, in an atmosphere of Turkish carpets, carved chairs, mirrors and alabaster statuary.

The most interesting ménage on the hills of Florence to Mrs. Dodge, however, as to many other visitors, was that of the Braggiottis, with their elfin children, the music they evoked, and their tribal ways. They had round pale faces, and Mrs. Dodge compared their eyes to dark pools with lotus petals. None of the *forestières* ever penetrated the cameolike exterior of Lily Braggiotti, although they were all well aware of the flamboyant and philandering Isidor. Wholly unlike in every way, these two had met at a musical soirée given in Paris by Lily's father, Sebastian Schlesinger, who was an amateur composer. They were married in Paris two weeks later and spent their honeymoon in Niagara Falls. Both were singers, and they decided that Italy would be their home. Braggiotti had Italian blood. His father, François Braggiotti, was of Venetian descent and had settled in Smyrna, dealing in figs, attar of roses and Oriental rugs. His business took him to the United States and in course of time he became an American citizen, but to many he seemed a Turk. He married Martha Chadwick, of Beacon Street, and Americans resident in Florence used to note the mingled characteristics in the fascinating Braggiotti children. Lily's father, Sebastian Schlesinger, was of German origin, and migrated to the United States to import and export steel as the great railroads were being built. He married Countess Berthe de Pourtalès, and Lily and her sister Bertha were born in Nahant, Massachusetts. For a time Schlesinger was the German consul in Boston.

The Braggiottis were already well established in Florence when the Dodges arrived. Schlesinger had added a large music room to their villa so that Isidor could teach music and give concerts. Lily also taught singing, and pupils came from all parts of Europe to study with them. Their lessons were expensive, and Lily sang completely off-key, but Isidor was famed for placing a voice correctly, as well as for his flamboyant manners and baroque attire. Mrs. Dodge considered Lily the "rarest, last flower of Jewish fineness and beauty, of loveliness and elegance." They were faddists and cultists, and when a swami turned up at the Villa Curonia, Mrs. Dodge, who found him too eccentric, knew that the place to send him was to the Braggiottis. She was right; they treated him like the messiah he thought he was. He was not strange to them, for all of them had gone through the barefoot phase, the sandal phase, the raw vegetable phase. The Braggiottis had strange meals, but even if the fare consisted only of nuts and raw carrots, it was served with great for-

mality by two servants in white. Like Raymond Duncan, Isadora's
expatriate brother, they gave up meat and finally abandoned all
cooked food in favor of raw vegetables and fruits. The couple's
children grouped around the table had the look of angels, for the
Braggiottis were a charmed circle.

No outsider could break up the family combination. When they
went out they moved en masse, or piled into a rickety phaeton with
a fringed top, and leaping, barking dogs followed them everywhere.
Although modern in its appointments, their villa was basically a
typical ancient building common amid the ilex, cypresses, pines,
and olive trees of the Florentine hills. Life was vivid and unconventional with this gifted family. Lily did beadwork endlessly, her wide
thoughtful eyes only half aware of the world around her.

But this was not the way that most of the American residents
around Florence lived, and it was certainly not the Dodges' way of
life. They had an excellent chef, a major domo, and half a dozen
other servants. The chef drove down into town in his pony cart to
do his shopping in the market. Mrs. Dodge encouraged the epicurean touch in her kitchen, and a visit to her villa was a visit deluxe.
It amused her to drive her friends around the countryside and to
show them where Pen Browning, the son of Robert and Elizabeth
Barrett Browning, lived in Asola in the house that his father's poem
Pippa Passes had hallowed. Mrs. Dodge knew the history of all the
villas and their assorted occupants, and her husband could enhance
their tours with architectural detail. Pen reminded Mabel of a small
red apple, with his plump figure, vivid blue eyes, webby eyelids, and
a small white moustache. He dressed in English checks and was simple and inarticulate.

When Eleanora Duse came to stay at the Villa Curonia she
brought her own bed, as was her custom, and it had to be put together. She and her hosts dined at a refectory table under the trees,
with candlelight making ghostly the sallow face of the great Duse.
The scent of gardenias was heavy in the air as they drank the wine
of Orvieto or of Montepulciano and ate spaghetti and ravioli with
thick crusty bread. Duse moved slowly and dramatically, even at the
table. She seemed to be brooding everlastingly, with her black lace
shawl covering her hair, her slender form wrapped in dark chiffon
at night, and homespun Capri wool in the daytime. Duse had abandoned the Florentine stage altogether by the time she visited the
Dodges, soon after the evening she faltered and the curtain was rung
down as D'Annunzio entered a box with Carlotta Rudini, his newest
interest, wounding his most famous love to the core.

Edward Gordon Craig, the illegitimate son of Ellen Terry and the lover of Isadora Duncan, often called at the Villa Curonia. He spent much of his time sprawling over café tables or wandering through the streets of Florence with his children, one of whom was the living image of Ellen Terry. His tangled brown hair streamed from under a low, wide-brimmed hat, and his pointed chin and delicate features gave him an eerie look, in Mabel's opinion. She was interested in his plan to start another renaissance in Florence and to recreate its great past. He persuaded the natives to make little dolls which he could use as puppets. The Americans were always interested in Gordon Craig, and in his long friendship with Isadora Duncan, by whom he fathered one of her two illegitimate children.

There were times when Mabel Dodge tired of entertaining impecunious artists and musicians, or helping them find a foothold, and then she would turn to old friends like Gladys Deacon, a brilliant and beautiful American who had engaged the interest of the Duke of Marlborough and stayed with him in Venice while the duchess, the former Consuelo Vanderbilt, grieved in London. Mabel had watched this romance from its beginning, when Gladys' mother lived in Rome. It was of great interest to the American expatriates that Consuelo and Gladys, who had gone to school together, should now be part of a triangle—and particularly since Consuelo had been forced by her ambitious mother to marry the duke.

An American heiress who lived in Florence in a villa at Settignano was Carrie Rand, whose mother, Mrs. E. D. Rand, organized and endowed the Rand School of Social Sciences in New York with the help of George Davis Herron, a bearded Congregational clergyman and educator who had abandoned his family to elope with Carrie. He called her the Modern Madonna as she moved about in velvet draperies, clasping her baby in her arms. She sat picturesquely at a large black piano playing Beethoven, with the flowing green sleeves of her Liberty gown sweeping the floor. Carrie's mother may have stood for the principles of the proletarian world, but her own silver and lace were much commented on in Florence. Forget-me-nots floated on geranium leaves in her silver finger bowls, and the spirit of wealth and privilege prevailed at their villa in the hills.

Henry Savage Landor, traveler and explorer, arrived intermittently at the Villa Curonia with some fresh tale of his travels, which Mabel Dodge believed, but the public usually doubted. His uncle, Walter Savage Landor, an artist whom he considered a "terrible old man," had lived in Como, Florence, and Paris, and young Henry was born in Florence. He returned to it like a homing pigeon from the far ends of the earth. He was short, slender, and insolent, making extravagant claims about his adventures, and the Dodges thought that he had come to look like an Asiatic.

The Dodges' most interesting expatriate visitor in some respects was Constance Fletcher, whose pseudonym was George Fleming. A homely, blue-eyed girl, originally from Salem, Massachusetts, she commanded the interest of Henry James, Oscar Wilde, and many of the writers of the day. She reviewed books for the *Times* of London and wrote successful plays. She dramatized *The Light That Failed* for Forbes-Robertson and wrote *The Canary* for Mrs. Patrick Campbell. Lord Lovelace, Byron's grandson, gave her his grandfather's miniature *The Letters,* referred to by Henry James in *The Aspern Papers.* Not even Mrs. Gardner at the Villa Barbaro could draw the intellectuals who swarmed around Constance Fletcher in the Palazzo Capello in Venice. She had strangely coquettish ways for a woman of New England background, and minced about on high heels, wearing diaphanous gowns. Her raddled skin belied her golden curls, and although so short-sighted that she walked into doors, she was too vain to wear glasses.

Her mother had eloped with handsome young Eugene Benson and had married him after being divorced by her husband. The Bensons settled at the Palazzo Capello in the 1870s and gave morning levees for expatriate society. Romantic Eugene strewed fresh rose petals over the marble stairs before his wife tripped down for these gatherings, and he continued this custom after her death. In fact, he turned the palazzo into something of a shrine to her memory. The atmosphere of mourning reached its climax when Eugene died, and Constance draped the main drawing room and the catafalque in black crepe.

After that she was on her own, and her *conversaziones* and customs were a source of wonderment to American travelers passing by. She visited the Dodges only once a year, but there was constant intercommunication between the salons of Rome, Florence, and Venice. In general, Mabel preferred the frank hedonists to the intellectuals, and she considered some of the Englishwomen on the hills tiresomely bookish. From their loggias the hill residents watched the sunset fade over Florence like a golden curtain. They cultivated rose gardens and moved in and out of big shadowy rooms with dim furniture in faded gold.

Periodically the Dodges went to Paris, where Edwin had many friends from his student days on the Left Bank. Mary Foote, an American author who illustrated her own novels, and Janet Scudder, a sculptor from Terre Haute, Indiana, remained vigorously

American in spite of the years they had spent in the Latin Quarter. Dressed in the height of fashion, perfumed and coifed to the last degree, Mabel Dodge would move gingerly around Miss Scudder's dusty studio with its wet clay, model stands, and plaster of Paris. Eventually Miss Scudder's *Frog Fountain* would be in the Metropolitan Museum and her *Fighting Boys Fountain* in the Art Institute of Chicago. Her graceful Dianas would adorn many of the formal Italian gardens of Tuxedo Park, Lenox, and Long Island.

Mrs. Dodge found Mary Shillito, her old school friend from Cincinnati, living with a Frenchwoman, Marcelle Senard, in a handsome apartment on the Avenue du Bois. With the death of her father, of department store fame, Mary inherited a large fortune and decided to settle abroad. But she veered away from the bohemianism that at times engulfed Mabel, and bought carefully and conservatively for a château she and Marcelle were building in the mountains near Lake Geneva. Like Mrs. Gardner they selected stone carvings, columns, arches, and pavements, and had old *boiseries* transported intact for walls and ceilings. Mrs. Dodge disliked the bold colors they used and their tendency to brighten the gold overlay. She preferred the "faded glory" and decay of the Venetian originals. Saint Bernard dogs provided an Alpine touch for Mary Shillito, who had found a new home in Europe after the death of her sister Violet.

In Paris she bought her gowns from Doucet, while Mabel shopped around for her characteristic turbans and intricate creations of lace, gold guipure, fur, and jeweled embroidery. She liked soft and misty effects, layers of chiffon and lace, and pastel-tinted peignoirs. When not wearing a turban, she usually chose a romantic hat with sweeping ostrich feathers in the Gainsborough tradition. In the afternoons they all skated at the Palais de Glace or had tea at Rumpelmayers. The prevailing perfumes were Houbigant's *Royal,* or *Chypre, Lilas,* or *Santal,* and American women spent lavishly on the luxury items along the Rue de Rivoli. Mabel smoked Macedonia cigarettes and sipped Quinquina Dubonnet, white Porto, or absinthe for aperitifs. Edwin took them to dine at Foyot's, Armenonville, or Le Voisin.

But in time he tired of his wife's bohemian friends, who constantly haunted their villa. Soon after Jo Davidson arrived to do a bust of Mabel, the Dodges decided to go their separate ways. It was time to start their son in an American school in any event, and Mabel had had enough of Europe. She was soon back in New York, conducting a salon in Greenwich Village and drawing in celebrities with the sure touch of the instinctive hostess.

In the Shadow of
Henry James

The American conception of compatriots abroad became more critical toward the close of the nineteenth century when Henry James created the unmistakable image of an authentic literary giant who was ready to foreswear his citizenship. His renunciation was not in a spirit of pique or rebellion. The Old World, he said, was his choice, his need, his life. His talents flowered as he lived in England, France, and Italy. He came to know the great men of his day, and to move with worldly authority in the most sophisticated social circles. To many he seemed a snob; he was certainly an Anglophile.

James's rejection of his own country ensured a hailstorm of criticism. An indirect defense of his act, however, came in course of time from Edith Wharton, the friend who knew him best and was also an expatriate. In *A Backward Glance* she wrote of James:

> The truth is that he belonged irrevocably to the old America out of which I also came, and of which—almost—it might paradoxically be said that to follow up its traces one has to come to Europe; as I discovered when my French and English friends told me, on reading *The Age of Innocence* that they had no idea New York life in the seventies had been so like that of the English cathedral town, or the French "ville de province" of the same date.

Both writers had had their first taste of Europe as children, but Mrs. Wharton never dissociated herself from her native country, in spite of the fact that she passed most of her years abroad and had a permanent home in Paris. She observed that James was neither happy nor at home on his return to the United States in 1904, 1905, and 1910. It seemed to her that he had thwarted his genius by living abroad and saw too late the mistake he had made. But between them they created a golden age of their own and gave the term *expatriate* a high literary polish at the turn of the century. Their prestige was undeniable. They were the "in" cosmopolitans, sought out by traveling Americans, commented on in the press, the favored guests of scholars and men of affairs. James moved about London like a native: a member of the best clubs; a friend of Gladstone, who had a weakness for visiting Americans; an associate of the notable writers and artists of the era. He followed the same pathways Sargent did, and the two men had good relations when they met.

At times he expressed doubts about the course he had followed. He said on one occasion, "The mixture of Europe and America which you see in me has proved disastrous." He wrote of the variant feelings of the cosmopolitan, the discomfort of seeing many lands and feeling at home in none.

> To be a cosmopolitan is not, I think, an ideal; the ideal should be to be a concentrated patriot. Being a cosmopolite is an accident, but one must make the best of it. If you have lived about, as the phrase is, you have lost that sense of the absoluteness and the sanctity of the habits of your fellow patriots . . . . There comes a time when one set of customs, wherever it may be found, grows to seem to you about as provincial as another; and then I suppose it may be said of you that you have become a cosmopolitan.

Regardless of the sharp arrows sometimes tossed at James for his apostasy, all the expatriates in Europe and the visiting Americans wished to meet him. He was cautious about giving invitations to his home, Lamb House in Rye, however. In England he felt completely at home. France attracted and charmed him, but there he felt a foreigner—a "moralist, puritan, and outsider." Italy fed his spirit as long as he lived. "At last—for the first time—I live," he exclaimed when he made his first entry into Rome in 1869, fresh from the "fogs, smoke, dirt, darkness, ugliness and brutal size of London"—an effect that chilled him at the time. But after he settled in London in 1876, he found that it was "more substantial to live upon . . . than the romance of Italy." With his literary career beginning to flower, he found London the "most possible form of life . . . the biggest aggregation of human life—the most complete compendium of the world."

Nevertheless from his first taste of Italian life he was permanently committed to its ambience, and Rome, Florence, and Venice were the cities where he lived at full pitch, passionately caught up in their art and history. His early impressions colored his first novel, *Roderick Hudson,* as he keenly observed the nature of the life spread out before him like a rich new canvas. He was to return many times and come to know Italy with intimacy and respect. Here he felt freed of "fixed and conscious identity, liberated from practical decision and responsibility." He found the beauties of Venice too distracting for concentrated work, and preferred Florence for writing. "The effort required for sitting down to a writing-table is heroic, and the brightest page of manuscript looks dull beside the brilliancy of your milieu," he commented. But Rome was the great "plum pudding" from every point of view. He was introduced to it in a lavish way by William Wetmore Story, whose home was a focus for Anglo-American life.

James stayed at the Hotel Inghilterra in the Via Bocca di Leone, where Robert and Elizabeth Barrett Browning had lived, and he had no sooner tramped around the city at high speed than he saw the pope driving past in a huge black-horsed coach, his ivory face like a cameo in a dimly lit chapel. He watched the women sinking to their knees, and the men removing their hats, as the mounted guards waved them back. James picnicked on the Campagna di Roma with Story's group and galloped by himself over the plains. Unlike his friend William Dean Howells, whose chief interest was architecture, and Nathaniel Hawthorne, who was not wholly committed to the works of art he saw, James found life and refreshment in the great masters, passing "exquisite hours, enveloped in light and silence" among them. His literary sympathies remained French, however, while Howells' were strongly Italian, but socially James would always feel most at home in England.

His brother, William James, recuperating after a long illness, joined him in Rome and Florence in the early 1870s, but had no yearnings to become an exile like Henry. William tired of churches and priests, and the Colosseum to this philosopher seemed nothing but "damned blood-soaked soil." On a visit to see it in the moonlight Henry James first thought of the Daisy Miller he would create—the exquisite-looking, beautifully dressed American girl he eventually brought to life with such devastating effect that for a generation she became as much a symbol of the American abroad as Sinclair Lewis's Dodsworth in the 1920s. Daisy was a child of nature, independent, heartless, scheming, snobbish, and relentless, and James's conception of her was an affront to the matchmaking mothers and adoring fathers of the era. An illness developing after a visit to the Colosseum was the end of the fictitious Daisy, and she was pictured as being buried romantically under spring flowers close to the graves of Keats and Shelley.

James's novel *Daisy Miller* and the play based on it, which he read to Isabella Stewart Gardner before it reached a producer, were widely discussed on both sides of the Atlantic. His *Transatlantic Sketches* were richly evocative of the mellow days in Italy, when even the decay in Venice was faded gold, and the misery was veiled in a violet mist. Although James did not admire John Ruskin, he wandered about with *Stones of Venice* as well as his Baedeker, enjoying the Palladian palaces and conscious of a different Venice from that seen by the more realistic Howells. He began *The Portrait of a Lady* in Florence in 1879, the year in which *Daisy Miller* came out, and it was there that he absorbed from Eugene Lee-Hamilton, Vernon Lee's half-brother, some of the material on which *The Aspern Papers* was based.

In the 1890s James was often in Italy, visiting Mrs. Gardner at the Villa Barbaro in Venice, or settling briefly at F. Marion Crawford's romantic compound in Sorrento. James visited Axel Munthe at Capri, and discussed with him the book Munthe later wrote, *The Story of San Michele*. The young American was highly critical of his compatriots as he observed them in the places he visited. In his early years abroad James was appalled by the "vulgarity" of the traveling Americans he saw in London and Paris, and he deplored their "unhappy poverty of voice, speech, of physiognomy." Many seemed to be ignorant, stingy, grudging in their appreciation of anything European, and determined to compare everything they saw to some American standard that existed only "in their own unscrupulous wind-bags."

James took careful note of the artists working in the galleries, the businessmen in the cafés, the shining girls like Daisy Miller, and a legion of well-off mothers determined to find titled husbands for their daughters. They were everywhere in the 1890s—Americans on the Grand Tour, and Americans who had lived abroad for years. They were insatiable in their quest for bric-a-brac and art treasures. Their sight-seeing was carefully mapped out for them. They walked a beaten track, ate in the most fashionable restaurants and cafés, listened to the same music, and reacted in conventional phrases to the art they were viewing. The quest for "culture" was painfully self-conscious as the young were shepherded from point to point. Children grew desperately fatigued and bored, and some, like John Singer Sargent, all their lives looked back with horror on their wandering childhoods, as their parents unfailingly showed up at the fashionable spots, seeking the company of people who seemingly did not want them.

This early indoctrination tended to make them worldly and art-conscious, however, and it enabled Sargent to be helpful to James in Italy, enlarging his understanding of classical art, just as James opened many doors for Sargent when he was well established in England. But Paris gave the young American writer his first taste of intense literary concentration on the prose masters. His letters from 1869 to 1870 and from 1875 to 1876 reflect what Paris meant to him creatively in those years.

The long association of Henry James and Mrs. Wharton began in the late eighties at the Paris home of Edward Darley Boit, a Boston artist whose watercolors were admired by Sargent. Soon the friendship of these two restless and brilliant expatriates highlighted the literary scene abroad and at home. Mrs. Wharton donned a tea-rose gown embroidered with iridescent beads from Doucet for the great occasion, but James did not notice her existence. He gave her equally short shrift at a later meeting at the Villa Barbaro in Venice, although at the time she was eager to tell him how much she admired *Daisy Miller* and *The Portrait of a Lady*. Later they became close friends, and by 1910 their lives, personal and literary, were closely intermeshed. Much as they differed in many respects, Mrs. Wharton always maintained that James was the most intimate friend she had ever had. But she disapproved of a good many things about him, including the renunciation of his American citizenship. They had many literary arguments, and she disagreed violently with many of his judgments; yet she found the "rarest understanding, the richest and most varied mental comradeship" in James. His slow manner of speaking, which some people took to be affectation, seemed to Mrs. Wharton to be a victory over a stammer. She found him ill at ease when he visited her in her New York home and at The Mount, her Italian villa close to Lenox, Massachusetts, on his first return to America in 1904. Wall Street bewildered him, and he told Edith that he was quite unable to use the "material," financial and industrial, of modern American life.

Both wrote about people with money and social status; both had a subtle bite behind their carefully fashioned prose. In her novels Mrs. Wharton viewed marriage sardonically, often combining stupid husbands with frivolous, worldly wives. James watched her through the breakup of her marriage to Edward Robbins Wharton, a Harvard graduate twelve years her senior. He shared in her long association with Walter Berry, the international lawyer resident in Paris who was a major force in her life until his death in 1927. When Mrs. Wharton's marriage ended in 1913, Berry became the romantic interest in her life. Thereafter she was the star of his set, which was known as *notre bande*. He had priceless books and collected objects of art.

France was her permanent home from 1910, and she was decorated for her work in World War I. Although she roamed across Europe at will, she was a hard worker, writing with great care but never with the involved sophistry James practiced in his later years. Her style became sharper and more lucid with each book. Her earliest story was published in *Scribner's Magazine* in 1891, when she was thirty, and the last was written in 1937, the year of her death. She turned out more than a score of novels and eighty-five short stories. Nearly all were written abroad, but most were American in mood, background, and character. *The Valley of Decision* came out in 1902, *The House of Mirth* in 1905, and *Ethan Frome* in 1911. When *The Age of Innocence* won the Pulitzer Prize in 1920, she became a commanding figure in the literary world. But *Ethan Frome,* which she wrote in Paris, reading each morning's work to Walter Berry in the evening, emerged as an American classic, although it was less successful at the time of publication than her earlier books. In this novel she wrote of a lonely hill region in New England with full understanding of the dialect, emotions, and the mental and moral attitudes of the people. She had studied these people and their environment perceptively on her drives around her Massachusetts home, The Mount, and Dr. Charles Eliot Norton of Harvard had enlightened her further.

Edith Wharton's intimate knowledge of New England came after her marriage, but as Edith Newbold Jones, growing up in New York City, she was frequently taken to Europe at an early age. Before she was four, she was playing in the Roman Forum, rolling hoops and skipping rope, with Daisy Terry, the little half-sister of F. Marion Crawford. They played hide and seek amid the stone benches of the Pincio, and stopped to sniff the violets and tulips on the steps of the Piazza de Spagna. Her parents, Mr. and Mrs. George Frederic Jones, toured Europe with their small daughter, giving her an "incurable passion for the road." She was always to remember from her childhood days the pools and fountains of the Alhambra, the orange groves of Seville, and the tower of the Giraldo.

Edith had her first dancing lesson in Paris with English and American friends. Their teacher was a former ballerina of the

Grand Opera named Mademoiselle Michelet. A flickering recollection of watching Empress Eugénie driving down the Champs Élysées with a mounted escort and outriders on her carriage, was one of Edith's memories. A tiny black lace bonnet with a tea rose over one ear crowned Eugénie's auburn hair, and the flounces of her taffeta billowed out around her. A small boy in uniform sat by her side.

When Edith's mother took her to a German spa, she learned from her Teutonic governess how to tat, knit, and string wild-flower garlands. She rode, swam, and romped like any little girl her age, but even as a child she was often in the company of famous people, and all her life she spoke French, Italian, and German with equal facility.

Her family returned to the United States when the Franco-Prussian War began, but the travel fever was already deeply embedded in little Edith. When she married in 1885, it was a simple matter to persuade her husband to go abroad. Although born in Boston, he was a Virginian, and he had no wish to live in New England. Mr. and Mrs. Wharton cruised through the Mediterranean on a chartered yacht, and from then on it was their custom to explore some new part of Italy each spring. Paul Bourget gave Mrs. Wharton a letter of introduction to Vernon Lee, the English writer who lived with her invalid half-brother, Eugene Lee-Hamilton, at the Villa del Palmerino, in a straggling village outside Florence. Their yellow house with its box-scented garden had open doors for Mrs. Wharton when she settled down to write *Italian Villas and Their Gardens*. Vernon Lee, whose *Eighteenth Century in Italy* had been Edith's own guidebook along the way, gave her help and advice, and in course of time she visited the villas of Florence, Siena, and Rome, then moved from Tuscany to Lombardy and took in Genoa and Venice. Her book became a working manual for landscape gardeners and students of architecture. It was one of the first of its kind and was done with distinction. It added substantially to the discoveries Catharine Sedgwick had made at Milan and Como three generations earlier.

Her journeyings early in the twentieth century included many happy days for Mrs. Wharton—in fact, "the happiest I was to know as regards literary hopes and achievements," she later wrote. She and her husband explored the byways in heavy carriages, often with the Bourgets, and in this way they traveled through the Bergamesque Alps, where she picked up Italian background for *The Valley of Decision*. Sometimes her husband would bicycle ahead to engage rooms and order dinner at inns along the way. Mrs. Wharton had a passion for finding the exceptional and the rare, and at times she traveled alone, absorbing the beauties of the countryside, and sauntering through the hill towns and villages with a keen eye for hidden treasure. She worked outside the scope of the guidebook and shared Bernard Berenson's instinct for scientific accuracy. She deplored the sentimental in art as in letters. Both Berenson and she had been students of Charles Eliot Norton in Cambridge, Massachusetts, where they had been lavishly exposed to his pre-Raphaelite predilections, and Norton had advised her on the sources she should consult for period background in writing *The Valley of Decision*. She studied the eighteenth century theater, music, costumes, and customs for the enrichment of this historical novel.

In later years, when Mrs. Wharton wrote her novels with an American background, her characters were likely to show up at the Villa d'Este, or in Como or Venice, for Italy was dear to her, and she was a close student of the culture of the Venetian eighteenth century. Few writers had given this period much thought, since the eighteenth century had seemed to belong to France. Vernon Lee was one of the few authorities who accepted the fact that Italian art had not ended with the Renaissance.

George Meyer, American ambassador to Rome in 1903, was one of the first Americans abroad to own a motorcar, and Mrs. Wharton was whirled around in this new contraption, which looked like a high-perched phaeton without hood or screen. She soon had a car of her own, and became an enthusiastic motorist. She was an insatiable traveler and one season chartered a sailing ship to take her to the West Indies.

It was easier for her American friends to understand her wish to travel and live abroad than it was for them to accept her success as a writer. It was something of an outré development for a fashionable American woman to write books, and particularly to turn a scathing eye on her own set—which she did, commandingly and with considerable perception. Her book *The House of Mirth* was appearing in the *Revue de Paris* when she and her husband settled on the Rue de Varenne after their Italian journeyings. This did not add to her family's peace of mind, but it did lead to her being taken into the inner circles of scholarship in Paris. Archibald Coolidge, who later became librarian at Harvard, was giving the Hyde Lecture that winter at the Sorbonne, and he introduced her to his academic friends, including Victor Bérard, director of the École des Hautes Études. In this way Mrs. Wharton by 1905 had gained entrée to the world of science and letters, closely guarded from the outsider, in which Benjamin Franklin had moved so harmoniously.

The writer soon had to choose her own alliances in this area of tight cliques and special interests. In university circles she found that she had a paralyzing effect on the scientists' wives, who regarded her as an intruder and a foreigner. She found some consolation in Gustave Schlumberger, archaeologist and historian of the Byzantine Empire, but she fared best and felt most at home in the literary salons of Paris. At Madame de Fitz-James's she was always sure to meet the men most prominent in the arts. Here she saw much of Paul Bourget, critic, poet, and novelist; of André Tardieu of *Le Temps*; Abel Bonnard, the writer; Jules Cambon, ambassador to the United States from 1897 to 1902; and the eloquent Paul Hervieu, novelist and playwright. Mrs. Wharton considered Madame de Noailles, Matilda Serao, the Neapolitan novelist, and Vernon Lee the three most eloquent women she had ever known.

There were always visitors from the United States to drop in on Mrs. Wharton. The old Bostonians, like Egerton Winthrop and Robert Minturn, observed her liaison with Berry with profound interest and some curiosity. The Minturn family had been associated with packet lines to Liverpool and London. They had had a hand in the creation of Central Park, and of the Union League Club. Robert was a member of *notre bande,* a small group of wits and intellectuals who met sometimes in Mrs. Wharton's salon in Paris and at other times in Queen's Acre, the home of Howard Sturgis near Windsor. The group included Percy Lubbock, English critic and essayist; Gaillard Lapsley, who would escape from his tutorial duties at Cambridge to join the other members of *notre bande;* Robert Norton, a close friend of Henry James's; and John Hugh-Smith, who liked to draw out George Moore on his opinion of James, Conrad, and Hardy. Wit, criticism, and sometimes cruel satire distinguished the gatherings of *notre bande*. Mrs. Wharton was particularly fond of Howard Sturgis, son of Russell Sturgis, an international banker who, although an American, spent most of his life in Europe. Howard Sturgis gave up literature for what Mrs. Wharton called days "methodically divided into brief moments of exercise and long hours of immobility." On her annual visit to Lamb House in Rye she found that a walk in the woods with Henry James and Howard Sturgis was an excruciating experience. James would go stumbling along with a heavy gait, stopping every few minutes "to propound a problem," and Sturgis would stand still altogether or make dashes into the bushes after his dog.

Mrs. Wharton preferred her motor drives with James. They were a passion with him, and he insisted on guiding his chauffeur through all the back lanes and obscure windings he could find. But her visits to Lamb House were stimulating, from the moment James greeted her in the hall with two solemn kisses until he sped her on her way back to Paris or America. She was less admiring of Lamb House than its owner was, although she conceded that its Georgian paneling was choice and that the Garden Room where he wrote, with its spectacular Palladian window, was an appropriate background for critical Mr. James. She liked the paneled walls with their old prints and bookcases.

Knowing Edith to be an epicure, he was always apologetic for the fare he offered her, and with cause. She thought it hopelessly frugal, and incredibly undistinguished. But she liked to watch him padding around, listening, muttering, groaning disapproval, or uttering paradoxes to his assembled guests. He always listened to the brilliant conversation of Howard Sturgis, a droll fellow and a perfect host.

While in England, Mrs. Wharton usually saw a good deal of Sir George Trevelyan, the historian, and of Mrs. Humphry Ward, the novelist, who admired her work and liked to steer her around in London's literary circles. As a friend of James and an American writer of real distinction, she was in and out of the drawing rooms of the Victorian era. But she considered Paris her true home, although she usually crossed the Atlantic each year and summered at The Mount until she sold it.

Henry White, a childhood friend of Edith's, was ambassador during her first year in Paris. His wife, the former Margaret Rutherfurd, and her two young brothers, Lewis and Winthrop, had been neighbors of hers at Newport, and they had played together as children. Mrs. Wharton enjoyed the visits of political celebrities, and she was particularly interested in Theodore Roosevelt. On his tour of 1909–10 she invited some of her friends to meet him at the Rue de Varenne. Jean Jules Jusserand helped her organize the party, and they decided not to invite governmental and university friends.

But Roosevelt took things into his own hands. He fastened on a member of the French Academy who specialized in one of his pet subjects, and completely ignored the friends Edith had invited to meet him. She considered the party a total flop. So did Berry, who was an intimate friend of Jusserand's and had been counsel at the French Embassy for many years.

Although her personal troubles were mounting in the years before World War I, Mrs. Wharton enjoyed to the full the beauty of provincial France, the still unravaged cornfields of Millet and Monet, the excitement of Paris itself—its violet-gray buildings, its statues and fountains. For an expatriate she felt extraordinarily at home in the French capital. Isadora Duncan, whom she had seen years earlier dancing at one of the Newport villas, was in her heyday and was popular in the American colony. Mrs. Wharton admired her unique style of dancing. She had become friendly with the Bernard Berensons after being introduced to them by Henry Adams in 1910, at a time when her husband's mental condition was deteriorating rapidly. She gave up their Massachusetts home, The Mount, because he did not like it, but by 1913 they were divorced.

In her later years Mrs. Wharton was in the habit of making an annual pilgrimage to I Tatti. Berenson had great respect for her artistic judgment, and he made more fuss about her than he did about any of his other guests, but he found her demanding, as did Mabel Dodge. Nicky Mariano, who presided at I Tatti after Mrs. Berenson's breakdown, disliked Mrs. Wharton at first and found her trying, but came to admire her. She commented on her fine eyes, good voice, and engaging laughter, but she found her movements nervous and jerky. She managed to make Nicky feel like a total outsider on her own ground, but Nicky watched her with respect when she read aloud to Berenson during quiet evenings in the library of I Tatti. "The curious thing about her is that she seems almost provincial in her awkwardness," Nicky wrote to Mary Berenson from Rome on May 21, 1932. This was an odd estimate of the cosmopolitan Mrs. Wharton, but she affected her own countrywoman, Mabel Dodge, in much the same way. Mabel commented on her "comic little provincialisms and 'Junkerisms.'" Consuelo Vanderbilt, who had gone to school with her in New York and had disliked her then, decided that she was prim as an old maid in her later years in spite of the "cosmopolitan, rather Bohemian, life she affected." She noticed that Mrs. Wharton took infinite pains with her dress, wearing a veil that "kept every hair in place."

In Nicky's opinion, Mrs. Wharton treated Berenson as if she were a "somewhat older, loving and pedagogical sister." His inviolable afternoon naps seemed a waste of time to her, robbing him of the best hours of the day. Like many of her other friends, he deplored her passion for picnics and outdoor expeditions. They were all inclined to duck the rituals on which she insisted, but she was considerate of her servants and thought that picnics made life easier for them.

When her yacht put in at Naples in 1926, she invited the Berenson party on board, and that same autumn she and Walter Berry, back from the lakes, joined them at Aosta. Edith was her most coquettish self on this occasion, done up in frivolous tea gowns and lace caps, her bed swamped with papers and books, her Pekingese dog asleep at her feet. All who visited her were required to show proper respect for gardens, one of her major interests, and for dogs.

She loved them all, and particularly the lapdog breed that became popular in the 1920s.

Berry, long an exile from his native land, died of a stroke in the spring of 1927, and Berenson asked Mrs. Wharton to spend the following Christmas with him at I Tatti, but instead she invited him to the Château-Sainte-Claire, her villa at Hyères. From then on it was his custom to spend each Christmas on the Riviera with Mrs. Wharton. Some of her other old friends would always be there, and she could count on Gaillard Lapsley, the American don at Trinity College, Cambridge, and Robert Norton, artist and poet. Percy Lubbock had deserted the old group to marry Lady Sybil Cutting after her divorce from Geoffrey Scott, who had been Berenson's secretary.

Mrs. Wharton was one of the great expatriate hostesses, presiding with feminine grace in elaborate gowns, and making a high ritual of dinner. The gastronomic whims of all her guests were considered. Her cuisine was of the best, but substitute foods were offered to the many faddists among her brilliant friends. When visiting other houses she liked to know who her fellow guests would be, and would turn down an invitation without hesitation if anyone of whom she disapproved chanced to be on the list. Mrs. Wharton was a knowing snob. She was intensely averse to avant-garde artists and writers, and had a strong sense of convention, although she could be damning in depicting it.

The Pavillon Colombe, her summer house near Paris, was choice in its eighteenth-century proportions. It had been the *nid d'amour* of Mademoiselle Marie Catherine Colombe, the eighteenth-century actress, but it did not charm Mrs. Wharton's guests like her villa at Hyères, with the sea, the sun, and the blue sweep of the Mediterranean. She liked to curl up by the fire in her frilly tea gowns and read with beautiful diction, or discuss the plot of something she was writing. Henry James, always intensely critical in spirit, affected her prose to some extent, but did not shake her convictions about the need for lucidity. She preferred reading the work of others to anything done by herself. The presence of outsiders made her manner stiff and forbidding. She would not surrender to oncoming age, and would tire herself out and become pettish and fussy trying to do too much rushing about. She died on August 11, 1937, at the Pavillon Colombe, and was buried close to Berry's grave in the Cimetière des Gonards at Versailles.

When Berenson learned of her death, he wrote to Nicky, "So poor Edith is dead and I feel dumb and numb and as if my bodily temperature had lowered to the freezing point." Her tantrums and caprices were forgotten at I Tatti. The good and delightful memories blossomed there. She was one expatriate who was remembered wherever she had been, and one whose fame grew in the decades after her death, although she was part of a world that was almost wholly dead by the 1970s.

The Henry James circle, of which she was so shining a part, included many of the prominent figures in American letters who came and went in the late nineteenth and early twentieth centuries. Most notable was William Dean Howells, a brilliant young man from Ohio who had written a campaign biography of Abraham Lincoln and who then landed the consulship in Venice for the years of the Civil War, 1861–1865. These posts in Italy usually went to artists of one kind or another, just as writers were more likely to be chosen for Britain and France.

Howells was already known to the American literati, and he had a distinguished career ahead of him in the world of letters. He was particularly respected in Boston and his native state, Ohio, when the post in Venice was offered to him. At first he was scathing and critical in his view of things European, deploring monarchical rule and many of the social customs he observed, but his years in Venice mellowed his viewpoint and he was a happy exile there, writing, enjoying leisurely hours in Saint Mark's Square, paying due reverence to the classical masters, but concerning himself more with the simple people. He left his own memorial in *Venetian Life and Italian Journeys,* the first realistic picture in American letters of the man in the street rather than the grandees and their art. He sought material among the fishermen and street vendors, the ragamuffins and glass blowers, the chimney sweeps and flower sellers. He had read all too much about the bridges and gondolas, the palazzos and canals, and he refused to romanticize this most romantic of cities.

The consular duties at Venice were few, and left him plenty of time to keep the diary that grew into a full-scale book. There were, however, matters of commerce to straighten out in a seaport town, and he had to keep a sharp eye for Confederate privateers. He was besieged by insistent mothers with marriageable daughters who presumably were studying music or art, and earnest-minded spinsters following the route marked by Ruskin, whom he disliked as much as he did Byron and Bernini. In fact he deplored the baroque in any shape or form. American widows came like homing pigeons to Venice, and Howells and his wife, living in a palace on the Grand Canal, came to know the expatriate in all his guises. Whenever he could, Howells mingled with the ordinary people in the back streets. From his windows he was constantly aware of the moving pageant along the Grand Canal, but he also heard the marching feet on the squares. He was a reporter and a realist, and his work was admired by his fellow authors.

Howells made so many trips to Europe and stayed for such long periods that he had expatriate status, but he always reacted in a lively way to anything concerning his native country. He was less enchanted with Spain than Washington Irving, and thought it a "wild, beautiful, ugly land." Berlin was a "fast, spiritless place," and Paris was the "most fascinating city in the world." In London he was shepherded around by Henry James, and he viewed it with considerable esteem.

"For forty years his English has been to me a continual delight and astonishment," said Mark Twain of Howells. But although the Ohioan knew how to debunk the romantic image, Twain was a past master at this process. His first appearance in Europe in 1867 was the opening gun in a major deflation of the travel legend, and of the American abroad. Conventional travel books grew dim when *The Innocents Abroad* came out, and thirty thousand copies were sold within six months. Bret Harte noted that "Mr. Mark Twain has used brickbats on stained-glass windows with damaging effect." Picture galleries and churches bored him, and he considered the vaunted civilization of Europe a "mere superstition." Italy was a "vast museum of magnificence and misery," and Venice seemed like a "half-submerged Arkansas town in a spring freshet." His good-natured and broad wit amused more than it hurt, and he became a popular figure in London, attending the court functions he ridiculed, and exchanging notes with a fellow realist and merry gentleman of the world, Sir Thomas Lipton, the tea magnate.

For all his skepticism, Mark Twain nevertheless succumbed to the charm of Italy in time, and the days passed like magic as he finished *Pudd'nhead Wilson* and worked on *Joan of Arc* in the Villa Viviani at Settignano. The view from his terrace overlooking Florence seemed "the most enchanting . . . picture on our planet." At times the city lost substance and became "just a faint soft dream, with domes and towers of air."

A trip to the Sandwich Islands in 1866 had started Mark Twain on his course as a traveler, popular lecturer, and entertainer. Thirty years later he took a trip around the world to pay off debts incurred when his publishing house failed. His native humor had penetrated to the far corners of the earth and had made the expatriate more understandable to the peoples of other countries.

Henry James was at Siena in the early 1890s when Mark Twain was busy on his terrace above Florence. James was visiting the Bourgets, who were living there at the time, and they all had a chance to view the Palio, a historic horse race in Siena. This time he also visited F. Marion Crawford at his magnificent villa overhanging the cliffs at Sorrento with its dramatic view of Capri and Salerno. Although James had no respect for Crawford's vast output of best-selling novels, he and Crawford were friends and moved in the same circles. None of the other expatriates knew Italy as Crawford did.

He was the son of Thomas Crawford, who had settled in Rome in 1834 and was regarded as the most important of the American sculptors. Thomas studied with the Dane Thorvaldsen, and his statues of Washington and Jefferson, his pediment of the Capitol in Washington, the bronze doors, and the "Armed Freedom" on top of the dome made him famous in his day. He had an army of marble cutters working in twelve studios among the ruins of the Baths of Diocletian during the 1840s and 1850s. Crawford married a banker's daughter from New York, and Marion was only four when his father died, but years later he recognized himself as one of the children on the bronze doors of the Capitol, which Crawford did not live to finish (the work was completed by William Henry Rinehart, a Baltimore sculptor).

The Crawfords lived in great style in the Villa Negroni as the tenants of Prince Massimo d'Azeglio, who was quartered below them. The children were told that they were looking out on the spot where Nero fiddled while Rome burned, but now Prince Massimo's vegetable garden covered this area, and by the 1930s it would all have been swallowed up by Mussolini's new railway station.

The Sargents and the Crawfords were close friends, and their children all played together, with young John Singer Sargent usually bottled up in a tight pepper-and-salt Eton jacket and round hat. In summer both families rode on donkeys to Lake Nemi and visited Roman families in their castles. After her husband's death Mrs. Crawford married Luther Terry, the painter, and Marion soon had a half-sister, Daisy Terry, who grew up to be the popular Mrs. Winthrop Chanler, author of *Roman Spring*. The Terrys lived in the Odescalchi Palace, and the children were entertained by such visitors as Edward Lear, who sang *The Owl and the Pussycat* to them.

As a youth Marion walked all over Italy with his tutor. He knew the wildest spots in Calabria and spent weeks in the Abruzzi mountains one year, working with the peasants in the vineyards and riding the loneliest mountain paths. A keen observer of the peasantry, he also knew both the papal and the princely nobility of Italy, and in time he became a Catholic convert. He was a prodigious worker, and all over Europe readers waited for the Crawford books, which were also serialized in American magazines. It did not worry him that James considered his works mere pot boilers. He knew where his audience lay, and it was huge.

Crawford had studied at Harvard, at Cambridge University, at Karlsruhe, and in Rome. He knew seventeen languages, including Sanskrit. He edited a paper in Allahabad for a time and was quite at ease in any part of the world, but Italy was his natural home. Crawford was a true expatriate, although his aunt, Julia Ward Howe, tried to make an American of him from time to time. He was ascetic in his own tastes, although his place at Sorrento had the trappings of an Arabian Nights' dream, and Mrs. Gardner, Henry James, and other visiting Americans enjoyed his sybaritic entertainments. His villa had spacious courts, a Moorish fountain, and a dramatic terrace overlooking the sea. A stone stairway led to a pier where he kept a schooner substantial enough to sail the Atlantic. His boatmen were elaborately costumed, like the rest of his staff, and the villagers, with violins, flutes, and guitars, played for his guests on the terrace after dinner. He had a passion for cruising and often went across to Capri, with gourmet fare on his ship for the inevitable picnics. Norman Douglas was struck by his intelligence and his militant Catholicism when Crawford took him on a cruise, stopping at Corsica, Elba, and other Tyrrhenian islands.

Crawford's parties were Oriental in their opulence. Statues done by his father shimmered in the garden under the play of Bengal lights. Great tents were covered with Oriental silks. His staff was picturesquely costumed. Early the next morning, however, Crawford would be hard at work in one of the caves that honeycombed his cliffs—a quiet spot for concentration. "A magnificent giant who lived up to his magnificence," said Joseph Pennell of Crawford.

It was almost forgotten at times that he was an American, so far had he traveled from his native inheritance, but his books sold as well in the United States as they did in Europe. At times he tired of his craft, and after writing six novels in fourteen months he told Mrs. Gardner that he must decide between selling his soul to meet the serial requirements and settling for the austere life of the true artist. He chose the mundane course, but he was not a happy man.

Neither was Bret Harte, another expatriate whose vivid stories of Western life were regional writing, and who lived abroad for years. Like a good many other authors he held consular posts, serving first in Germany and then in Scotland. The last seventeen years of his life were spent in England, and he died there, like Stephen Crane, an exile whose life burned out from tuberculosis at the end of a hectic stay in Europe.

Crane's expatriate years were brief and highly charged, like everything else in his life. They were spent close to two of his idols, Henry James and Joseph Conrad, who visited him often at Brede Manor, the fourteenth-century mansion he had rented in Surrey for next to nothing. It looked as if it were haunted by bats and owls, and was rotted with mildew and moths. Furniture was sparsely scattered through ten vast rooms, and Mexican blankets hung decoratively on the walls. Crane rolled dice in the manorial hall, wearing cowboy trousers and a gray flannel shirt. He wrote like fury in this environment to meet his debts. After one New Year's house party he hemorrhaged badly. Nevertheless, his guests danced on until dawn, and breakfasted on gammon and beer, scarcely aware how ill their host was.

Crane soon died in a sanitarium in the Black Forest. He was only twenty-eight, but in one fiercely productive decade—in the 1890s —he had electrified the literary world with *The Red Badge of Courage,* a realistic approach to the much romanticized Civil War. Ford Madox Ford wrote of it, "One awakened one morning in the nineties in England and *The Red Badge of Courage* was out; by noon of the same day it filled the universe. There was nothing you could talk of but that book." Half a century later Hemingway viewed it as the truest of the "how it was" books. Crane set the pattern for the tough, debunking war books of the 1940s, 1950s, and 1960s. He lived by Emerson's dictum: "Congratulate yourselves if you have done something strange and extravagant and broken the monotony of a decorous age." Conrad thought that Stephen's temperament "made old things new and new things amazing."

Crane was a Methodist minister's son who became a well-known war correspondent and adventurer in the closing days of the century. He covered the Greco-Turkish and Spanish-American wars, setting a precedent for the journalist authors of today, who divide their time between America and other countries. Lincoln Steffens, George Kennan (uncle of the diplomat with the same name), and other militant correspondents were coming into view at the time, a pattern that continued without a break through World War I and in the years that followed. To H. L. Mencken, Stephen Crane was the man with whom twentieth-century American letters began.

The Changing Arts

Long before the expatriates of the 1920s settled on the Left Bank, Gertrude Stein and her brother Leo from Allegheny, Pennsylvania, were conspicuous Americans abroad, surrounded by the surrealist artists as well as by writers. Like Ezra Pound, a close friend, Gertrude was one of the early exiles of the twentieth century and had been living abroad since 1902. Her *Three Lives* came out in 1908, and she was well ahead of the writers who swept into view after World War I, but her fame grew during the 1920s.

Miss Stein had considerable influence with young artists and writers, and the Stein ménage at 27 Rue de Fleurus was a museum of modern art. With the work of Cézanne, Matisse, Picasso, Renoir, Monet, Gauguin, and Toulouse-Lautrec hung in their atelier, the Steins were important figures in the life of Paris. Leo was the original collector, buying their paintings for a song, but he and Gertrude soon quarreled about the relative merits of their finds. Leo turned cold to his former idols, Matisse and Cézanne, and considered Picasso's cubism "an utter abomination." Gertrude's name, however, became firmly associated with the development of Picasso's work.

Visitors of all nationalities flocked to the Stein studio early in the century to study the strange new pictures. Some scoffed; others went away impressed and conscious of a new movement in art. The artists themselves became the great attraction at these Saturday evening gatherings. Picasso was often there with his mistress, Férnande Olivier. Matisse, spectacled and with a reddish beard, would engage in long discussions with Leo, and tall Georges Braque would hang and adjust the pictures. Guillaume Apollinaire would be there with his painter friend, Marie Laurencin. Alfred Maurer, an American among the Frenchmen, would hold up sputtering matches to show off Cézanne's work. He and Patrick Henry Bruce were two Americans convinced from the start that the cubists were the new breed to follow. It soon meant réclame to have Gertrude Stein buy and display one's work. She could interest such other rich Americans as Mabel Dodge Luhan in the work of these men. Her own taste, however, was erratic, and her friendship with Matisse, whom she had called *cher maître,* chilled as she became more committed to the work of Picasso.

When she described Madame Matisse in *The Autobiography of Alice B. Toklas* as having a "long face and a firm large loosely hung mouth like a horse," Matisse was furious, and he and several other artists offered a "Testimony Against Gertrude Stein" in *Transition.* They gave Michael Stein, Gertrude's older brother, credit for having been the first American collector of Matisse's work. Miss Stein's association with Picasso began around 1905, and she crossed Paris each day to pose for him at his studio on the Rue Ravignan. His mistress, Férnande, read aloud the *Fables of La Fontaine* during the sittings, which in the end numbered eighty or more. Picasso found Gertrude a difficult subject, and he went off to Spain leaving her portrait unfinished. On his return he brushed in the features without seeing her again. The result was the masklike Picasso of Gertrude now in the Metropolitan Museum of Art. It marked his transition from the Rose Period to cubism. Gertrude's comment on it, in her book *Picasso,* published just before World War II, was, "For me, it is I, and it is the only reproduction of me which is always I, for me."

Jo Davidson and Jacques Lipchitz did busts of her, but although she was well known to the prewar artists, her association with American writers living in Paris did not develop noticeably until the 1920s. At this time she became the patron saint of some, serving them choice pastries and fine liqueurs when their funds were low and hectoring or praising them, according to her mood. Most of her visitors disliked the formidable Alice B. Toklas, who cooked divinely, ran the Stein household, and was a hostile watchdog for the Stein interests.

Gertrude was a massive figure, usually garbed in brown corduroy.

Her hair was brushed crisply back from her deeply furrowed face. She wore sandals with turned-up toes and decked herself at times with incongruous mosaic brooches. Like some of her more eccentric contemporaries Gertrude dabbled in the psychic and had picked up some medical knowledge at Johns Hopkins University. Her manner was hearty, and when amused, she roared with laughter. She could also shout in anger. She ate huge steaks, was full of vitality, and showed insatiable interest in people with talent. Janet Flanner of *The New Yorker,* an expatriate of her generation, who was still writing in 1969, noted when Gertrude died in 1946, "she pulled her pictures from the stem, in the ateliers where they grew four decades ago." And *The Nation* commented editorally, "The world will be a duller place without her; her sins harmed no one; at this moment she is sitting in the Elysian fields talking to Samuel Johnson, the only man who could ever be her match."

Her companion and alter ego, Miss Toklas, was slim, dark, and melancholy in appearance. She favored Javanese prints and barbaric jewelry. Heavy Oriental earrings swung almost to her shoulders, and she spent hours polishing her nails.

The ways of this strange household were closely observed by the expatriate writers, and for a time Hemingway was a favorite guest, but in the end he could not endure Miss Stein. In the early days of their association they took long walks together discussing his writing problems, and she liked to think that she was his mentor. He was never out of touch with her and seemed eager for her advice and approval. Gertrude thought him extraordinarily good-looking and a "good listener," which was something she demanded in her favorites. When he first visited her he liked to walk up to her flat through the Jardin du Luxembourg. Leo by this time had gone off to live in Florence, and Hemingway found his two hostesses offering him choice and bountiful fare. He commented on the liqueurs distilled from purple plums and wild raspberries, and served from cut-glass carafes—a change from his squalid apartment, with no furniture but a mattress on the floor and a baby carriage for his son, John Hadley Hemingway, commonly known as Bumby. The whine of the sawmill in the courtyard below was a constant obbligato to his work, and the floating sawdust clouded the air.

Although Hemingway disliked Gertrude's clothes and general getup intensely, he was won by her conversation. It amazed him, however, that she was so consistently critical of the writers in their set. In the three or four years that he saw her, he could not remember hearing her speak well of any writer who had not applauded her own work except Ronald Firbank, Scott Fitzgerald, and Sherwood

Anderson, to whom she was devoted. She thought that no one else in America could write such clear and passionate sentences. Hemingway remained cold to Anderson, however, an attitude that Gertrude did not approve. She liked Anderson's nature even better than his prose.

She was particularly hostile to Joyce and seemed to be jealous of his influence with the young American writers. It entertained her to talk to Hemingway about the "lost generation," her own phrase for the bright young men drowning their talents in drink. The irascible Robert McAlmon got on well with her. Both were Trollope fans. Both liked autobiography and biography, but it soon was apparent to McAlmon that Miss Stein was interested only in people who sat before her and listened. She was dogmatic and would not brook opposition or even a contrary opinion from anyone. She conducted a monologue and pontificated, reiterated, and stammered in her conversation as in her writing. But McAlmon thought her "more human and a better specimen" than Amy Lowell, although he considered both "doubting and spoiled rich children."

She and Hemingway drifted apart through the middle years of the twenties. She bore no animosity but deplored his growing obsession with sex and violent death. Although she had spent many hours with him discussing bullfighting, a subject in which she was interested, too, she thought that he went too far in his preoccupation with violence and that it impaired his talent. To Gertrude Stein Hemingway's work declined after he was twenty-five and was never again as good as his early short stories. She liked to think that she had had some influence on his work, and a year after he met her, before disillusionment had set in, he observed, "It was a vital day for me when I stumbled upon you."

Gertrude Stein had independent means, which enabled her to play the role of patron. Ezra Pound could handle her better than most, and after he moved from London to Paris in 1921 and settled on the Rue Notre-Dame-Des-Champs near the Luxembourg Gardens, he would come tearing into her atelier—his long hair flying, his reddish beard jutting from his chin, his shirt wide open at the neck—and plump down on one of her fragile chairs. Her own seat had thronelike proportions, and she occupied it like a Buddha or, as one of her expatriate friends observed, like a Roman emperor. Gertrude liked Pound's propensity for organizing groups—he had been involved with the imagists and the vorticists, and it was natural that he should turn with enthusiasm to the Dadaists. Gertrude valued his wide acquaintance with the poets and authors of Britain.

He was ubiquitous in the haunts of the expatriates, but one of his own favorite restaurants was named Émile's.

When André Breton pushed the Dadaist cause in the early twenties, some of the expatriates were convinced that it expressed the spirit of the period. Its manifesto had been written in 1918 in Switzerland by Tristan Tzara, a Romanian who had given the movement life at the Cabaret Voltaire in Zurich two years earlier. Malcolm Cowley wrote of it, "I began to feel that the Dada movement was the very essence of Paris. It existed on a level far below Joyce's ambition and Valéry's high researches into the metaphysics of self, but at least it was young and adventurous and human." By 1924 it had succumbed to the inroads made by surrealism. Some of the American artists were wholly skeptical about this break with tradition. Thomas Hart Benton, who had studied at the Académie Julien from 1908 to 1911 and had served as a private in World War I, turned his back on the new abstract trends and went home to do his sturdily native paintings of people and life in the West. Grant Wood made a similiar choice and found another way to fame in the native idiom.

Musicians gathered around Gertrude Stein, too. Virgil Thomson, who had been music critic of the New York *Herald Tribune,* wrote the music for her *Four Saints in Three Acts,* and George Gershwin's *American in Paris,* a hit in 1928, was a salute to the period. George Antheil battered away at his strange instruments over Sylvia Beach's bookshop before his *Ballet Méchanique* made a sensation at the Théâtre des Champs Elysées, to be presented later with less éclat and applause at Carnegie Hall in New York. Its discordant, deafening quality made it one of the most discussed productions of the period, but not the best loved, except among George's friends on the Left Bank, notably Ezra Pound.

Gertrude drove around Paris in a high, antiquated car, and she was unmistakable wherever she went. Mabel Dodge Luhan preferred seeing her in her Paris setting to having her descend on the Villa Curonia from Fiesole as she did on one occasion, with dusty feet and clammy attire. Miss Stein had walked under the steaming Tuscan midday sun in a heavy brown corduroy kimono and was a troublesome and demanding guest. Mabel, a lion hunter herself, could count on meeting celebrities at the Stein ménage in Paris. Both women would sometimes show up at Janet Scudder's studio in the Latin Quarter, where they were likely to run into the peering, dogmatic English art critic, Roger Fry. Miss Scudder was from Terre Haute, Indiana, and was "one of the wayfarers from the sticks" whom Mabel Dodge Luhan thought Fry liked to patronize. Mabel felt that he wished to blend her friends on the Left Bank with rich Mary Shillito from Cincinnati, who, unlike Miss Stein, had a Gainsborough, a Filippo Lippi, a Rembrandt, and an exquisite Memling set up on an easel in her substantial home on the Avenue du Bois. Fry was scornful, deeming them fakes.

A stern critic of the drinking on the Left Bank was Isadora Duncan's brother Raymond, whose colony at Neuilly and shops on the Rue Saint Honoré and the Boulevard Saint-Germain were part of the expatriate life of the period. He expected his American guests to get drunk on joy when he served his own brand of punch, spiked with spices and fruits. When a party of forty sneaked in their own gin and brandy, hiding it under the hall table, he thought they were intoxicated from his punch. Before he became a Spartan, living chiefly on nuts and fruits, Raymond liked to drop in at Gertrude's place to enjoy her pastries. It always surprised her that he should have changed so much, and she recalled the time, as she studied him in his toga, tunic, and sandals, when he was worldly and a dandy, with the crease in his trousers impeccable, and his hair, now pinned in gray braids like a crown around his small head, brushed with military precision. In those days he had worn a carnation in his buttonhole, drunk sherry, and smoked big black cigars.

But on Duncan's return from his lofty mission to Greece, where he had worked with the inspired Isadora to build a temple to the dance, his hands were rocklike from all the stones he had carried and the manual work he had done. The temple was never finished; it remained one of the empty dreams of the 1920s. Raymond's speech suggested the Middle West, although the Duncans came from California and had once been neighbors there of Gertrude Stein. The four Duncan children—Isadora, Augustin, Raymond, and Elizabeth—went their separate ways in Paris, and Augustin soon returned to America. They were of considerable interest to their fellow expatriates, and Raymond's colony at Neuilly, with its goats shepherded through the byways of Paris, was much discussed. When the goats' bells rang, the French children came out with wooden bowls for fresh milk drawn for them by a goatherd.

Isadora was a true expatriate who had cut herself off completely from her native country and rarely returned to the United States, even to give dance recitals. She went first to London in 1897 to take dancing lessons with Ketti Lanner, and three years later she migrated with her mother, her two brothers, and her sister to England. In the years that followed she won her way in Paris, London,

Berlin, Vienna, Budapest, Moscow, Athens, and briefly in New York. She knew the raptures of great ovations and the chill contempt of those who thought that she posed but did not dance.

Her personal life was as fascinating as her art, for the two were indistinguishable. There were no half-measures in her life, and her love affairs were notorious. She had a genius for causing trouble, to such a degree that even the members of her own family were discouraged. Isadora lived a vagabond life when she was not wrapped in luxury, but her great tragedy was the drowning in 1913 of her two children, Patrick and Deirdre, when the car in which they were riding plunged into the Seine.

While the war raged in France and Belgium, Isadora moved her students from Germany and England to the United States. For a time she had a dance studio in New York, and Otto Kahn leased the Century Theater for her for a season. She was back in Paris in 1916, again the expatriate, and her audience went wild over her interpretation of the "Marseillaise." She repeated this dance at the Metropolitan Opera House when she returned to New York, but the patriotic note faded from her life as she became more and more committed to the thinking of the Russian revolutionaries. She danced in the Bolshoi Theater on the fourth anniversary of the Bolshevik Revolution, and by that time she had fallen in love with Sergei Esenin, a tall young poet with deep-set blue eyes and a mop of flaxen curls. He was the peasant poet laureate of the new republic, but he was also an epileptic subject to fits of madness, and their life together was stormy. They shocked Boston with their display of the Red flag and Isadora's partial disrobing as she danced. She gave her last performance at Carnegie Hall in 1923, and she never returned to the United States after that, but she became a familiar figure in the cafés of Paris.

The scenes with Esenin in Paris, Venice, and Leningrad were notorious, and he hanged himself in 1925. Newspaper correspondents felt sorry for the beautiful Isadora as they watched her rapid decline, but some grew tired of humoring her. Floyd Gibbons, the Chicago newspaperman who wore a white patch over one eye because of a war injury, staged a noisy brawl with her in the Sélect. The gendarmerie were called in to restore order. The Isadorables, a group of her most gifted students, continued to spread Isadora's fame and keep her name alive as they danced on both sides of the Atlantic. Elizabeth ran her dancing school in Potsdam but the star herself was reduced to scrounging a meal or a drink when she could from traveling Americans. She gave her last recital at the Théâtre Mogador in

1927 and went to work on her autobiography. Shortly before her death in that same year she gave three summer programs in Nice —two with Cocteau, who accompanied her dancing with his spoken verse. She held a taper for hours outside the United States Embassy on the night that Sacco and Vanzetti died, having shared in the demonstrations of the protesters earlier. She died as she had lived—dramatically. Starting out on a trial spin of a new car in Nice, she flung a brightly embroidered scarf around her neck. It was two yards long, and the heavy fringe caught in the rear wheel of the low, two-seated racing car. As the car started her neck was broken.

Her body lay in state in Raymond's studio, and the purple cape she had worn when dancing Chopin's "Funeral March" and Liszt's "Les Funerailles" was spread across her coffin. Paris was full of American soldiers, for American Legion Day was being celebrated with a great parade. The American residents were out in force, and the Stars and Stripes floated everywhere. In the end Raymond draped his sister's coffin with the American flag. More than ten thousand persons gathered for her funeral, and among them were the artists and writers, American and French, who had believed in Isadora, the artist, the creator, the innovator, a revolutionary force in the arts. Yvette Guilbert spoke for the artists of Paris when she wrote her farewell to Isadora: "Genius of flesh and of blood, human superhuman, may Olympus greet you." In America *The New Yorker* had noted before her death that Isadora Duncan had come "like a figure from the Elgin marbles . . . the first artist to appear uncinctured, barefooted and free . . . she has danced before Kings and Peasants. She has danced from the Pacific to London, from Petrograd to the Black Sea, from Athens to Paris and Berlin."

She was only forty-nine when she died. Her life had been packed with drama, triumph, and more often despair. Much of the heartbreak and occasional exaltation of the confirmed expatriate were Isadora's as she turned in bitterness from her native land. Although she had been a destructive force to herself and to others, she had influenced the dance tradition of her generation, and her personality was as deeply impressed on the public as her art.

The Left Bank was a natural setting for her, and even in the midst of surrounding revelry she shut herself up and worked with all the intensity of her high-powered nature. During her early days in Paris she developed her theory that the solar plexus was the seat of power in dancing instead of the base of the spine. Her conception was revolutionary in its way, and she made it the central principle of her school of dancing. For a time she joined forces with Loie

Fuller, the American girl who had developed the serpentine dance, with shimmering effects of moths and flames. They made a strange combination, with Isadora's strong individual style that took no heed of an ensemble effect. She was at odds also with the classical effect of the Russian ballet at a time when the Bolshoi Ballet was sweeping Europe and the United States.

The cultists were in high gear all through the 1920s, and Georges Gurdjieff was the pet guru of the period. Expatriates instinctively gravitated to movements of all kinds, and he offered nepenthe by incantation. The delicate Katherine Mansfield, deeply committed to the Gurdjieff philosophy, brought other writers to his Institute for the Harmonious Development of Man. Already in the last stages of tuberculosis, Miss Mansfield died there, but not before a number of American writers had explored the wonders offered by Gurdjieff in the woods of Fontainebleau. His votaries built houses in the forest. They chopped wood. They lived on bread and soup, and had some of the community spirit of Brook Farm and other nineteenth-century communal colonies in the United States.

Gurdjieff taught that man has four distinct personalities: the automatic functioning; natural heredity; heredity and circumstances during his preparatory formation; and the being, himself, when all his qualities are fully developed. "All the separate beings must harmonize," he said, as he led his votaries through rhythmical exercises. "All other people are simply automatons, machines or mechanical toys set in motion by external forces."

Isadora inevitably sought the new sensations provided at the guru's school of philosophy. Other American expatriates, like Jane Heap and Margaret Anderson, who edited the *Little Review,* became involved. Like Raymond Duncan, Gurdjieff wore turbans and sandals as he drew in disciples of many nationalities, all repeating numbers and words in their own languages, like incantations. While a pianist played, the pupils sat in the circle repeating certain words until they were hypnotized and swayed as they spoke. Gurdjieff had been a hypnotist in the East before he appeared suddenly in Paris. The more cynical among the expatriates observed that the incantations seemed to be helped along by the bottles of armagnac placed in the center of the circle, and systematically emptied by the swaying circle. When McAlmon, over a drink of Pernod, asked the guru who paid for the armagnac, he was told that "the spirit provides."

But Gurdjieff had a genius for attracting people of wealth. He was identified with Piotr Uspenski, the Russian writer and mystic known as Ouspensky, when he established a colony near Nyack, New York. The history of both men was obscure, but they flour-

ished in the way that some of the gurus do today. When Gurdjieff
was persuaded to visit America in the 1920s by some of the well-to-
do tourists passing through Paris, he continued his incantations and
exercises at a fashionable New York hotel. However, he excited less
interest than bustling little Émile Coué, the Troyes pharmacist who
practiced hypnotism and autosuggestion by his own system of psy-
chotherapy, known as Couéism. Not only the expatriates, but Americans at home, were soon repeating, "Every day in every way I'm getting better and better." Coué's visit to America was a great success,
but he died in 1926, and his incantations, like those of Gurdjieff,
were lost in the days of the Depression. World War II, the rise of
new philosophies, the rebirth of the old interest in extrasensory perception, and gurus like Maharishi stirred up the same sort of interest in the 1960s that had surrounded the earlier mystics. Repeatedly
in history American expatriates have been drawn to the mystical,
the exotic, the far-out movements of the time, always in quest of
stimulants to satisfy the fierce creative spirit that burned within
them. Some sought this release on the Left Bank, much as Americans had flocked earlier to the hydrotherapy establishment run by
Dr. Vincenz Priessnitz at Gräfenberg in the Silesian woods during
the 1840s. His cold-water cure, nude bathing, beds of straw, and a
simple diet of brown bread, butter, and milk drew some of the most
fashionable Americans, as well as a number of the permanent expatriates. Dr. Elizabeth Blackwell, who took treatments there in the
mid-nineteenth century, was struck by the number of her countrywomen who blazed with diamonds and fashionable gowns at dinner
time, but otherwise seemed to live in a manger while undergoing
the cure.

Hydrotherapy, like mesmerism, hypnotism, automatic writing,
and spiritualism, fed the expatriate discontent, filled up empty
hours, and promised more positive living. The spas, beloved by all
expatriates, toned up their bodies, and Priessnitz and those who followed him offered women some of the benefits they get today at the
health clinics in Switzerland, or in America at such beauty centers as
Maine Chance and at the reducing farms.

The desire for freedom, self-expression, and fulfillment that had
started many of the expatriates on their quest abroad made them
easy victims for quackery of all kinds. It soothed them as the days
slipped by without achievement of any kind, when the lotus spirit
gradually eroded the hard core of ambition common to the American heritage. The expatriates of the 1920s opened the door to an
easier way of life and escape from drudgery. The sons of the men

who had worked strenuously in the nineteenth century to build up their fortunes fell with ease into the seductive pattern of following the sun, finding the idyllic escape spots, indulging in the sports of the hour. The expatriate spirit so highly developed during this period marked a decisive break in the sturdy American way of life.

Among the most enduring of the expatriates linked to the changing arts is Peggy Guggenheim, who flourished on the Left Bank in the 1920s, became an art collector in the 1930s, and in 1969, at the age of seventy, dazzled art lovers in New York with her collection of modern paintings and sculpture brought from her eighteenth-century palazzo in Venice to the Guggenheim Museum on Fifth Avenue. Peggy was an international character long before she was a collector. Her loves, her marriages, her pranks, were legendary on the Left Bank and in London. As the wife first of Laurence Vail, painter and writer, and then of Max Ernst, the refugee artist whom she helped to bring to America, she had plenty of exposure to the arts and had traveled in Italy studying Renaissance art with books by Berenson to guide her. Until 1938, however, she did not give thought to any school beyond the Impressionists.

In a moment of boredom in London, between her two marriages, Miss Guggenheim decided to open an art gallery. She called it Guggenheim Jeune, and she exhibited the work of Brancusi, Arp, Kandinsky, Yves Tanguy, and other surrealists. Although it closed within a year and a half, her interest in these men and their work had been keenly developed, and when she came home in 1942, as World War II raged, she opened a much discussed gallery in New York called Art of This Century. Here she launched Jackson Pollock, Robert Motherwell, and William Baziotes. Pollock was a carpenter who worked at her uncle's museum, then on East Fifty-fourth Street. She concentrated on his progress with all the intensity of her nature, and watched his explosive brushwork with some degree of awe, but without any conception of the prices his work would fetch in the future.

After the war, divorced from Ernst, she gave up this unique gallery and went back to Europe, where she had lived for twenty-one years. This time she established herself in the widest palazzo on the Grand Canal, with gardens and an art gallery. Here she held court and became one of the better known Americans abroad. In Italy the surrealists were almost unknown when Peggy gave them dazzling promotion. She felt that she had at last found official recognition when asked to show her entire collection at the twenty-fourth *biennale* in Venice in the 1950s. But true to form Peggy arrived at this ceremonious affair without hat, stockings, or gloves, and promptly covered her head with enormous marguerite blossoms and earrings made from Venetian glass beads.

From her earliest years Peggy was considered the *enfant terrible* of her family. She had had a severe blow when her father, Benjamin Guggenheim, went down with the *Titanic* before she was fourteen years old. While working near Grand Central Station in a bookshop run by her cousin Harold Loeb, she met Laurence Vail, and through him she was soon in Paris and an accepted member of the bohemian set on the Left Bank. Their marriage was stormy. Vail sometimes beat her, and in retrospect Peggy confessed, "I've been lucky with everything in life but love." Ernst left her for a woman artist whom she had discovered, and Peggy had earlier left Vail for an extended affair with an English writer named John Holms.

In the 1920s she wandered all over Europe, giving and attending parties, haunting the cafés, sharing in madcap pranks, circulating where that era's equivalent of Jet Setters convened. When she came to rest at last in Venice, she installed all modern comforts in her palazzo but kept the fourteenth-century atmosphere intact, except for her bed, which has a silver headboard designed by Alexander Calder. Everything about Peggy bespeaks her love of life and her zest for the unconventional. Her gondoliers wear turquoise, her palazzo color, and she shops by motorboat. Her museum is open to the public two days a week.

During World War II Léger tried to have her art collection preserved by the Louvre, but no interest was shown in Peggy Guggenheim or her paintings. She finally managed to get it into the United States, but it was some time before members of her family realized the value of her buying operations in the field of art. Full recognition did not come until her overwhelming reception in 1969, when more than a thousand art lovers and social celebrities assembled at the Guggenheim Museum to welcome and applaud her. Mildly subdued by the passing years, the effervescent Peggy, who had shocked and baffled her family and friends for a lifetime, was reaping the harvest of her hard and intelligent work on behalf of the unknown artist. The twentieth-century paintings and sculpture on display were hailed by some art critics as among the most distinguished of their kind in the world. Cubism, futurism, surrealism, abstract-expressionism, all were represented in the display of work by Picasso, Miró, Mondrian, Moore, Klee, Chagall, Braque, Calder, Giacometti, Kandinsky, Duchamp, Pollock, Léger, De Kooning, and many others.

When her treasures were taken back to Venice, Peggy followed them, with the knowledge that her collection will become part of the Solomon R. Guggenheim Museum when she dies. It will not be dispersed but will remain intact in the palazzo and will be known as the Peggy Guggenheim Collection. The Frank Lloyd Wright building on Fifth Avenue, which she once described as a "huge garage" with a rising ramp that "coils like an evil serpent," will have her paintings on exhibition except during the tourist season in Venice, when they are a great attraction there.

In her seventies when she opened her New York exhibition, Peggy Guggenheim was still brisk, animated, and dauntless in manner—a permanent expatriate taking another look at her native land and enriching it with treasures from abroad.

Life on the Left Bank

Genius has flowered repeatedly among American exiles. The late nineteenth century was rich in this respect, but the term *expatriate* took on a special meaning in the 1920s because of the number of gifted writers and artists settled in Paris during this decade. Individualistic though they were, they created a group effect, whereas historically the expatriates had been the isolated few, the men and women who had broken with convention or who had been driven by their own particularity to seek new environments.

When the scene shifted from Rome and Florence to Paris in the early twentieth century, the Left Bank became renowned for a remarkable surge of creative work that changed the world of letters in the course of a decade. New names that are part of the American heritage today came into view. Little magazines lighted small flames of creativity. Abstract art made inroads on the traditional standards of the past. Above all, Ernest Hemingway, F. Scott Fitzgerald, and a bright coterie of associates shook up the literary world, as both writers and personalities. Their influence and charisma were deeply felt for the next half century.

The era was well chronicled. Many of the expatriates worked intermittently for the Paris *Herald* and the Paris edition of the Chicago *Tribune*. These newspapermen were close to the new world taking shape and form on the Left Bank. It was an unquenchable harvest, nourished by World War I. Even before the United States entered the war, patriotic fervor spread across the campuses of Yale, Harvard, and Princeton. Young men signed up with the British and Canadian forces, with the Foreign Legion, the American Ambulance Service, and the Norton-Harjes ambulance corps, which caught young Ivy Leaguers even before they had graduated. Some, like Ernest Hemingway, drove ambulances on the Italian front, or served with the Red Cross or the Salvation Army. As Malcolm Cowley, one of their number, put it, "They found death among the flowers, danger in spring, the sweet wine of sentiment neither spiced with paradox nor yet insipid, the death of being real, the danger near at hand."

It was the era of Rupert Brooke, of youth's rendezvous with death, of the poppies of Flanders fields. By chance, men whose names soon would become household words in America drove ambulances or trucks in 1916 and 1917. Among them were Hemingway, John Dos Passos, Dashiell Hammett, E. E. Cummings, William Seabrook, Malcolm Cowley, Louis Bromfield, Robert Hillyer, Sidney Howard, Harry Crosby, Julien Green, and John Howard Lawson. Alexander Woollcott and Harold Ross, who would join forces in the establishment of *The New Yorker,* edited the *Stars and Stripes* after the United States entered the war. A young Ohioan named Joel Sayre, who would later become well known as an author and magazine writer, joined the lonely Canadian expedition to Siberia.

Many of the bright young men stayed on to become long- or short-term expatriates. Stephen Vincent Benét took classes at the Sorbonne and wrote *John Brown's Body* in Paris. Rosemary, his wife, worked for the Paris *Herald.* Dos Passos, moving restlessly across the map of Europe, sputtering political revolt, wrote *Three Soldiers,* one of the most acclaimed of the major war novels. It was drawn from his experiences as an ambulance driver. But in course of time the eager, voluble Dos Passos moved to the right, as his colleagues, made cynical by the bitter fruits of war and the political negotiations that followed, veered to the left in a sharp parting of the ways. Thornton Wilder, a quiet man who did not flaunt his gifts, divided his time between France and Italy and maintained the expatriate tradition into the 1960s. Another survivor of the ambulance corps, E. E. Cummings, turned out *The Enormous Room* at this time. After serving with the Royal Air Force, William Faulkner returned in 1925 to go tramping through France and Italy, but he saw no more of Europe until 1950, when he went to Stockholm to accept the Nobel Prize. Oxford, Mississippi, remained his home as his talents flowered.

Archibald MacLeish, a young scholar from Illinois destined to become a well-known poet, Librarian of Congress, and political figure, took his family to Paris in 1923 and stayed for five years. He later viewed this as the period of crystallization of his literary interests. He was one of many young Americans who found inspiration abroad and were able to make good use of their gifts on their return home. Glenway Westcott, a handsome youth from Wisconsin who became known at the University of Chicago for the Byronic cloak that he wore with great dash, remained abroad after many of the others had returned to America. His novels included *The Grandmothers,* which was critically acclaimed when it was published in 1927. Morley Callaghan, a Canadian writer whose *Strange Fugitive* had just been published with considerable flourish, reached the Left Bank in 1929. Although he did not linger long in Paris, he consorted with the literary men of the hour and left his "memories of tangled friendships" with Hemingway, Fitzgerald, and others in *That Summer in Paris,* published in 1963. Matthew Josephson, a youth from Brooklyn whose book *The Robber Barons* would create a sensation in 1934, and Malcolm Cowley, a Pennsylvanian who would be one of the first to leave the Left Bank, but later wrote about it evocatively in *Exile's Return,* were among the gifted young men who discussed life and letters at the Dôme, the Flore, the Café de la Rotonde, the Sélect, the Coupole, the Deux-Magots, and other haunts irrevocably linked with these days of carefree expatriation.

But the exiles of the 1920s worked as well as drank and lounged the hours away. Their habits were restless and uneven. They wrote in fitful bursts, or with long periods of concentration, as in the case of Hemingway. Once in Europe, they could move with freedom while their funds held out. A magazine acceptance, a picture sold, a windfall from home, and they were off to look at the flowering almond trees of Avignon, to cross to Algiers, to bicycle in Holland, to tramp in the Tyrolean Alps or spend long periods in Giverny, where Claude Monet, still busy painting in his eighties, looked with mild alarm at the wandering Americans who intruded on his world of golden haystacks.

Sooner or later they all returned to the Left Bank, to pursue interrupted romances, to pick up their letters at the Dôme, to compare notes on the mounting tide of prosperity at home, and to congratulate themselves on being far removed from the disastrous results of prohibition, the ignominy of the Scopes trial, and the hot fevers of the struggle between the Fundamentalists and Modernists of the church. They gloried in H. L. Mencken's barbed attacks on the puritanical heritage of America and felt that they had found freedom away from it all. But Sinclair Lewis, an expatriate whose second wife, Dorothy Thompson, found him always as American as ham and eggs, made the cynical comment that many of the writers lingered on in Paris because the wine was cheap, the girls pretty, the crêpes suzette exalted, and the Place de la Concorde beautiful.

True enough, their lives had fluidity, constant novelty and change, a drifting away from moorings, a welcome escape from the corroding responsibilities of life. Their studios, attics, and hotel rooms might be cold and cheerless, the lighting inadequate for writing and reading, the plumbing defective or nonexistent, the telephone an insoluble problem, but the horse chestnuts flowered in the spring, the Tuileries blazed with seasonal color, Les Halles was a wonderland displaying the produce of provincial France, and the art showings were always provocative. The Left Bank was a surging mass of talent, romance, heartbreak, defeat, and great dreams, which in the end outdistanced the shattered marriages, alcoholism, drug addiction, and debauchery that were also part of its history at this time.

Before long the nebulous figures moving uneasily through the disorderly life of the Left Bank would emerge as pacesetters and innovators in American letters. Their doings, and the way in which some of their masterpieces were conceived and produced, would be chronicled for years to come. They had their own publications, and they caught the limelight more immediately than the expatriates of the late nineteenth century, who emerged only gradually in memoirs of the period. Not until the 1960s would American expatriates again become so visible a moving body, but by then the picture would be international in spirit.

The characters Hemingway used in *The Sun Also Rises* were well-known habitués of the Left Bank, just as George du Maurier used Whistler and other members of the old Latin Quarter in his *Trilby*. In the 1920s Trilby had her counterpart in Kiki of Montparnasse, who went from one café to another, her pale face dabbed with bright circles of rouge, her sparkling eyes always responsive to American intonations. Kiki, who was Man Ray's model, knew the writers, the artists, and the musicians, and rejoiced in their moments of triumph just as she cheered them in the long hours of depression. When Kiki wrote her memoirs she had the unique distinction of a Hemingway preface, in which he said that she had dominated the 1920s even more positively than Queen Victoria had the Victorian age. He expressed his admiration for her "fine face" and "wonderfully beautiful body."

Kiki's vogue as a courtesan and model faded as Montparnasse changed in character, but she was a symbol to the public of the wastrel ways and dissipation of the loungers of the period. Americans at home read of endless drinking sprees and uninhibited parties, but did not feel the bitterness toward them that was directed at Henry James when he became a British subject. American traditions were being so thoroughly debunked at home and abroad at this time that the disillusioned expatriates could back up some of their grievances about life in the United States. And as fresh, creative work and a dynamic style in letters emerged from the American group in Paris, they were regarded with interest and curiosity. A whole new generation of writers was in the making—a recurrent experience after great wars and revolutions.

On the Right Bank things were different, but there, too, the American influence became pervasive in the 1920s. The war had left its aftermath in the Peace Conference and the reconstruction operations that brought officials pouring into the French capital. Statesmen, economists, bankers, engineers, scientists of all kinds, correspondents, scholars, and businessmen representing all the states in the Union, were omnipresent. Many of them spent years abroad, expatriates of substance and established habits.

They were in and out of the American Embassy. The Fourth of July and other national holidays were formally celebrated, and Thanksgiving turkey was eaten with New England fervor. They had their own banks and schools, their library and excellently run hospital at Neuilly. American doctors, dentists, and lawyers were part of the community, and American bankers and real estate agents gave them reassuring support in the lush days of the Harding and Coolidge administrations. The Chamber of Commerce, Rotary Club, American Legion, and other fraternal organizations flourished. The American Women's Club, luxuriously housed in Passy, had more than a thousand members, and musicians, painters, sculptors, and writers were cultivated in the name of art. On Sundays the pews of the American Cathedral were filled with formally dressed churchgoers whose accents were unmistakable. The American Methodist Memorial Church in Montparnasse had its own baseball and basketball leagues, and American residents of any faith could find a place to worship.

The newspaper people consorted with all groups, from the heiresses who had made international marriages to the wildest characters of the Left Bank. They were heavily involved with the growing legions of well-off American tourists who arrived like a conquering army each summer, to spend millions on clothes, jewels, and luxuries of all kinds.

The dividing line between groups became blurred as the permanent residents were caught up in the bright whirl of American jazz, the cabarets of Montmartre, the fashion houses, the automobiles coming from Detroit, the swift pace of the 1920s. The women who had driven ambulances, worn uniforms, learned to smoke and bob their hair, had escaped from the traditional setting. They were tasting *la vie bohème* and they liked it, as they danced the Charleston, wore knee-length skirts, flourished long cigarette holders, and had closely shingled hair.

But the visiting hordes were creating a new image, too, of an America not altogether in the tradition of Babbitt. Europeans took note of their assorted accents, customs, clothes, and optimistic outlook on life. It was another variation of the Grand Tour, but with more emphasis on worldly pleasure and less on the museums and antiquities of Europe. The escapees from the land of prohibition were inclined to settle for gourmet food and vintage wines consumed at leisure, and to do their sightseeing at lightning speed. The rogues on the Left Bank were soon insisting that their affluent compatriots, laden with dollars and plagued by thirst, were the real drinkers and high livers of the period. The Left Bank set at least had something to show in the way of artistic output when the great spree was ended and life settled into the stark outlines of reality.

They approved Sinclair Lewis's definition of the American Babbitt and added their own touches to the picture of a reckless, extravagant, heedless, boastful generation, dancing on the brink of hell, as it turned out later. But there was no denying the American popularity created by the Hoover Commission and by the work of some of the American missions and philanthropic societies. Hoover was the man of mercy, distributing food and supplies in the war-battered countries. American businessmen were regarded with fresh interest by a variety of European statesmen. The resident expatriate was treated with respect, and his business operations were encouraged. Not since the days of Franklin, Adams, and Jefferson had merchants of all kinds worked with such concentration to build up trade, and the early operations were miniscule in comparison with the postwar drive of the 1920s and the large-scale operations of big corporations.

A massive union of interests, born out of the pressures and consequences of the war, opened up new channels of communication and understanding. Many Europeans had come to view America as a land of millionaires, with yachts cruising in the Mediterranean and villas on the Riviera. The international marriages of the late nine-teenth and early twentieth centuries had spread a false patina over the American image. But some of the brides who had married titles yearned to go home. The sturdy pioneering tradition of their ances-tors made them less susceptible to the gloss and idiom of Europe than some of the nouveau riche and ambitious mothers who had forced their marriages.

The rich widows who took châteaus, hired gigolos as escorts, and squandered their inheritance in the 1920s did little to change the image of extravagance and pretension. The same breed of cosmopo-lite who would fly to Acapulco or the Greek Islands, to Sardinia, Portugal, or the Caribbean in the 1960s, sought the Riviera in the 1920s. It was the land of wine and roses, of turquoise urns and sun-soaked days, then back to the Ritz, the Crillon or the Continen-tal, and the life of Paris again. Diplomats tried to keep pace with the constant demand for official recognition and invitations to the best parties.

The students found their own world around the Sorbonne, as they had always done, and they had their special place in the life of Paris, acknowledged and understood. Americans flocked to take courses at this ancient institution, at a time when the Rhodes schol-ars were also flourishing in England. The students were a harmoniz-ing influence in the expatriate world and they created a trend that would grow stronger in the 1940s, 1950s, and 1960s as Fulbright and Guggenheim scholars, and many others with special grants, attended the universities of Europe, from Oslo to Grenoble, and from Oxford to Athens. The expatriate world of the student, like that of the writer, has recurred with one generation after another, and has given depth to the expatriate legend.

The artists and writers, traditionally regarded as a class apart, were a tightly knit group on the Left Bank and had little to do with the scrubbed-up sculptors and painters who sipped Pernod at the American Women's Club. The favorable exchange rate in the early 1920s certainly helped keep the expatriates happy in Europe. The devalued franc in France and inflation in Germany ran a mad course for a time and gave the impoverished writers a sense of affluence until the exchange was eventually stabilized. Americans could live in high style in Berlin, haunt the beer gardens of Munich, absorb the Vien-nese postwar atmosphere, and stop off in war-torn Belgium on their way back to Paris, all for the price of a song. The writers took full ad-vantage of this while it lasted; some had houses, servants, and cars like the more prosperous resident Americans. Others continued to freeze in garrets, but gloried in the fact that they looked out on the roofs of Paris, the solid outlines of Notre Dame, the needle point of the Eiffel Tower, and the white and gold glitter of Sacré Coeur.

Early in the 1920s they settled in formidable numbers in the Saint-Germain section. One group had come straight from Greenwich Village and continued their customary way of life. Their loves and their feuds were merely enhanced by the novelty of their surroundings. Harold Stearns of the *New Republic,* who had turned his back on the United States with emphatic shouts of renunciation, settled in Montparnasse and was often one of Hemingway's drinking companions. Alfred Kreymborg, already writing some of the poetry that would make him well-known, stayed at the same hotel as Harold Loeb, who looked like John Barrymore, and edited the little magazine *Broom.* Loeb tried to push Hemingway's publishing interests when he was still almost unknown. He also shared Hemingway's interest in the gray-eyed Englishwoman Lady Duff Twysden, who became known the world around as Lady Brett Ashley in *The Sun Also Rises.* Duff, as her friends called her, had a thin cameolike face, with thoughtful gray eyes and blonde hair, closely cropped. Hemingway was impressed with her capacity to drink and her steady nerves after hours of indulgence. She was thirty-two and in the process of being divorced from Sir Roger Thomas Twysden when Hemingway began to study her personality. Her son Anthony was being brought up by her husband's family.

Before settling in Paris, Loeb had worked in the Washington Square Bookshop, and on the Left Bank he continued to seek the company of Margaret Anderson and Jane Heap, two lively American girls who kept stirring things up while they edited the *Little Review.* Miss Anderson said she would cheerfully go to jail for publishing Joyce, should the need arise. The Brasserie Lutétia was a favorite gathering place for this group, as they held endless conferences about the little magazines they were nurturing, and which of the writers should be featured, and how much they should be paid.

The English influence was pervasive on the Left Bank too, with Ford Madox Ford trying to repeat in Paris the success he had had in London with the *English Review.* His drinking parties were legendary, and his manners were gross. After dinner he would take his guests to a *bal musette* behind the Panthéon. Hemingway, corresponding for the Toronto *Star,* was getting to be known around Montparnasse, although it was understood that he was a worker who would let nothing stand in the way when he decided to finish a writing task.

None could ignore the presence of Gertrude Stein when she showed up with majestic arrogance. They were all accustomed to the sight of Raymond Duncan in his toga and sandals, and his sister Isadora, the beautiful, the dramatic, the doomed, who danced and drank and loved all over Paris. Emma Goldman, back from Russia in a state of disillusionment, moved glumly among the expatriates but fared better when she crossed to London and was taken up by Rebecca West.

George Biddle, artist and critic from Philadelphia; Jo Davidson and Paul Manship, both sculptors; Sisley Huddleston, the English author; George Slocombe, then correspondent for the *Daily Herald* of London; Sally and William Bird, who specialized in fine printing, book binding, and hand-set type; Clotilde Vail and her brother, Laurence Vail, an artist who was then married to Peggy Guggenheim, art collector and rich American playgirl, all belonged to this early group. The score mounted as others arrived—Louis Bromfield, a newspaperman well on his way to substantial literary success, and Ludwig Lewisohn, the German novelist and critic who settled in America in 1890 but became a resident of France in the late 1920s. Eugene O'Neill, winning the Nobel Prize for literature and the Pulitzer Prize for drama in the 1920s, showed up inevitably on the Left Bank, although he did not linger there. Harriet Monroe, who had gained wide recognition as the editor of *Poetry* magazine in Chicago, for a time seemed to be in the mood to settle into the expatriate pattern but decided to return to America before she succumbed completely to the slow drift of lotus land. She urged the young poets whose work she fostered to hasten back to the United States for inspiration in the native idiom. Her first meeting with Ezra Pound, whose work she valued, was in the Stryx, a Swedish café popular with the American expatriates. They drank fine old Madeira together and discussed poetry. Julien Green, the novelist, born of American parents but Gallic in his work and thinking, and George Santayana, Spanish by birth but closely linked with Harvard, had expatriate status at this time; both were frequently seen with other American writers, but neither one belonged to the convivial set.

Malcolm Cowley bicycled and fished at Giverny, where he lived for a time, going in to Paris once a week to catch up on the latest art showing, to attend a concert, or to drop in at Sylvia Beach's bookshop or at the Dôme; to chat with Robert Coates, who would later be a bright star on *The New Yorker;* with Harold Loeb, or with Robert McAlmon, the cynical Kansan who published the work of Hemingway, Fitzgerald, Ezra Pound, Bob Coates, William Carlos Williams, and Gertrude Stein before they became widely known.

To his own surprise Cowley found himself in jail on Bastille Day in 1923 after he had assaulted the proprietor of the Rotonde on a dare from Laurence Vail. Bands played and Chinese lanterns swung from the trees as Cowley led a group of roisterers in a parade of his own along the Boulevard Montparnasse, going from café to café and picking up new followers along the way. He looked the complete bohemian, with espadrilles, a frayed blue shirt, and a reckless air. Tourists wearing Lanvin and Vionnet gowns, and hung with jewels, thought it another phase of bohemia, but Cowley was obsessed with the idea that he must beat up the surly guardian of the Rotonde, a starchy fellow whom no one liked. He stood for the conventions and would not let women smoke on the premises, or appear hatless on the terrace.

When the deed was done, neatly and with surprise tactics, Bob Coates suggested that they all go back to the friendlier atmosphere of the Dôme, but the gendarmerie stepped in and arrested the bewildered Cowley. Next day Zelda and Scott Fitzgerald, along with other well-heeled expatriates, showed up in court to testify on his behalf. None had seen what had happened, but they were rich, beautiful, and persuasive people, with much to say about the hostility of the victim. Cowley was freed and at once became something of a public character. He was entertained by the bright wits of the moment and was asked to contribute to the magazines linked with the Dadaist movement. But the expatriate world did not hold him. He returned home in 1923, the first member of this colony to desert it.

Cowley was a critic of T. S. Eliot's *The Waste Land* when it came out in 1922, dedicated to Ezra Pound. Although it won the *Dial* prize for poetry and had sensational success, his fellow exiles were scathing about its merits. Cowley thought that its symbolism, learning, and metrical structure suggested that the contemporary scene lacked color, that only the past mattered. "We were new men, without inherited traditions, and were entering a new world of art . . . although we did not see our own path, we instinctively rejected Eliot's," Cowley commented.

Eliot reached eminence a little ahead of his fellow exiles, but he was soon the target of their antagonism. A native of St. Louis and a graduate of Harvard in 1910, he had stunned his generation with the poems that began to appear in 1917 and reached a crescendo in *The Waste Land*. Earlier, determined as always to help a compatriot, Ezra Pound worked with Natalie Clifford Barney, a rich young American who had a small Greek temple in her Paris garden and prided herself on her literary salon, to raise money to help the bored young bank clerk in London. Eliot's success, however, was so swift and spectacular that he was well able to take care of himself. When he became a British subject in 1927, he was attacked as the first of the expatriates since James to give up American citizenship. But his work continued to affect a generation of Ivy League college and prep school students. He was the poet of the bright young people.

When *Ulysses* came out in the early 1920s, Joyce and Eliot were the big names in the expatriate world, and their appearance on the Left Bank was always a matter of great interest to the American residents. James Joyce could usually be found at Sylvia Beach's Shakespeare and Company bookshop on the Rue de l'Odéon, a haven and sometimes a home for the writers, who found it easy to slip across from the terrace of the Deux-Magots or the other cafés near Saint-Germain-des-Prés, and settle down to the warmth and comfort of her back parlor, where tea was served by firelight. Slim, brown-haired Sylvia, lovingly handling her books and encouraging their authors, was the daughter of the Reverend Sylvester Beach, and she had touching faith in the wild young writers who used her shop for their own ends. When Hemingway was too poor to join her rental library, she sent him out loaded down with books to read on his various trips. "No one that I ever knew was nicer to me," he said of her.

Her clergyman father, who considered Sylvia a simple-minded and sincere young woman, had some explaining to do on the home front about the characters who haunted her shop. She knew the fake poets, the derelicts, the adventurers, the dreamers, the spongers, and somehow she seemed to sense where talent lay. In course of time her bookshop became a well-known institution that any bookseller might envy. On her walls were the early photographs of such men as Hemingway, Fitzgerald, Pound, Joyce, and others whose names would live. Walt Whitman's manuscripts were displayed, and the new books guaranteed to lure the tourists were prominently exhibited in her windows. She made shrewd use of this showcase for her literary friends. She sold all their publications, including poems in a hundred languages. She pushed George Antheil's *Ballet Méchanique,* for he had a studio above her shop and she had long listened to the din from above. She gave extraordinary promotion to Joyce's haphazardly punctuated *Ulysses,* 300,000 words long. And she featured the little magazines sparked with revolt. Pound was responsible for *Exile,* Ford Madox Ford for the *Transatlantic Review,* and Elliot Paul and Eugene Jolas for *Transition. This Quarter,* which made its appearance in 1925, was directed chiefly by Ernest Walsh, the Irish-American poet who had been seriously injured in the war, and Ethel Moorhead, a Scot who had studied painting in

Paris with Whistler. The first issue was dedicated to Ezra Pound, and during its span its contributors included Hemingway, Pound, Kay Boyle, Djuna Barnes, and Morley Callaghan.

Sylvia Beach, an important link in this community, would move about her shop in a brown velveteen jacket and kilted skirt, joking with her customers and feeding them literary gossip. Aside from the charm of her shop, her special claim to fame lay in the way she fostered the art of James Joyce. She met him when she was working in La Maison des Amis des Livres, where Dadaism had its start, and Gide, Claudel, Louis Aragon, André Breton, Valéry Larbaud, and Jules Romains were customers. Such was her faith in Joyce that from their first meeting she determined to publish his book at all costs. Her own shop grew out of this resolution. She introduced him to the American writers, typed stretches of his manuscript, enlisted the interest of the newspapers in his behalf, and finally published his *Ulysses*. The first edition was a paperback that sold for sixty cents and had many typographical errors. But tales of its eroticism traveled fast, and soon the conservative booksellers on the Right Bank were offering it to the American tourists. It became the conversation piece of the literary world and a lasting classic.

Few of the expatriates who circled around Joyce in Sylvia's shop expected much of the book. However, they enjoyed the author when he was in an amiable mood, which was not often, and they liked his relaxed, fresh-complexioned wife, Nora. Mary and Padraic Colum, understanding Celts, never tired of hearing him read, and would nod approvingly as he repeated one word in twenty-nine languages. He picked up a dash of the worldly spirit in Paris, and although at first he disapproved sternly of all the carousing he learned to drink insatiably at times, as he suffered excruciating pain with his eyes, worried about money and his sight, and indulged in true Celtic despondency. Through it all Sylvia, the minister's daughter who avoided the cafés and never drank, encouraged Joyce and indulged his fondness for birthday celebrations and fetes of one kind or another. Saint Patrick's Day was honored in high style with a dinner party at the Trianon, given for William Carlos Williams, the doctor-poet from Rutherford, New Jersey, who had taken a sabbatical year abroad. Joyce sang Irish songs on this occasion, something he liked to do when he was in a good mood. Robert McAlmon, from the Far West, bellowed cowboy songs and spirituals. Clotilde Vail was expert at the blues, and Peggy Guggenheim, the young and dashing heiress always ready to foot the bill at a party, did her best to shock them all.

One American who moved helpfully but abrasively among them

was McAlmon, poet and short story writer who gave the more gifted of the coterie recognition. With William Carlos Williams he founded the magazine *Contact,* which was published for three years. His *Contact* editions featured the early work of Hemingway, and Ezra Pound, Robert Coates, Gertrude Stein, Hilda Doolittle, Ford Madox Ford, Mina Loy, and William Carlos Williams all came under his wing in this form at one time or another. He was difficult to work with, and some of the writers dreaded his icy blue-eyed gaze and the tight set of his lips. Moody and arrogant, he could not endure any criticism of his own work, nor would he accept advice or compromise on any subject.

McAlmon was of Scottish descent. He was born in Kansas and spent his youth in South Dakota. He arrived in Paris in 1921, just as the American expatriates were settling in Montparnasse. Unlike most of the others he had money, for he was married to the novelist Bryher Ellerman, daughter of Sir John Ellerman, a British shipping magnate. She was completely alien to their surroundings, and they were desperately unhappy, but her income enabled McAlmon to indulge his literary interests and back ventures in which he believed. He attached himself whenever possible to Eliot, Pound, and Joyce, and made a wary study of Hemingway and Fitzgerald. He disliked Hemingway, and Hemingway frankly detested him.

McAlmon moved around the continent with ease, and in Florence he stayed with Norman Douglas, the author of *South Wind,* which was drawing the attention of the traveler to Capri. He was bored by Douglas, although he thought his book amusing. Douglas, in turn, deplored McAlmon's lack of reverence for tradition, age, and convention. McAlmon found Florence dry, dusty, and uninteresting after the vivid life on the Left Bank. The expatriates there lived in villas and rarely appeared in the cafés. In Paris it was his custom to spend most of his time in the cafés and newspaper offices. He was a hard drinker and had some of the swagger of the early Wild West. He was handsome, trimly built, and showy, strutting about with wide-brimmed hats and a turquoise earring in one ear.

McAlmon's marriage had broken up by 1930. He no longer had an endless supply of money. The men he had helped had moved up the ladder, and because he had never been popular he was more or less forgotten. He returned to the United States to write in the desert of the golden days of the 1920s in Paris. His book was published in Europe in 1938 but did not come out in America until 1967. *Being Geniuses Together* was revised and rounded out for American publication by Kay Boyle, the member of his circle who had always been loyal to him. She wrote of him that he "spoke for his generation in a voice that echoes, unacknowledged, in the prose of Hemingway and that of other writers of his time." He died a lonely man in 1956 at Desert Springs, California, and few but Sylvia Beach knew that he had retyped the last fifty pages of Joyce's *Ulysses* himself, for he believed so thoroughly in the book. Sylvia was almost equally forgotten when she died in 1962. It was several days before she was found in a flat near the old site where she had worked for so many years. Her shop was gone. Her sight was gone. But Janet Flanner, a fellow expatriate, commented in *The New Yorker* that Sylvia Beach was a "friend to writing."

Miss Boyle, who was closest to McAlmon, was one of the most distinguished and enduring of the expatriates in Paris. Years after the others returned to the United States, she remained abroad. She lived and loved and became politically involved, and no one had more inner knowledge of the Left Bank characters than she. Originally Kay came from Cincinnati, a simple and spontaneous girl who was desperately ambitious but thought she could never get anywhere because she had not gone to college. She read Rebecca West's *The Judge* with awe and admiration, memorizing the text for inspiration. Kay lived happily in abject poverty in Greenwich Village, and sauntered out into the sunlight with bright dabs of rouge on her cheeks and great hoop earrings from Woolworth's dangling from her ears. She was only eighteen when she married a Frenchman, Robert Brault, and sailed with him for France in 1923, expecting to be gone for a few months only. She did not return to the United States until 1941, after the fall of France. But her French relatives were stiff and formal, and they did not approve of Kay's spontaneous American ways. Life was difficult for her, as she cooked and shopped and gave dinner parties, while writing *Plagued by the Nightingale*.

Her marriage did not last, and she left her husband to live with Ernest Walsh when he was in the last stages of tuberculosis. She bore him a child posthumously, and soon became deeply embroiled with her compatriots on the Left Bank. She tried her hand at many things, but Eugene Jolas and Robert McAlmon encouraged her to write. For a time she worked in Sylvia Beach's shop. Then she joined Raymond Duncan's colony and was surprised to find that his tunics and rugs had not been woven on hand looms in Neuilly, as Raymond maintained, but had been done a decade earlier in Greece. The soles and thongs of the sandals actually came from a shop off the Boulevard Saint-Germain and were only stitched by Raymond's disciples. The batiks were dyed in the back garden, but the prices remained sky-high.

When she became well established among the writers, Kay described the period as "one of the gravest crisis in letters, of furious schism and revolution in the arts." In her view Joyce, Jolas, Williams, Walsh, and the "troubled vision of the Surrealists prepared the way for the anti-novel, the anti-hero, for the type of poetry that Cummings was writing, and the quite new type of novel of Céline." Out of oblivion the revolution retrieved the work of Kafka, Rimbaud, and Lautreamont, Miss Boyle added.

She found inspiration in the encouragement McAlmon gave her. He considered Kay and Katherine Anne Porter better writers than Katherine Mansfield, although not so well publicized. But by 1932 the brilliant Miss Porter was downgrading Hemingway as a fraud with a point of view as superficial "as any memoirs of an ex-wife." She said flatly that he "never created one plausible human being." Miss Boyle did not share this conviction. Her own life moved on into other channels, and in 1951 she was in Germany with a new husband, an Austrian baron with the military government. Her revival of the McAlmon legend in the 1960s was a matter of interest to the survivors of the literary life of the 1920s, but the doings on the Left Bank paled in the world of war, riots, Hippies, and draft evaders. The expatriate life of the 1960s had grimmer undertones, or completely frivolous ones, with the comings and goings of the Jet Set.

The offices of the Paris *Herald* and the Chicago *Tribune* harbored their share of transient talent, and their staffs knew where the creative workers were to be found at any given moment. The Chicago paper had a small circulation, and at times was merely given away at the hotels, but it had more literary flavor than the Paris *Herald,* which devoted its columns to social and business events, the kind of news that would interest the prosperous tourists, the diplomats, and the permanent residents. On the Chicago *Tribune* Waverley Lewis Root, Jr., directed the literary criticism, and close attention was paid to the writers of the era. Both establishments became legendary, and their graduates ranged from James Vincent Sheean and Floyd Dell to Elliot Paul and Whit Burnett. They were always in the thick of things, and they differed from the other expatriates in having inescapable deadlines to meet. Much as they consorted with the émigrés of the Left Bank, they resisted persuasion to stay for the end of a drinking bout. The few who failed to follow this rule soon disappeared.

Sheean, a big, blond, pink-cheeked youth from the Middle West, was fresh from covering the famous Stillman divorce case in New York. Later he would find a notable place in American letters, but in the 1920s he was a carefree expatriate who never failed to catch the violets tossed into the audience by Raquel Meller, the melancholy Spanish singer who popularized the song "Fleur du Mal." Sheean was a friend of John Reed, the flaming revolutionary dedicated to the Bolshevik cause, and of his wife, the beautiful Louise Bryant, an ardent suffrage worker. The handsome young correspondent soon became friendly with Sinclair Lewis and Dorothy Thompson, and later married Diana Forbes-Robertson, the niece and biographer of Maxine Elliott.

The newspapermen could be ruthless in publicizing the exploits of their friends on the Left Bank, and Elliot Paul's quarters at the Hôtel du Caveau on the Rue de la Huchette were something of an expatriate center. All manner of visiting Americans looked him up, and his writing colleagues were in and out of his quarters from 1923 until the end of the golden days. As a writer finding literary success beyond his daily round for the Chicago *Tribune,* he was keenly alive to the special charms of Paris. Walking home from his office at dawn after a hard night's work, he watched Nôtre Dame loom into soft outline through a flood of rose. The lamps on the bridges and along the avenues and boulevards glowed pink and lemon. The crisp, cool air blew over sleeping Paris and switched his thoughts from the news of the day to the eerie charm of his surroundings. However chilly and austere his digs at the Hôtel du Caveau, he was always alive to the shifting scene around him—to the first of the *bateaux* appearing on the Seine with a load of shivering passengers; to the revival of life on the café terraces as spring decked Paris in blossoms and tender green; to the wide leaves of the plane trees spreading their luxuriant shade over the pavements.

Paul, with his pointed beard and impudent air, was a maverick who worked in the end for the *Herald* as well as the *Tribune.* He liked to act as host, to organize parties and play the accordion for his guests. He became in time a self-appointed promoter for the expatriate life, and he coped better with the obscurities of Gertrude Stein and James Joyce than most of his colleagues. There were wits among them who thought that the new style was all posture and affectation. The surrealists and the Dadaists were more of a joke to them than anything else.

The correspondents lived chiefly in the Saint-Germain and Montparnasse regions, and when their night's work was ended, they often stayed in their offices to play poker, or they went to Les Halles for food and drink, and sometimes for copy. Some would wind up at the Chien Qui Fume to watch the tourists capering and romping in evening clothes after a night on the town, for by 1924 the doings of the American tourists were prime copy. They were all over Europe, dancing in the nightclubs of Paris, attending Nancy Cunard's highpaced parties in Venice, catching the bullfights at Pamplona, foxtrotting at tea dances in Berlin, where a dollar went as far as ten elsewhere. It was the Grand Tour all over again, but within the reach of a much greater assortment of people, from the schoolteachers who had always found their way to Europe, to the big manufacturers and founders of substantial fortunes across the United States.

All over the map of Europe the correspondents roamed too— expatriate in spirit, yet always linked with home, a breed by themselves and ever conscious of the growing sweep of talent around them. They rejoiced when one of their number hit a big story, or carried out a particularly difficult assignment. But as the decade advanced, the feeling for Americans chilled in France, and the correspondents had awkward questions to answer about President Coolidge and his vice president, Charles G. Dawes. Reparations were the big issue of the hour, and Owen D. Young, Frank B. Kellogg, and J. P. Morgan, all involved in these negotiations with conquered Germany, were discussed at length by men of affairs, hoping to learn something from the correspondents. The gangsters in the United States, operating at high gear in the speakeasy days, did not help the country's prestige abroad, nor did the depredations of the Ku Klux Klan. Over the Dingo Bar and Harry's New York Bar, or at Joe Zelli's in Montmartre, the expatriates, the permanent residents, and the floating population of newspaper correspondents exchanged notes on the American scene.

Paris was becoming noticeably Americanized as Frenchmen tried to distinguish between the accents of New England and the South, Brooklyn and the Middle West, Texas and San Francisco. American coffee and pancakes were to be found here and there, and American films, American jazz, motorcars, cameras, and chewing gum were in demand. The Ritz Bar (Cambon side) was the haunt of the knowing. The great restaurants of the hour were Foyot's, Prunier's, and Lapérouse. The Café de Paris, the Tour d'Argent, and Weber's were still in high esteem. But in the 1920s innocents from the United States were lured into all manner of restaurants guaranteed to give them the best food in France.

The Folies Bergère had an overnight sensation when Josephine Baker flipped her green ostrich feather plume and became a star. Life dimmed for her, but in 1969 she was again in the headlines, living in a Riviera villa with her integrated family of twelve adopted children. Princess Grace and Prince Rainier were backing her in her humane work. Interest in Negroes grew as Florence Mills and her Blackbirds flourished at Les Ambassadeurs. Bricktop's place in Montmartre drew the American crowd. Chalk-faced Kiki wandered around the cafés, exchanging notes at times with Florence (Flossie) Martin, an old Ziegfeld girl. Nina Hammett, an English artist, sang ballads in Joe Zelli's bar.

Paris was alive with press agents who promoted fashion houses and restaurants, acted as guides, steered women through the perils of shopping for a fat commission, provided gigolos, and encouraged publicity of the right sort. The stars of Hollywood were coming over in shoals and were always good for interviews in the *Herald* and *Tribune*. An enterprising newspaperman thought up the "Whoopee Tours," which were symbolic of the time, and involved a searching look at the night life of Paris.

Mary Margaret McBride, a blue-eyed girl from Missouri who would become famous on radio as Martha Deane, was all over the city catching the highlights of the period. She appeared in Paris when the New York *Mail* merged with the *Globe* under Munsey's guiding hand, and her job was gone. With Helen Josephy she pinned down during these expatriate years much of the prevailing atmosphere in her books *Paris Is a Woman's Town* and *London Is a Man's Town*.

By 1925 the *Herald* was playing fashion and society to the hilt, and Vionnet, Patou, Chanel, and Lanvin were catching the lush American trade. May Birkhead, who had attracted the attention of James Gordon Bennett, dynamic editor of the *Herald,* with her work on the sinking of the *Titanic,* had become the society empress of the American press in Europe. Miss Birkhead, a native of Louisiana, who had earned a trip abroad by sewing shirts, chanced to be on the *Carpathia,* the ship that picked up the *Titanic* survivors. She rounded up stories and sketches of their experiences and gave Bennett the kind of international beat in which he delighted. As society editor of the *Herald* she followed the visiting Americans from one resort to another—going to Deauville or Le Touquet in August, to Biarritz in September, to the Riviera in February, and concentrating on Monte Carlo in March. Fashion and society became firmly meshed with this sort of reporting, and it set a pattern for the future.

This new type of journalism had been encouraged before World War I by one of the most famous of American expatriates, James Gordon Bennett, Jr., who left New York in a hurry in 1877 after a duel with the brother of the girl to whom he was engaged. He did not return in forty years, except for brief visits of a few days at a time. But he soon became famous as the most daring of journalists —a flamboyant and erratic editor who encouraged experimentation with the automobile and airplane, who backed new inventions and established the Commercial Cable Company with John W. Mackay. He was responsible for the discovery of Dr. Livingstone by Henry M. Stanley in the heart of Africa, and for other great stories of adventure, exploration, and scientific advances.

His hard-working, churlish father had failed to break the barriers of New York society, but the younger Bennett became the most cosmopolitan of editors, consorting with royalty, financiers, and other celebrities of the era. He was a yachtsman who cruised the Mediterrean as Aristotle Onassis would later, with shiploads of fascinating guests. He remained a bachelor until he was seventy-three, when he married the widow of Baron George de Reuter, of the Reuter news agency family. His wife was a Philadelphia girl, the former Maud Potter, who had long been his friend. His widow survived him by twenty-eight years and was one of the rich expatriate widows, living in Europe until she died in 1946 at the Bennett house on the Avenue d'Iéna.

In his bachelor days Bennett caused more uproar in Paris at times than the vagabonds of the Left Bank. He drove without clothes through the streets of Paris in a tallyho on one occasion. On another he ripped off the tablecloths at Maxime's, danced on the wreckage he had caused, and later paid handsomely for these moments of eccentricity. When he invited the Duchess of Marlborough and some of her friends to board his yacht on the Riviera, they suddenly found themselves heading off for Egypt, a trip they had not anticipated. He apologized, and they swung around in the Mediterranean. But at all times he kept a tight grip on his papers in New York and Paris, directing his editors from his villa at Beaulieu, from his cruising yacht, from his shooting box in the Highlands, or from other distant parts of the world, as he traveled erratically. He spent money with a free hand where the interests of the *Herald* were concerned, and he played the role of statesman when American interests were involved. "If a nation is friendly to America, I wish the *Herald* to be friendly to that nation, but if a nation shows an unfriendly policy, I wish the paper to adopt an unfriendly tone," he decreed. "This may not be patriotism, but it is the course I wish the *Herald* to follow." He added that he considered himself a watchdog for American foreign policy.

Bennett paid his staff poorly, even though he spent fabulous sums to back expeditions and innovations. When the Paris *Herald* first came out, it had four pages and was loaded with personal items. He announced that he would hire all the brains he wanted for twenty-five dollars a week. He became the employer of men of intellectual drive and many gifts who would become well known in the literary world. He opened a business office at 49 Avenue de l'Opéra, close to the Café de la Paix, with a conspicuous sign advertising his paper at that crossroads of American life in Paris.

His appearances in the Paris office were always dreaded, and some of the men he employed had a pact with his butler to tip them off when he was on his way in. But his appearances when the *Herald* was on its way up were few and far between. The Caliph, the Mogul, the Sybarite, as his irreverent staff referred to him, would be hunting in Austria, sunning himself on the Riviera, or sailing up the Nile. However, his paper was firmly established as a link between the American residents in Paris and the rest of the world. He featured Christmas supplements containing the work of France's leading writers. He issued illustrated editions on the Paris art salons. The special supplement, the comics, rotogravure effects, and linotype all were part of the Bennett tradition in Paris. But he showed himself to be the true newspaperman when World War I broke out. As France mobilized in the summer of 1914, he was left with two printers, one stereotyper, and three or four men in the composing room. But the *Herald* came out every day, with its skeleton staff, and his staff men in uniform received full pay. Bennett urged anyone who wished to bow out to do so. "This place will be under the protection of the Stars and Stripes," he said, "and I will defy these Prussians to disregard it. In any event, the paper comes out."

It did, and the Paris *Herald* was eagerly read by the French as the zeppelin raids began and the cannon fire of Big Bertha was directed at the city. Bennett walked to and from his office every day, when automobiles, carriages, and horses were requisitioned by the government. He raged editorially against the Germans and flaunted the slang term *Boche,* meaning square-headed and stupid, until it became common usage. He died within a few months after the United States entered the war, and it was after his time that the more noted expatriates flowed in and out of the *Herald* office. But he had contributed richly himself to the legendary world of the American exile.

Joseph Pulitzer, roaming the globe in his yacht—soundproofed from the clamor of the world, yet communicating swiftly and by the hour with Park Row and the American public—was in essence and spirit an expatriate. He was rarely at home or in American waters. He sought restlessly for peace and quiet, yet stirred up conflict as he fought the battles of the underprivileged, unearthed corruption through his brilliant staff, fired editors at will, wrote sharp-edged editorials, and competed with the formidable William Randolph Hearst; with stately Whitelaw Reid, who had followed Horace Greeley as owner of the *Tribune;* and with Adolph Ochs, looming as the master practitioner among them. Ochs challenged Bennett in the foreign field, where the *Herald's* strength chiefly lay.

Frank A. Munsey had become owner of the *Herald* by the time the expatriates of the 1920s poured in, and peace and reconstruction activities were underway. The French were turning to sports, and the Olympic games in 1924 brought waves of Americans into Paris. Sparrow Robinson, an amateur athlete who had gone to Europe with the Y.M.C.A., wrote a column "Sporting Gossip," which was a feature of the *Herald* for the next twenty years. He commented on the life of Americans in Europe as well as on sports events. Eugene O'Neill, settled for a time near Tours, said that he went to the village every morning to get the *Herald* because he could not settle down to his day's work until he had read what Sparrow had to say. William O. McGeehan, of the New York *Herald Tribune,* Westbrook Pegler, then of the Chicago *Tribune,* and other stars of journalism from Park Row were in and out of the Paris newspaper offices as Gertrude Ederle swam the Channel and Suzanne Lenglen clinched honors on the tennis courts. The transatlantic flights were thrilling events for the correspondents in Paris, and the night in 1927 when Lindbergh landed at Le Bourget was one of the unforgettable moments in expatriate life. An era was born, as again in the space achievements of the 1960s. It was the decade of aviation. It was also the decade of the crash. The expatriates sensed the approach of disaster, and many headed for home.

Hemingway and Fitzgerald

Ernest Hemingway was a presence on the Left Bank before he won a reputation as a writer. He was not a man to be overlooked in any gathering. His firm, robust body and tough, defensive manner made him conspicuous among the languid, the cynical, the eccentric, and the conventionally handsome expatriates who hung around the cafés. Although the master drinker and idler when he wished to be, he was immune to dalliance when he felt the urge to write. None of the playboys could divert him from his purpose when the spirit moved him to work, or when he felt that things were going well. He could rid himself of parasites, gossips, and bores more easily than his more malleable friend, F. Scott Fitzgerald, or other good-natured members of the expatriate community.

Hemingway felt that he was on top of the world during these days of inspiration in Paris. He was a productive, careful worker, and when he was busy he chose the cafés where he was least likely to be bothered by his fellows. He knew that the Sélect would mean chatter about horses and racing with Harold Stearns, and there was danger there, since he liked racing, gambling, tennis, and boxing. The revolutionaries liked the Rotonde, and the painters and writers who worked all day favored the Dôme, so Hemingway chose his bistros with forethought. When in dead earnest, he would retreat to the

Closerie des Lilas, and he wrote much of *The Sun Also Rises* over *café crème* at this quiet hideaway. With a horse chestnut and rabbit's foot in his pocket for luck, he hunched his broad shoulders over a marble-topped table and wrote and rewrote in blue French notebooks. The Closerie was close to 113 Rue Notre-Dame-des-Champs, where he lived at the time. There were tables out under the trees, and the American writers who liked to see and be seen rarely came to the bistro. The old coffee club tradition of England in the eighteenth century had its logical sequel in the cafés of the Left Bank, as in the bars and restaurants of the 1960s most favored by the floaters of the international set. The wanderer of each generation had to find a place to mingle with his fellows, to drink, to talk, and to absorb the native atmosphere. Cafés were the inevitable gathering ground.

Poets had once favored the Closerie des Lilas, and many of the wounded French veterans of World War I also came in for a drink. Some of the men wore the Croix de Guerre and the Médaille Militaire; a few were amputees. They mingled with the middle-aged patrons and glanced through the papers and magazines strung on rods. Hemingway observed them closely. He had the interest of the journalist in his fellow human beings, and as correspondent for the Toronto *Star* he was alert to what went on around him. But until the smashing success of *The Sun Also Rises* in 1926, he was just another member of the expatriate community, and sometimes a rather troublesome one. His work found publication at times in the little magazines. It appeared in *This Quarter, Transition,* and *TransAtlantic Review.* McAlmon took note of his literary style, but did not like him. Ezra Pound was a firm friend, and Hemingway thought him the kindest man he had ever known. Pound lived on the same street at this time, and his studio was warm and comfortable. Hemingway would drop in and take casual note of the paintings done by Japanese artists whom Pound knew.

Hemingway was not a man who cared to have his work torn apart, but he considered Pound a critic of judgment and kindness, and he wrote of Ezra, "His own writing, when he would hit it right, was so perfect, and he was so sincere in his mistakes . . . and so kind to people that I always thought of him as a sort of saint. He was also irascible but so perhaps have been many saints."

Pound warned Ernest not to take offense at Ford Madox Ford's rude ways, but Hemingway found his "heavy, wheezing, ignoble presence" unendurable and was barely civil to him when they met inevitably at the Left Bank parties. He was equally averse to Wyndham Lewis, but Pound was more involved than the other Americans on the Left Bank with the writers who had come over from London.

Hemingway's passion for sports and for speed was not in keeping with the expatriate spirit of the Left Bank. He believed in keeping physically fit, and he exercised regularly. He walked vigorously along the quais and would approach the cafés with a suggestion of the jogger's trot. But he could also dawdle over the bookstalls on the quais, watch the fishermen dangle their rods over the Seine, and stand outside Michaud's to watch Joyce and his wife, Nora, order a hearty meal. Hemingway had some hungry hours on the Left Bank, when he could afford only the cheapest Corsican wine, but he was always ready to gamble his last cent on a horse. When he had money, he went to the races, and he boxed regularly, inciting some of his less muscular colleagues to keep fit in this way. His lust for speed grew with the years, and as he prospered, he became an enthusiastic observer of the six-day bicycle races and of road-racing in the mountains.

A trip to Spain in 1924 changed the course of his life and made him a bullfight aficionado. On his return his friends noticed that he had become obsessed with the subject, and that he was apt to indulge in shadow fighting, doing imaginary cape work and sword thrusts, as if the toro were at hand. This was not out of character, since he had amused his friends before by shadow boxing as he approached them. He considered himself unbeatable as a boxer, and when Morley Callaghan arrived from Toronto, they had bouts together, and one notable one, which brought Hemingway into conflict with Fitzgerald.

Callaghan was writing about sports at the time, with some concentration on prize fighters, gangsters, and tough, silent characters. Hemingway thought the Canadian was imitating his style, and there was a slight mist of suspicion between them, but Callaghan was the first formidable opponent he had had. Pound urged Hemingway to teach him to box, and his enthusiasm for this sport, as for bullfighting, conveyed itself to more impressionable colleagues. Fitzgerald, assigned to referee a bout between Hemingway and Callaghan, muffed the task for reasons never well defined, but the incident stirred up a controversy on the Left Bank in 1929 that left echoes in literary circles for years. Fitzgerald and Callaghan each viewed the bout differently. Callaghan had knocked Hemingway down so that he lay sprawled on his back. Fitzgerald let the round continue for four minutes, one minute overtime. Ernest thought that his friend Scott had done this on purpose. When it was over, Scott whispered to Callaghan, "Don't you see I got fascinated watching? I forgot all about the watch. My God, he thinks I did it on purpose. Why would I do it on purpose?"

Messages whizzed back and forth across the Atlantic after the New York *Herald Tribune* published a version of the fight that became controversial. Callaghan felt that the incident had soured the relationship of the two men, although they kept up a show of friendship. He liked both Hemingway and Scott and wrote of them, in his book *That Summer in Paris,*

> Hemingway in his prime, the man I knew in Paris, the author of the early books and *A Farewell to Arms,* was perhaps the nicest man I had ever met . . . . In the good days he was a reticent man, often strangely ingrown and hidden with something sweet and gentle in him. But I was glad to hear that in the last year of his life out in Sun Valley, he talked to the photographer so affectionately about those days in Paris with Scott and me, and sent me at last his warm regards.

"That summer in Paris" was 1929. Both authors had helped to start Callaghan on his writing career, but he drifted so far away from Hemingway that he did not congratulate his famous colleague on winning the Nobel Prize.

Hemingway and Fitzgerald were the two who towered over their expatriate fellows during the hectic 1920s. But as Hemingway came to the front, Fitzgerald declined in popularity. It was a gradual descent, characterized by unlimited drinking, endless partying, and a flashing existence all over Europe. Hemingway blamed the beautiful Zelda Sayre Fitzgerald, a soft-eyed girl from Montgomery, Alabama, for Scott's ruin, and Zelda's friends blamed Scott and some of his wild compatriots. But her schizophrenic history was already well defined as she moved restlessly among the glittering play children of their world. Some detected her oncoming madness before Scott did, or at least before he would accept the fact.

The Fitzgeralds lived on a much more lavish scale than their friends on the Left Bank. Profits from the play based on *The Great Gatsby* were filling the family coffers. As the young Princetonian tasted the wine of success, he quickly became a worshipper of Hemingway's work, as different from his own as night from day. They met in 1925 coming out of the Dingo Bar in the Rue Delambre, and Hemingway thought the gilded youth, who had become legendary, was in poor shape physically. His face seemed slightly puffy, but his tailoring was impeccable except for a Guard's tie, which Hemingway thought he had no right to wear. He decided that Scott looked like a boy with a rather handsome face—"fair wavy hair, a high forehead," friendly excited eyes, and a "delicate long-lipped Irish mouth that, on a girl, would have been the mouth of a beauty." His capable hands and well-modeled chin commended themselves to Hemingway, the accomplished fighter. Ernest knew that Scott could box, as well as write, and drink, and charm all whom he met.

Soon the two men were close friends, and Fitzgerald became little short of idolatrous about the lean, spare style of the new master. He was unqualified in his praise, sometimes to Hemingway's embarrassment. Ernest was not given to praise or to criticism of another man's work. He had a major talent for silence, and when he disliked something, he made no comment. But he genuinely admired *The Great Gatsby* and wrote in *A Moveable Feast,* published in 1964,

> When I had finished the book I knew that no matter what Scott did, nor how he behaved, I must know it was like a sickness and be of any help I could to him and try to be a good friend. He had many good, good friends, more than anyone I knew. But I enlisted as one more, whether I could be of any use to him or not. If he could write a book as fine as *The Great Gatsby* I was sure that he could write an even better one. I did not know Zelda yet, and so I did not know the terrible odds that were against him. But we were to find them out soon enough.

Fitzgerald, already well established with Scribner's publishing house and George Horace Lorimer, editor of the *Saturday Evening Post,* was so eager to help the lesser known writer that Hemingway found him "cynical and funny and very jolly and charming and endearing." Fitzgerald could laugh at his own work, but he pounced on anyone who downgraded the work of Hemingway. Scott saw it as a new form of art. It was not the sort of thing he could do himself, but he divined that it was a fresh style in letters.

The two men got to know each other well and to size up their natural weaknesses on a trip they took together to Lyons soon after meeting. Hemingway decided as he watched Scott fall apart that he had a chemical intolerance for liquor, and would go ashen and helpless on quantities that Hemingway would not even feel. He also decided that Scott was a hypochondriac, and quite irrationally prejudiced against the French and Italians. Fitzgerald wavered about the English, alternately admiring them and deploring their conventional ways.

Fitzgerald's quick and total revival after a drinking bout also amazed Hemingway. Scott was always intent on getting some work done, but the moment would pass unfulfilled. When drunk, he would look up Hemingway and take "almost as much pleasure interfering with my work·as Zelda did interfering with his. This continued for years but, for years too, I had no more loyal friend than

Scott when he was sober," Hemingway wrote. When he visited the Fitzgeralds at their furnished flat at 14 Rue Tilsitt, Ernest had his first glimpse of Zelda, already acquiring a hazy fame of her own, and of their daughter, Scotty, who one day would become a popular writer and hostess in Washington. Zelda was suffering from a hangover at the time, a commonplace in the expatriate colony, but her blonde hair and tautly drawn features suggested the beauty for which she was noted. Hemingway disliked her on sight. He commented on her "secret smile" and what seemed to him to be the "predatory eyes of a hawk." Scott watched her closely and was protective at times. He would tell her to go to bed when she seemed to be tired and would explain that she had to get up early in the morning to take ballet lessons. This became lifelong therapy for Zelda, who kept up her ballet lessons when she lived in the South after having a total breakdown.

It was apparent to her husband's friends that she longed to assert herself, that she felt she could write, that she wished to be recognized. With burning intensity she would insist, "I write prose. It's good prose." When *Scribner's Magazine* printed one of her stories, she was elated and talked about it constantly. When Scott was working on *Tender Is the Night,* he was despondent about the slow pace at which he proceeded. Callaghan thought that actually he worked harder than Hemingway did, and that he had fantastic energies stored within him. "What power of concentration while at the same time he watched over the wife whom Hemingway had called crazy," Morley commented. He recalled a night they spent talking at the Lilas under the chestnut trees. Scott had brought Mary Blair, who had been married to Edmund Wilson, to dinner, and he was talking in his frank, joyous way about the writing set. Sinclair Lewis was the man of the hour.

"Do you know I predate Sinclair Lewis," he announced suddenly. "I predate him as a writer. I had a success with *This Side of Paradise* before he had any success. I was an established writer before Lewis was. What do you think of that?"

The violins were playing under the chestnut trees. The tune was "Ramona," and they all felt nostalgic. Fitzgerald took off the pearl gray hat he always wore at a jaunty angle and in a whimsical way settled it on Callaghan's head. "You poor old guy," said Callaghan, with a touch of pity. There were later scenes when Callaghan visited the Fitzgeralds, and found Zelda "pale, haggard, dark patches under her eyes," with the overhead hall light shining on her blond head and showing up the ravages of her face. Afterward Callaghan realized that he had walked in on the scene that Fitzgerald later used in

Tender Is the Night, involving a man he had wrongly accused of theft, a police interrogation, and his embarrassment in the presence of other Americans.

"In those days," Callaghan wrote,

> whenever Scott did something ridiculous, he was caught red-handed. But worse, he suffered for things he didn't do; he had a knack of making himself always look worse than he was . . . . On the other hand, it was intolerable to Ernest to be in a bad light. Yet such was his nature, and his attractiveness, that he only needed to wait; in the course of time, no matter what he had done, he would manage to emerge in a good light.

Whether falling flat on his face, or letting dollar bills drift like petals to the floor in a nightclub, Scott remained an object of commanding interest to visiting Americans. His colleagues liked him for his generosity and his willingness to extol work other than his own. Callaghan thought that as much as anyone he had ever known Fitzgerald had a "conception of an aristocracy of talent." Hemingway upheld the vogue he had created for the stripped, staccato sentence, the virtue of repetition, which Gertrude Stein liked to think he had learned from her.

The animosities, feuds, and jealousies among the expatriates were considerable, as well as the assorted romances, changing of wives, and casual love affairs. Fitzgerald had a theory that Hemingway needed a new woman for each big book, and no one was surprised when he broke with the faithful Hadley Richardson, divorced her, and married Pauline Pfeiffer in 1927. "There was one for the stories and *The Sun Also Rises,*" commented Scott. "Now there's Pauline. *A Farewell to Arms* is a big book. If there's another big book I think we'll find Ernest has another wife." It was no secret in the select group that Lady Brett of *The Sun Also Rises* was Lady Duff Twysden, an Englishwoman who seemed strangely alien to the spirit of Montparnasse. McAlmon took her big bare studio when she went off to Spain. He failed to find her either witty or amusing, and she had the habit of becoming haughty at dangerous moments.

Hemingway rewrote the first half of *The Sun Also Rises* at Schruns in the Vorarlberg in Austria. He reveled in the trails through the orchards and fields of the hillside farms and the warm houses with their great stoves and big wood piles covered with snow. But the years with Hadley were coming to an end. He took the first draft of the book to New York to show to Max Perkins of Scribner's, a connection made for him by Fitzgerald. Then he returned to Austria to complete the final draft, and he did not show it to Fitzgerald until it was completely finished. "I remember joking with him about it, and him being worried and anxious to help as always once a thing was done," Hemingway recalled in *A Moveable Feast*. "But I did not want his help while I was rewriting."

In 1926 he visited the Fitzgeralds on the Riviera at Juan-les-Pins and showed Scott his revision of *The Sun Also Rises*. The Fitzgeralds were enjoying profits from Scott's play. Zelda was looking particularly gorgeous, with her skin a "lovely gold color" and her "hawk's eyes clear and calm." But a chance remark she made persuaded Hemingway that she was insane. She asked him, in all seriousness, whether he did not think Al Jolson was greater than Christ. "Scott did not write anything any more that was good until after he knew that she was insane," he commented.

Hemingway grew away from his fellow writers as his own success became overwhelming. In course of time he turned against Fitzgerald. But he was always friendly to Joyce. He liked Dos Passos and felt that the young Chicagoan understood the types in *Three Soldiers*. McAlmon and Hemingway were on edge with each other from the day they met at Ezra Pound's house in Rapallo. McAlmon thought him consciously hard-boiled, case-hardened, and old; and again sensitive, young, and naive, wishing to be brave, yet on the defensive. Both Ford Madox Ford and McAlmon were unpopular, but McAlmon had helped so many on their way up that he held a niche of his own. They all liked Ezra Pound. Fitzgerald could not stand McAlmon, and McAlmon despised Hemingway. Joyce was one of the few who could tolerate McAlmon. The feuds and quarrels, the scrapes and achievements of the elite among the writers made literary gossip at home and abroad.

Owen Johnson resisted the assumption that Fitzgerald had been the first to depict the doings of the flapper and the jazz age. His own novel *The Salamander*, published in 1913, had been the first, he claimed. But the legends about Fitzgerald and other writers flourished like tropical blossoms as tourists swarmed over Paris and lounged in the cafés, hoping for glimpses of the geniuses of the Left Bank. "The bums," Hemingway noted, "could be seen in the cafés in the forenoons." The workers came out only at night.

Caresse and Harry Crosby, a well-off poet and publisher, lived in an old mill on the Duc de La Rochefoucauld's estate near Paris. Hart Crane, the Ohio poet, Douglas Fairbanks, Sr., and other American celebrities of the day would roll up in the afternoon to drink and listen to jazz. Both Europe and America were being swept by this strange new music. Radio was carrying it over the airways. Records were selling by the million. Crosby, who took opium pills, flitted uneasily from point to point, moving through Italy and Spain, crossing to Africa, tasting the sturdy seafaring life of the Basque coast, playing baccarat at Deauville, turning up periodically in the art galleries and bookshops of Paris—the playboy who could never find nepenthe. He died at home after his expatriate years, in the "maw of violence" that Fitzgerald had foreseen for him. In 1929 he and a young married woman named Mrs. Josephine Bigelow were found dead at the Hotel des Artistes in New York in a double suicide pact. Hart Crane, another of the playboys of the period, slipped off the *Orizaba* in 1932 on his way home from Mexico.

The more gifted of the expatriates lived with such intensity that they moved ahead to fame or sank into ruin. Fitzgerald thought he could do better if he holed in on the Riviera to work, but ultimately he died in Hollywood. Pound settled in Rapallo. He was missed on the Left Bank, but many of his old associates visited him in his Italian home. Some scattered to islands in the old tradition of escape when they left Paris at the end of the 1920s—to Majorca and Capri, Corsica, the isles of Greece, the South Sea Islands, in the fashion of Gauguin and later of James Michener. Africa drew many, as Negro dances, music, and masks—popularized in the nightclubs of Paris and Harlem—focused attention on the arts of the black man and his native music. The little oasis of Bou Saada brought some to the edge of the Sahara Desert. Algiers became as popular with American expatriates as Marrakesh in the 1940s and 1950s. They explored the Tripolitan coast and found new beauties on the Dalmatian coast of Yugoslavia. They visited Persia, Abyssinia, or Central Africa. Some, like Sinclair Lewis and Theodore Dreiser, went to Russia in 1927, drawn by the mysterious events and conflicting passions of the days following the Bolshevik Revolution.

The tourists had made Paris as obnoxious to some of the writers as their native country, and the publication of Sinclair Lewis' *Main Street, Babbitt,* and *Elmer Gantry* during the 1920s made the image of babbittry one to be avoided by the American abroad. Lewis was a confirmed expatriate—perhaps the most famous of them all— but he never associated himself in any way with the exiles of the Left Bank. They, in turn, were contemptuous of his literary style, deeming it commonplace, and they disliked his Middle Western point of view. He stayed in the best hotels and dined in the best restaurants. Never one of the indigent, he was by all odds the most observant of the exiles. He tramped the boulevards alone, and he also liked to drink alone. His tall, angular figure, with his pock-marked face and nervous, mottled hands, caused more of a stir on the Right

Bank among the American tourists than it did on the Rive Gauche. After *Babbitt* came out, the tourists moved with more care, lowered their voices, subdued their boasting, minded their manners.

Djuna Barnes, the proud, beautiful girl from New York State, who was poet, playwright, and dreamer, snubbed Lewis when he appeared in the Gypsy Bar. She had not liked a story he had written making fun of what he called "hobohemia," nor did she admire his work. McAlmon recalled an uncomfortable evening when Lewis showed up with his first wife, Grace, at the Stryx, a popular Swedish restaurant. Lewis said to him, "Bob, I want you to meet Gracie. People say she is difficult, but maybe you won't find her so." McAlmon took her to the bar and over gin fizzes she suddenly asked him three questions: Did he think Lewis the greatest American writer? Was he a fine artist? Was he America's first?

The questions came so quickly that McAlmon did not answer, and Grace turned away and refused to drink. At that time McAlmon had not read any of Lewis' books, and his short stories had not impressed him. He and Lewis had something of the same Midwestern background, and he was scornful of the echoes of Main Street he heard quoted everywhere. "He gives to the traveling salesman, the fake-superior pseudo intellectual, and to the Europeans, a picture of America which they like to believe in order to feel their superiority," McAlmon said of Lewis. "He fits in with Mencken and his Americans, but before him there had been Stephen Crane, Henry James, and at the time, Dos Passos had drawn wholly and in a characterized way several human beings in his *Three Soldiers.*"

McAlmon deemed Edith Wharton's *Ethan Frome* to be worth more than all that Lewis had written. When Lewis won the Nobel Prize in 1930, he referred to his old tormentors of the Left Bank as "a little insane." He had brought ridicule on himself at the Dôme when an admirer told him his characterization was better than Flaubert's but his style was inferior to that of the French master. Intoxicated at the time, and standing up as he talked, Lewis insisted that he not only depicted character better than Flaubert but also had a better style.

"Sit down," someone shouted. "You're just a best seller."

This was the coup de grâce, and Lewis was crushed. McAlmon commented bitterly, "The world has become accustomed to seeing the Nobel Prize given to writers of second or third rank. It is pleasing to the populace, the mediocre."

But together Sinclair Lewis, Henry Mencken, and George J. Nathan had shaken up a generation with their pointed inroads on tradition, convention, and national custom. The debunking school had taken hold in postwar America as surely as the Hemingway genre had been born, but neither group had much respect for the other. Americans as a whole were more deeply aware of Lewis in the 1920s than they were of Hemingway. Red Lewis seemed incurably bumptious to his fellow expatriates, and when he drank he was difficult and quarrelsome. He, too, became a wanderer, always looking for the perfect place to settle. He went from country to country, taking notes insatiably, drinking insatiably, yet writing only about his homeland, and remaining completely American in all his ways and thoughts. He believed he had found happiness in Germany when Dorothy Thompson, the brilliant correspondent running a newspaper bureau in Berlin, drew him there. After a swift and insistent courtship by Lewis, they were married in 1928. Some hectic years at home and abroad followed, with the birth of a son, Michael, and the rise of Dorothy as a woman of political power.

After their divorce in 1942 Lewis again became the wandering expatriate. He returned to his own Minnesota for a time, just as Glenway Westcott had to his native Wisconsin in 1927. But the charm did not work in either case. The expatriate spirit held firm. Lewis died alone in Rome, with no friend near him but his secretary. The lonely man from Sauk Center, Minnesota, who had stirred up American letters, enraged his fellow countrymen, and been revered by them, was on the front page of papers all over the world when he died, but for a long time he had been the forgotten man of letters. Students of the 1960s, bred on avant-garde writings of a new order, wondered what all the fuss had been about in the distant 1920s when Lewis and even Hemingway were such idols.

There were few solid friendships among writers in these years of their germinal writing. If the confirmed expatriates could not live on American soil, they chose nearly always to write about the land from which they had sprung and the people they had known from childhood. Few wrote convincingly of the foreign milieu in which they lived, except for the descriptive backgrounds used by Hemingway and others.

This fact was pointed up by Sam Spewack, first a newspaper correspondent, later a successful playwright, collaborating with his wife Bella. The expatriate dream he had cherished for years dissolved in 1926 when he headed home at the height of his journalistic career. "The fact is that no matter how long you live in a foreign country you are never part of it. You remain an outsider," Sam wrote in a *Saturday Evening Post* article entitled "Four Years in Europe Made Me an American." Growing up on the lower East Side he had heard his parents speak of the glories and culture of Europe. He was twenty-two when he went abroad, and in the years that followed he traveled all over Europe. He talked to Lenin and Trotsky. He watched the French legions occupy the Ruhr. He saw the Communist uprising in the same region and listened skeptically to the false promises of statesmen. Spewack zoomed to the top of his field, working for the New York *World*. But when he made his choice and returned home, he said, "I was convinced that Europe was not the place to live; that the Europe of 1926 offers no culture not obtainable in America while it despises the new culture which America is producing. . . . Europe is standing still. It is looking backward."

This was the expatriate story in reverse. Spewack, witty, shy, and brilliant, returned to America, made a fortune with plays, traveled abroad when he wished to, but his expatriate years had served to strengthen his faith in his own country. Louis Bromfield, another correspondent, who with his wife, Mary, ran a cosmopolitan ménage at Senlis, close to Paris, entertaining the celebrities and wits of the period, returned before World War II to the home of his ancestors in Ohio. Malabar Farm became known around the world for its technical efficiency and great acres. The Bromfield guest list still sparkled with well-known names, and Lauren Bacall and Humphrey Bogart were married there in 1945. At Senlis it had been Leslie Howard, Douglas Fairbanks, and Ina Claire, but a new generation was on the scene. Nothing in Bromfield's later years compared with the romantic days at Senlis, but his work at Malabar Farm had patriotic undertones, and he found that in spirit he had never been far away from his native land. Expatriatism could be more a state of mind than a matter of geography.

Nomads at Large

The escapists are everywhere today. The whole world is their playground. The islands, which beguiled even the early whaling captains, are still the most cherished of havens, but they make their oases everywhere—in the desert, in the jungle, on snow-capped mountains and solitary plains. The old-time image of the resident American permanently abroad has changed with the constant rush across the world of the Jet Set, the fashionables who follow the sun, the latest sport, the newest casino or resort hotel, the last word in high-paced living. They have taken possession of the most halcyon isles, stripping them of their solitude, their simplicity, their low prices, and beating the old-style expatriate at his own game.

Their restless quest for luxury and pleasure, for exotic parties and social momentum, makes them a race apart, the marionettes of the society and gossip columns, familiar but only half-real to the quiet people who travel for travel's sake. They are not a wholly new breed, but they have more money and mobility than their ancestors who traveled on a statelier basis. They can move fast from point to point, and new diversions open up for them almost overnight. They are well named the Jet Set, since they travel like meteors—from Acapulco to Gstaad, from Honolulu to Tangier, where Barbara Hutton, the Woolworth heiress, has one of her many mansions.

They build Arabian palaces and go on safaris. With half their time spent in the expatriate world, they keep their American passports constantly in use.

The history of the expatriate is inseparable from the mystique of far islands. The trade winds bearing the scent of spices, the crescent beaches and jade waters, the blaze of blossoms and the languid ways of the natives, have lured artists and writers of all nations, and the earliest sailors from America were touched by their drawing power. This trend took root in the literary world when Robert Louis Stevenson wrote of the native life of Samoa. He had sailed from San Francisco on a health cruise that took him to the Marquesas Islands, Tahiti, Molokai, Honolulu, and the Gilbert Islands, and ended up in contented exile with his American wife at Samoa from 1889 until his death in 1894. Tusitala, or the Teller of Tales, as the natives knew him, lived at Vailima, five hundred feet above sea level, during his long fight against tuberculosis. His influence was far-reaching in the United States.

Lafcadio Hearn, born on the Greek island of Santa Maura and an American journalist from the age of nineteen, did much to foster interest in escape to the Orient. After working in Cincinnati and New Orleans, and contributing to *Century Magazine* and *Harper's Weekly,* he taught English in Japanese schools and married a native girl. He was a true expatriate because he became a Japanese citizen, using the name Yakumo Koizumi. He wore native robes and tried to interpret the Japanese to his fellow countrymen. This came in the late nineteenth century, when a general interest in Oriental art was developing in the United States, and Japanese prints and Chinese porcelains were greatly prized in American homes.

The highly stylized writings of Pierre Loti added fuel to this fire. The French naval officer and novelist, whose stories were infused with delicately done local color, became the rage, and the young were urged to read him for style. He romantically evoked the image of the Orient for many Americans with his *Madame Chrysanthème, Les Derniers Jours de Pékin, Fantôme d'Orient, The Marriage of Loti,* and other works in his highly individualistic style. He was married for a time to a European woman, Judith Gautier, daughter of Théophile Gautier, leader of the Parnassians, but the Oriental image surrounded him constantly, and Americans found seduction in his writings. George Biddle, author and artist from Philadelphia, who had been a wandering expatriate for years, spent two years in the early twenties on Tahiti.

The South Sea Islands, and Tahiti in particular, had become the new paradise as Gauguin, James Norman Hall—working in collaboration with Charles B. Nordhoff—and James A. Michener wrote richly and creatively in this setting. Hall's *Faery Lands of the South Seas,* followed by the lusty *Mutiny on the Bounty, Pitcairn Island,* and *Men Against the Sea,* would keep a generation of cinema fans enthralled, aside from an assorted multitude of readers. Hall and Michener gave the South Sea Islands at different times a special aura for those who sought escape.

World War II made a difference to the romantic islands of the South Pacific, with new roads, military installations, health measures, and a general quickening of the business tempo. But Samoa, the only United States territory south of the Equator, hung on to its languor and was fighting drastic changes in 1969. Pago Pago, with its easygoing Polynesian way of life, its Sadie Thompson tradition, felt threatened by television, the constant flow of tourists, and an invasion of Hippies. A naval and fueling station and an airfield had brought sleepy Pago Pago into the central stream of life, while the natives still clung devotedly to their natural ways, to copra drying, their fishing and their taro fields. They were only mildly stirred when the astronauts, back from their trip to the moon, landed in their vicinity.

Majorca was early tagged one of the blessed isles of escape, when Chopin, suffering from tuberculosis like Robert Louis Stevenson, sought its mild climate and singular beauty with George Sand. Many Americans since then have made Majorca a retreat, living on its terraced slopes, with a vista all around them of almond, fig, and lemon trees, sloping down to a palm-fringed coastline. The dean of island writers, Robert Graves, an Englishman who chose to live in a house without telephone or car, writing on an eighteenth-century French escritoire with ivory inlay, was responsible for many Americans settling there. In 1929 he retired to a house he had built in a flowering hillside village after his valedictory autobiography, *Goodbye to All That.*

Many of the expatriates of the 1920s, including Gertrude Stein, tried Majorca for brief stays. Today the ranks have thinned as other islands have gained in popularity, but writers are still drawn by the mellow climate and the economical aspects, while other resorts soar in costs until they can be enjoyed only by the affluent. William L. Laurence, the veteran science reporter of *The New York Times* who shared in the mission when the first atomic bomb was dropped and gave the world its earliest description of this cataclysmic event, now finds quiet and peace on Majorca. Faye Emerson, once the daughter-in-law of Franklin D. Roosevelt, and a stage and television personality in New York, gardens in the soft winds and gentle sun of her chosen island. She has done over an old Spanish farmhouse, and she misses little about her native country except perhaps the glory of the autumn leaves in New England, which she still longs to see. Miss Emerson has returned to America only once in five and a half years. She still gets offers to work again in television and pictures, but she says firmly, "I'm completely retired and having a marvelous time. I don't regret anything I ever did, but I know that I'll never go back. . . . I have a beautiful garden which I love to work in. I read books, travel and have many friends."

Anne Sinclair Mehdevi, an American writer who married a Persian in 1945, has since lived most of the time on Majorca. American residents show interest, too, in the presence of aging Joan Miró, seventy-six years old and ever busy in the white stucco studio designed for him by José Luis Sert in 1956, next door to his two-hundred-year-old stone farmhouse. Sometimes he listens to the music of Bach, sometimes to that of the Beatles. The Hippies have not made headway on Majorca, but both they and the Jet Set turned their attention in 1968 to Ibiza, closest to Spain of the Balearic Islands, as a tiny gem for retreat, staked out by Stavros Niarchos from his yacht. Portugal has been running away with the honors for happy tourism, and the sun-swept beaches of Algarve in the south, and wooded valleys of the north, draw a growing number of Americans. Estoril, with its new casino and its fine Tomaris Beach, catches the international set, while immaculate Lisbon, with its seventeenth-century houses, winding cobblestone streets, flower merchants, and fresh-faced people, has great appeal for the traveler. South of the Tagus estuary American travelers find lagoons ideal for fishing, boating, water-skiing, and skin-diving, a contrast to the dark pine forests, alive with game.

Portugal, with its ancient architecture and its thoroughly modern conveniences, picked up international glitter in the autumn of 1968 with extravaganzas given by Mrs. Pierre Schlumberger and Mrs. Antenor Patino. Mrs. Schlumberger, with roots in New York and Houston and an oil equipment fortune behind her, entertained more than a thousand guests, including many of the most famous names in the arts, fashion, and society, at her sixteenth-century house, adorned for the occasion with synthetic Roman columns. A carpeted stone bridge led to a blue-tiled swimming pool, and the top names in contemporary sculpture were represented in the sculpture garden. It took four months to put up the party pavilion and one night for the rose petals to fade after the most discussed party since Truman Capote's historic bash in New York in 1966. Douglas and Mary Lou Fairbanks were there, as well as the Duchess of

Windsor and most of the fashion leaders of Europe and America.

Spain retains its classic place in the expatriate world, its glories extolled by Washington Irving in the early eighteenth century, by Hemingway in the 1920s, and by James Michener, author of *Iberia,* in the 1960s. Michener returns to enjoy its fiestas and flamenco dancing, an expatriate without strings, the writer who roams the world. The Countess of Quintanilla and Romanones, with houses in Madrid and Marbella, was Aline Griffith of Pearl River, up the Hudson and not far from New York, when fate whirled her into the international milieu and endowed her with two of the oldest titles in Spain. Pascualete, a thirteenth-century stone house four hours' drive from Madrid, is her country retreat, and there she and her husband raise racehorses, ducks, lambs, and chickens. With the money she made from her book about Pascualete, called *The Earth Rests Lightly,* she bought looms for her rug factory in Santa Marta. The weaving is done by the local women on a cooperative basis, and the rugs are in the Spanish home the Duchess of Windsor has at Marbella and on Audrey Hepburn's floors.

The countess's own story is one of high adventure. Fresh from school she joined the OSS and led the adventurous life of a spy during World War II. Since her marriage to Count Luis Quintanilla she has become the mother of three sons, and has also figured on the international list of best-dressed women. Members of the fashionable set, seeking novelty and seclusion, have made Marbella an expatriate retreat, from the Windsors to Baron and Baroness Hubert von Pantz. The baroness is an American heiress who believes in having houses in the most fashionable spots. Her best known is the Schloss Enzesfeld, an Austrian castle once owned by a Rothschild. But the adventurers and writers have also found in Spain cause for inspiration or indignation, and Robert Ruark, a New York newspaperman and author who died in London in 1965, wrote some of his best sellers in Spain.

The islands seem to be traditionally the more natural refuge of the literary or artistic expatriate, but the speed with which the traveler now reaches his destination may have robbed some of them of their romance. For twenty centuries it was the custom to cross from Naples to Capri by rowboat, barge, steamer, or motorboat. Now a hydrofoil or helicopter whirls one to the ancient playground of Tiberius and Augustus within a matter of minutes. Americans first began to flock to Capri after Norman Douglas' book *South Wind* came out in 1917. For a time it seemed a focus of expatriate life, as all the wandering tribes passing through Italy crossed to its fabulous shore to watch the grotesque parade in the Piazzetta, to visit the

Blue Grotto, to climb the heights to Anacapri, or to loaf at the romantic swimming pool owned by Gracie Fields, the aging English music-hall entertainer. The bells of the baroque church toll for the movie stars today as they did for monarchs, adventurers, and long-term expatriates in an earlier era. The outlandish costumes of Capri no longer seem so odd in a world attuned to all variations of freakish attire.

Sicily, with its Greek ruins, has long been an isle of escape. When British and American tourists began invading Taormina a century ago, they were following the Normans, the Saracens, the Byzantines, the Romans, and the Greeks. Seven hundred feet above the sea, broad lava-rock steps lead to cobbled streets and piazzas where Americans buy all manner of bibelots from crusader puppets to Sicilian donkey carts. Expatriates lounge at the Wonderbar and the Mocambo, and listen to rock and roll, and to electric guitars in a setting of ancient magnificence. Through broken arches they view the Greco-Roman theater, the cypresses and beaches below, and in the distance the smoky cone of Mount Etna. Few Americans have settled permanently in this volcanic, magnificent, and historic island, although it was essential in the itinerary of the leisured traveler of an earlier era. Today, like Capri, it is more of a stopover for the transient.

Interest for the time being has shifted to the isles of Greece, an old tradition, alive again in the 1960s. Popularized by Lord Byron in the nineteenth century and again in the headlines of 1969, when Jacqueline Kennedy married Aristotle Onassis on the island of Skorpios, the expatriate spirit has always been nourished in Greece and its islands. Corfu, the largest of the seven that make up the Ionian group—Paxos, Leukas, Ithaca, Cephalonia, Zante, and Cerigo—has an ancient history of expatriate adventure. Signs of its four centuries of occupation by the Venetians contrast today with its thoroughly American air of modern motels, marinas, hotels, restaurants, and taverns. The Georgian mansions of the British remain and cricket is still played, but the American feeling grows more noticeable in this beautiful island with its olive groves and Venetian flavor.

The fad for one isle of escape or another goes far back in American travel history. In the nineteenth century expatriates turned to the Sandwich Islands, before they became the Hawaiian Islands, or to the South Sea Islands, the Canary Islands, Majorca, or Sicily. It took time once to travel as far as Honolulu, but planes now bring more than a million tourists a year to Hawaii. The languid beach life has been stepped up beyond belief. Hotels and condominiums rise against the blue skyline, and Diamond Head looks diminished in the distance. Unemployment is at its lowest ebb, and the expatriate on the Hawaiian Islands no longer lives a life of leisure. The shower blossoms and bougainvillea are as lush as ever; the air is filled with fragrance; Waikiki Beach, small but exciting, has not lost its magic, but shopping centers and high-rise buildings are death to an ancient dream. Between 1960 and 1967 the islands absorbed 107,401 nonmilitary new residents. But the Hawaiians themselves in increasing numbers said "Aloha" to their lovely surroundings as they sought new lands themselves.

Now somber Sardinia has joined the charmed circle of isles of escape, as people grope for the unknown. They are drawn to the Sporting Club at Porto Rotondo, the crescent-shaped village facing the port. Wild boar, stags, the eagle, and vultures still make their home in the rocky hills, while the villagers pursue their tuna, lobster, and sardine fishing.

But islands no longer ensure peace of mind for the escapist. The ancient belief that a body of water separating one from the mainland would assuage romantic suffering was obviously an impossible dream. Swaying palms and scarlet oleanders close to turquoise waters are soothing, but they do not wipe out human ills. Now the most primitive spots have become the most fashionable, with thatched and coral houses renting for fantastic sums. The quest is for yet another little island that has not been reached by a cruising ship. Once James Thurber found peace to write and draw on Bermuda. Hemingway sought solitude in Cuba, after roaming the world. William Styron finds moments of quiet on Martha's Vineyard, and Nantucket remains a haven for artists and writers. Block Island, Shelter Island, and other lonely islands along the Eastern seaboard provide the isolation of difficult communication.

The Caribbean has become the favorite playground and retreat of people of wealth, and its islands are now familiar to all kinds of American travelers, who can leave their offices and land on enchanted islands in the space of a few hours. Aruba and Antigua, where the Paul Mellons have a home, are quiet and fashionable. Marietta and Ronald Lambert Field Tree have a compound, Heron Bay, in Barbados, and Mrs. Elsie Woodward, one of New York's most honored dowagers, winters nearby. Jamaica and the Virgin Islands are high on the traveler's list, with yachting and deep-sea fishing, water-skiing, snorkeling, treasure hunts, and Laurance Rockefeller's Little Dix Bay, a luxurious resort on a buccaneer shore. Americans dance the calypso to the rhythm of steel bands, dine by candlelight in a seventeenth-century café in Curaçao, or engage in a swinging flamenco in picturesque San Juan. But they know that they are never far away from it all, as Robert Louis Stevenson was on Tahiti or Lafcadio Hearn in Japan. With their worries often unrelieved they can be home in a few hours from the golden sands and green crystal shallows of any of the isles of escape.

They are on firmer ground at mainland resorts, like Acapulco, where Merle Oberon, married to Bruno Pagliai, the Mexican industrialist, and Sloan Simpson, once the wife of Mayor William O'Dwyer of New York City, are golden girls leading the expatriate life. Merle Oberon, a former film star, rules her empire like a queen, and during the Olympic Games of 1968 was official hostess to Prince Philip in her white marble palace overlooking Acapulco Bay. She is the beautiful exile, circa 1970—rich, jeweled, chic, with her own palace and many servants at her command. In the mood of her era she cruises on a friend's yacht from Naples to Greece, to Istanbul, to Rhodes, to Beirut, to Israel, to Crete, and back to Never Never Land.

Life at Acapulco has become the wanderers' dream—it is the "in" place of the day. They congregate at the swimming pool of the Villa Vera Racquet Club as they once did at Gracie Fields's place on Capri. They sail up the coast to watch the hazardous cliff-diving from the Quebrada rocks. They parachute behind speedboats, go skin-diving, water-skiing, surfing, and game-fishing. They keep a tight hand on fashion, and shop in the old town for the newest things. Or they sit in the moonlight in the gardens of Ghalal, the Pagliais' Moorish house, and consort with oilmen, stage stars, the granddaughters of Henry Ford, or with Paul Getty, Jr., son of the richest American of the expatriate world, safely grounded in England. Eleanor Lambert, czarina of the fashion world, is among them, dispensing hospitality and keeping a weather eye on the rich flow of fashion around her. Her Casa Leonor is in Las Brisas, and she is never far from the hostess of the hour, the newest turn in fashion, or the best parties, some of which she masterminds. Martha Gellhorn, once married to Ernest Hemingway, is a contemporary expatriate whose latest book, *The Lowest Trees Have Tops,* is a novel dealing with a colony of refugees in a Mexican mountain village. The expatriate life is nothing new for Martha.

To Americans resident in Mexico the Acapulco setting seems dreamlike, when the sun goes down in fiery splendor, the lights blossom, and the Mexican bands stir up the revelers. Life is simpler but even more intense at Puerto Vallarta, where Richard Burton, with his wife, Elizabeth Taylor, near at hand, made *Night of the Iguana.* Miss Taylor is another of the great stars who increasingly spends her time away from the United States. Her settings are as various as her moods, and the whole world recognizes her memorable face.

Perhaps the most noted of all the contemporary American exiles are the Duchess of Windsor—Wallis Warfield, a Baltimore girl for whom a king gave up a throne—and Princess Grace of Monaco, a Philadelphia girl who helps to conduct a principality, sends her children to the local schools in Monte Carlo, and has turned her face against all cinema offers, famous though she was as a star.

The Duchess of Windsor is an exile for obvious reasons. She fits into the ancient pattern of dislodged royalty, although her case is without historical parallel. No husband ever gave up so great an empire to live a wandering and expatriate life with the woman he loved. Since the duke will not live in England without full recognition of his American wife, the Windsors call Paris their home. But their weekend retreat, the Moulin de la Tuilerie, was up for sale for more than a million dollars in 1969. For years the exiled duke has used the mill as a retreat from the world. Surrounded by the memorabilia of his princely days, in rooms exquisitely furnished by his knowing wife, he has found solace in his land, his garden, his writing, and the companionship of his wife and many friends. The Windsors move with the seasons—to Marbella, to Palm Beach, with brief stops in New York and Baltimore. Even before her marriage to the Duke of Windsor, Wallis Warfield had spent much of her life abroad. Her second husband, Ernest Simpson, lived most of the time in England.

Princess Grace's case is different. She gave up a brilliant film career for a prince and evidently has found it a happy exchange. She spends little time in her native land, except for brief annual visits to Philadelphia and New York. She and her children have dual citizenship, Monegasque and American. Not for a moment has Princess Grace foresworn her American heritage, but her life is now fashioned in the Continental pattern, and she prefers the disciplined French training for her children. She has worked constructively at her job and is the leading spirit in the Monegasque Red Cross. Her gift for promoting Prince Rainier's realm is quite pronounced. The palace, with a hundred servants, runs like clockwork, and American, French, and Italian dishes are served. She supports the ballet and all the musical and artistic events likely to help Monaco.

Always beautiful to look at, the sports-loving American in the daytime, the diademed princess by night, she is an international figure of charm and distinction. If she welcomes Cary Grant or Jimmy Stewart at the palace, it's only a lingering echo of the days when she made pictures with them that thrilled the American public. As one of the most radiant stars of the screen she won an Oscar in 1954 for *The Country Girl*. Grace Kelly married Prince Rainier two years later, and now they have three children—Prince Albert, Princess Caroline, and Princess Stephanie. In defining her own status, she says, "I am now part Monegasque and part American and sometimes I feel I'm not one or the other but somewhere in the middle."

Hope Cooke, a Sarah Lawrence girl who became the Maharanee of Sikkim, has the most eerie of all expatriate settings in her mountain fastness. It seemed like Shangri-la when she married the maharajah, but the terrors of the modern world have shaken the little kingdom. The maharanee encourages native crafts and has been zealous in working for the health of the people. The Hippies were not allowed to invade her husband's realm. She rarely comes to the United States, and when she does it is as an ambassador to spread enlightenment about the Sikkimese and to display the crafts of the native women.

Princess Lee Radziwill, the sister of Mrs. Aristotle Onassis, is another American expatriate who has lived for years in England, the wife of Stanislas Radziwill, a Polish prince. She belongs to the international set and counts among her special friends Truman Capote and Rudolf Nureyev, the ballet dancer. The princess has stage ambitions but has not yet met with success. She accompanied her sister, then Mrs. John F. Kennedy, on an official trip to India, and is often at her side in moments of crisis.

Today the picture in London and on the Continent is young and swinging. Some of the older duchesses of American origin are still in circulation, but the social play lies in the hands of such dashing hostesses as the Vicomtesse de Rozière in Paris and the popular Duchesse d'Uzès, who was Peggy Bedford Bancroft d'Arenberg not so long ago, a princess whose husband died in 1967. An assortment of bright young Americans were as expert at snagging titles in the 1960s as they were in the 1890s. Debrett's still tells the enlightening tale of transatlantic unions. The Duchess of Rutland was Frances Sweeney, the Marchesa Lily Gerini was Lily Poli of New Haven, the Princess Chigi della Rovere was Marian Berry, and the Countess Alvise de Robilant was Elizabeth Storck. Baroness Philippe de Rothschild was Pauline Fairfax Potter, and Lady Ogilvy was Virginia Ryan of New York. The number of Italian and Greek alliances multiply, and titles abound. Countess Edward Bismarck, who spends much of her time on Capri, has long been one of America's most beautiful and regal expatriates. As Mrs. Harrison Williams she always made the list of best-dressed women. Green-eyed, soignée, uncommunicative, she is noted also for her tact and discretion.

One of London's most energetic American exiles is Mrs. Tom Montague Meyer, the former Fleur Cowles, who was once married to Gardner Cowles. Mrs. Meyer works hard as an artist, writer, philanthropist, and party giver for visiting Americans. No one is allowed to criticize the United States within Mrs. Meyer's hearing. She calls herself a "practicing American." In moving to London in 1955 she found what she wanted after a controversial existence—"exchanging the goldfish bowl for the incredible privacy of England."

Mrs. Meyer, whose husband's fortune is made from timber, has a country house in Sussex and a flat in London. She paints on weekends, working as she entertains friends. She has illustrated a book of animal stories and moves in the bright milieu of *Harper's Bazaar* and the fashion magazines of Britain, as does Pamela Colin, another dashing young New Yorker, who works for *Vogue* in London and is closely identified with the court set. Mrs. Meyer's special interest is work for the facially disfigured. She also applies her bright wits to helping the American Museum in Bath, an institution not duplicated anywhere outside of the United States. Aside from her philanthropic work she specializes in great parties, like a number of other American women abroad.

A much traveled and independent American girl who joined the expatriate ranks by marriage in 1968 is Sharman Douglas, daughter of a former ambassador at the Court of Saint James's. After many years of moving restlessly from one side of the Atlantic to the other, Miss Douglas married Andrew Hay, a Scot, but continued to circulate in Princess Margaret's set, where she had always been popular. No less close to the royal family is Douglas Fairbanks, Jr., who, like Charlie Chaplin, lives as an expatriate. These two stars of the cinema settled abroad for entirely different reasons. Chaplin sought political haven in Switzerland many years ago. Fairbanks refuses to call himself an exile and enjoys life on both sides of the Atlantic.

Like all screen stars, Fairbanks moves from continent to continent, but he has become so much a part of the court life in Britain that he lives in the manner of an Englishman. He has more than a superficial claim to this, since his father happened to be of English birth. But Fairbanks' business interests today are American, and he is a familiar figure in Hollywood, Palm Beach, Acapulco, or on a Caribbean island. He lives in England avowedly because he prefers the British way of life, but he has the best of both worlds. His children have been educated in England, and one of his daughters has married an Englishman. Although his mother and father were closely linked with Charlie Chaplin in the great days of Hollywood, there is no similarity in the status of the two men today. Charlie Chaplin burned his bridges when he left the United States. Douglas Fairbanks is a welcome figure in Britain or the United States.

Chaplin has bitterness in his heart, frequently expressed, for the country he foreswore, and his pictures have suffered from the blight he created for himself. His consummate art was legendary around the world for many years, and in most countries he is still considered the prince of comedians. Chaplin leads a formal and conventional life in Switzerland with his wife, Oona, the daughter of Eugene O'Neill. They have raised a large family, some of whom have rebelliously moved away from their father's cold domination and toward Hippie land, causing some public uproar. He has been severe with his children, and is much preoccupied with his professional life. His oldest son by an earlier wife, the late Sydney Chaplin, made headway on the American stage without his father's assistance, and he was Barbra Streisand's first vis-à-vis in *Funny Girl*.

In recent years Anthony Quinn has spent much of his time in Italy, living at the Villa Vigna San Antonio, in the Castelli Romani wine country southeast of Rome. He cultivated his own vineyard while making pictures, and spent much time with his four sons, Francesco, Daniel, Anthony, and Lorenzo. His wife Iolanda is Italian. Quinn, like all the film stars, is always ready to pack up and go on location. American stars are a community of their own today in Rome, and many take refuge in Switzerland—to rest, to ski, to seek beauty and rejuvenation at the health clinics. Audrey Hepburn, first married to Mel Ferrer, in her latest marriage to an Italian psychiatrist maintains her expatriate status, but her occasional presence in America to work on films causes something of a stir.

Positano, with its Renaissance architecture, is a center for music and art, and the Harkness Ballet, established by the wealthy Rebekkah Harkness, is identified now with Spoleto. Some of the old nineteenth-century spirit infuses the various American groups in Italy today, but with the emphasis on the new Mod World, and not on the Renaissance tradition.

American film producers lead an expatriate existence much of the time. The theatrical world is a shifting one as the stars move from point to point—Africa today, Australia tomorrow. The brooding shadow of Orson Welles hangs over the English studios at times, and he rarely returns to America, although he visits Spain and Italy. John Huston has gone one step further and has taken out citizenship in Ireland. This film producer, director, actor, and writer has found peace on his estate near Galway. As Master of Fox Hounds he qualifies as a country squire. Tall, shambling Huston, identified with some of Hollywood's most noted productions, had no particular reason for giving up his American citizenship. After living for a time in Ireland, he came to think it felt more like home than Hollywood did. His two children went to the local grade schools, continued their education at prep schools in England, and one has gone on to Trinity College. Many of the stars have been accused of living abroad in order to escape taxation; Huston has been under heavy fire in this respect. William Holden has his Mount Kenya game ranch in Africa and his apartment in Geneva, but his life, like that of other stars, is peripatetic.

Another successful producer and writer, who gave thirty years of his life to Hollywood and is now contentedly established on Grosvenor Square in London, is Nunnally Johnson, the wit from Georgia, who entered the writing field on Park Row in the 1920s. He has since sampled life in many parts of the world and has had a succession of popular films. Norman Krasna, also a Park Row graduate and Hollywood producer, finds Lausanne a paradise, with time to read, no telephone to annoy him, and fishing and golf close at hand. But the life of the producer is much like the life of the star—he can summon life's luxuries wherever he goes.

Olivia de Havilland qualifies as a true expatriate since she married Pierre Galante, of *Paris-Match*. They are legally separated but continue to live under the same roof, and she prefers to bring up her children in France. Deanna Durbin, a memorable young star of the 1940s with a nightingale voice and sparkling personality, lives in total retirement as a French housewife near Paris. She is happy with her home and children, and no longer worries about keeping down her weight, a problem that stood for a time between her and her career.

Almost as mobile as the producers and stars of stage and screen are American writers today—at least those who have flourished financially. Irwin Shaw calls Klosters in Switzerland his home, but he summers in Italy and never has any trouble finding his way to New York or Hollywood. He considers the skiing and mountain air fine for his children, who are trilingual, speaking English, French, and Italian like natives. The fact that his wife is Italian tends to keep him firmly based in Europe.

Marc Slonim, a survivor of the earlier generation of expatriates, also lives in Switzerland and has clear views on the differences between the exiles of the 1960s and the 1920s. He believes the day of the convinced expatriate is past. No longer is there the bitter rejection of the United States felt by the writers of fifty years ago, however critical they may be of the Vietnam war. Slonim, Irwin Shaw, James Jones, and Henry Miller are the writers who have stayed most consistently abroad. Styron tried France for two years. John Cheever took a year in Italy. John Hersey goes wherever he has an assignment, and John Gunther roves the world for his *Inside* books on countries and cities. Tennessee Williams and Truman Capote are apt to turn up in any part of the world, but never for long, since both are gadflies. James Baldwin goes where his work for the black community leads him, and he is often in Paris.

One long-time expatriate is Paul Bowles, a literary wanderer and music composer who has written in Italy, Spain, France, South America, Algiers, and on an island off the coast of Ceylon, which he bought in 1952. When Gertrude Stein suggested that Bowles try Tangiers, he found a number of American residents already there. Eugenia Bankhead, sister of the late Tallulah, had gone ashore for a visit and never rejoined her ship. Mary Rogers, daughter of Will Rogers, and Princess Martha Ruspoli of Cincinnati were two other compatriots already settled there. So was William Burroughs, the novelist, who has sought many retreats. Tangiers, Marrakesh, Casablanca, have all been expatriate havens at one time or another.

Mary McCarthy spends most of her time in Paris now, with visits to Venice, Vietnam, or other areas where her work takes her. Katherine Anne Porter passed her expatriate years in Mexico, with rich results in *Ship of Fools*. Firmly based in England are two American women writers of substance who occasionally visit the United States to lecture or attend to editorial matters. Virginia Cowles, daughter of Dr. Edward Cowles, a New York psychiatrist of the 1920s, is a social historian of the English scene. Emily Hahn, a versatile girl from Chicago with a scientific training, who has traveled the world over, lived for years in China, and writes today on a variety of subjects. She has never found that her years of exile have neutralized her sharp awareness of all things American. Her married name is Mrs. Charles Boxer, and she sent her only child to Vassar. Her work has appeared frequently in *The New Yorker,* a magazine that in 1969 still had perhaps the most enduring of all the expatriates on its staff.

Janet Flanner is one of a group of three women—the other two being Maria Jolas and Natalie Clifford Barney—whose expatriate status reaches back to the 1920s and who are still living in Paris. Miss Flanner is a native of Indianapolis who settled in Paris in 1922 after a brief period in Greenwich Village. Three years later she became the permanent correspondent of *The New Yorker,* and Harold Ross, its founder, named her Genêt. For more than forty years her impeccable prose and sophisticated viewpoint from Paris have graced the magazine's pages. For half of this time she has lived on the top floor of the Continental Hotel, with the gardens of the Tuileries, the dome of the Invalides, and the Eiffel Tower for a view, and she faces the projected demolition of the hotel with dismay. She likes to recall that the Empress Eugénie spent the last years of her life at the Continental.

Now silver-haired, with chiseled features and an inherent sense of style, Miss Flanner is representative of the generation that sought aesthetic satisfaction abroad, and she found it in rich measure as she studied the architecture, civilization, and arts of France; visited the palaces and gardens; observed the ways of the people. Starting her day with Chinese tea and croissants, she has lived in the Continental manner and has never regretted her life of exile. No observer has been more alert than Miss Flanner to the gradual Americanization of Paris. She views the snack bars and hot dogs grilled on French rolls with an understanding eye, and takes note of the new linguistic jargon of the young, half-French, half-American. Her essays on Parisian life have been fresh and keen, but she has shown her greatest skill in political commentary and her appraisal of the arts. She has watched the expatriates come and go, while maintaining her own steady pace, an American daughter of Quaker parents with an infallible instinct for the *mot juste.*

Miss Barney, whose Friday afternoons were a literary institution in the 1920s, has now passed ninety and is living with many memories at 20 Rue Jacob. The pavilion in her garden where she used to receive Proust, Joyce, Anatole France, Colette, and Gertrude Stein, is a dim little landmark in a sea of noisy traffic. She deplores the cocktail party of today, for Miss Barney's technique was always that of the salon. But she is not forgotten. Young authors aware of her legendary history drop in, and Truman Capote and Mary McCarthy are among her callers. When revisiting his old Parisian haunts in recent years, Ezra Pound revived the bright days of the 1920s for her. More surprisingly, in the spring of 1969, at the age of eighty-four, he appeared on his old campus at Hamilton College, Clinton, New York, to receive an honorary degree.

Tall and impressive as in the days when she edited *Transition* with her husband Eugene, Maria Jolas lives today on the Rue de Rennes and recently paid her first visit to the United States in eighteen years. A Louisville girl who went to Berlin in 1913 to study singing with Lilli Lehmann, the German soprano, Mrs. Jolas settled in Paris in 1919 and became part of the expatriate sweep that followed World War I. She married Jolas in 1926 and after a brief stay in New Orleans they were back in Paris to push the avant-garde movement in art. They rented for $120 the vine-entwined house that later became the home of De Gaulle. Jolas fought in both World Wars, and during the occupation Maria and her two daughters lived in a château near Vichy. When war broke out, the girls were sent back to the United States, but in the end they married Frenchmen. Mrs. Jolas never thinks of herself as an exile, although she rarely sees her native land. She views herself merely as an American who lives in France.

Early in 1969 an old colleague who wrote for *Transition* died of cancer in New York. Josephine Herbst, from Sioux City, Iowa, who once worked for Mencken's *Smart Set,* lived in Germany during the political turmoil of the Weimar Republic and three years later met Hemingway, McAlmon, and the novelist John Herrmann, whom she married and later divorced. Radical politics and modern literature were Miss Herbst's dominant interests, and her dispatches from Germany, Spain, and Cuba were considered sensational in her era. She was one of the few women correspondents allowed to report from the front-line villages during the 1937 Civil War in Spain.

Another survivor of Mrs. Jolas' generation, Arthur Moss, died at the American Hospital at Neuilly in February 1969. He edited the *Gargoyle,* one of the first of the expatriate magazines of the 1920s, and pushed the young artists and writers who were following new paths at the time. Moss settled in Paris in 1921 and was eighty when he died. At much the same time Eric Hawkins, retired managing editor of the Paris *Herald,* now known as *The International Herald Tribune,* was hailed on his eightieth birthday in Paris, but he died in 1969, a few months after Moss. Hawkins went to work on the *Herald* in 1915, the day after the *Lusitania* was sunk by a German submarine. He had lived through it all—from the expatriates of the 1920s to the expatriates of the 1960s, and he had proved to be a singularly enduring one himself.

The Expatriate
World Today

Of the two and a half million Americans, representing more than 1 percent of the nation's population, who currently live around the world, the great majority have official status of one kind or another. They are no longer the troubadours of the arts, although the volunteer spirit is dominant in the Peace Corps and some of the other organizations. The spirit of adventure, the longing to see the world, the patriotic spirit, all have their place in this great army of exiled Americans. For some it's heaven; for others it's hell. For the wives and families it often spells loneliness and severe disorientation, unless they chance to view it as expanded opportunity and the rich educational experience it seemed to earlier generations.

As the world grows more disordered, and Americans abroad suffer severely from their national unpopularity, they are not necessarily the happiest breed. The old tradition that exile meant freedom from care and responsibility has no parallel in the war-swept world of today. And the switch from British to American omnipresence in large areas has involved the creation of a vast network of bureaucracy and officialdom.

Almost without exception the Americans abroad cling to their native passports, however long they stay away, however critical they may be of events at home. The largest group are the members of the armed forces and the employees of government agencies. With their families they are an impressive force in themselves. The second group includes the businessmen and technical experts, the doctors, teachers, and writers, the social service workers, missionaries, and experts in assorted fields. The smallest group of all takes in those who live abroad for one reason only—because they wish to— and here artists and political dissidents prevail. But it is the scientist, the technical expert, and the businessman who are of sterling value in the expatriate world today, as they were after the Revolution. The development of the ego is a dim pursuit in the midst of chaos. Practical help and business know-how are expected of the resident American.

Aside from the transient population, which makes its own rules as it goes along, Americans abroad increasingly show signs of solidarity, and American wives of foreign husbands do everything possible to keep their citizenship intact and preserve their passports. With the fast communication of today Americans organize their own political committees in the capitals of Europe during presidential years, as they did in the cases of Barry Goldwater, Lyndon B. Johnson, and Nelson Rockefeller. They have been known to stage civil rights marches, and some have figured noisily in antiwar and campus demonstrations in England, France, and Mexico. Many express themselves as they might at home. They even have their own lobby in Washington—The League of Americans Residing Abroad— with headquarters in Washington and Paris, and a cause made to order: taxation without representation.

The majority, however, are dedicated to exuding charm, tact, and friendliness rather than to stirring up trouble. This attitude is sometimes—although not always—a reciprocal game. American expatriates can be tiresome, too, by dwelling on the superior creature comforts of their own land, their climate, and the American way of doing things—from fixing the plumbing to brewing a satisfying cup of coffee. The expatriate of the 1920s was intrigued by the guttering candle that scarcely illuminated the page, the little bricks that warmed his room, the lumpy mattress, and the abysmal toilet arrangements. The contemporary expatriate, particularly if he is Hollywood-bred, demands something better, and if it fails to materialize he is annoyed, unless he happens to belong to the Hippie brigade, in which hygiene is of minor importance.

Women are the unsung expatriates who down the years have settled by the thousands in various outposts of the world, spending the greater part of their lives away from their native shores, sending their children to schools of many kinds, and coping with language and housekeeping problems. The international schools run in various capitals have not always been satisfactory, although some supply the credits needed to get the young into American colleges. From the earliest times, when Abigail Adams and other women of her kind accompanied their husbands abroad on government missions, down to those who are settled in the outposts today, the history of these American wives has of necessity been one of major adjustment and consummate tact. The exiled wife is in a class by herself. Language barriers make it difficult for her to socialize in certain parts of the world. Indeed, many families have returned to the United States because the wives could not make the necessary adjustment.

The scenic beauties pall after a time; the sun beats too relentlessly on them, and they long for the bronzed woods of New England. Their children are always a little alien to the surrounding scene, and the mothers are never too sure that their offspring will be stouthearted Americans after having lived overseas. They miss their electrical equipment, their gleaming kitchens, their superb supermarkets, except in the few places where such benefits exist. They are critical of the medical and dental care offered them, and they are affronted by the dirt and unhygienic conditions they encounter at many of the foreign posts.

Above all, the wives miss the companionship of their kind: the long summer days on friendly tree-lined streets in Portland, the big anniversaries like Thanksgiving and the Fourth of July so artificially celebrated abroad; their clubs, their community work, their fashions, and the forms of entertainment that are most familiar to them. Unlike the members of the Jet Set, who share in all the worldly pleasures abroad as well as at home, the average exiled wife can be lonely and adrift. At least four hundred American women have married Frenchmen abroad, and a number are the wives of Italians. Many romances begun in Florence and Rome, from the Junior year abroad, or other educational activities, have resulted in American wives coping with large households in the Italian hills.

Their husbands are often engaged in stimulating work, and for the men the foreign picture is apt to be bright and challenging. They go out into the world each day. They make friends and work their way around language difficulties because they must. They keep in touch with the embassies, American libraries, and all official bases. They have access to many sports and live on a much less competitive level in business than they would at home. As Americans abroad they have a sense of power, in spite of the antagonism that they meet in many areas. Expense accounts sometimes pave the way for more luxury than they have at home. They speak with some authority and are far from close surveillance. The British treat them with great politeness. The Swiss let them alone. The Italians are vociferously friendly, and the French are as critical, aloof, and cynical as in the days of Thomas Jefferson. They are exposed to ambivalent feelings in Germany and are well received in the Netherlands and the Scandinavian countries.

Outside western Europe the course is rocky and uncertain, as governments fall and political alignments change. The pot boils—in Africa and the Near East, as well as in Vietnam. Tanzania, the first nation in the world picked for a Peace Corps delegation, abandoned the program early in 1969, when the number of volunteers dropped from four hundred to eleven. The eighth country to send the Peace Corps home since 1961, Tanzania complained that too many of the volunteers were teachers, and not enough were technicians. Often the mission on which they are engaged counts—for or against them. Dr. Thomas Dooley, on an errand of mercy, won his way in Laos. An architect like Edward Durell Stone, who designed an embassy in New Delhi faintly reminiscent of the Taj Mahal, made an impression in India. An electronics expert is a welcome arrival. American bankers and lawyers have new functions and subtle power in the expatriate field. But all are closely linked to the home base today, by telephone and airplane. This close communication is what makes the status of the exile so different now from what it was a century ago, or even in the days of Henry James.

Coming in the wake of the steamship, the railroad, and the automobile, the airplane took the world by storm, although its development was slow. Cross-channel flights between London and Paris were put on a commercial basis after World War I. Lindbergh's transatlantic flight gave impact to all the scattered advances in aviation, and twelve years later Pan American's *Dixie Clipper* carried twenty-two passengers successfully from Port Washington, Long Island, to Marseilles, with stops at the Azores and Lisbon. World War II interrupted this service for the civilian, but after 1945 developments were rapid. Today air service is universal and swift, and its lowered cost has brought long-distance flights within range of people of moderate means. In a sense the airplane has made the term expatriate an anachronism. There is no such person any longer in the literal sense of the word, unless he is deeply determined not to return to his native shores under any circumstances. When it took months to move around the globe, as in the case of Robert Louis Stevenson, and the artistic world was not running with gold as it is today, it was easier to settle for a lifetime away from America. Moreover, today's exiles are more disillusioned with their foreign surroundings than the men and women of the 1920s, and they think more fondly of home. They can no longer say that America is lacking in culture, is wholly materialistic, is not the place where the artist can thrive. The evidence against this is too convincing.

Here and there are Americans of great wealth who have found their own formulas for life abroad. Most notable of this breed is J. Paul Getty, one of the richest men in the world, and the most inflexible of expatriates. Holed up in his fortresslike mansion—Sutton Place in Surrey—he is now restoring the Castello Odescalchi in Rome, which was once owned by Mrs. Luther Terry and was familiar to Henry James and other expatriates of the 1890's.

The writers and artists are still instinctive expatriates, but with a difference: They no longer go abroad to starve in garrets and freeze in barren lodgings. All that they need for their artistic education is in their own land. In general, the writer or artist who goes abroad today does it in style, on the earnings his books and paintings have brought him. He skis at deluxe resorts and goes skin-diving in the bluest of waters, along with the traditional yachtsman. He stays at the best hotels, and consorts with the fashionables of the international set. His swift visits to the United States often involve literary transactions with publishers and Hollywood producers.

The old quest for isolation to pursue artistic expression is not in the contemporary mood, when all men are asked to be brothers, although James Jones, author of *From Here to Eternity,* thinks he finds a deeper quiet on the Île Saint-Louis in Paris than he could anywhere in his own land. And Man Ray, painter, photographer, and one of the founders of the Dadaist movement, is back in Paris after a return to the United States and a term in Hollywood. He arrived in Paris in 1921 and made it his home. It is again his home, and he is just as unkempt and careless in his attire as he was in the days when Gertrude Stein labeled Man Ray and his colleagues "The Lost Generation."

The big changes came after the crash of 1929, when the writers and artists scattered and the tourist influx tapered off. By degrees a new generation of writers moved into view—the voices of the Depression, like John Steinbeck with *The Grapes of Wrath.* Most authors of the period were slightly touched by the influence of Hemingway, who continued his expatriate existence in Spain, France, Switzerland, Germany, Austria, Italy, Africa, and Cuba, before he ended his life with a shotgun in Idaho in 1961. Between the 1920s, when he had been the most notable of expatriates, and his literary decline and suicide, he continued to make headlines, both as adventurer and writer. The note of death and violence, which had begun when he was wounded by a canister explosion in the valley of the Piave while serving as an ambulance driver in World War I, ran clear through his subsequent life history.

In the late thirties, allying himself with the Loyalists in Spain, Hemingway continued to be the idol of the writers who threw themselves into the Spanish Civil War with fierce belief in what they were doing. His history was one of constant movement, of safaris, exploration, bullfights, deep-sea fishing, and racing. Bernard Berenson quoted him as saying that "to love killing was doubtless a sin . . . . Yet he had hated the Nazis and the Fascists so much that he had actually enjoyed killing them." He was on the scene for the liberation of Paris, and on many occasions later said that he had personally freed the Travelers Club. He celebrated at the Ritz with Fitzgerald, and the conviviality continued with Ira Wolfert, John Reinhart, Charles Wertenbaker, Irwin Shaw, and Helen Kirkpatrick, all fellow writers who had watched Paris being freed from the Germans.

Hemingway's plane crashed in Uganda in 1954 when he was on a safari, and he was thought to be dead. His injuries were serious, and one major accident seemed to follow another in his life. His books came out periodically but with dwindling interest on the part of the public. His *Across the River and into the Trees* in 1950 did not cause a ripple, but four years later he received the Nobel Prize. He was reaching back to his great days in the 1920s when he wrote his reminiscences of Paris, *A Moveable Feast,* in the fall of 1957 and the spring of 1958, shortly before the signs of a nervous breakdown, which ended in his suicide, were apparent.

He was married four times—to Hadley Richardson, the auburn-haired girl from St. Louis who was his wife as he moved toward fame in the 1920s; to Pauline Pfeiffer, an Arkansas girl who worked for the Paris edition of *Vogue;* to Martha Gellhorn, a strong-willed and ambitious girl who would become well known as a writer and correspondent; and to Mary Welsh, a diminutive blonde from Minnesota who was married to Noel Monks, an Australian reporter in London, when Hemingway first met her. Hadley, who was a comforting wife for the young author, was the only one of the four not involved in the world of letters. Hadley bore a son, John Hadley Hemingway, known as "Bumpy," and Pauline had two sons, Patrick and Gregory.

A world-famous figure by the 1940s, Hemingway had moved away from many of his old associates. This was another war decade, with a great exodus, not only to Europe but to distant parts of the world —to Korea, to Japan, to the Philippines. Although this was the mandatory expatriation of war, many servicemen married in distant places and turned their backs on the United States. At the same time there was a much-discussed expatriate flow to America—the refugees fleeing from Hitler and Mussolini, the Spanish republicans, the Austrians, and the Jewish writers who enriched the literary picture in America. New York was something like Paris in the 1920s, with the gifted of many races seeking refuge. However, most of the French and Belgians returned when the lights went on again in Paris.

While the shadow of the dictators lay over Europe, a new generation of war correspondents flowered in response to such drama as the world had scarcely known. The work of many merged eventually into the radio and television coverage of news, as in the case of Edward R. Murrow. A new pattern was set for the interpretive emphasis and personal opinion that dominate the airways, papers, and magazines today.

The feats of the Civil War correspondents in the 1860s, and of Lincoln Steffens, George Kennan, and Stephen Crane at the turn of the century, paled in comparison with those of prominent correspondents of later on. Among the best-known journalists of the period were: Edwin L. James, master of the graceful dispatch for *The New York Times;* Ralph Barnes of the New York *Herald Tribune,* who died on duty in an airplane crash; William L. Shirer, whose book *The Rise and Fall of the Third Reich* stands as the classic in its field; Leland Stowe, whose work on the Nazi invasion of Norway catapulted him to fame; William L. Laurence, of *The New York Times,* who watched the first atom bomb being dropped; John Gunther, whose days of newspaper correspondence in Europe led to his *Inside* books; and Edgar Ansel Mowrer, a full-time expatriate who spent practically all his life abroad, and who was thrown out of Berlin by Hitler, out of Russia by Stalin, and out of Spain by Franco. These writers and countless others were a new breed, and from their years of exile flowed much realistic writing when they translated their experiences into books and magazine articles. Home for these men was usually where they hung their hats, and in recent years that has been anywhere from the North Pole to Vietnam.

After World War II the tourists and a new bureaucracy, born out of the New Deal, flooded Europe with Americans of all ages—some to work, some to play, all to spend. The expatriate life expanded and became more unified than it had been since the 1920s. As Janet Flanner pictured it in *The New Yorker:*

The vanguard of the biggest influx of American tourists since the great season of 1929 is now becoming visible and audible everywhere in Paris. They are as welcome as they are valuable, for Nôtre-Dame, the Place de la Concorde, Ste. Chapelle and other architectural gems are once again being given their prewar evening floodlights. . . . The Café de Flore serves as a drugstore for pretty upstate girls in unbecoming blue denim pants and their Middle Western dates, most of whom are growing hasty Beaux-Arts beards. Members of the tourist intelligentsia patronize the Rue du Bac's Pont-Royal bar.

The lights were on again. The dreamers were back. The French cabinet was debating the wisdom of distributing Coca-Cola on a large scale, and it was gravely pointed out by the legislators that already "American chewing-gum wrappers strew Paris boulevards . . . tractors plow French fields, that du Pont stockings sheathe Parisienne legs, that Frigidaires chill gourmet foods."

Colette became president of the Goncourt Academy—the first woman to reach this eminence in letters. Sylvia Beach was missing from her old haunts, but a James Joyce exhibition was given in a new Left Bank bookshop called La Hune. Opulent Americans buying on the Rue de la Paix and along the Rue de Rivoli were rubbing shoulders with an exotic new assemblage of Hindu women in saris; of small, exquisite Chinese women in rich brocades; of Turks, Iranians, Israelis, and Arab chiefs in robes. Their own good grooming and high fashion were being challenged by the stunning women from South America, with fortunes at their command. But by 1957 Janet Flanner noted that American tourists were giving Paris the go-by because of high prices, a condition that continued for the next decade and was not helped by De Gaulle's anti-American policies in the 1960s.

In Rome the picture was dim after World War II, as many American girls who had held good government jobs and wished to stay on in Italy were cast adrift. Some went home on freighters. Others stayed to paint, to write, to walk their dogs in the Borghese Gardens and duck the pinchers on the Via Veneto. The great days of happy exile for the film set were yet to come, but the tourists returned to their endless parade through Rome, Florence, Venice, and Naples, with fresh sights to see—Monte Cassino, the beach at Salerno, the wreckage in the northern mountains, and other echoes of the war. In Germany it was the same story, from Buchenwald to flattened Hamburg. Because of the long occupation many young American servicemen married and decided to stay abroad, a fairly common situation today.

Things were less happy for the blacks abroad, as at home, although they made headway in many directions. Their established tradition as entertainers both helped and hindered them. Although they wanted to step into other roles, to become scholars and men of business, they found that the public still expected them to sing and dance, to play jazz and always to entertain, when they were not fulfilling menial functions. For many, their natural gifts meant fame and fortune; for the others the picture was dim. Richard Wright made this shockingly plain in his *Native Son*. Paris became the special haven of the blacks who had left America because of racial intolerance, but in time they found places for themselves in Berlin, Munich, Madrid, Rome, Copenhagen, and Amsterdam. Their art was valued in London, too.

Negroes had brought jazz from New Orleans to New York in a wild blaze of popularity during the years of World War I, and the Cotton Club in Harlem, one of the most popular resorts of the 1920s, sent many on their way to Europe. The jazz bands brought bright fresh talent into view, and Josephine Baker and Florence Mills with her Blackbirds were sensations in Paris. Miss Baker went into eclipse during World War II but was back at the Folies-Bergère in 1949, as its leading lady, this time with a pagoda headdress instead of her derrière plume. The Saint-Germain-des-Près quarter had become what Montparnasse had been after World War I. The little *boîtes* in eighteenth-century cellars were still suffocatingly hot, and blacks from Africa were now singing and dancing with an emphasis of their own. Their songs were being collected; their art was being exhibited.

The American blacks had their own colonies in various cities, their own stars, who were accepted around the world. Three Negro singers—Mattiwilda Dobbs, Reri Grist, and Gloria Davy—went to Europe for better opportunities in opera. They found them. Miss Dobbs was the first American Negro singer to be heard at La Scala, and the third to be signed at the Metropolitan in New York. She married a Swede and divides her time between Stockholm, Majorca, and Hamburg. Mae Mercer, a North Carolinian with a Cherokee Indian mother, sings spirituals all over Europe. Dean Dixon, whose reputation was already made when he arrived in Europe in 1949, managed to break the prejudice against a black man conducting a symphony orchestra. He had to go to Europe to effect this end. Bud Powell, Albert Nicholas, and Kenny Clarke are popular with audiences abroad. All of the expatriate blacks put Paris first as the place they would rather be, although some have sought lower prices in Spain and Italy. Sammy Davis, Jr., Harry Belafonte, Lena Horne, and all the other noted black artists of the stage and films command attention everywhere.

The French take a different view of the blacks from Africa and the blacks from America. Political feeling enters into this. There were fifteen hundred Afro-Americans in Paris in the late 1960s, only half as many as in the years after World War II when the GI Bill of Rights made it possible for them to go anywhere, and they instinctively went to Paris. Labor law restrictions controlling the number of jazz musicians allowed to enter France figure in this decline. They still do not marry into conservative French families. French mothers show prejudice in this respect, but many American Negroes have white American or English wives or sweethearts.

When Richard Wright, with his wife, Ellen, who is now a literary agent, went to Paris in 1946, he became a stormy focus of impassioned writing and racial discontent until his death. Together they popularized the Café de Tournon, and it and Monaco became centers for the young black artists and writers to discuss their work, to gossip and sip apéritifs, as Hemingway's generation did at the Sélect and the Coupole in Montparnasse. But with James Baldwin and other black writers of the 1960s coming and going, this picture has changed, and restaurants serving "soul food" have come into fashion. They are tourist bait, serving collard greens, red beans and rice, fried chicken, and fried catfish. Politicians, stage stars, GIs, and the regular American arrivals see native atmosphere in the "soul food" theme, either in song or gastronomically. Leroy Haynes's restaurant close to the Place Pigalle features chitterlings, grits, fried chicken, and ribs. Writers haunt his place for atmosphere. James Jones and Françoise Sagan are apt to turn up at Juan Romer's bar off Saint-Germain-des-Près.

But the more serious-minded blacks avoid such displays, and Richard Wright's daughter, Julia Hervé, a journalist who spent two and a half years in Ghana with her French husband during the Nkrumah regime, is an impatient activist who believes it is foolish to sit around tables "speculating about a brave new world." Madame Hervé stands for action and has no time for the cafés, even those most closely identified with her parents.

Richard William Gardner Smith, an old friend of Wright's, heads the Paris colony of blacks. He went to Paris in 1951, declaring that he could not take the small facts of life in the United States any longer. Earlier he had been with the NAACP in Philadelphia; then he was a member of CORE, along with William Mauldin and William Worthy. When he was twenty, he wrote Last of the Conquerors in Philadelphia, and then Anger at Innocence. Smith is one of a number of blacks abroad today who feel guilty because they are not at home fighting their cause on home ground. His wife was a teacher at a French *lycée*. One of his children was born in Paris, the other in Africa. He has no wish to have either of them grow up in the United States. Eldridge Cleaver remains a controversial figure in absentia.

Next to the musical and stage celebrities who share most of the deluxe haunts of their white colleagues, the best-off blacks in Paris are the writers. Few starve in garrets today. They live in steam-heated apartments, dine often at Leroy Haynes's restaurant, and have their place in the artistic world of the French capital. They like to relax in the Living Room, run by Art Simmons, the black pianist, on the Right Bank. Negro women, too, are finding an outlet for their literary and artistic talents in Paris. Carlene Hatcher Polite, who lives in a modern apartment on the Left Bank with her two daughters, writes without any racial bitterness. She went to Paris to complete her first novel, *The Flagellants,* and has an endowment to follow it with another. Mrs. Polite is an articulate feminist who believes with Simone de Beauvoir that the problems of the blacks are similar to women's problems of self-determination, and that no member of her sex can produce the best that is in her while she feels herself to be a second-class citizen.

Margaret Just Butcher, author of *The Negro in American Culture,* has official status as assistant cultural affairs officer at the American embassy. She lectures in France on Negro writing and civil rights, and is one of many attractive American blacks who are working usefully, and to their own satisfaction, in the foreign field. Hazel Scott, the singer and pianist from Trinidad who was married to Adam Clayton Powell, Jr., prefers Paris to London, and she thinks that the blacks fare well in Italy and the Scandinavian countries.

It took Chester Himes, detective-story writer, many years to find success in his field. He has tried working and living in Paris, in the south of France, in Denmark, and has finally wound up in Barcelona. Things moved faster for Alexander Haley, who found fame by compiling *The Autobiography of Malcolm X.* Since then he has been a transatlantic traveler, lecturing, seeing publishers and Hollywood producers. The contemporary taste for books on the problems of the blacks has kept many writers busy and in funds. Haley lives part of the time near Cagnes on the Riviera. In Paris he may be found at Leroy Haynes's popular rendezvous. He has made a business of tracing his own roots back to Gambia in West Africa, and of trying to identify the slave ship that brought his forefathers to America.

James Baldwin has said that if he had been a drummer and not a writer, he would never have returned to the United States. "The danger of being an expatriate is that you are very likely to find yourself living, in effect, nowhere," he told Ernest Dunbar, who became a writer for *Look* in 1954 and has made a serious and balanced study of the whole situation in *The Black Expatriates: A Study of American Negroes in Exile.*

Dunbar found that many of the black Americans in Paris, Stockholm, Rome, Berlin, Zurich, and Frankfurt had tried for careers not open to them in the United States. Some had met with fair success, and Eddie Barnett, a specialist in fashion photography, had made it all the way. Dunbar noticed that in Africa even the shade of one's skin made a difference, and one could be accepted or rejected by this standard. When an Afro-American woman marries an African, she soon learns most emphatically that he is the boss. Dunbar gleaned from Bill Sutherland—one of the founders of CORE, who later served as personal secretary to K. A. Gbedemah of Ghana, and as assistant secretary in the Ministry of Information in Tanzania—that the practical approach in political matters was better than the idealistic one.

Much of the prejudice in hotels, bars, and restaurants stems from colonial rule in Africa, and presents special regional problems, according to Dunbar. Many of the blacks he interviewed in Africa showed signs of deep disappointment and disillusionment. Ed Smith, who kept a diary, *Where to, Black Man?*, while working for the Peace Corps in Ghana, felt the hopelessness of bringing together the black African and the black American. He returned to the United States to work with the Student Nonviolent Coordinating Committee, since renamed the Student National Coordinating Committee.

The picture of black exiles in other parts of the world is brighter, and in Saigon the integration of the armed forces, and the abandonment of color bars in most government agencies and civilian bodies overseas, has made a difference. Negroes have proved themselves to be good and loyal soldiers, and they have been given opportunities as career soldiers and as civilian administrators, technicians, and professionals of one kind or another. Most of them are enlisted men of lower rank, however, and their death rate is high. Nevertheless, their reenlistment rate in the army is three times higher than that of white soldiers.

Black women, too, have benefited by the technical training given overseas, and they help to keep the administrative and industrial machinery moving in the Far East. They flourish in secretarial jobs, and one, Mrs. Ursula Holmes of Washington, has risen to be chief of administration for the Army Inspector General's Office in South Vietnam.

Romance flourishes in the Far East, and the beautiful Thai girls are alluring to the black soldiers. Some marry and talk of becoming permanent exiles. A Negro runs the Chao Phya, a luxurious hotel in Bangkok for American officers. An army sergeant's wife, who lived in a housing project in Queens when at home, now has a villa well staffed with servants in Bangkok. Life is better for some of the blacks who have turned to civilian occupations than it ever was in ghettos in America. A number run businesses of their own and no longer think in terms of returning to America. Others find that the far fields are not necessarily the green fields for them, and they long for home, just like many of the white exiles around the world. Their children are not always happy in so different an environment. *

While some of the blacks have found new opportunities and precise technical training in the armed forces, a small percentage of white and black youths resist the thought of military service and seek self-exile rather than wait to be drafted. Canada and Sweden have received most of these escapees, and the Canadian government has ruled that deserters are free to enter. Students from Long Island to Arizona have made brief visits to Toronto, Montreal, and Vancouver to scout for jobs and sound out their welcome. Many have returned to stay, although of more than four thousand who went to Canada in 1968 a number returned to the United States. Others were encouraged to stay by the Toronto Anti-Draft group, left-wingers who issued a manual giving advice about life in Canada, immigration laws, and what to do about finding jobs. Antiwar groups provide money, shelter, and transportation for the deserters. This underground railway is composed of pacifist and religious organizations, campus radicals, camp counsellors, and business and professional people.

Some of the Canadian colleges have welcomed these resistant youths, and a few young men have landed teaching posts. However they work generally as hospital orderlies, cooks, or clerks. The population as a whole has been hospitable to them, and many residents have taken them into their homes. They have government assurance that they are welcome now. But American-owned companies in Canada give them the cold shoulder. One way draft resisters have discovered to place themselves beyond the reach of the draft board is to renounce their American citizenship and take up residence outside the United States before they become draft delinquents. This renunciation makes them stateless for five years, until they become Canadians. If Canada deports them, they are automatically returned to the United States.

Deserters to Sweden receive twenty dollars a week under the Swedish welfare system, and they have been made welcome except where their militancy has caused disorder. They work with the draft evaders in France, turning out booklets and papers under the general title "The Second Front." The American Deserters Committee in Stockholm prepares material designed to encourage further desertions. Its general approach is opposition to "American economic imperialism" and support for the black liberation movement in the United States. The committee gives legal advice to new deserters, helps them with housing and jobs, and encourages them to maintain a high degree of protest.

Eighteen of the first hundred deserters to Sweden have since left, and those who remain have received permanent residence permits and asylum on humanitarian grounds. Fifteen of this group are blacks. At a lawn party given at the United States Embassy on the Fourth of July 1968, some of the deserters were involved in a fracas that ended with seven being held overnight by the police.

Draft evasion is a problem that did not seriously ruffle American university life until the Vietnam war, when protests became widespread. There was no draft at the time of the War of 1812. During the Mexican War one Dartmouth senior raised the question, "Is War a Sin?" and argued that it was not, if necessary. But the Civil War roused such burning feeling that the subject was seriously discussed on the campuses at that time, and Harriet Beecher Stowe, who was the wife of Calvin Ellis Stowe, a professor, advocated draft resistance and emigration to Canada for the slaves. The Spanish-American War began and ended too swiftly to engage the students in much discussion of its aims, and World War I evoked a blaze of patriotic response from the leading universities in the country. Young men were eager to go to Europe and fight in this war. The picture had changed, however, by the time World War II broke out, and Peter Keir, the Dartmouth valedictorian of 1941, remarked, "The same men who taught us that war is bad now tell us to go fight one. We are simply resigned—resigned to the fact of a world war that must in one way or another involve us personally." A year later Charles Pearson, valedictorian for the class of 1942, was telling his classmates that it "was thrilling to be so needed." A month after graduation 80 percent of his class was in service, and Pearson died in a plane crash in the Pacific.

Two decades have intervened, and now there are draft evaders and Hippies as well as eager volunteers. Thousands of the young have made their own expatriate world, and there has never been anything like it in the history of the United States. This great exodus of boys and girls from average homes to all parts of the globe, existing on pot and pleasure, not caring where they live, or eat, or sleep, has baffled all observers. They talk of high ideals and a new and wonderful world as they lounge on rock ledges outside the Matala caves in Crete, sun themselves on the Spanish Steps in Rome, or get high on hashish in Tangiers.

Some have college degrees. Most of them have been exposed to the accepted American principles of hygiene. Yet the first impression of the Hippies is of a dirty, shaggy, unkempt army, shuffling along like vagrants. Their habiliments are as curious as their manners. Wherever they are found—from San Francisco to Istanbul, in the African jungle or the Himalayan foothills—they are a discordant, curious assemblage, with a language of their own and strange music to match their mood.

Many have left San Francisco's Haight-Ashbury and New York's East Village to stray far from their native land, to build up an expatriate existence that so far has eluded them. Sikkim kept them out. They are unwelcome nearly everywhere they go. They plant themselves in restless clusters, forage for what they can get, and drowse the days away in apathy. No youth movement has ever been so widespread, so strange, so destructive to the well-being of its participants. Nowhere have they settled as uniquely as in the caves of Matala, well known to the ancients, once a burial ground and also a leper colony. The youths cook outdoors, hang their washing in the sun, and roll up in sleeping bags in forty or fifty caves at night. Behind their heavy beards some of the youths have handsome, clean-cut features and large, unblinking eyes. At times they burst into song, or strum their guitars. The villagers stare at them unbelievingly as they drive their donkeys, laden with hay, along the rutted roads close to the caves. Flowering cherry trees give the scene a moment of beauty, but the Hippies do not seem to care. They have had fewer problems in Crete than in their wanderings in Africa, where they have met with many rebuffs and have been expelled at various points.

The Hippies tend to set up their own standards and institutions. They think they are politically significant and that America owes them a secretary of youth in the cabinet. Some believe they foster good relations as they travel, but they show little interest in anything outside of their own cacophony. They are self-obsessed, self-ab-

297

sorbed, and are always ready to sling arrows at their native country. Yet, like American expatriates everywhere, they cherish their passports and keep a link with the embassies.

On their journey through New Delhi they sparked The Cellar, India's first authentic discothèque. It was opened by a young Sikh, and Joan Baez was one of its early entertainers. After her came Aretha Franklin, Wilson Pickett, and Otis Redding. Its Indian sponsors went back to wearing the kurta, the collarless Indian shirt affected in the East Village and Haight-Ashbury, but abandoned long ago by the native university students in favor of Western dress.

The Club Vagabond near Lausanne is one of their favorite haunts, and they have followed the Jet Set to Ibiza in Spain, where they can get beds for fifty cents a night, or a bedroll for nothing. They touch bottom at the Gulhane Hotel in Istanbul, where a corrugated roof covers the canvas that is known as The Tent. Here up to seventy-five of the wanderers roll into sleeping bags at twenty-five cents a night, and the air is heavy with the smoke of hashish. Candles flicker precariously on top of matchboxes, and a Hippy makes eerie music with his guitar.

In Rome Dr. Georges Boyer, a French lay missionary and Franciscan, who had observed the Hippie invasion of the stately Piazza Navona, opened an apartment for their use a block from the Bernini Fountain. Girls and boys sleep in separate rooms. Guests get breakfast and are encouraged to bathe, shave, and cut their hair. Dr. Boyer has yet to find out why these strange brigades of Hippies act as they do. They give many reasons for their flight as far as possible from home, or they clam up and say nothing at all. They are sometimes the children of parents gifted in the arts, and most are convinced that they must live as they wish, make their own decisions, follow their star. They are drawn to Buddhism, to yoga, to Zen philosophy and macrobiotic diets. They turn up in guru circles and go in for incantation. Some have been known to work in moments of emergency. In Greece they have sold blood. In France they have picked grapes in the vineyards. They do odd jobs around cafés and bars. Housewives sometimes regard them with sympathy and give them square meals. The embassies in a pinch will call their parents collect, and raise funds for them to travel home. But usually they want to stay lost, so far as their families are concerned. They live by this compelling purpose, resistant to the disciplines of home and conventional life. Some are thoughtful sojourners, sincerely believing they are chasing a dream. They can be clever and idealistic, and many have a strange beauty, with their long streaming hair, their unfathomable eyes, the soft bloom of their skin, belied by the wild disarray and confusion of their costumes. A considerable number are rude, dirty, intractable young egotists, who seem to find their only pleasure in consorting with others like themselves. Only a few pull out and go home, to cope with the dull old issue of conformity and the "horrors" of life in America.

But the Hippies are in a class by themselves, a phenomenon matching the far-out developments of the 1960s. There has never been anything like them in the nation's history, and they are not to be confused with the young American students who concentrate with the old enthusiasm on the classical sources of learning, as in the days of Washington Irving and Henry James. Paris, Rome, and Florence are still the fountainheads, but the range is now worldwide. A total of 21,597 young Americans were scattered around the world in 1969, students as hungry for learning as their more disciplined ancestors.

They might be spotted in New Zealand, Korea, or Pakistan. Iran had 11, Japan had 57, and Israel had 144. Seventeen anthropological students worked in the Fiji Islands, and fifty-two classical and archaeological students were at work in Greece. Twenty-five were in South Africa and one in Indonesia. Others were studying in Finland, Turkey, Czechoslovakia, and all over Latin America. In the eighteenth and nineteenth centuries expatriate students often had patrons at home, or affluent families behind them. In the world of today they have government grants and aid from foundations, as well as family backing.

In Britain a new group of provincial universities are open to those who cannot manage Oxford, Cambridge, or London University. Edinburgh, Aberdeen, and Saint Andrews continue to welcome American students, as they always have. Foreign students in London have become adept at finding bed-sitting rooms, or "pads" of one kind or another. They can always warm up in the libraries or the British Museum, the cinema or the chain lunchrooms. And when spring and the primroses bloom together they find delight in their bicycle trips, in punting, hiking, and motoring. As hostelers they can sleep in ancient castles haunted by ghosts. The student population from America is a well-understood body of pilgrims in Britain.

The Sorbonne has not lost its magic for the exiled student, and Grenoble is still good for skiing as well as scholarship. Italy remains the golden dream it always was for the student. The young still haunt the American Academy in Rome and the Società Dante Alighieri. They meet the students of many lands at the Italian University for Foreigners in Perugia, and in Florence they cluster around the Centro di Cultura per Stranieri, which is part of the University of Florence.

They are not as prone to read Dante and linger over the love legend of the Brownings as their nineteenth-century ancestors, but they still work hard at art and archaeology, at languages and all the fine arts. The old romantic magic is at work more visibly in Italy than elsewhere. Girl students prefer Florence, but its faded glory leaves many of the young men cold. Rome is for fast living and leisurely learning. Venice is for all to see and enjoy. The students still gather at the American Express offices to pick up their mail and cash their checks from home. They read American papers on board the darting barges known as *vaporetti,* for they rarely have time to rock in gondolas. They tear along the roads in fast cars or on motorcycles. They take off for the Alps to ski. They throw coins in the Trevi Fountain and make love in the moonlit Colosseum.

The young studying abroad, like students everywhere today, see themselves as the hope of the future, and their drive is so strong that none can deny the radical change in their ways and thinking. In some respects they have the same basic goals as the travelers of the nineteenth century—to return to their native land enriched by their years abroad, with something to add to a constantly changing civilization. But the young of the 1970's have found new horizons. They react passionately to the needs and aspirations of other people around the world. While they do not covet the expatriate image, many are prone to seek foreign service and join the growing army of Americans who live and work abroad.

Notes

CHAPTERS 1 AND 2

Americans Abroad and Diplomacy in Europe

Stewart Mitchell (ed.), *New Letters of Abigail Adams, 1788–1801;* Charles Francis Adams (ed.), *Familiar Letters of John Adams and His Wife, Abigail Adams, During the Revolution* and *Memoirs of John Quincy Adams;* Henry Adams, *The Education of Henry Adams* and *The Life of Albert Gallatin;* Samuel Flagg Bemis, *The Diplomacy of the American Revolution;* Dorothie Bobbé, *Abigail Adams, the Second First Lady;* Allen Dulles, *The Craft of Intelligence;* Foster Rhea Dulles, *Americans Abroad;* Elizabeth F. Ellet, *The Women of the American Revolution;* Manfred S. Guttmacher, "Catherine Macaulay and Patience Wright: Patronesses of the American Revolution," *Johns Hopkins Alumni Magazine,* vol. 24, 1936; James Gallatin, *The Diary of James Gallatin, secretary to Albert Gallatin, the Great Peacemaker, 1813–1827;* Edward Everett Hale and Edward Everett Hale, Jr., *Franklin in France;* John Bigelow (ed.), *Autobiography of Benjamin Franklin;* Leonard W. Labaree (ed.), *The Autobiography of Benjamin Franklin;* Luther Samuel Livingston, *Franklin and His Press at Passy;* James Parton, *Life and Times of Benjamin Franklin;* Willis Steell, *Benjamin Franklin of Paris, 1776–1785;* Elkanah Watson, *Men and Times of the Revolution: or Memoirs of Elkanah Watson;* Janet Whitney, *Abigail Adams;* Constance Wright, *Madame de Lafayette;* Anne Cary Morris (ed.), *The Diary and*

Letters of Gouverneur Morris, Minister of the United States to France; George Ticknor, *Life, Letters and Journals of George Ticknor,* vol. 1; William Henry Wilkins, *Mrs. Fitzherbert and George IV;* Shane Leslie, *Mrs. Fitzherbert: A Life Chiefly from Unpublished Sources;* George Pellew, *John Jay;* William Jay, *The Life of John Jay;* Gilbert Chinard, *Honest John Adams;* Margaret L. Brown, "Anne Willing Bingham," *Bermuda Historical Quarterly,* August 1949, and "William Bingham, Eighteenth-Century Magnate," *Pennsylvania Magazine of History and Biography,* vol. 61, 1937.

CHAPTER 3
Jefferson in Paris

Adrienne Koch and William Peden (eds.), *Life and Selected Writings of Thomas Jefferson;* Julian P. Boyd, Lyman H. Butterfield, and Mina R. Bryan (eds.), *Jefferson Papers, 1779–1780,* vols. 15, 16, and 17; Saul K. Padover, *Jefferson* and *The Complete Madison;* Gilbert Chinard, *Thomas Jefferson, the Apostle of Americanism* and *Honest John Adams;* Bernard Mayo (ed.), *Jefferson Himself, the Personal Narrative of a Many-Sided American;* Edward Dumbauld, *Thomas Jefferson, American Tourist;* James Truslow Adams, *The Living Jefferson;* Daniel J. Boorstin, *The Lost World of Thomas Jefferson;* Paul Leicester Ford, *Thomas Jefferson;* Marie Kimball, *Jefferson: The Scene of Europe 1784–1789;* Andrew A. Lipscomb (ed.), *The Writings of Thomas Jefferson,* Vol. 1; George C. Williamson, *Richard Cosway, R. A.;* Gordon Langley Hall, *Mr. Jefferson's Ladies;* Helen Claire Bullock, *My Head and My Heart, a Little History of Thomas Jefferson and Maria Cosway;* Charles Francis Adams (ed.), *Memoirs of John Quincy Adams* and *Familiar Letters of John Adams and His Wife, Abigail Adams, During the Revolution;* Samuel Flagg Bemis, *The Diplomacy of the American Revolution;* Beatrix Cary Davenport (ed.), *A Diary of the French Revolution 1752–1816 by Gouverneur Morris;* Beverley Waugh Bond, *The Monroe Mission to France;* James Gallatin, *A Great Peacemaker;* Stuart Gerry Brown (ed.), *Autobiography of James Monroe;* Arthur Styron, *The Last of the Cocked Hats: James Monroe and the Virginia Dynasty;* Brand Whitlock, *Lafayette;* Elisabeth de Nolde, *Madame de Staël and Benjamin Constant;* Margaret Leland Goldsmith, *Madame de Staël;* John Trumbull, *The Autobiography of Colonel John Trumbull, Patriot-artist, 1756–1843;* Elkanah Watson, *Men and Times of the Revolution;* George Ticknor, *Life, Letters and Journals of George Ticknor,* vol. 1; Joseph Green Cogswell, *Life of Joseph Green Cogswell as Sketched in His Letters;* Katharine Susan Anthony, *Dolley Madison, Her Life and Times;* S. G. Tollentyre, *The Friends of Voltaire;* Julian P. Boyd, "Two Diplomats between Revolutions," *Virginia Magazine of History and Biography,* vol. 66, 1958; Julia Truitt Bishop, "Angelica Schuyler Church and Her Work," New Orleans *Times-Picayune,* March 3, 1935; Meade Minnegerode, "Stephen

Jumel, Merchant," *Saturday Evening Post,* May 31, 1914; William Cary Duncan, *The Amazing Madame Jumel;* Leonard Falkner, *Painted Lady;* Henry Shelton, *The Jumel Mansion;* Ishbel Ross, *Charmers and Cranks;* Jumel papers in The New-York Historical Society.

CHAPTER 4

The Artist's Quest

John Galt, *The Life and Studies of Benjamin West; Letters and Papers of John Singleton Copley and Henry Pelham 1739–1776;* J. T. Flexner, *America's Old Masters; Gilbert Stuart, a Great Life in Brief; John Singleton Copley;* and *A Short History of American Painting;* Joseph McSpadden, *Famous Painters of America;* George Champlin Mason, *The Life and Works of Gilbert Stuart;* Jared Bradley Flagg, *The Life and Letters of Washington Allston;* Richard Henry Dana, Jr. (ed.), *Washington Allston;* E. P. Richardson, *Washington Allston;* John Trumbull, *The Autobiography of Colonel John Trumbull, Patriot-artist, 1756–1843;* Elkanah Watson, *Men and Times of the Revolution: or Memoirs of Elkanah Watson;* George Ticknor, *Life, Letters and Journals of George Ticknor,* vol. 1; Rembrandt Peale, *Notes in Italy;* William Henry Wilkins, *Mrs. Fitzherbert and George IV;* Shane Leslie, *Mrs. Fitzherbert: A Life Chiefly from Unpublished Sources;* Washington Irving, *Life and Letters of Washington Irving,* edited by his nephew, Pierre M. Irving, vol. 4; *Life and Selected Writings of Thomas Jefferson,* edited by Adrienne Koch and William Peden; Charles Edwards Lester, *The Artists of America;* Willis Steell, *Benjamin Franklin of Paris, 1776–1785;* Samuel Flagg Bemis, *The Diplomacy of the American Revolution;* John Bigelow (ed.), *Autobiography of Benjamin Franklin;* Manfred S. Guttmacher, "Catherine Macaulay and Patience Wright: Patronesses of the American Revolution," *Johns Hopkins Alumni Magazine,* vol. 24, 1936; Van Wyck Brooks, *The Dream of Arcadia: American Writers and Artists in Italy 1760–1915;* Francis Haskell, *The Age of the Grand Tour;* Abigail Adams, *New Letters of Abigail Adams, 1788–1801,* edited by Stewart Mitchell; Marie Kimball, *Jefferson: The Scene of Europe 1784–1789;* Ruel Pardee Tolman, *The Life and Works of Edward Greene Malbone 1777–1807,* The New-York Historical Society, 1958.

CHAPTER 5

Literary Pilgrims

Washington Irving, *Life and Letters of Washington Irving,* edited by his nephew, Pierre M. Irving, vol. 4, and *Spanish papers and other miscellanies;* John Dunton, *The Life and Errors of John Dunton,* vol. 1; James Russell Lowell, *Lowell's Impressions of Spain,* compiled by Joseph Gilder, and *Letters of James Russell Lowell,* edited by Charles Eliot Norton; Samuel Longfellow, *Life of Henry Wadsworth Longfellow,* vol. 2; *Longfellow's Prose Works,* vol. 1; Newton Arvin, *Longfellow: His Life and Work;* Van Wyck Brooks, *The Dream of Arcadia: American Writers and Artists in Italy 1760–1915* and *The World of Washington Irving;* Edwin H. Cady, *William Dean Howells, Dean of American Letters,* 2 vols.; Ernest Hartley Coleridge (ed.), *Letters of Samuel Taylor Coleridge,* vol. 2; Charles T. Congdon, *Reminiscences of a Journalist;* J. Fenimore Cooper, *Letters and Journals,* edited by James Franklin Beard, and *Traveling Bachelor;* Clara Crowinshield, *Diary: European Tour with Longfellow 1835–1836;* Margaret Denny and William H. Gilman (eds.), *The American Writer and the European Tradition;* Ralph Waldo Emerson, *Journals of Ralph Waldo Emerson,* edited by Edward Waldo Emerson and Waldo Emerson Forbes, vol. 3; Mrs. Anne (MacVicar) Grant of Laggan, *Letters from the Mountains;* Gordon S. Haight, *George Eliot, a Biography;* Nathaniel Hawthorne, *English Notebooks, vol. 2,* and *French and Italian Notebooks,* vol. 3; George Sidney Hellman, *Washington Irving Esquire, Ambassador at large from the New World to the Old;* Mildred Howells (ed.), *Life in Letters of William Dean Howells,* 2 vols.; *The Journals of Francis Parkman; Letters of Charles Eliot Norton,* with biographical comment by his daughter, S. Norton, and M. A. De Wolfe Howe; F. Marion Crawford, *A Lady of Rome, Salve Venetia,* and *Sant' Ilario;* Julia Ward Howe, *Reminiscences 1819–1899;* Margaret (Terry) Chanler, *Roman Spring: Memoirs;* James Fenimore Cooper, *Gleanings in Europe,* edited by Robert Ernest Spiller; William Wetmore Story, *Conversations in a Studio,* vol. 2; Harriet Beecher Stowe, *Sunny Memories of Foreign Lands;* Bayard Taylor, *Views Afoot* and *At Home and Abroad;* George Ticknor, *Life of William H. Prescott;* Maisie Ward, *Robert Browning and His World,* 2 vols.; Lilian Whiting, *Kate Field;* Ishbel Ross, *Charmers and Cranks;* Stanley T. Williams, *The Life of Washington Irving,* 2 vols.; Nathaniel Parker Willis, *Pencillings by the way; The Reminiscences of William C. Preston,* edited by Minnie Clare Yarbrough; Edward Lind Morse (ed.), *Samuel F. B. Morse: His Letters and Journals;* Anna Brownell Jameson, *The Memoirs of the Life of Anna Jameson;* Samuel Langhorne Clemens, *A Tramp Abroad, Travelling with the Innocents Abroad,* and *The Travels of Mark Twain;* George Washington Greene, *Biographical Studies;* David H. Donald, *Charles Sumner and the Coming of the Civil War;* Edward Lillie Pierce, *Memoirs and Letters of Charles Sumner,* 4 vols.

CHAPTER 6

The Italian Mystique

Henry James, *Italian Hours,* illustrated by Elihu Vedder; Henry James, *Autobiography* and *William Wetmore Story and his Friends;* James Jackson Jarves, *Italian Rambles;* William Dean Howells, *Tuscan Cities* and

Roman Holidays and Others; Annie Fields, *Authors and Friends;* Joseph Wechsberg, "Rome's Caffè Greco," *Gourmet,* April 1969; F. Marion Crawford, *A Lady of Rome, Salve Venetia,* and *Sant' Ilario;* Millicent Bell, *Edith Wharton and Henry James;* Otto Henry Bacher, *With Whistler in Venice;* Bernard Berenson, *The Venetian Painters of the Renaissance;* Phillips Brooks, *Letters of Travel;* Elizabeth Barrett Browning, *The Letters of Mrs. Browning;* Maisie Ward, *Robert Browning and his World;* Margaret (Terry) Chanler, *Roman Spring: Memoirs;* Norman Douglas, *South Wind;* Maud (Howe) Elliott, *My Cousin, F. Marion Crawford: The Story of an Artist,* and *Uncle Sam Ward and his Circle;* Jared Bradley Flagg, *The Life and Letters of Washington Allston;* James Thomas Flexner, *America's Old Masters;* Nathaniel Hawthorne, *French and Italian Notebooks* and *The Marble Faun;* Louise (Hall) Tharp, *The Peabody Sisters of Salem;* Harriet Goodhue Hosmer, *Harriet Hosmer Letters and Memories,* edited by Cornelia Carr; Julia Ward Howe, *Reminiscences 1819–1899;* Gertrude Reese Hudson (ed.), *Browning to his American friends: letters between the Brownings, the Storys and James Russell Lowell, 1841–1890;* Anna Brownell Jameson, *Visits and Sketches at Home and Abroad; The Memoirs of the life of Anna Jameson* and *The Diary of an Ennuyée;* Princess Cantacuzene, *My Life Here and There;* Samuel Longfellow, *Life of Henry Wadsworth Longfellow,* vol. 2; Mabel Dodge Luhan, *European Experiences;* John Henry Middleton, *The Remains of Ancient Rome;* Eleanor Clark, *Rome and a Villa;* Samuel Osgood, *Thomas Crawford and Art in America;* Francis Parkman, *The Journals of Francis Parkman;* Elizabeth Pennell, *Nights: Rome, Venice in the Aesthetic Eighties; London, Paris, in the Fighting Nineties;* E. P. Richardson, *Washington Allston;* Eugene Schuyler, *Italian Influences;* Catharine M. Sedgwick, *Letters from abroad to kindred at home;* Leonora Cranch Scott (ed.), *The Life and Letters of Christopher Pearse Cranch;* Van Wyck Brooks, *The Dream of Arcadia: American Writers and Artists in Italy 1760–1915;* William Wetmore Story, *Conversations in a Studio,* vol. 2; Harriet Beecher Stowe, *Sunny Memories of Foreign Lands,* 2 vols., and *Agnes of Sorrento;* Constance Fenimore Woolson, *The Front Yard and other Italian stories;* Leon Edel, *Henry James,* 4 vols.; J. Fenimore Cooper, *Letters and Journals;* Charles Edwards Lester, *The artist, the merchant and the statesman of the age of the Medici, and of our own times;* Edwin H. Cady, *William Dean Howells: Dean of American Letters,* 2 vols.; William Cullen Bryant, *Letters of a Traveller;* Francesca Alexander, *Roadside Songs of Tuscany,* edited by John Ruskin; Lucia Gray Swett, *John Ruskin's Letters to Francesca and Memoirs of the Alexanders;* William James Stillman, *The Autobiography of a Journalist;* Rembrandt Peale, *Notes on Italy;* Frances Boott Greenough (ed.), *Letters of Horatio Greenough to his brother, Henry Greenough;* Charles Eliot Norton, *Notes of Travel and Study in Italy* and *The Correspondence of Thomas Carlyle and Ralph Waldo Emerson;* Alma Lutz, *Emma Willard;* Elihu Vedder, *The Digressions of V., written for his own fun and that of his friends;* Eugene Plon, *Thorvaldsen: his life and works;* Henry Boynton, "Hiram Powers," *New England Magazine,* vol. 20, no. 5; "Letters of Hiram Powers to Nicholas Longworth Esquire 1856–1858," *Historical and Philosophical Society of Ohio Quarterly,* Cincinnati, 1906; Nathalia Wright (ed.), "The Letters of Richard Henry Wilde to Hiram Powers," *Georgia Historical Quarterly,* September 1962.

CHAPTER 7

Students and the Grand Tour

Sylvester W. Beach, "The American Student in Paris," *Independent,* September 1902; H. G. D. Wright, "Americans in Europe as seen from a Consulate," *North American,* 1903; Eliot Gregory, "Rolling Stones," *Century,* 1902; Franklin Matthews, "Our Annual Travel in Europe," *Chautauqua,* 1896; "The Traveller," *Chautauqua,* 1887; Booth Tarkington, "Some Americans Abroad," *Everybody's,* 1907; "The Wandering American," *Smart Set,* June 1901; Taft family correspondence, Library of Congress; Elizabeth and Anna Blackwell correspondence, Library of Congress; Joseph Wechsberg, "The Grand Tour—as It Was," *Saturday Review,* January 6, 1968; Francis Haskell, *The Age of the Grand Tour;* Edward Lillie Pierce, *Memoirs and Letters of Charles Sumner;* Henry Cabot Lodge, *Early Memories;* Karl Schriftgiesser, *The Gentleman from Massachusetts: Henry Cabot Lodge;* George Ticknor, *Life, Letters and Journals of George Ticknor;* Elkanah Watson, *Men and Times of the Revolution; or Memoirs of Elkanah Watson;* Mrs. Anne Grant of Laggan, *Letters from the Mountains;* Henry Greenleaf Pearson, *James S. Wadsworth of Geneseo;* Washington Irving, *Life and Letters of Washington Irving,* vol. 4; James Russell Lowell, *Lowell's Impressions of Spain;* Francis Parkman, *The Journals of Francis Parkman;* William C. Preston, *The Reminiscences of William C. Preston;* Nathaniel Hawthorne, *English Notebooks,* vol. 2; *French and Italian Notebooks,* vol. 3; Nathaniel Parker Willis, *Pencillings by the way;* Bayard Taylor, *Views Afoot;* Catharine M. Sedgwick, *Letters from abroad to kindred at home;* Harriet Beecher Stowe, *Sunny Memories of Foreign Lands;* William Tudor, *Letters of the Eastern States;* James Sloan, *Rambles in Italy in the years 1816, 1817, 1818 by an American;* Elizabeth Pennell, *Nights: Rome, Venice in the Aesthetic Eighties; London, Paris, in the Fighting Nineties;* Robert W. Burgess, *Reminiscences of an American Scholar;* Julia Ward Howe, *Reminiscences 1819–1899;* William Dean Howells, *Venetian Life, Tuscan Cities,* and *Seven English Cities;* Van Wyck Brooks, *The Dream of Arcadia: American Writers and Artists in Italy 1760–1915;* Edward Everett Hale, *Seven Spanish Cities, and the way to them;* Joseph Green Cogswell, *Life of Joseph Green Cogswell as sketched in his letters;* Rev. John Overton Choules, *The Cruise of the Steam Yacht North Star;* J. Fenimore Cooper, *Travelling Bachelor;* Foster Rhea Dulles, *Americans Abroad;* Horace Greeley, *Glances at Europe;* Frances Scott Greenough (ed.), *Let-*

ters of Horace Greeley to his brother; Alice Ford, *John James Audubon;* Wayne Andrews, *Germaine: A Portrait of Madame de Staël.*

CHAPTER 8

Political Refugees

Liverpool newspaper clippings, State Archives, Montgomery, Alabama; Varina Davis correspondence with British journalists and authors, Confederate Museum, Richmond; Arthur Marvin Shaw, "The Family Sorrows of Jefferson Davis," *Alabama Historical Quarterly,* vol. IX, 1947; Virginia Frazer Boyle's manuscript, including Steven S. Cummins' recollections of the Davis family, Confederate Museum, Richmond; correspondence of Robert Toombs, Alexander H. Stephens, and Howell Cobb, 2 vols., ninth report of the Historical Manuscripts Commission, 1913; Jefferson Davis, *The Rise and Fall of the Confederate Government,* 2 vols.; Varina Davis, *Jefferson Davis: A Memoir by his Wife,* 2 vols.; Hudson Strode, *Jefferson Davis,* 3 vols.; Ishbel Ross, *First Lady of the South* and *Rebel Rose;* William M. Robinson, *The Confederate Privateers;* Robert Douthat Meade, *Judah P. Benjamin;* Theodore Roosevelt, *Diaries of Boyhood and Youth;* Varina Davis papers, Confederate Memorial Hall, New Orleans; Varina Davis papers, Duke University; Kimbrough papers, Library of Congress; Nancy Mayes Crump correspondence, Library of Congress; Jefferson Davis papers, Library of Congress; Lord Newton: *Lord Lyons: a record of British Diplomacy;* Rose O'Neal Greenhow (Confederate Agent) papers, National Archives; Louis A. Sigaud, "Mrs. Greenhow and the Rebel Spy Ring," *Maryland Historical Magazine,* September 1946; Thomas E. Taylor, *Running the Blockade;* Rose O'Neal Greenhow, *My Imprisonment and the First Year of Abolition Rule at Washington; The Works of James Buchanan,* edited by J. B. Moore; Steven S. Cummins, *Confederate Veteran,* March 1929; Chiles Clifton Ferrell, "The Daughter of the Confederacy," publications of the *Mississippi Historical Society,* vol. 1, 1898; William Howard Russell, *My Diary North and South;* Diana Fontaine Maury Corbin, *Life of Matthew Fontaine Maury;* Richard L. Maury, *A Brief Sketch of the Work of Matthew Fontaine Maury by his Son;* Richardson Wright, *Forgotten Ladies;* Dr. John W. Burgess, *Reminiscences of an American Scholar;* files of *Harper's New Monthly Magazine, Harper's Weekly, Leslie's Illustrated,* and *Blackwood's Edinburgh Magazine* during 1860s and 1870s.

CHAPTER 9

The Ladies Travel

Margaret Fuller, *Memoirs of Margaret Fuller,* 2 vols.; Katharine Susan Anthony, *Margaret Fuller;* Margaret Bell, *Margaret Fuller;* Margaret

Fuller's correspondence in New York *Tribune* during the Risorgimento, 1848 and 1849; Julia Ward Howe, *Margaret Fuller* and *Reminiscences 1819–1899;* Margaret Fuller, *Love Letters of Margaret Fuller;* Madeleine B. Stern, *The Life of Margaret Fuller;* Leopold Wellicz, "The Friendship of Margaret Fuller d'Ossoli and Adam Mickiewicz," *Polish Institute of Arts and Sciences in America Bulletin,* vol. 4, 1945–46; Mary King Waddington, *My First Years as a Frenchwoman;* Gordon S. Haight, *George Eliot;* Margaret Leland Goldsmith, *Madame de Staël;* Jessie Benton Frémont, *Souvenirs of my Times;* Catharine M. Sedgwick, *Letters from abroad to kindred at home;* Harriet Beecher Stowe, *Sunny Memories from Foreign Lands;* Mary Merwin Phelps, *Kate Chase, Dominant Daughter;* Thomas Graham Belden and Marva Robins Belden, *So Fell the Angels;* Royal Cortissoz, *The Life of Whitelaw Reid;* Larz Anderson, *Letters and Journals of a Diplomat;* Ishbel Ross, *Proud Kate, Rebel Rose, Child of Destiny, Angel of the Battlefield, The General's Wife,* and *Charmers and Cranks;* Kate Field, *Ten Days in Spain;* Lilian Whiting, *Kate Field;* Margaret (Terry) Chanler, *Roman Spring: Memoirs;* Charles T. Congdon, *Reminiscences of a Journalist;* Clara Crowinshield, *Diary: European Tour with Longfellow, 1835–1836;* Foster Rhea Dulles, *Americans Abroad;* Van Wyck Brooks, *The Dream of Arcadia: American Writers and Artists in Italy 1760–1915;* Maud (Howe) Elliott, *The Story of an Artist, John Elliott* and *My Cousin, F. Marion Crawford;* Annie Fields, *Authors and Friends;* Arthur B. Fuller (ed.), *Margaret Fuller at Home and Abroad;* Harriet Hosmer Letters and Memories, edited by Cornelia Carr; Lord Newton, *Lord Lyons; a record of British Diplomacy;* Anna Brownell Jameson, *Memoirs and Loves of the Poets;* Elizabeth Blackwell, *Pioneer Work in Opening the Medical Profession to Women;* Joanna Johnston, *Mrs. Satan;* Emanie Sachs, *The Terrible Siren;* Theodore Tilton, "Victoria Woodhull," *Golden Age,* 1871; M. A. De Wolfe Howe, *A Venture in Remembrance;* Zula Maud Woodhull, "Affinities," *Westminster Review,* April 1899; Wayne Andrews, *The Vanderbilt Legend;* G. S. Darewin, *Synopsis of the Lives of Victoria Woodhull and Tennessee Claflin;* Lady Cook (Tennessee Claflin), *Talks and Essays;* Madeleine Legge, *Two Noble Women;* Victoria Claflin Woodhull, *And the Truth Shall Make you Free;* Madeleine B. Stern, *Purple Passage;* Clara Barton, *The Red Cross: A History of This Remarkable International Movement in the Interest of Humanity;* George Kennan, *Campaigning in Cuba;* Francis Tiffany, *Life of Dorothea Lynde Dix;* Mrs. Frank Leslie, "Scenes in Sun-Lands," *Frank Leslie's Monthly,* March 1862; "Cuban Bygones," *Frank Leslie's Popular Monthly,* December 1898; Mrs. E. G. Squier, "The Ladies of Lima," *Frank Leslie's Chimney Corner,* June 3, 1865; Mrs. Frank Leslie, *Are Men Gay Deceivers?* and *Rents in Our Robes;* files of *Woodhull & Claflin's Weekly,* of *The Humanitarian,* of *Demorest's Monthly Magazine,* of *Harper's Weekly,* of *Peterson's,* of *Frank Leslie's Illustrated Weekly,* and *Frank Leslie's Illustrated Newspaper;* William Crookes, "Notes of an Enquiry into the Phenomena called Spiritual," *Journal of Science,* January 1874; A. Leah Fox Underhill,

Rochester Knockings; W. G. Langworthy Taylor, *Katie Fox and the Fox-Taylor Record.*

CHAPTER 10

Sargent and Whistler

William Howe Downes, *John S. Sargent, His Life and Work;* Charles Merrill Mount, *John Singer Sargent;* Joseph Walker McSpadden, *Famous Painters of America;* James Thomas Flexner, *A Short History of American Painting;* Leon Edel, *Henry James. The Treacherous Years: 1895–1901,* vol. 4; Shaw Desmond, *The Edwardian Era;* James Laver, *Edwardian Promenade;* Shane Leslie, *Long Shadows;* Ellery Sedgwick, *The Happy Profession;* Louise (Hall) Tharp, *Mrs. Jack, A Biography of Isabella Stewart Gardner;* Morris Carter, *Isabella Stewart Gardner and Fenway Court;* Mrs. Jack Gardner's correspondence with John Singer Sargent and James A. McNeill Whistler, in the Isabella Stewart Gardner Museum; William Rothenstein, *Men and Memories: Recollections of William Rothenstein, 1900–1922;* Aline Saarinen, *The Proud Possessors;* Ishbel Ross, *Charmers and Cranks* and *Silhouette in Diamonds;* Consuelo Vanderbilt Balsan, *The Glitter and the Gold;* Cecilia Beaux, *Background with Figures;* Margaret Breuning, *Mary Cassatt;* Frederick A. Sweet, *Sargent, Whistler, and Mary Cassatt;* Julia M. Carson, *Mary Cassatt;* Mabel Dodge Luhan, *European Experiences;* A. K. McComb (ed.), *The Selected Letters of Bernard Berenson;* Horace Gregory, *The World of James McNeill Whistler;* Arthur Jerome Eddy, *Recollections and Impressions of James A. McNeill Whistler;* Elizabeth Luther Cary, *The Works of James McNeill Whistler;* Nancy R. Bell, *James McNeill Whistler;* Otto Henry Bacher, *With Whistler in Venice;* Hesketh Pearson, *The Man Whistler;* Julia Ward Howe, *Reminiscences 1819–1899;* George du Maurier, *Trilby;* Eugene Exman, *The House of Harper;* Elizabeth R. and Joseph Pennell, *The Life of James McNeill Whistler;* Foster Rhea Dulles, *Americans Abroad;* Dana H. Carroll, *The Freer Collection for the Nation: The Whistler Peacock Room,* publication 4024 of the Smithsonian Institution, 1951; Henry Huntington, *Memories: personages, people, places;* Alexander Gardiner, *Canfield: the True Story of the Greatest Gambler;* George Brinton McClellan Harvey, *Henry C. Frick, the Man;* files of *Harper's Magazine, Frank Leslie's Illustrated Magazine,* and *Punch* for 1870s; "Tough Dandy," *Newsweek,* January 22, 1968.

CHAPTER 11

Collectors and Patrons

Mrs. Jack Gardner's correspondence with John Singer Sargent, James A. McNeill Whistler, Henry James, F. Marion Crawford, Henry Adams, and F. Hopkinson Smith, in the Isabella Stewart Gardner Museum, Boston;

Nelson Lansdale, "Mrs. Gardner's Palace of Paintings," *Horizon,* July 1959; George L. Stout, "Mrs. Gardner's Legacy on the Fenway," *Museum News,* May 1960; Morris Carter, *Isabella Stewart Gardner and Fenway Court;* Louise (Hall) Tharp, *Mrs. Jack, a Biography of Isabella Stewart Gardner;* Aline Saarinen, *Proud Possessors;* Ishbel Ross, *Charmers and Cranks* and *Silhouette in Diamonds;* Bernard Berenson, *The Selected Letters of Bernard Berenson,* edited by A. K. McComb; Nicky Mariano, *Forty Years with Berenson;* Sylvia Sprigge, *Berenson: A Biography;* S. N. Behrman, *Duveen;* James H. Duveen, *The Rise of the House of Duveen;* Frederick A. Sweet, *Miss Mary Cassatt* and *Sargent, Whistler, and Mary Cassatt;* George Biddle, *An American Artist's Story;* Cecilia Beaux, *Background with Figures;* William Rothenstein, *Men and Memories: Recollections of William Rothenstein, 1900–1922;* Edith Wharton, *A Backward Glance;* Forbes Watson, *Mary Cassatt;* Mabel Dodge Luhan, *European Experiences;* Leon Edel, *Henry James. The Treacherous Years: 1895–1901,* vol. 4; Louisine W. Havemeyer, *Sixteen to Sixty: Memoirs of a Collector;* Maud (Howe) Elliott, *The Story of an Artist, John Elliott;* Ellery Sedgwick, *The Happy Profession;* Frederick Lewis Allen, *The Great Pierpont Morgan;* Belle d'Acosta Greene, *The Pierpont Morgan Library;* George Brinton McClellan Harvey, *Henry C. Frick, the Man;* Henry Huntington, *Memories: personages, people, places;* Harvey O'Connor, *Mellon's Millions: The Biography of a Fortune: The Life and Times of Andrew Mellon;* Arthur Jerome Eddy, *Recollections and Impressions of James A. McNeill Whistler;* Mary Berenson, *A Modern Pilgrimage;* Logan Pearsall Smith, *Unforgotten Years;* Ralph Barton Perry, *On All Fronts;* George Santayana, *Persons and Places;* George Santayana, *Letters,* ed. Daniel Cory; W. Swanberg, *Citizen Hearst;* Oliver Carlson and Ernest Sutherland Bates, *Hearst, Lord of San Simeon;* John K. Winkler, *W. R. Hearst, an American Phenomenon;* Mrs. Potter Palmer's correspondence, Chicago Historical Society; Sara T. Hallowell correspondence, Chicago Historical Society; Raoul Heilbronner catalogs, Library of Congress; William Walton, "Miss Mary Cassatt," *Scribner's Magazine,* vol. 19, 1896; Wayne Andrews, "The Lady from Allegheny City," *The New York Times,* December 18, 1966; George Moore, "Memories of Degas," *Burlington Magazine,* London: 1918, vol. 32; "Henry Clay Frick, Pioneer, Patriot, and Philanthropist, 1849–1919," *Western Pennsylvania Historical Magazine,* September to December 1949; Degas *Letters,* edited by Marcel Guérin; J. B. Manson, *The Life and Work of Edgar Degas;* Dana H. Carroll, *The Freer Collection for the Nation;* Gloria Braggiotti, *Born in a Crowd;* Virginia Woolf, *Roger Fry;* William James Stillman, *The Autobiography of a Journalist.*

CHAPTER 12

The International Set

Jennie Churchill, *The Reminiscences of Lady Randolph Churchill, by Mrs. George Cornwallis-West;* Winston S. Churchill, *My Early Life* and

Lord Randolph Churchill; Ralph G. Martin, Jennie: The Life of Lady Randolph Churchill. Vol. 1, The Romantic Years 1854–1895; Anita Leslie, The Remarkable Mr. Jerome; René Kraus, Young Lady Randolph: The Life and Times of Jennie Jerome; Margot Asquith, The Autobiography of Margot Asquith; Consuelo Vanderbilt Balsan, The Glitter and the Gold; Cornelius Vanderbilt, Jr., The Vanderbilt Feud; Cleveland Amory, Who Killed Society?; Wayne Andrews, The Vanderbilt Legend: The Story of the Vanderbilt Family 1794–1940; E. F. Benson, King Edward VII; George Cornwallis-West, Edwardian Hey-Days; Virginia Cowles, Edward VII and his Circle; Shaw Desmond, The Edwardian Era; Lady Elizabeth Eliot, Heiresses and Coronets; Diana Forbes-Robertson, My Aunt Maxine; Henry James, Daisy Miller; Lucy Kavaler, The Astors: A Family Chronicle of Pomp and Power and The Private World of High Society; James Laver, Edwardian Promenade; Shane Leslie, Salutation to Five; Elizabeth Longford, Queen Victoria; Mabel Dodge Luhan, European Experiences; Elisabeth Marbury, My Crystal Ball; Princess Catherine Radziwill, The Royal Marriage Market of Europe and It Really Happened; Princess Cantacuzène, My Life Here and There and Revolutionary Days; Ishbel Ross, Silhouette in Diamonds and Charmers and Cranks; Countess Marguerite Cassini, Never a Dull Moment; Lucius Beebe, Boston and the Boston Legend; Madeleine B. Stern, Purple Passage; Frances Evelyn Warwick, Discretions; Edith Wharton, A Backward Glance; Stephen Birmingham, Our Crowd; Stewart Holbrook, The Age of the Moguls; Florence Jaffray Hurst Harriman (Mrs. J. Borden Harriman), From Pinafores to Politics; Royal Cortissoz, The Life of Whitelaw Reid; Samuel Langhorne Clemens, A Connecticut Yankee in King Arthur's Court; Following the equator, a journey round the world; and The Innocents Abroad; Ellin Berlin, Silver Platter, a Portrait of Mrs. John Mackay; Boni de Castellani, How I Discovered America; Confessions of the Marquis de Castellani; John William Tebbel, The Marshall Fields: a Study in Wealth; Marchioness Grace Elvina Trillia Curzon, Reminiscences; Nancy Astor, My Two Countries.

CHAPTER 13
In the Shadow of Henry James

Louis Auchincloss, Edith Wharton and The Edith Wharton Reader; Millicent Bell, Edith Wharton and Henry James; Van Wyck Brooks, The Dream of Arcadia: American Writers and Artists in Italy 1760–1915; The Letters of Robert Browning and Elizabeth Barrett Browning; F. Marion Crawford, A Lady of Rome; Mary Anderson de Navarro, A Few Memories; Edith Wharton, A Backward Glance, Roman Fever, and Italian Backgrounds; Hanna Kiel (ed.), The Bernard Berenson Treasury; Kay Boyle and Robert McAlmon, Being Geniuses Together; Edwin H. Cady, William Dean Howells: Dean of American Letters, 2 vols.; Shaw Desmond, The Edwardian Era; Leon Edel, Henry James, 4 vols.; Maud (Howe) Elliott, My Cousin, F. Marion Crawford; Julia Ward Howe, Rem-

iniscences 1819–1899; Horace Gregory, *The World of James McNeill Whistler;* William Howe Downes, *John S. Sargent, His Life and Work;* Gordon S. Haight, *George Eliot;* Henry James, *Henry James Autobiography, Daisy Miller, Italian Hours, Portrait of Places, William Wetmore Story and his Friends,* and *Hawthorne;* Morton Dauwen Zabel (ed.), *The Art of Travel: Scenes and Journeys in America, England, France, and Italy from the Travel Writings of Henry James;* James Jackson Jarves, *Italian Rambles;* Anna Brownell (Murphy) Jameson, *Studies, Stories, and Memoirs* and *The Diary of an Ennuyée;* Charles Eliot Norton (ed.), *Letters of James Russell Lowell;* Percy Lubbock, *Portrait of Edith Wharton;* Mabel Dodge Luhan, *European Experiences;* Nicky Mariano, *Forty Years with Berenson;* Ralph Barton Perry, *On All Fronts;* Ralph G. Martin, *Jennie: The Life of Lady Randolph Churchill.* Vol. 1, *The Romantic Years 1854–1895.* William Wetmore Story, *Conversations in a Studio,* vol. 2; Maisie Ward, *Robert Browning and his World,* vol. 2; Constance Fenimore Woolson, *The Front Yard, and other Italian Stories;* R. W. Stallman, *Stephen Crane;* Thomas Beer, *Stephen Crane;* Edwin H. Cady, *William Dean Howells: Dean of American Letters,* 2 vols.; Graham Greene, *Collected Essays;* Margaret (Terry) Chanler, *Roman Spring: Memoirs;* Louise (Hall) Tharp, *Mrs. Jack: A Biography of Mrs. Isabella Stewart Gardner* and *The Peabody Sisters of Salem;* Cleveland Amory, *The Proper Bostonians;* Lucius Beebe, *Boston and the Boston Legend;* Mary Augusta Arnold Ward (Mrs. Humphry Ward), *A Writer's Recollections;* Ford Madox Ford, *Henry James, a Critical Study;* Gertrude Stein, *Four in America.* Introduction by Thornton Wilder; Charles Eliot Norton, *Notes of Travel and Study in Italy;* William James Stillman, *The Autobiography of a Journalist;* Granville Hicks, "The Intense Aristocrat," *Saturday Review,* August 3, 1968.

CHAPTER 14
The Changing Arts

Elizabeth Sprigge, *Gertrude Stein: Her Life and Work;* Alice B. Toklas, *The Autobiography of Alice B. Toklas* and *What Is Remembered;* John Malcolm Brinnin, *The Third Rose: Gertrude Stein and Her World;* Gertrude Stein, *Wars I Have Seen;* Ernest Hemingway, *A Moveable Feast;* Mabel Dodge Luhan, *European Experiences;* James R. Mellow, "The Stein Salon was the First Museum of Modern Art," *New York Times Magazine,* December 1, 1968; Robert McAlmon and Kay Boyle, *Being Geniuses Together;* Malcolm Cowley, *Exile's Return;* Edward Gordon Craig, *Gordon Craig: The Story of His Life;* "Gordon Craig, The Theater's Chief Revolutionary," *Theater Arts Monthly,* New York: 1927, vol. 11; Janet Flanner, *An American in Paris; Profile of an Interlude Between Two Wars;* Mary Desti, *The Life of Isadora Duncan;* Isadora Duncan, *My Life;* Allan Ross MacDougall and Irma Duncan, *Isadora Duncan's Russian Days and Her Last Years in France;* Allan Ross MacDougall, *Isa-*

Notes

dora: A Revolutionary in Art and Love; Isadora Duncan correspondence in Irma Duncan dance collection, New York Public Library; Ernest Newman, "Dances of Isadora Duncan," *Living Age,* June 1921; Nelia Pavlova, "Essenine and Isadora Duncan," *Revue Mondiale,* January 1930; Countess Marguerite Cassini, *Never a Dull Moment;* Mabel Dodge Luhan, *Movers and Shakers;* Petr Demianovich Uspenskii, *The Fourth Way: A Record of Talks and Answers to Questions Based on the Teachings of G. I. Gurdjieff;* Georges Ivanovitch Gurdjieff, *All and Everything;* Charles Norman, *Ezra Pound;* "Ezra Pound Visits his Alma Mater," *New York Post,* June 9, 1969; Peggy Guggenheim, *Confessions of an Art Addict* and *Out of This Century;* Henry Ehrlich, "Guggenheim's Art to America," *Look,* April 4, 1969; Hilton Kramer, "20th-Century Masters Dominate Guggenheim Collection," *The New York Times,* January 16, 1969; Richard F. Shepard, "Peggy Guggenheim Entrusts Art Here," *The New York Times,* March 25, 1969; Angela Taylor, "At the Guggenheim Party for Cousin Peggy and her Art," *The New York Times,* January 16, 1969; "Peggy's Back in Town," *Newsweek,* January 27, 1969; Elberta Brandes Gratz, "The Art of being Peggy," *New York Post,* January 18, 1969.

CHAPTER 15
Life on the Left Bank

Henry Hazlitt, "In Defense of Expatriates," *Century Magazine,* January 1930; H. A. Phillips, "In Defense of Our Literary Expatriates," *Bookman,* June 1927; Eugene Bagger, "Uprooted Americans," *Harper's Magazine,* September 1929; H. Stearns, "Apologia of an Expatriate," *Scribner's Monthly,* March 1929; Frances Warfield, "Innocence Abroad," *Scribner's Magazine,* October 1928; Francis P. Miller and H. D. Hill, "Europe as a Playground," *Atlantic Monthly,* August 1930; H. Motherwell, "The American Tourist Makes History," *Harper's Magazine,* December 1929; Louis Bromfield, "Vintage Expatriate," *Saturday Review,* March 19, 1927; Sam Spewack, "Four Years in Europe made me an American," *Saturday Evening Post,* May 29, 1926; Maude Parker Child, "Expatriated Americans," *Saturday Evening Post,* June 13, 1925; W. T. Upton, "Our Musical Expatriates," *Musical Quarterly,* January 1928; Joseph Wood Krutch, "Was Europe a Success?" *The Nation,* September 1934; *Literary Digest:* "Pan America, the Cry of Expatriates," September 7, 1929; "Shall Arts Run to Europe?", March 2, 1929; and "Whom America Has Failed," May 26, 1928; Ernest Hemingway, *A Moveable Feast, The Sun Also Rises,* and *A Farewell to Arms;* John Dos Passos, *Journeys Between Wars, The Best Times: An Informal Memoir,* and *Three Soldiers;* Malcolm Cowley, *Exile's Return;* Glenway Westcott, *Goodbye Wisconsin;* Morley Callaghan, *That Summer in Paris;* Robert McAlmon and Kay Boyle, *Being Geniuses Together;* Margaret C. Anderson, *The Fiery Fountains, The Little Review Anthology* (ed.), and *My Thirty Years War: An Autobiography;* Julien Green, *Diary 1928–1957;* Harold

313

Loeb, *The Way It Was;* Harold E. Stearns, *America and the Young Intellectual* and *Civilization in the United States, an Inquiry by Thirty Americans;* George Biddle, *An American Artist's Story;* Charles Norman, *Ezra Pound;* Don C. Seitz, *The James Gordon Bennetts, Father and Son;* Richard O'Connor, *The Scandalous Mr. Bennett;* Al Laney, *Paris Herald;* Elliot Paul, *The Last Time I Saw Paris;* Caresse Crosby, *The Passionate Years;* Mary Margaret McBride and Helen Josephy, *Paris is a Woman's Town* and *London is a Man's Town;* Frank Harris, *My Life and Loves;* Sisley Huddleston, *Paris: Salons, Cafés, Studios;* Janet Flanner, *An American in Paris; Profile of an Interlude Between Two Wars;* Tex Burbank, *Thornton Wilder;* Matthew Josephson, *Life Among the Surrealists, a Memoir:* Ford Madox Ford, *Memories and Impressions;* Don Carlos Seitz, *Pulitzer, His Life and Letters;* Ernest Walsh, *Poems and Sonnets, with a Memoir by Ethel Moorhead;* Oliver Carlson and Ernest Sutherland Bates, *Hearst, Lord of San Simeon;* Djuna Barnes, *Selected Works;* Margaret Anderson, *The Unknowable Gurdjieff;* Kiki, *Les Souvenirs de Kiki;* Patino Abatino, *Josephine Baker Vue par la Presse Française;* Eugene Jolas, *I Have Seen Monsters and Angels;* Bruce Kellner, *Carl Van Vechten and the Irreverent Decades;* Vincent Sheean, *Personal History;* files of the *Paris Herald, Chicago Tribune* (Paris edition), *Transition,* and *Transatlantic Review.*

CHAPTER 16
Hemingway and Fitzgerald

Ernest Hemingway, *A Moveable Feast, The Sun Also Rises,* and *A Farewell to Arms;* Carlos Baker, *Ernest Hemingway: A Life Story;* Alden Whitman, "Biographer Evaluates Unpublished Hemingway," *The New York Times,* January 10, 1969; Brian Glanville, "Speaking of Books: Silence, Exile and Cunning," *The New York Times Book Review,* January 5, 1969; "Speaking of Books: In the Vault with Hemingway," *The New York Times Book Review,* September 1968; Kay Boyle, *Generation Without Farewell;* Robert McAlmon and Kay Boyle, *Being Geniuses Together;* Morley Callaghan, *That Summer in Paris: Memories of Tangled Friendships with Hemingway, Fitzgerald, and Some Others;* Robert D. Stephens, *The Public Voice;* Elliot Paul, *The Last Time I Saw Paris;* Alice B. Toklas, *The Autobiography of Alice B. Toklas;* Elizabeth Sprigge, *Gertrude Stein: Her Life and Work;* Malcolm Cowley, *Exile's Return;* F. Scott Fitzgerald, *Tender is the Night, Six Tales of the Jazz Age,* and *The Stories of F. Scott Fitzgerald: A Selection of 28 Stories with an Introduction by Malcolm Cowley;* Janet Flanner, *Interlude Between Two Wars;* Willa Cather, *Willa Cather in Europe; Her Own Story of the First Journey;* Vincent Sheean, *Personal History;* Sinclair Lewis, *From Main Street to Stockholm: Letters 1919–1930,* edited by Harrison Smith; Mark Schorer, *Sinclair Lewis: An American Life;* Vincent Sheean, *Dorothy and Red;* V. F. Calverton, "Sinclair Lewis: An American Phenomenon," Paris: *New Review*, January and February, 1931; Dorothy Thompson, *"I Saw Hitler!"*, *Culture under the Nazis*, and *Let the Record Speak;* Edgar Ansel Mowrer, *Triumph and Turmoil;* William L. Shirer, *Berlin Diary: The Journal of a Foreign Correspondent, 1934–41* and *The Rise and Fall of the Third Reich: A History of Nazi Germany;* Leland Stowe, *They Shall Not Sleep;* R. W. Stallman, *Stephen Crane;* Mark Sullivan, *Our Times. The Twenties*, vol. 7; Kenneth Macfarlane Walker, *Venture with Ideas: Meetings with Gurdjieff and Ouspensky;* Andrew Turnbull, *Scott Fitzgerald;* Tex Burbank, *Thornton Wilder;* Charles Norman, *Ezra Pound;* Thomas Beer, *Stephen Crane;* Harold Loeb, *The Way It Was;* Harold E. Stearns, *America and the Young Intellectual* and *Civilization in the United States, an Inquiry by Thirty Americans;* Sara Mayfield, *The Constant Circle: H. L. Mencken and his Friends;* Matthew Josephson, *Infidel in the Temple: A Memoir;* Al Laney, *Paris Herald;* Caresse Crosby, *The Passionate Years;* Zelda Fitzgerald, *Save Me the Waltz;* Martha Gellhorn, *The Face of War;* Eugene Jolas, *I Have Seen Monsters and Angels;* Joseph Hergesheimer, "Good-by Europe," *Saturday Evening Post*, January 7, 1933; William Harlan Hale, "Grand Tour New Style," *Atlantic Monthly*, December 1932; Thomas Craven, "New Innocents Abroad," *Forum*, April 1930; Gilbert Seldes, "Tramps —Are We?" *Saturday Evening Post*, June 11, 1932; "Europe is America's New World," *Literary Digest*, June 6, 1936; Eugene Bagger, "Uprooted Americans," *Harper's Magazine*, September 1929; Sam Spewack, "Four Years in Europe Made Me an American," *Saturday Evening Post*, May 29, 1926; Ellen Bromfield Geld, *The Heritage;* files of *Paris Herald, Chicago Tribune, The Transatlantic Review, This Quarter*, and *Transition*.

CHAPTER 17

Nomads at Large

Lafcadio Hearn, *In Ghostly Japan* and *The Japanese Letters of Lafcadio Hearn;* Pierre Loti, *Madame Chrysanthème* and *Le Mariage de Loti;* Robert Louis Stevenson, *Island Nights' Entertainments;* James Norman Hall, *The Far Lands, My Island Home*, and *Faery Lands of the South Seas;* James A. Michener, *Hawaii, Tales of the South Pacific*, and *Iberia;* the Duke of Windsor, *A King's Story: The Memoirs of the Duke of Windsor;* Wallis Warfield, Duchess of Windsor, *The Heart Has Its Reasons: The Memoirs of the Duchess of Windsor;* Geoffrey Bocca, *The Woman Who Would Be Queen: A Biography of the Duchess of Windsor;* Gant Gaither, *Princess of Monaco: The Story of Grace Kelly;* Brian Connell, *Knight Errant: A Biography of Douglas Fairbanks, Jr.:* Charles Chaplin, *My Trip Abroad* and *My Autobiography;* Robert Balmain Mowat, *Americans in England;* Lanfranco Rasponi, *The International Nomads;* Harlan Cleveland, Gerard J. Magone, and John Clarke Adams, *The Overseas Americans;* John Bainbridge, *Another Way of Living;* Letitia Baldridge, *Of Diamonds and Diplomats;* Janet Flanner, *An American* in Paris: Profile of an Interlude Between Two Wars and Paris Journal 1944–1965; Mary T. McCarthy, The Stones of Florence and Venice Observed; Nathalia Clifford Barney, Selected Writings; John Steinbeck, "Yank in Europe," Holiday, January 1956; Joseph Wechsberg, "The American Abroad," Atlantic Monthly, November 1957; G. Maranon, "Exiles," Atlantic Monthly, January 1961; V. S. Pritchett, "Party of One," Holiday, November 1960; Newsweek, "Simmering Island in the Caribbean," April 6, 1959, and "Living like ex-Kings," May 18, 1959; Joseph Wechsberg, "The Grand Tour—as It Was," Saturday Review, January 6, 1969; Mary Simons, "The Loving World of Anthony Quinn," Look, January 4, 1969; Herbert R. Lottman, "Literary Life in Paris," Saturday Review, November 27, 1967; Mary Hemingway, "Harry's Bar in Venice," Holiday, June 1968, and "Hemingway's Spain," Saturday Review, March 11, 1967; Robert Trumbull, "American Samoa Keeps Old Ways," The New York Times, February 16, 1969; John Bainbridge, "Students, Sojourners, Beatniks Abroad," Holiday, July 1968; Aline Griffith, Countess of Quintanilla, The Earth Rests Lightly; Stephen Birmingham, "The Indulgent Coast," Holiday, July 1968; Brian Glanville, "Speaking of Books: Silence, Exile and Cunning," The New York Times Book Review, January 5, 1969; "Hawaii," Look, April 29, 1969; Gaia Servadio, "Italian Sexport to Scotland," Life, June 7, 1968; Frank Shea, "Corfu: From Caesar to Constantine," Saturday Review, March 8, 1969; Joyce Haber, "A Visit to Merle Oberon's Castle," New York Post, January 28, 1969; Anne Sinclair Mehdevi, "Robert Graves's Secret Vice Pays Off," The New York Times, October 30, 1966; Doris Lilly, "Sardinia Will Swing," New York Post, May 15, 1968, and "New Island in the Sun," September 10, 1968; "Portugal Thrives in the Sun," The New York Times, November 3, 1968; Suzy Says, in the New York Daily News, April 25, May 16, September 3, 1968; February 4, March 12, 13, and 17, and June 5 and 8, 1969; Kay Gardella, "A Place in the Sun," New York Daily News; "Father for Today," Time, July 26, 1968; J. Bryan, "Estoril, Home of Throneless Exiles," Holiday, January 1961.

CHAPTER 18
The Expatriate World Today

International Educational Exchange reports, State Department; annual Survey of International Travel, 1956–1968, Department of Commerce; Thomas Thompson, "The New Odyssey," Life, July 19, 1968; Ernest Dunbar, The Black Expatriates: A Study of American Negroes in Exile; John A. Williams, The Man Who Cried I Am; Richard Wright, Native Son; Ed Smith, Where to, Black Man? An American Negro's African Diary; Margaret Parton, "Rejected U.S.A.," Ladies' Home Journal, September 1959; "College Seniors and the War," The New Yorker, July 20, 1968; "Why Good Sons Become Draft Dodgers," Ladies' Home Journal, August 1967; John M. Lee, "Many Deserters Active in Sweden," The

New York Times, July 15, 1968; Lawrence Fellows, "Peace Corps Quietly Folding up in Tanzania," *The New York Times,* April 10, 1968; Edward Cowan, "Draft Dodgers Find Life in Canada Is Not Easy," *The New York Times,* April 10, 1968; John A. Williams, "The U.S.—a Nice Place to Visit," *Saturday Review,* January 27, 1968; Herbert Lottman, "The Action is Everywhere the Black Man Goes," *The New York Times,* April 21, 1968; Thomas A. Johnson, "Negro Expatriates Finding Wide Opportunity in Asia," *The New York Times,* April 30, 1968; Joseph Lelyveld, "The Kurta Makes a Comeback in India," *The New York Times,* September 2, 1968; John Bainbridge, *Another Way of Living;* "Guadalajara has an American flavor from its University to its Ice Cream Cones," *The New York Times,* March 10, 1969; "Doctor's Order for Hippies in Rome: Hospitality," *The New York Times,* April 5, 1969; "Prospero's Progress," *Time,* May 23, 1969; "Josephine Baker is Beset by More Woes," *The New York Times,* March 13, 1969; E. Gilbert, "New Faces in Expatriate Colony," *The New York Times Magazine,* December 8, 1963.

Bibliography

ADAMS, ABIGAIL. *New Letters of Abigail Adams, 1788–1801,* edited by Stewart Mitchell. Boston: Houghton Mifflin Company, 1947.

ADAMS, CHARLES FRANCIS (ed.). *Familiar Letters of John Adams and his wife, Abigail Adams, during the Revolution.* Boston: Houghton Mifflin Company, 1875.

————. *Memoirs of John Quincy Adams.* Philadelphia: J. B. Lippincott Company, 1874–79.

ADAMS, HENRY. *The Education of Henry Adams.* Boston: Houghton Mifflin Company, 1918. Vols. 1-3.

————. *The Life of Albert Gallatin.* Philadelphia: J. B. Lippincott, 1879.

ADAMS, JAMES TRUSLOW. *Revolutionary New England, 1691–1776.* Boston: The Atlantic Monthly Press, 1923.

————. *The Living Jefferson.* New York: Charles Scribner's Sons, 1936.

ALEXANDER, FRANCESCA. *Roadside Songs of Tuscany,* edited by John Ruskin. Orpington, Kent: G. Allen, 1885.

ALLEN, FREDERICK LEWIS. *The Great Pierpont Morgan.* New York: Harper & Brothers, 1949.

AMORY, CLEVELAND. *Who Killed Society?* New York: Harper & Brothers, 1960.

AMORY, MARTHA BABCOCK. *The Domestic and Artistic Life of John Singleton Copley.* Boston: Houghton Mifflin Company, 1882.

Bibliography

ANDERSON, LARZ. *Letters and Journals of a Diplomat,* edited by Isabel Anderson. New York, London: Fleming H. Revell Company, 1940.

ANDERSON, MARGARET C. *The Fiery Fountains.* New York: Hermitage House, 1951.

———(ed.). *The Little Review Anthology.* New York: Hermitage House, 1953.

———. *My Thirty Years' War: An Autobiography.* New York: Covici, Friede, 1930.

———. *The Unknowable Gurdjieff.* London: Routledge & Kegan Paul, 1962.

ANDREW, OLIVER. *Portraits of John and Abigail Adams,* Cambridge: Belknap Press of Harvard University Press, 1967.

ANDREWS, ALLEN. *The Splendid Pauper.* Philadelphia: J. B. Lippincott Company, 1968.

ANDREWS, WAYNE. *Germaine: A Portrait of Madame de Staël.* New York: Atheneum, 1963.

———. *The Vanderbilt Legend: The Story of the Vanderbilt Family, 1794–1940.* New York: Harcourt, Brace & Company, 1941.

ANTHONY, KATHARINE SUSAN. *Margaret Fuller.* New York: Harcourt, -Brace & Howe, 1920.

ARVIN, NEWTON. *Longfellow: His Life and Work.* Boston; Little, Brown & Company, 1963.

ASQUITH, MARGOT. *The Autobiography of Margot Asquith.* London: Thornton Butterworth, 1920.

ASTOR, NANCY. *My Two Countries.* Garden City, N.Y.: Doubleday, Page & Company, 1923.

AUCHINCLOSS, LOUIS. *Edith Wharton.* Minneapolis: University of Minnesota Press, 1961.

———(ed.). *The Edith Wharton Reader,* New York: Charles Scribner's Sons, 1965.

AUGER, HELEN. *An American Jezebel.* New York: Brentano's, 1930.

BACHER, OTTO HENRY. *With Whistler in Venice.* New York: The Century Company, 1908.

BAINBRIDGE, JOHN. *Another Way of Living.* New York: Holt, Rinehart and Winston, 1968.

BAKER, CARLOS. *Ernest Hemingway: A Life Story.* New York: Charles Scribner's Sons, 1969.

BALDRIDGE, LETITIA. *Roman Candle.* Boston: Houghton Mifflin Company, 1956.

———. *Of Diamonds and Diplomats.* Boston: Houghton Mifflin Company, 1968.

BALSAN, CONSUELO VANDERBILT. *The Glitter and the Gold.* New York: Harper & Brothers, 1952.

BARNES, DJUNA, *Selected Works.* New York: Farrar, Strauss and Cudahy, 1962.

BARNEY, NATHALIA CLIFFORD. *Selected Writings,* edited by Miron Grindea. London: Adam Books, 1963.

BARTON, CLARA. *A Story of the Red Cross: Glimpses of Field Work.* New York: D. Appleton & Company, 1924.

————. *The Red Cross, A History of this Remarkable International Movement in the interest of Humanity.* Washington: American Nation Red Cross, 1898.

BEAUX, CECILIA. *Background with Figures.* Boston: Houghton Mifflin Company, 1930.

BEEBE, LUCIUS. *Boston and the Boston Legend.* New York: D. Appleton-Century Company, 1935.

BEECHER, HENRY WARD. *Star Papers.* New York: J. C. Derby, 1855.

BEER, THOMAS. *Stephen Crane.* New York: Alfred A. Knopf, 1923.

BEHRMAN, S. W. *Duveen.* New York: Random House, 1951.

BELDEN, THOMAS GRAHAM and MARVA ROBINS. *So Fell the Angels.* Boston: Little, Brown & Company, 1956.

BELL, MARGARET. *Margaret Fuller.* New York: Albert and Charles Boni, 1930.

BELL, MILLICENT. *Edith Wharton and Henry James.* New York: G. Braziller, 1965.

BELL, NANCY R. *James McNeill Whistler.* London: G. Bell & Sons, 1904.

BEMIS, SAMUEL FLAGG. *The Diplomacy of the American Revolution.* New York: D. Appleton-Century Company, 1935.

BENSON, E. F. *King Edward VII.* London: Longmans, Green Company, 1933.

BERENSON, BERNARD. *The Bernard Berenson Treasury,* selected and edited by Hanna Kiel. New York: Simon & Schuster, 1962.

————. *The Selected Letters of Bernard Berenson,* edited by A. K. McComb. Boston: Houghton Mifflin Company, 1964.

————. *The Passionate Sightseer: From the Diaries, 1947–1956.* New York: Simon & Schuster, 1960.

————. *The Venetian Painters of the Renaissance.* New York: G. P. Putnam's Sons, 1894.

BERENSON, MARY. *A Modern Pilgrimage.* New York: D. Appleton & Company, 1933.

BERLIN, ELLIN. *Silver Platter.* New York: Doubleday & Company, 1957.

BIDDLE, GEORGE. *An American Artist's Story.* Boston: Little, Brown & Company, 1939.

————. *Tahitian Journal.* Minneapolis: University of Minnesota Press, 1968.

BIGELOW, JOHN (ed.). *Autobiography of Benjamin Franklin.* Philadelphia: J. B. Lippincott, 1868.

BIRMINGHAM, STEPHEN. *Our Crowd.* New York: Harper & Row, 1967.

BIZARDEL, YVON. *American Painters in Paris.* Translated by Richard Howard. New York: The Macmillan Company, 1960.

BLACKWELL, ELIZABETH. *Pioneer Work in Opening the Medical Profession to Women.* New York: E. P. Dutton & Company, 1895.

BOBBÉ, DOROTHIE. *Abigail Adams, the Second First Lady.* New York: Minton, Balch & Company, 1929.

Bibliography

BOCCA, GEOFFREY. *The Woman Who Would Be Queen: A Biography of the Duchess of Windsor*. New York: Rinehart & Company, 1954.

BOND, BEVERLEY WAUGH. *The Monroe Mission to France*. Baltimore: The Johns Hopkins Press, 1907.

BOORSTIN, DANIEL J. *The Lost World of Thomas Jefferson*. New York: Henry Holt & Company, 1942.

BOYLE, KAY, and MCALMON, ROBERT. *Being Geniuses Together*. Garden City, N.Y.: Doubleday & Company, 1968.

BOYLE, KAY. *Generation Without Farewell*. New York: Alfred A. Knopf, 1960.

―――. *The Smoking Mountain*. New York: Alfred A. Knopf, 1963.

―――. *365 Days*, edited by Kay Boyle, Laurence Vail, and Nina Conarain. New York: Harcourt, Brace & Company, 1936.

BRADFORD, GAMALIEL. *The Quick and the Dead*. Boston: Houghton Mifflin Company, 1931.

BRAGGIOTTI, GLORIA. *Born in a Crowd*. New York: Thomas Y. Crowell Company, 1957.

BREUNING, MARGARET. *Mary Cassatt*. New York: Hyperion Press, 1944.

BRINNIN, JOHN MALCOLM. *The Third Rose: Gertrude Stein and her World*. London: Weidenfeld and Nicholson, 1960.

BROOKS, PHILLIPS. *Letters of Travel*. New York: E. P. Dutton & Company, 1894.

BROOKS, VAN WYCK. *The Dream of Arcadia: American Writers and Artists in Italy, 1760–1915*. New York: E. P. Dutton & Company, 1958.

―――. *The Pilgrimage of Henry James*. New York: E. P. Dutton & Company, 1925.

―――. *The World of Washington Irving*. New York: E. P. Dutton & Company, 1944.

BROWN, STUART GERRY (ed.). *Autobiography of James Monroe*. Syracuse, N.Y.: Syracuse University Press, 1959.

BROWNE, J. ROSS. *An American Family in Germany*. New York: Harper & Brothers, 1866.

BROWNING, ELIZABETH BARRETT. *The Letters of Mrs. Browning*, edited by Frederic G. Kenyon. New York: The Macmillan Company, 1897.

―――. *The Letters of Robert Browning and Elizabeth Barrett Browning, 1845–1846*. New York: Harper & Brothers, 1899.

BRYANT, WILLIAM CULLEN. *Letters of a Traveller*. New York: G. P. Putnam's Sons, 1869.

BULFINCH, ELLEN SUSAN (ed.). *Charles Bulfinch*. Boston: Houghton Mifflin & Company, 1896.

BULLOCK, HELEN CLAIRE. *My Head and My Heart: A Little History of Thomas Jefferson and Maria Cosway*. New York: G. P. Putnam's Sons, 1945.

BURBANK, TEX. *Thornton Wilder*. New York: Twayne Publishing Company, 1961.

BURGESS, ROBERT W. *Reminiscences of an American Scholar*. New York: Columbia University Press, 1934.

BUTLER, NICHOLAS MURRAY. *Across the Busy Years.* New York: Charles Scribner's Sons, 1939.

CADY, EDWIN H. *William Dean Howells: Dean of American Letters.* 2 vols. Syracuse University Press, 1956 and 1958.

CALLAGHAN, MORLEY. *That Summer in Paris: Memories of Tangled Friendships with Hemingway, Fitzgerald and Some Others.* New York: Coward-McCann, 1963.

CANTACUZÈNE, PRINCESS. *My Life Here and There.* New York: Charles Scribner's Sons, 1921.

————. *Revolutionary Days.* Boston: Small, Maynard & Company, 1919.

CARLSON, OLIVER, and BATES, ERNEST SUTHERLAND. *Hearst, Lord of San Simeon.* New York: The Viking Press, 1936.

CARR, CORNELIA (ed.). *Harriet Goodhue Hosmer Letters and Memories.* New York: Moffat, Yard and Company, 1912.

CARROLL, DANA H. *The Freer Collection for the Nation.* New York: Marchbanks Press, 1923.

CARSON, JULIA M. *Mary Cassatt.* New York: David McKay Company, 1966.

CARTER, MORRIS. *Isabella Stewart Gardner and Fenway Court.* Cambridge, Mass.: The Riverside Press, 1925.

CARY, ELISABETH LUTHER. *The Works of James M. Whistler: A Study.* New York: Moffat, Yard & Company, 1907.

CASSINI, MARGUERITE. *Never a Dull Moment: The Memoirs of Countess Marguerite Cassini.* New York: Harper & Brothers, 1956.

CASTELLANI, BONI DE. *How I Discovered America: Confessions of the Marquis de Castellani.* New York: Alfred A. Knopf, 1924.

CATHER, WILLA. *Willa Cather in Europe: Her Own Story of the First Journey.* New York: Alfred Knopf, 1956.

CHANLER, MARGARET (TERRY). *Roman Spring: Memoirs.* Boston: Little, Brown & Company, 1934.

CHANLER, WINTHROP. *Winthrop Chanler's Letters, Collected by His Wife, Margaret Terry Chanler.* New York: privately printed, 1951.

CHAPLIN, CHARLES. *My Autobiography.* New York: Simon & Schuster, 1964.

————. *My Trip Abroad.* New York: Harper & Brothers, 1922.

CHINARD, GILBERT. *Thomas Jefferson, the Apostle of Americanism.* Boston: Little, Brown & Company, 1929.

————. *Honest John Adams.* Boston: Little, Brown & Company, 1933.

CHOULES, REV. JOHN OVERTON. *The Cruise of the Steam Yacht North Star, a Narrative of the Excursions of Mr. Vanderbilt's Party.* Boston: Gould and Lincoln, 1854.

CHURCHILL, JENNIE. *The Reminiscences of Lady Randolph Churchill, by Mrs. George Cornwallis-West.* New York: The Century Company, 1908.

CHURCHILL, WINSTON S. *My Early Life.* New York: Charles Scribner's Sons, 1930.

————. *Lord Randolph Churchill.* New York: The Macmillan Company, 1906.

Bibliography

CLARK, ELEANOR. *Rome and a Villa*. Garden City, N.Y.: Doubleday & Company, 1952.

CLEMENS, SAMUEL LANGHORNE. *A Connecticut Yankee in King Arthur's Court*. New York: C. L. Webster and Company, 1889.

————. *Following the equator; a journey round the world*. Hartford, Conn.: The American Publishing Company, 1897.

————. *The Innocents Abroad*. Hartford, Conn.: The American Publishing Company, 1869.

CLEVELAND, HARLAN; MANGONE, GERARD J.; and ADAMS, JOHN CLARKE. *The Overseas Americans*. New York: McGraw-Hill, 1960.

COGSWELL, JOSEPH GREEN. *Life of Joseph Green Cogswell as sketched in his letters*. Cambridge, Mass.: Riverside Press, 1874.

COLERIDGE, SAMUEL TAYLOR. *Letters of Samuel Taylor Coleridge*, edited by Ernest Hartley Coleridge. Vol. 2. Boston: Houghton Mifflin & Company, 1895.

CONGDON, CHARLES T. *Reminiscences of a Journalist*. Boston: J. R. Osgood and Company, 1880.

CONNELL, BRIAN. *Knight Errant: A Biography of Douglas Fairbanks, Jr.*, London: Hodder and Stoughton, 1955.

COOK, TENNESSEE CLAFLIN (LADY). *Talks and Essays*. London: The Roxburghe Press, 1897.

COOPER, JAMES FENIMORE. *Gleanings in Europe*, edited by Robert Ernest Spiller. New York: Oxford University Press, 1928–30.

————. *Letters and Journals*, edited by James Franklin Beard. Cambridge: Belknap Press of Harvard University Press, 1960.

————. *Travelling Bachelor*. New York: W. A. Townsend & Company, 1859.

COPLEY, JOHN SINGLETON. *Letters and Papers of John Singleton Copley and Henry Pelham, 1739–1776*. Boston: Massachusetts Historical Society, 1914.

CORBIN, DIANA FONTAINE MAURY. *A Life of Matthew Fontaine Maury*. London: Sampson Low, Marston and Searle, 1888.

CORNWALLIS-WEST, GEORGE. *Edwardian Hey-Days*. New York: G. P. Putnam's Sons, 1931.

CORTISSOZ, ROYAL. *The Life of Whitelaw Reid*. New York: Charles Scribner's Sons, 1921.

COWLES, VIRGINIA. *Edward VII and his Circle*. London: Hamish Hamilton, 1956.

COWLEY, MALCOLM. *Exile's Return: A Narrative of Ideas*. New York: The Viking Press, 1951.

————. *Writers at Work*. New York: The Viking Press, 1958.

CRAIG, EDWARD GORDON. *Gordon Craig: The Story of His Life*. New York: Alfred A. Knopf, 1968.

CRAWFORD, F. MARION. *Salve Venetia and Sant' Ilario*. New York: The Macmillan Company, 1905.

————. *A Lady of Rome*. New York: The Macmillan Company, 1906.

CRAWFORD, MARY MACDERMOTT. *Madame de Lafayette and her Family*. New York: J. Pott & Company, 1907.

CROCKETT, ALBERT STEVENS. *When James Gordon Bennett Was Caliph of Bagdad*. New York: Funk & Wagnalls Company, 1926.

CROSBY, CARESSE. *The Passionate Years*. New York: Dial Press, 1953.

CROWINSHIELD, CLARA. *Diary: European Tour with Longfellow, 1835–1836*, edited by Andrew Hilen, Seattle: University of Washington Press, 1956.

CURTI, MERLE. *The Growth of American Thought*. New York: Harper & Brothers, 1943.

CURZON, GRACE ELVINA TRILLIA (MARCHIONESS). *Reminiscences*. London: Hutchinson & Co., 1955.

DANA, RICHARD HENRY, JR. (ed.). *Washington Allston*. New York: Baker and Scribner, 1850.

DAREWIN, G. S. *Synopsis of the Lives of Victoria C. Woodhull and Tennessee Claflin*. London: J. H. Corthesy, 1891.

DAVIS, VARINA. *Jefferson Davis, A Memoir by his wife*. 2 vols. New York: Belford Company, 1890.

DE NAVARRO, MARY ANDERSON. *A Few Memories by Mary Anderson*. New York: Harper & Brothers, 1896.

DENNIS, ALFRED PEARCE. *Gods and Little Fishes*. Indianapolis: The Bobbs-Merrill Company, 1924.

DENNY, MARGARET, and GILMAN, WILLIAM H. (eds.). *The American Writer and the European Tradition*. Minneapolis: Published for the University of Rochester by the University of Minnesota Press, 1950.

DE NOLDE, ELISABETH. *Madame de Staël and Benjamin Constant*. New York: G. P. Putnam's Sons, 1907.

DESMOND, SHAW. *The Edwardian Era*. London: Rockcliff Publishing Corporation, 1949.

DESTI, MARY. *The Life of Isadora Duncan, 1921–1927*. New York: Horace Liveright, 1929.

DONALD, DAVID H. *Charles Sumner and the Coming of the Civil War*. New York: Alfred A. Knopf, 1960.

DOS PASSOS, JOHN. *Journeys Between Wars*. New York: Harcourt, Brace & Company, 1938.

———. *The Best Times: An Informal Memoir*. New York: New American Library, 1966.

———. *Three Soldiers*. New York: Doubleday, Doran & Company, 1921.

DOUGLAS, NORMAN. *South Wind*. New York: Dodd, Mead & Company, 1926.

DOWNES, WILLIAM HOWE. *John S. Sargent, His Life and Work*. Boston: Little, Brown & Company, 1925.

DREISER, THEODORE. *A Traveler at Forty*. New York: The Century Company, 1913.

DULLES, ALLEN. *The Craft of Intelligence*. New York: Harper & Row, 1963.

DULLES, FOSTER RHEA. *Americans Abroad*. Ann Arbor: University of Michigan Press, 1964.

Bibliography

Du Maurier, George. *Trilby*. New York: Harper & Brothers, 1894.

Dumbauld, Edward. *Thomas Jefferson, American Tourist: A Jefferson Profile as Revealed in His Letters, Selected and Arranged, with an Introduction by Saul K. Padover*. Norman, Oklahoma: University of Oklahoma Press, 1946.

Dunbar, Ernest. *The Black Expatriates*. New York: E. P. Dutton & Company, 1968.

Duncan, Isadora. *My Life*. New York: Boni & Liveright, 1927.

Dunton, John. *The Life and Errors of John Dunton*. Vol. 1. London: J. Nicholson, and Bentley, 1818.

Duveen, James H. *The Rise of the House of Duveen*. New York: Alfred A. Knopf, 1957.

Eddy, Arthur Jerome. *Recollections and Impressions of James A. McNeill Whistler*. Philadelphia: J. B. Lippincott Company, 1904.

Edel, Leon. *Henry James*. 4 vols. Philadelphia: J. B. Lippincott Company, 1953–1969.

Eliot, Lady Elizabeth. *Heiresses and Coronets*. New York: McDowell, Obolensky, 1959.

Ellet, Elizabeth F. *Queens of American Society*. New York: Charles Scribner & Company, 1867.

———. *The Women of the American Revolution*. 3 vols. New York: Baker & Scribner, 1850.

Elliott, Maud (Howe). *My Cousin, F. Marion Crawford*. New York: The Macmillan Company, 1934.

———. *The Story of an Artist, John Elliott*. Boston: The Riverside Press, 1930.

———. *Uncle Sam Ward and his Circle*. New York: The Macmillan Company, 1938.

Emerson, Ralph Waldo. *Journals of Ralph Waldo Emerson*, edited by Edward Waldo Emerson and Waldo Emerson Forbes. Vol. 3. Boston: Houghton Mifflin Company, 1909–1914.

Exman, Eugene. *The House of Harper*. New York: Harper & Row, 1967.

Falkner, Leonard. *Painted Lady*. New York: E. P. Dutton & Company, 1962.

Faulkner, Harold U. *From Versailles to the New Deal*. New Haven: Yale University Press, 1950.

Field, Kate. *Ten Days in Spain*. Boston: J. R. Osgood & Company, 1875.

Fields, Annie. *Authors and Friends*. Boston: Houghton Mifflin & Company, 1898.

Fitzgerald, F. Scott. *Six Tales of the Jazz Age*. New York: Charles Scribner's Sons, 1960.

———. *The Stories of F. Scott Fitzgerald: A selection of 28 with an Introduction by Malcolm Cowley*. New York: Charles Scribner's Sons, 1961.

———. *Tender is the Night*. New York: Charles Scribner's Sons, 1951.

Fitzgerald, Zelda. *Save Me the Waltz*. New York: Charles Scribner's Sons, 1932.

FLAGG, JARED BRADLEY. *The Life and Letters of Washington Allston.* New York: Charles Scribner's Sons, 1892.

FLANNER, JANET (GENÊT). *An American in Paris: Profile of an Interlude Between Two Wars.* New York: Simon & Schuster, 1940.

———. *Paris Journal 1944–1965,* edited by William Shawn. New York: Atheneum, 1965.

FLEXNER, JAMES THOMAS. *America's Old Masters.* New York: The Viking Press, 1939.

———. *A Short History of American Painting.* Boston: Houghton Mifflin Company, 1950.

———. *Gilbert Stuart: A Great Life in Brief.* New York: Alfred A. Knopf, 1955.

———. *John Singleton Copley.* Boston: Houghton Mifflin Company, 1948.

FORBES-ROBERTSON, DIANA. *My Aunt Maxine.* New York: The Viking Press, 1964.

FORD, ALICE. *John James Audubon.* Norman: University of Oklahoma Press, 1964.

FORD, FORD MADOX. *Henry James, a Critical Study.* New York: Octagon Books, 1964.

———. *Memories and Impressions.* New York: Harper & Brothers, 1911.

FORD, PAUL LEICESTER. *Thomas Jefferson.* Boston: A. W. Elson & Company, 1904.

FREEMAN, JAMES E. *Gatherings from an Artist's Portfolio.* New York: D. Appleton & Company, 1877–83.

FRÉMONT, JESSIE BENTON. *Souvenirs of My Times.* Boston: D. Lothrop & Company, 1887.

FULLER, ARTHUR B. (ed.). *Margaret Fuller at Home and Abroad.* Boston: Crosby, Nichols and Company, 1856.

FULLER, MARGARET. *Love Letters of Margaret Fuller 1845–1846.* New York: D. Appleton & Company, 1903.

FULLER (OSSOLI), MARGARET. *Memoirs of Margaret Fuller.* 2 vols. Boston: Sampson and Company, 1852.

GAITHER, GANT. *Princess of Monaco: The Story of Grace Kelly.* New York: Henry Holt & Co., 1957.

GALLATIN, JAMES. *The Diary of James Gallatin, Secretary to Albert Gallatin, the Great Peacemaker, 1813–1827.* New York: Charles Scribner's Sons, 1916.

GALT, JOHN. *The Life and Studies of Benjamin West.* London: T. Cadell and W. Davies, 1820.

GARDINER, ALEXANDER. *Canfield: The True Story of the Greatest Gambler.* New York: Doubleday, Doran & Company, 1930.

GARRATY, JOHN ARTHUR. *Henry Cabot Lodge, a Biography.* New York: Alfred A. Knopf, 1953.

GELD, ELLEN BROMFIELD. *The Heritage.* New York: Harper & Brothers, 1962.

Bibliography

GELLHORN, MARTHA. *The Lowest Trees Have Tops*. New York: Dodd, Mead & Company, 1969.

————. *The Face of War*. New York: Simon & Schuster, 1959.

GIBBS, PHILIP. *People of Destiny*. New York: Harper & Brothers, 1920.

GOLDHURST, WILLIAM. *F. Scott Fitzgerald and His Contemporaries*. New York: World Publishing Company, 1963.

GOLDMAN, ERIC F. *The Crucial Decade*. New York: Alfred A. Knopf, 1959.

GOLDSMITH, MARGARET LELAND. *Madame de Staël*. London: Longmans, Green & Company, 1938.

GRANT, MRS. ANNE (MACVICAR) of Laggan. *Letters from the Mountains*. London: Longman, Hurst, Rees, 1806.

GRANT, J. P. (ed.). *Memoir and Correspondence of Mrs. Grant of Laggan*. London: Longman, Brown, Green and Longmans, 1844.

GREELEY, HORACE. *Recollections of a Busy Life*. New York: J. B. Ford & Company, 1868.

————. *Glances at Europe*. New York: Dewitt & Davenport, 1851.

GREEN, JULIEN. *Diary 1928–1957*. Translated by Anne Green. New York: Harcourt, Brace & World, 1964.

GREENE, BELLE D'ACOSTA. *The Pierpont Morgan Library*. New York: privately printed. The Plandome Press, 1930.

GREENE, GEORGE WASHINGTON. *Biographical Studies*. New York: G. P. Putnam, 1860.

GREENE, GRAHAM. *Collected Essays*. New York: The Viking Press, 1969.

GREENE, LAURENCE. *The Era of Wonderful Nonsense*. Indianapolis: Bobbs-Merrill Company, 1939.

GREENHOW, ROSE O'NEAL. *My Imprisonment and the First Year of Abolition Rule at Washington*. Boston: Charles C. Little and James Brown, 1844.

GREENOUGH, FRANCES BOOTT (ed.). *Letters of Horatio Greenough to his brother, Henry Greenough*. Boston: Ticknor and Company, 1887.

GREGORY, HORACE. *The World of James McNeill Whistler*. New York: Thomas Nelson & Sons, 1959.

GRIFFITH, ALINE (Countess of Quintanilla). *The Earth Rests Lightly*. New York: Holt, Rinehart and Winston, 1963.

GUÉRIN, MARCEL (ed.). *Degas Letters*, translated by Marguerite Kay. Oxford: B. Cassirer; distributed in the United States by Studio Publications, 1948.

GUGGENHEIM, PEGGY. *Confessions of an Art Addict*. New York: The Macmillan Company, 1960.

————. *Out of This Century. The Informal Memoirs of Peggy Guggenheim*. New York: The Macmillan Company, 1960.

GUNTHER, JOHN, and QUINT, BERNARD. *Days to Remember*. New York: Harper & Brothers, 1956.

GURDJIEFF, GEORGES IVANOVITCH. *All and Everything*. New York: Harcourt, Brace and Company, 1950.

HAIGHT, GORDON S. *George Eliot: A Biography.* New York: Oxford University Press, 1968.

HALE, EDWARD EVERETT. *Seven Spanish Cities, and the way to them.* Boston: Roberts Brothers, 1883.

————, and HALE, EDWARD EVERETT, JR. *Franklin in France.* Boston: Roberts Brothers, 1888.

HALL, GORDON LANGLEY. *Mr. Jefferson's Ladies.* Boston: Beacon Press, 1966.

HALL, JAMES NORMAN. *The Far Lands.* Boston: Little, Brown & Company, 1950.

————. *My Island Home: An Autobiography.* Boston: Little, Brown & Company, 1952.

————. *Faery Lands of the South Seas.* New York: Harper & Brothers, 1921.

HARRIMAN, FLORENCE JAFFRAY HURST (MRS. J. BORDEN HARRIMAN). *From Pinafores to Politics.* New York: Henry Holt & Company, 1923.

HARRIS, FRANK. *My Life and Loves.* New York: Grove Press, 1963.

HARVEY, GEORGE BRINTON McCLELLAN. *Henry C. Frick, the Man.* New York: Charles Scribner's Sons, 1928.

HASKELL, FRANCIS. *The Age of the Grand Tour.* New York: Crown Publishers, 1967.

HAVEMEYER, LOUISINE W. *Sixteen to Sixty: Memoirs of a Collector.* New York: Metropolitan Museum of Art, 1961.

HAWTHORNE, NATHANIEL. *English Notebooks,* vol. 2; *French and Italian Notebooks,* vol. 3. London: Oxford University Press, 1841.

————. *The Marble Faun.* Boston: Ticknor and Fields, 1860.

HEARN, LAFCADIO. *In Ghostly Japan.* Boston: Little, Brown & Company, 1899.

————. *The Japanese Letters of Lafcadio Hearn, with an Introduction by Elizabeth Bisland.* Boston: Houghton Mifflin Company, 1910.

————. *Two Years in the French West Indies.* New York: Harper & Brothers, 1890.

HELLMAN, GEORGE SIDNEY. *Washington Irving Esquire, Ambassador at Large from the New World to the Old.* New York: Alfred A. Knopf, 1929.

HEMINGWAY, ERNEST. *A Moveable Feast.* New York: Charles Scribner's Sons, 1964.

————. *A Farewell to Arms.* New York: Charles Scribner's Sons, 1929.

————. *By-line: Ernest Hemingway, Selected Articles and Dispatches of Four Decades,* edited by William White. New York: Charles Scribner's Sons, 1967.

————. *The Sun Also Rises.* New York: Charles Scribner's Sons, 1928.

HOLBROOK, STEWART H. *The Age of the Moguls.* Garden City, N.Y.: Doubleday & Company, 1953.

HOLROYD, MICHAEL. *Lytton Strachey.* Vol. 2, *The Years of Achievement, 1910–1932.* New York: Holt, Rinehart and Winston, 1968.

HORTON, PHILIP. *Hart Crane: The Life of an American Poet.* New York, W. W. Norton & Company, 1937.

HOWE, JULIA WARD. *Margaret Fuller.* Boston: Roberts Brothers, 1883.

―――. *Reminiscences 1819–1899.* Boston: Houghton Mifflin Company, 1899.

HOWE, M. A. DE WOLFE. *A Venture in Remembrance.* Boston: Little, Brown & Company, 1941.

HOWELLS, MILDRED (ed.). *Life in Letters of William Dean Howells.* 2 vols. New York: Doubleday, Doran & Company, 1928.

HOWELLS, WILLIAM DEAN. *Roman Holidays and Others.* New York: Harper & Brothers, 1908.

―――. *Seven English Cities.* New York: Harper & Brothers, 1909.

―――. *Tuscan Cities.* Boston: Ticknor and Company, 1886.

―――. *Venetian Life.* New York: Hurd and Houghton, 1866.

HUDDLESTON, SISLEY. *Paris: Salons, Cafés, Studios.* Philadelphia: J. B. Lippincott Company, 1928.

HUDSON, GERTRUDE REESE (ed.). *Browning to his American friends; letters between the Brownings, the Storys, and James Russell Lowell, 1841–1890.* New York: Barnes & Noble, 1965.

HUNTINGTON, HENRY, *Memories: Personages, People, Places.* London: Constable and Company, 1911.

IRVING, WASHINGTON. *Life and Letters of Washington Irving,* edited by his nephew, Pierre M. Irving. Vol. 4. New York: G. P. Putnam's Sons, 1864.

―――. *Spanish papers and other miscellanies,* edited by Pierre M. Irving. New York: G. P. Putnam's Sons, 1866.

JAMES, HENRY. *Daisy Miller.* New York: Harper & Brothers, 1879.

―――. *Essays in London and Elsewhere.* New York: Harper & Brothers, 1893.

―――. *Hawthorne.* New York: Harper & Brothers, 1879.

―――. *Henry James Autobiography,* edited by Frederick M. Dupee. New York: Criterion Books, 1956.

―――. *Italian Hours.* Boston: Houghton Mifflin Company, 1909.

―――. *Portraits of Places.* Boston: J. R. Osgood and Company, 1884.

―――. *William Wetmore Story and His Friends.* Boston: Houghton, Mifflin Company, 1903.

JAMESON, ANNA BROWNELL. *Memoirs and Loves of the Poets.* Boston: Ticknor and Fields, 1857.

―――. *Memoirs of the Life of Anna Jameson.* Boston: Roberts Brothers, 1878.

―――. *The Diary of an Ennuyée.* New York: Harper & Brothers, 1834.

―――. *Visits and Sketches at home and abroad.* New York: Harper & Brothers, 1834.

JARVES, JAMES JACKSON. *Italian Rambles.* New York: G. P. Putnam's Sons, 1883.

JAY, WILLIAM. *The Life of John Jay; with selections from his correspon-*

dence and miscellaneous papers, by his son. New York: J. and J. Harper, 1833.

JEFFERSON, THOMAS. *Life and Selected Writings of Thomas Jefferson,* edited by Adrienne Koch and William Peden. New York: The Modern Library, 1944.

————. *Papers, 1779–1780,* edited by Julian P. Boyd, Lyman H. Butterfield, and Mina R. Bryan. Vol. 3. Princeton, N.J.: Princeton University Press.

————. *Jefferson Himself, The Personal Narrative of a Many-sided American,* edited by Bernard Mayo. Boston: Houghton Mifflin Company, 1942.

————. *The Writings of Thomas Jefferson,* edited by Andrew A. Lipscomb. Vol. 1. Washington, D.C.: Monticello Edition, issued under the auspices of the Thomas Jefferson Memorial Foundation, 1904.

JOHNSON, JOANNA. *Mrs. Satan.* New York: G. P. Putnam's Sons, 1967.

JOLAS, EUGENE. *I Have Seen Monsters and Angels.* Paris: Transition Press, 1938.

JOSEPHSON, MATTHEW. *Infidel in the Temple: A Memoir.* Alfred A. Knopf, 1967.

————. *Life Among the Surrealists, a Memoir.* New York: Holt, Rinehart and Winston, 1962.

KAVALER, LUCY. *The Astors: A Family Chronicle of Pomp and Power.* New York: Dodd, Mead & Company, 1966.

————. *The Private World of High Society.* New York: D. McKay Company, 1960.

KELLNER, BRUCE. *Carl Van Vechten and the Irreverent Decade.* Norman: University of Oklahoma Press, 1968.

KENNAN, GEORGE. *Campaigning in Cuba.* New York: The Century Company, 1899.

KIKI. *Les Souvenirs de Kiki,* edited by Henri Broca. Paris, 1929.

KIMBALL, MARIE. *Jefferson: The Scene of Europe 1784–1789.* New York: Coward-McCann, 1950.

KIRK, CLARA MARBURG. *William Dean Howells: Traveler from Altruria, 1889–1894.* New Brunswick, N.J.: Rutgers University Press, 1962.

KRAUS, RENÉ. *Young Lady Randolph: The Life and Times of Jennie Jerome, American Mother of Winston Churchill.* Toronto: Longmans, 1944.

LABAREE, LEONARD W. (ed.). *The Autobiography of Benjamin Franklin.* New Haven: Yale University Press, 1964.

LANEY, AL. *Paris Herald.* New York: D. Appleton-Century Company, 1947.

LAVER, JAMES. *Edwardian Promenade.* London: Edward Hulton, 1958.

LEGGE, MADELINE. *Two Noble Women.* London: Phelps Bros., 1893.

LESLIE, ANITA. *The Remarkable Mr. Jerome.* New York: Henry Holt & Company, 1954.

LESLIE, MRS. FRANK. *Rents in our robes.* Chicago: Belford, Clarke and Company, 1888.

LESLIE, SHANE. *Mrs. Fitzherbert: A Life Chiefly from Unpublished Sources*. London: Burns, Oates, 1939.

———. *Long Shadows*. London: John Murray, 1966.

———. *Salutation to Five*. London: Hollis & Carter, 1951.

LESTER, CHARLES EDWARDS. *The Artists of America*. New York: Baker & Scribner, 1846.

———. *The artist, the merchant and the statesman of the age of the Medici, and of our own times*. New York: Paine & Burgess, 1845.

LEWIS, SINCLAIR. *From Main Street to Stockholm: Letters 1919–1930*, edited by Harrison Smith. New York: Harcourt, Brace & Company, 1952.

LIVINGSTON, LUTHER SAMUEL. *Franklin and His Press at Passy*. New York: The Grolier Club, 1914.

LODGE, HENRY CABOT. *Early Memories*. New York: Charles Scribner's Sons, 1913.

LOEB, HAROLD. *The Way It Was*. New York: Criterion Books, 1959.

LONGFELLOW, HENRY WADSWORTH. *Longfellow's Prose Works*. Vol. 1. Boston: Ticknor and Fields, 1846.

LONGFELLOW, SAMUEL. *Life of Henry Wadsworth Longfellow*. Vol. 2. Boston: Ticknor and Fields, 1886.

LONGFORD, ELIZABETH. *Queen Victoria*. New York: Harper & Row, 1965.

LONGWORTH, ALICE ROOSEVELT. *Crowded Hours*. New York: Charles Scribner's Sons, 1933.

LORD, WALTER. *The Good Years*. New York: Harper & Brothers, 1960.

LOWELL, JAMES RUSSELL. *Letters of James Russell Lowell,* edited by Charles Eliot Norton. New York: Harper & Brothers, 1894.

———. *Lowell's Impressions of Spain,* compiled by Joseph Gilder. Boston: Houghton Mifflin Company, 1899.

LUBBOCK, PERCY. *Portrait of Edith Wharton*. New York: D. Appleton-Century Company, 1947.

LUHAN, MABEL DODGE. *European Experiences*. New York: Harcourt, Brace & Company, 1935.

LUTZ, ALMA. *Emma Willard*. Boston: Houghton Mifflin Company, 1929.

LYONS, RICHARD B. P. *Franco-German War 1871*. London: Harrison & Sons, 1871.

MCALMON, ROBERT. *Being Geniuses Together, 1920–1930*. Recollections and with supplementary chapters by Kay Boyle. Garden City, N.Y.: Doubleday & Company, 1968.

———. *McAlmon and the Lost Generation: A Self-portrait*. Lincoln, Nebraska: University of Nebraska Press, 1962.

MCBRIDE, MARY MARGARET, and JOSEPHY, HELEN. *London Is a Man's Town*. New York: Coward-McCann, 1930.

———. *Paris Is a Woman's Town*. New York: Coward-McCann, 1929.

MCCARTHY, MARY T. *Venice Observed*. New York: Reynal & Company, 1956.

———. *The Stones of Florence*. New York: Harcourt, Brace & Company, 1959.

MacDougall, Allan Ross, and Duncan, Irma. *Isadora Duncan's Russian Days and her Last Years in France.* New York: Covici, Friede, 1929.

———. *Isadora: A Revolutionary in Art and Love.* Edinburgh and New York: T. Nelson, 1960.

McSpadden, Joseph Walker. *Famous Painters of America.* New York: Thomas Y. Crowell Company, 1907.

Manson, J. B. *The Life and Work of Edgar Degas,* edited by Geoffrey Holme. London: The Studio, Ltd., 1927.

Marbury, Elisabeth. *My Crystal Ball.* New York: Boni and Liveright, 1923.

Mariano, Nicky. *Forty Years with Berenson.* New York: Alfred A. Knopf, 1966.

Martin, Ralph G. *Jennie: The Life of Lady Randolph Churchill.* Vol. 1, *The Romantic Years 1854–1895.* Englewood Cliffs, N.J.: Prentice-Hall, 1969.

Mason, George Champlin. *The Life and Works of Gilbert Stuart.* New York: Charles Scribner's Sons, 1879.

Maurois, André. *Adrienne: The Life of the Marquise de Lafayette.* New York: McGraw-Hill Book Company, 1961.

Maury, Richard L. *A Brief Sketch of the Work of Matthew Fontaine Maury by His Son.* Richmond: Whittet & Shepperson, 1915.

Mayfield, Sara. *The Constant Circle: H. L. Mencken and His Friends.* New York: Delacorte Press, 1968.

Meade, Robert Douthat. *Judah P. Benjamin.* New York: Oxford University Press, 1943.

Michener, James A. *Hawaii.* New York: Random House, 1959.

———. *Tales of the South Pacific.* New York: The Macmillan Company, 1962.

———. *Iberia.* New York: Random House, 1968.

Middleton, John Henry. *The Remains of Ancient Rome.* London and Edinburgh: A. & C. Black, 1892.

Moore, J. B. (ed.). *The Works of James Buchanan.* Philadelphia: J. B. Lippincott Company, 1908.

Morris, Gouverneur. *A Diary of the French Revolution, 1752–1816,* edited by Beatrix Cary Davenport. Boston: Houghton Mifflin Company, 1939.

Morris, Lloyd. *Postscripts to Yesterday.* New York: Random House, 1947.

Morse, Edward Lind (ed.). *Samuel F. B. Morse: His Letters and Journals,* edited by his son. Boston: Houghton Mifflin Company, 1914.

Mount, Charles Merrill. *John Singer Sargent.* New York: W. W. Norton and Company, 1914.

Mowat, Robert Balmain. *Americans in England.* Boston: Houghton Mifflin Company, 1935.

Mowrer, Edgar Ansel. *Triumph and Turmoil.* New York: Weybright and Talley, 1969.

Bibliography

NEWTON, LORD. *Lord Lyons: A Record of British Diplomacy.* London: E. Arnold, 1913.

NORMAN, CHARLES. *Ezra Pound.* New York: The Macmillan Company, 1960.

NORTON, CHARLES ELIOT. *Letters of Charles Eliot Norton,* with biographical comment by his daughter, S. Norton, and M. A. De Wolfe Howe. Boston: Houghton Mifflin Company, 1913.

————. *The Correspondence of Thomas Carlyle and Ralph Waldo Emerson.* Boston: Houghton Mifflin & Company, 1894.

————. *Notes of Travel and Study in Italy.* Boston: Ticknor and Fields, 1860.

O'CONNOR, HARVEY. *Mellon's Millions; The Biography of a Fortune: The Life and Times of Andrew Mellon.* New York: The John Day Company, 1933.

O'CONNOR, RICHARD. *The Scandalous Mr. Bennett.* Garden City: Doubleday & Company, 1962.

OSGOOD, SAMUEL. *Thomas Crawford and Art in America.* New York: J. F. Trow & Son, 1875.

PADOVER, SAUL K. *Jefferson:* New York: Harcourt, Brace & Company, 1942.

————(ed.). *The Complete Madison.* New York: Harper & Brothers, 1953.

PARKMAN, FRANCIS. *The Journals of Francis Parkman.* New York: Harper & Brothers, 1947.

PARTON, JAMES. *Life and Times of Benjamin Franklin.* New York: Mason Bros., 1864.

PATINO, ABATINO. *Josephine Baker vue par la presse française.* Paris Editions. Isis, 1931.

PAUL, ELLIOT. *The Last Time I Saw Paris.* New York: Random House, 1942.

PEALE, REMBRANDT. *Notes on Italy.* Philadelphia: Carey and Lea, 1831.

PEARSON, HENRY GREENLEAF. *James S. Wadsworth of Geneseo.* New York: Charles Scribner's Sons, 1913.

PEARSON, HESKETH. *The Man Whistler.* New York: Harper & Brothers, 1953.

PELLEW, GEORGE. *John Jay.* Boston: Houghton Mifflin Company, 1898.   ·

PENNELL, JOSEPH and ELIZABETH R. *The Life of James McNeill Whistler.* Philadelphia: J. B. Lippincott Company, 1911.

PENNELL, ELIZABETH. *Nights: Rome, Venice, in the Aesthetic Eighties: London, Paris, in the Fighting Nineties.* Philadelphia: J. B. Lippincott Company, 1911.

PERRY, RALPH BARTON. *On All Fronts.* New York: Vanguard Press, 1941.

PHELPS, MARY MERWIN. *Kate Chase, Dominant Daughter.* New York: Thomas Y. Crowell Company, 1935.

PHILLIPS, CATHERINE COFFIN. *Jessie Benton Frémont, a Woman Who Made History.* San Francisco: printed by John Henry Nash, 1935.

PIERCE, EDWARD LILLIE. *Memoirs and Letters of Charles Sumner*. Boston: Roberts Bros., 1877–1893.

PLON, EUGENE. *Thorvaldsen: his life and works*. Boston: Roberts Bros., 1873.

PRESTON, WILLIAM C. *The Reminiscences of William C. Preston*, edited by Minnie Clare Yarbrough. Chapel Hill: The University of North Carolina Press, 1933.

PUTNAM, SAMUEL. *Paris Was Our Mistress: Memoirs of a Lost and Found Generation*. New York: The Viking Press, 1947.

RADZIWILL, PRINCESS CATHERINE. *It Really Happened*. New York: The Dial Press, 1931.

———. *The Royal Marriage Market of Europe*. New York: Funk & Wagnalls Company, 1915.

RASPONI, LANFRANCO. *The International Nomads*. New York: G. P. Putnam's Sons, 1966.

RICHARDS, LAURA E. *Abigail Adams and Her Times*. New York: D. Appleton & Company, 1917.

——— and HOWE, MAUD. *Julia Ward Howe, 1819–1910*. 2 vols. Boston: Houghton Mifflin Company, 1915.

RICHARDSON, E. P. *Washington Allston*. Chicago: University of Chicago Press, 1948.

ROBINSON, HENRY MORTON. *Fantastic Interim*. New York: Harcourt, Brace & Company, 1943.

ROBINSON, WILLIAM M. *The Confederate Privateers*. New Haven: Yale University Press, 1928.

RONALDSHAY, EARL OF. *The Life of Lord Curzon*. London: E. Benn, Ltd., 1928.

ROOSEVELT, THEODORE. *Diaries of Boyhood and Youth*. New York: Charles Scribner's Sons, 1928.

ROSS, ISHBEL. *An American Family: the Tafts 1678–1964*. Cleveland, Ohio: World Publishing Company, 1964.

———. *Charmers and Cranks*. New York: Harper & Row, 1965.

———. *Child of Destiny*. New York: Harper & Brothers, 1949.

———. *First Lady of the South*. New York: Harper & Brothers, 1958.

———. *Ladies of the Press*. New York: Harper & Brothers, 1936.

———. *Proud Kate*. New York: Harper & Brothers, 1953.

———. *Rebel Rose*. New York: Harper & Brothers, 1954.

———. *Silhouette in Diamonds: The Life of Mrs. Potter Palmer*, New York: Harper & Brothers, 1960.

———. *The General's Wife*. New York: Dodd, Mead & Company, 1959.

ROTHENSTEIN, WILLIAM. *Men and Memories*. New York: Coward-McCann, 1932.

RUSSELL, WILLIAM HOWARD. *My Diary North and South*. New York: Harper & Brothers, 1954.

SAARINEN, ALINE. *The Proud Possessors*. New York: Random House, 1958.

SACHS, EMANIE. *The Terrible Siren*. New York: Harper & Brothers, 1928.

Bibliography

SANTAYANA, GEORGE. *Persons and Places*. New York: Charles Scribner's Sons, 1963.

————. *Letters*, edited with an introduction and commentary by Daniel Cory. New York: Charles Scribner's Sons, 1965.

SCHORER, MARK. *Sinclair Lewis*. New York: McGraw-Hill, 1961.

SCHRIFTGIESSER, KARL. *The Gentleman from Massachusetts: Henry Cabot Lodge*. Boston: Little, Brown & Company, 1944.

SCHUYLER, EUGENE. *Italian Influences*. New York: Charles Scribner's Sons, 1901.

SCOTT, LEONORA CRANCH (ed.). *The Life and Letters of Christopher Pearse Cranch*. Boston: Houghton Mifflin Company, 1917.

SEDGWICK, CATHARINE M. *Letters from abroad to kindred at home*. New York: Harper & Brothers, 1841.

SEDGWICK, ELLERY. *The Happy Profession*. Boston: Little, Brown & Company, 1946.

SEITZ, DON CARLOS. *Joseph Pulitzer, His Life and Letters*. New York: Simon & Schuster, 1924.

————. *The James Gordon Bennetts, Father and Son*. Indianapolis: Bobbs-Merrill Company, 1928.

SHEEAN, VINCENT. *Dorothy and Red*. Boston: Houghton Mifflin Company, 1963.

————. *Personal History*. Garden City, N.Y.: Doubleday & Company, 1935.

SHELTON, HENRY. *The Jumel Mansion*. Boston: Houghton Mifflin Company, 1916.

SHIRER, WILLIAM L. *Berlin Diary: The Journal of a Foreign Correspondent, 1934–41*. New York: Alfred A. Knopf, 1941.

————. *The Rise and Fall of the Third Reich: A History of Nazi Germany*. New York: Simon & Schuster, 1960.

SLOAN, JAMES. *Rambles in Italy in the years 1816, 1817, 1818, by an American*. Baltimore: N. G. Maxwell, 1818.

SMITH, ED. *Where to, Black Man?* Chicago: Quadrangle Books, 1967.

SMITH, LOGAN PEARSALL. *Unforgotten Years*. Boston: Little, Brown & Company, 1939.

SPARKS, JARED. *The Life of Gouverneur Morris*. Boston: Gray and Bowen, 1832.

SPILLER, ROBERT ERNEST. *The Oblique Light: Studies in Literary History and Biography*. New York: The Macmillan Company, 1968.

SPRIGGE, ELIZABETH. *Gertrude Stein: Her Life and Work*. New York: Harper & Brothers, 1957.

SPRIGGE, SYLVIA. *Berenson: A Biography*. London: George Allen & Unwin, 1960.

STALLMAN, R. W. *Stephen Crane*. New York: G. Braziller, 1968.

STEARNS, HAROLD E. *America and the Young Intellectual*. New York: George H. Doran Company, 1921.

————. *Civilization in the United States, an Inquiry by Thirty Americans*. New York: Harcourt, Brace & Company, 1922.

STEELL, WILLIS. *Benjamin Franklin of Paris, 1776–1785.* New York: Minton, Balch & Company, 1928.

STEIN, GERTRUDE. *Four in America.* Introduction by Thornton Wilder. New Haven: Yale University Press, 1947.

———. *Wars I Have Seen.* New York: Random House, 1945.

STERN, MADELEINE B. *The Life of Margaret Fuller.* New York: E. P. Dutton & Company, 1942.

———. *Purple Passage.* Norman, Oklahoma: University of Oklahoma Press, 1953.

STILLMAN, WILLIAM JAMES. *The Autobiography of a Journalist.* Boston: Houghton Mifflin Company, 1901.

STORY, WILLIAM WETMORE. *Conversations in a Studio.* Vol. 2. Boston: Houghton Mifflin Company, 1890.

STOWE, HARRIET BEECHER. *Agnes of Sorrento.* Boston: Houghton Mifflin Company, 1862.

———. *Sunny Memories of Foreign Lands.* 2 vols. Boston: Phillips, Sampson and Company, 1854.

STOWE, LELAND. *They Shall Not Sleep.* New York: Alfred A. Knopf, 1944.

STRODE, HUDSON. *Jefferson Davis.* 3 vols. New York: Harcourt, Brace & Company, 1955–64.

STYRON, ARTHUR. *The Last of the Cocked Hats: James Monroe and the Virginia Dynasty.* Norman, Oklahoma: University of Oklahoma Press, 1945.

SULLIVAN, MARK. *Our Times 1900–1925.* Vol. 6, *The Twenties.* New York: Charles Scribner's Sons, 1935.

SWANBERG, W. *Citizen Hearst: A Biography of William Randolph Hearst.* New York: Charles Scribner's Sons, 1961.

SWEET, FREDERICK A. *Sargent, Whistler, and Mary Cassatt.* Chicago: The Art Institute, 1954.

———. *Miss Mary Cassatt.* Norman, Oklahoma: University of Oklahoma Press, 1966.

SWETT, LUCIA GRAY. *John Ruskin's Letters to Francesca and Memoirs of the Alexanders.* Boston: Lothrop, Lee and Shepard Company, 1931.

TAYLOR, BAYARD. *By-ways of Europe.* New York: G. P. Putnam's Sons, 1869.

———. *Views Afoot.* Philadelphia: D. McKay, 1848.

TAYLOR, T. (ed.). *Charles Robert Leslie's Autobiographical Recollections.* Boston: Ticknor and Fields, 1860.

TAYLOR, THOMAS E. *Running the Blockade.* New York: Charles Scribner's Sons, 1896.

TAYLOR, W. G. LANGWORTHY. *Katie Fox and the Fox-Taylor Record.* New York: G. P. Putnam's Sons, 1933.

TEBBEL, JOHN WILLIAM. *The Marshall Fields: A Study in Wealth.* New York: E. P. Dutton Company, 1947.

THARP, LOUISE (HALL). *Mrs. Jack: A Biography of Isabella Stewart Gardner.* Boston: Little, Brown & Company, 1956.

——. *The Peabody Sisters of Salem.* Boston: Little, Brown & Company, 1950.

——. *Three Saints and a Sinner.* Boston: Little, Brown & Company, 1956.

THOMPSON, DOROTHY. *Let the Record Speak.* Boston: Houghton Mifflin Company, 1939.

——. *"I Saw Hitler."* New York: Farrar & Rinehart, 1932.

——. *Czechoslovakia on the Record.* New York: Listy Publishing Company, 1938.

THORON, WARD (ed.). *The Letters of Mrs. Henry Adams, 1865–1883.* Boston: Little, Brown & Company, 1936.

TICKNOR, GEORGE. *Life of William H. Prescott.* Boston: Ticknor and Fields, 1864.

——. *Life, Letters and Journals of George Ticknor.* Vol. 1. Boston: James R. Osgood & Company, 1876.

TIFFANY, FRANCIS. *Life of Dorothea Lynde Dix.* Boston: Houghton Mifflin Company, 1882.

TOKLAS, ALICE B. *The Autobiography of Alice B. Toklas.* New York: Harcourt, Brace & Company, 1933.

TOLLENTYRE, S. G. (pseudonym). *The Friends of Voltaire.* New York: G. P. Putnam's Sons, 1907.

TOLMAN, RUEL PARDEE. *The Life and Works of Edward Greene Malbone, 1777–1807.* New York: New-York Historical Society, 1958.

TRUMBULL, JOHN. *The Autobiography of Colonel John Trumbull, Patriot-artist, 1756–1843,* edited by Theodore Sizer. New Haven: Yale University Press, 1953.

TUDOR, WILLIAM. *Letters of the Eastern States.* New York: Kirk and Mercein, 1820.

TURNBULL, ANDREW. *Scott Fitzgerald.* New York: Charles Scribner's Sons, 1962.

UNDERHILL, A. LEAH FOX. *Rochester Knockings.* Buffalo: G. H. Derby, 1851.

USPENSKII, PETR DEMIANOVICH. *The Fourth Way: A Record of Talks and Answers to Questions Based on the Teachings of G. I. Gurdjieff.* New York: Alfred A. Knopf, 1957.

——. *In Search of the Miraculous: Fragments of an Unknown Teaching.* New York: Harcourt, Brace & Company, 1949.

VANDERBILT, CORNELIUS, JR. *The Vanderbilt Feud.* London: Hutchinson & Co., 1957.

VEDDER, ELIHU. *The Digressions of V., Written for His Own Fun and That of His Friends.* Boston: Houghton Mifflin & Company, 1910.

WADDINGTON, MARY KING. *My First Years as a Frenchwoman 1876–1879.* New York: Charles Scribner's Sons, 1914.

WALKER, KENNETH MACFARLANE. *Venture with Ideas: Meetings with Gurdjieff and Ouspensky.* London: Jonathan Cape, 1951.

WALSH, ERNEST. *Poems and Sonnets: With a Memoir by Ethel Moorhead.* New York: Harcourt, Brace & Company, 1934.

WARD, MAISIE. *Robert Browning and His World*. 2 vols. New York: Holt, Rinehart and Winston, 1969.

WARD, MARY AUGUSTA ARNOLD (MRS. HUMPHRY WARD). *A Writer's Recollections*. New York: Harper & Brothers, 1918.

WATSON, FORBES. *Mary Cassatt*. American Artists Series. New York: Whitney Museum of Modern Art, 1932.

WATSON, ELKANAH. *Men and Times of the Revolution: or Memoirs of Elkanah Watson*. New York: Dana and Company, 1856.

WARWICK, FRANCES EVELYN (MAYNARD), Countess of Greville. *Discretions*. New York: Charles Scribner's Sons, 1931.

———. *Life's Ebb and Flow*. New York: William Morrow and Company, 1929.

WECTER, DIXON. *The Saga of American Society*. New York: Charles Scribner's Sons, 1937.

WELLICZ, LEOPOLD. *The Friendship of Margaret Fuller d'Ossoli and Adam Mickiewicz*. New York: *Polish Institute of Arts and Sciences in America Bulletin*. Vol. 4, 1945–46.

WESTCOTT, GLENWAY. *Good-bye Wisconsin*. New York: Harper & Brothers, 1928.

WHARTON, EDITH. *A Backward Glance*. New York: D. Appleton-Century Company, 1934.

———. *Italian Backgrounds*. New York: Charles Scribner's Sons, 1905.

———. *Italian Villas and their Gardens*. New York: The Century Company, 1904.

WHITING, LILIAN. *Kate Field*. Boston: Little, Brown & Company, 1899.

———. *The Brownings: Their Life and Art*. Boston: Little, Brown & Company, 1911.

WHITLOCK, BRAND. *Lafayette*. New York: D. Appleton & Company, 1929.

WHITNEY, JANET. *Abigail Adams*. Boston: Little, Brown & Company, 1947.

WILKINS, WILLIAM HENRY. *Mrs. Fitzherbert and George IV*. New York: Longmans, Green & Company, 1905.

WILLIAMS, JOHN A. *The Man Who Cried I Am*. Boston: Little, Brown & Company, 1967.

WILLIAMS, STANLEY T. *The Life of Washington Irving*. 2 vols. New York: Oxford University Press, 1935.

WILLIAMSON, GEORGE C. *Richard Cosway, R. A.* London: G. Bell & Sons, 1897.

WILLIS, NATHANIEL PARKER. *Pencillings by the way*. Philadelphia: Carey & Lea, 1836.

WINDSOR, THE DUKE OF. *A King's Story: The Memoirs of the Duke of Windsor*. New York: G. P. Putnam's Sons, 1951.

WINDSOR, WALLIS (WARFIELD), DUCHESS OF. *The Heart Has Its Reasons: The Memoirs of the Duchess of Windsor*. New York: D. McKay Company, 1956.

WOLFE, THOMAS. *Letters of Thomas Wolfe*, edited by Elizabeth Nowell. New York: Charles Scribner's Sons, 1956.

Bibliography

WOODHULL, VICTORIA CLAFLIN. *And the Truth Shall Make you Free.* London: Blackfriars, 1894.

WOOLF, VIRGINIA. *Roger Fry: A biography.* New York: Harcourt, Brace & Company, 1940.

WOOLSON, CONSTANCE FENIMORE. *The Front Yard and other Italian stories.* New York: Harper & Brothers, 1895.

WRIGHT, CONSTANCE. *Madame de Lafayette.* New York: Henry Holt & Co., 1959.

WRIGHT, RICHARD. *Native Son.* New York: Harper & Brothers, 1940.

WRIGHT, RICHARDSON L. *Forgotten Ladies.* Philadelphia: J. B. Lippincott Company, 1928.

ZABEL, MORTON DAUWEN (ed.). *The Art of Travel: Scenes and Journeys in America, England, France and Italy from the Travel Writings of Henry James.* Garden City, N.Y.: Doubleday & Company, 1958.

Index

Anthony, Joseph, 39
anti-novel, the, 247-248
antiquities, 55
  Greek, 66, 272, 299
  Roman, 46, 49, 65, 89, 90
anti-slavery, *see* slavery
Anville, Duchesse d', 16
Apollinaire, Guillaume, 222
Appleton, Thomas Gold, 67
Aragon, Louis, 245
archaeology, classical, 47, 67, 90
Arenberg, Peggy d' (d'Uzès), 276
Argyll, Duke of, 106
armed forces abroad, *see* servicemen
Armenonville (Paris), 203
Armory Show (New York), 167
Armour, Philip Danforth, 190
Arnauld, Abbé, 25
Arp, Hans, 231
"Arrangement in Gray and Black" (Whistler), 147-148
art collectors, *see* collectors of art
Art Institute (Chicago), 203
artists abroad, 2-7 *passim*, 26, 36-44, 49, 55-68 *passim*, 71, 142-150, 198, 201, 207, 234, 238-242 *passim*, 255, 282, 284, 287-288
Artois, Comte d' (Charles X), 33
Ascot, 188, 193-194
Aspern Papers, The (James), 202, 207
Asquith, Herbert H., 1st Earl, 195
Asquith, Margot (Tennant), 175
Astley's (London), 21
Astor, Caroline Schermerhorn, 193
Astor, John Jacob, 32
Astor, Mrs. John Jacob, 173
Astor, Lady Nancy (Langhorne), 187
Astor, Viscount William Waldorf, 187
Astor collection, 72
Astor family, 33
Atlantic Monthly, 127
Audubon, John James, 99-100
Aulne, Baron de l', 11, 24-25
Aurora Leigh (Browning, E. B.), 65
Auteuil (Paris), 15, 192
Autobiography of Alice B. Toklas, The (Stein), 222
Autobiography of Malcolm X (Haley), 293
automobile, the, 192, 194, 198, 211-212, 225, 227-228, 239, 250-251, 300
aviation, 137-138, 251, 254
Azeglio, Prince Massimo d', 218

Babbitt (Lewis), 239, 263-264
Bacall, Lauren, 266
Backward Glance, A (Wharton), 204
Baedeker, 100, 207
Baez, Joan, 298
Baillie, Joanna, 87, 91
Baker, Josephine, 181, 250, 291
Baldwin, James, 280, 292-294
Balfour, Arthur, 175, 195
ballet, 194, 209-210, 229, 260, 275, 278
Ballet Méchanique (Antheil), 225, 244

Balsan, Consuelo, *see* Vanderbilt, Consuelo
Balsan, Jacques, 189
Balzac, Evelina, 127
Bancroft, Dr. Edward, 21, 95
Bancroft, George, 62, 72
Bancroft, John, 168
Bankhead, Eugenia and Tallulah, 280
Bannister, John, 27
Barbaro, Villa, 6, 144, 153-155, 202, 207-208
Barbizon school, 125, 162
Barlow, Ernesta, 158
Barlow, Samuel, 158-159
Barnard, Frederick, 143
Barnes, Djuna, 245, 264
Barnes, Ralph, 289
Barnett, Eddie, 294
Barney, Natalie Clifford, 243, 280-281
Barrett-Leonard, Mrs. C. E., 113
Barrie, Sir James, 188
Barry, Marie Jeanne Bécu du, 26
Barrymore, John, 241
Bartolozzi, Francesco, 26
Barton, Clara, 141
Battle Hymn of the Republic (Howe), 125
Bayreuth Festival, 184
Baziotes, William, 231
Bazus, Baroness de, 138-139
Beach, Rev. Sylvester, 244
Beach, Sylvia, 6, 225, 242-247 *passim*, 290
Beardsley, Aubrey, 82, 145-146
Beatles, the, 270
Beaton, Cecil, 147
Beatty, Lord David, 170
Beautiful People, the, 17, 175, 195
Beauvoir, Simone de, 293
Beaux, Cecilia, 5, 164, 168-170
Beecher, Henry Ward, 62, 136-137
Beekman family, 33
Beerbohm, Max, 86
Being Geniuses Together (McAlmon), 246
Belafonte, Harry, 291
Bell, Alexander Graham, 134
Belle Irlandaise, La (Courbet), 163
Bellerophon, the, 33
Belmont, Alva, *see* Vanderbilt, Alva
Belmont, Mr. and Mrs. Oliver, 189
Benét, Rosemary and Stephen V., 235
Benjamin, Judah, 104, 114-119
Benjamin, Natalie and Ninette, 117
Bennett, James Gordon, 251-252
Bennett, James Gordon, Jr., 5, 86, 251-253
Bennett, Maud (Potter, Reuter), 252
Benson, Mr. and Mrs. Eugene, 202
Bentham, Jeremy, 31
Benton, Thomas Hart, 225
Bérard, Victor, 211
Berenson, Bernard, 5, 50, 83, 151-161, 163, 211, 214-216, 231, 288
Berenson, Mary (Costelloe), 154-155, 157-158, 160-161, 214
Berenson, Rachel (Perry), 158
Beresford-Hope, A. J. B., 109
Berlin, Irving, 165

DATE DUE

12-9-14			
GAYLORD			PRINTED IN U.S.A.